Two Views of
Little Round Top

Two Views of Little Round Top

A Pivotal Engagement During the Battle of Gettysburg, July 1st-3rd, 1863 During the American Civil War

ILLUSTRATED

The Attack and Defense of Little Round Top

Boyd Vincent

The Attack and Defense of Little Round Top

and

Strong Vincent and His Brigade at Gettysburg July 2, 1863

Oliver W Norton

Two Views of Little Round Top
A Pivotal Engagement During the Battle of Gettysburg, July 1st-3rd, 1863 During the American Civil War
ILLUSTRATED
The Attack and Defense of Little Round Top

by Boyd Vincent

The Attack and Defense of Little Round Top

and

Strong Vincent and His Brigade at Gettysburg July 2, 1863

by Oliver W Norton

FIRST EDITION

Leonaur is an imprint of Oakpast Ltd

Copyright in this form © 2017 Oakpast Ltd

ISBN: 978-1-78282-628-6 (hardcover)
ISBN: 978-1-78282-629-3 (softcover)

http://www.leonaur.com

Publisher's Notes

The views expressed in this book are not necessarily those of the publisher.

Contents

The Attack and Defense of Little Round Top *by Boyd Vincent*	7
The Attack and Defense of Little Round Top *by Oliver W Norton*	23
1. Introduction	25
2. The Historians	28
3. The Official Reports	133
4. Attack and Defense of Little Round Top	222
5. Biographical	252
6. Letters and Papers	268
7. The Warren Letters	280
8. Appomattox	303
Strong Vincent and His Brigade at Gettysburg *by Oliver W Norton*	311

The Attack and Defense of Little Round Top
A paper read before the Ohio Commandery of the
Loyal Legion February 3, 1915
By Boyd Vincent

THE ATTACK AND DEFENSE OF LITTLE ROUND TOP.

We Americans like to boast of our democratic spirit; but we are often most amiably inconsistent in it. We do not "dearly love a lord"; we cannot abide a caste; we want no aristocracy of mere privilege. Yet we do believe, as thoroughly as any people on earth, in an aristocracy of real merit; and we do rightly pride ourselves on any honourable inheritance we may have in such ancestral worth. My own good old father, born on a farm, was a fine example of such inconsistency. He fairly scorned the idea of a privileged ancestry.

Asked once if he had not a family coat-of-arms: "Oh, yes," he replied; "let me tell you about it. It's a currycomb and a sawbuck; both rampant!"

That wasn't so bad, either; considering that that old soldier-hero Cincinnatus himself left a plough to serve the state, and then went back to it. And yet, after my father's death, I found among his papers a lengthy genealogy of his ancestors, written by himself, in which he had not failed to note whatever was really worthy in any of them. So much stronger is human nature than human prejudice.

I think this feeling of family pride is always particularly strong in the case of a soldier-ancestor or relative. That famous old oracle, Dr. Johnson, came very near the truth when he said:

Every man thinks meanly of himself for not having been a soldier.

But no one has put the matter better than our own late and lamented companion, General Beatty, when he said once before this Commandery:

> The most enduring legacy any man can leave his children, and the one they will esteem most highly, is a good military record. ... If there has been a soldier in the family, it is the one thing the family never forgets—the one thing the family biographer never fails to mention. In short the father's military record is the son's patent of nobility.

I think we all agree to that.

Now, there are two purposes of our Order which we have in common with most of the fifty other American societies of honour: first, the perpetuation of the memory of the services of the Original Companions; and, second, the perpetuation of the principles for which they fought. In all this we hereditary companions have our bounden and grateful part—and one which we can always be doing. But there is also another practice of our Order which has been almost a part of its life so far, and that is in calling out the personal reminiscences, by its Original Companions, of their own observations and experiences in the war.

In these, of course, we hereditary members have no real share. But I have thought that where, as in my own case, the Original Companions from whom we derive did not live to speak of what they themselves saw and knew, it might not perhaps be considered altogether unreasonable or unbecoming in us to speak, for them, of the things in which they bore their personal part. At any rate, it is on this assumption that I venture to say something tonight about this particular fight for "Little Round Top," Gettysburg, in which my brother, General Strong Vincent, took part.

What I shall say is practically a summary of one of the more recent volumes of our Civil War literature. It was published in 1913, and is entitled *The Attack and Defense of Little Round Top, Gettysburg*. Its author is Oliver W. Norton, a successful and retired business man of Chicago, a member and ex-commander of our Illinois Commandery, and a member of our commandery-in-chief. The value of this book as an authority consists in two facts: first, that the author, although long entirely blind, has unearthed and brought together original reports and letters of leading men in that fight, most of which were unknown to the historians, and some of which have never before been published; and, second, the fact that the author was himself a personal eye witness of new and important incidents which he relates, connected with some critical moments in that fight.

At the time, he was brigade bugler, mounted, and bearer of the brigade's headquarters flag. As it was his duty to be always near his brigade commander, Colonel Vincent, he had, in this way, exceptional opportunities of hearing what was said and seeing what was done. When the fight was on, however, and until his services as colour bearer were again needed, he seized a musket and fought in the ranks with his regiment.

But, to begin with, let me now briefly recall the principal facts which led up to this particular fight.

******

In the summer of 1863, Lee undertook to divert the Federal offensive from Richmond, and to take the offensive himself against Washington. He also hoped to pass around Washington's main defences on the Potomac and attack it on the flank or rear. In order to do this, he marched northward, first into Maryland and then into Pennsylvania; also carrying the war in this way into the enemy's country. But first Hooker, and then Meade, keeping himself all the while between Lee and Washington, marched northward, too. almost exactly parallel with Lee. Finally, as Lee had decided to give battle, when the advance corps of the two armies met near Gettysburg on July 1st, there was a preliminary struggle, in which Major-General Reynolds of our First Corps was killed.

On July 2nd, the main bodies of both armies began to arrive, and as the commanders-in-chief chose their positions, the two lines of battle were still practically those on which the two armies had marched. That is to say, each line stretched, generally, in a north and south direction, Lee's army facing east and Meade's facing west. Gettysburg lay well to the north, between the two lines. But Lee's advance columns had, on July 1st, passed through Gettysburg or around it, and so to the east of it, as far as Gulp's Hill, where that day's battle was fought; and from there Lee's line on July 2nd extended back around the town and then nearly straight southwardly along Seminary Ridge for three or four miles.

Meade's line, on the other hand, taking advantage of the higher land, was in the shape of a horseshoe, with the convex side toward the enemy; or, perhaps, more like a fish-hook, with the barb and main curve at Gulp's Hill, the straight shank lying southwardly along Cemetery Ridge, with the ground rising steadily higher, until the line terminated at the bold and rough elevations since known as the Two Round Tops. The two armies were thus separated by a valley nearly a mile wide, filled in its upper part with flourishing farms, but widening and deepening at its lower end southwardly into rocky and heavily wooded hills and ravines. Through the centre of this valley, from north to south, and about midway between the two armies, ran the Emmittsburg Road.

In the early morning of July 2nd neither Lee nor Meade was ready to strike again. Each was awaiting the arrival of the rest of his army. Meanwhile Meade had posted Sickles' Corps at the extreme left of the Union line, on Cemetery Ridge, reaching almost as far as the Little Round Top. But Sickles, for some reason—probably because the intervening woods obstructed his view of the enemy's position and movements—soon moved part of his corps, *viz.*, Humphrey's Division, forward to the Emmittsburg Road, near a peach orchard, still facing this part of his line westward toward the enemy's line on Seminary Ridge. Birney's Division, however, he faced southward—that is, down the valley and partly across it—with his line at right angles with Humphrey's, and reaching from Humphrey's left on the Emmittsburg Road back to the famous "Devil's Den" of rocks, which lay in front of Little Round Top but was still separated from that by a considerable distance. Both Round Tops were thus left entirely unprotected.

About two o'clock Meade, inspecting his lines, told Sickles he had moved too far out. When Sickles offered to withdraw to his former position: "I wish to God you could sir," replied Meade; "but you see those people don't intend to let you." For Longstreet's artillery had just opened on Birney's position—(But this is anticipating slightly—for the sake of a story!)

Now Longstreet's Corps was on the extreme right of the Confederate line, so facing, but also far outstretching, the left of the Union line. During the morning, Lee wanted Longstreet to begin his attack. But Longstreet hesitated, for several reasons. Part of one of his divisions—Hood's—had not arrived. Another of his divisions—Pickett's—was also still to come up. Longstreet said to Hood:

"The general (meaning General Lee) is a little nervous this morning; he wishes me to attack; I do not wish to do so without Picket, I never like to go into battle with one boot off."

But about three o'clock Longstreet decided not to wait any longer for Pickett, and ordered a direct frontal attack up the Emmittsburg Road on Birney's position. Just about this time Law's scouts had reported to him, and he to Hood, that Meade's left did not reach Little Round Top; that there were no Union troops at all on Big Round Top, still further to the left; that it was thus possible for the Confederates to march out of sight and unhindered, clear around the lower or southern side of Big Round Top; outflank and attack Meade in the rear; capture his commissary and ammunition trains, parked in the hollow of his horseshoe line, and so demolish his whole position.

Under these circumstances—that is, with the manifest advantage of such a plan—Law entered a formal protest to Hood, and Hood, in his turn, to Longstreet, against the uncertain, but certainly costly, frontal attack on Birney which had been ordered. No less than three separate times and by three separate messengers Hood made this protest to Longstreet—the only one. Hood said, he ever made. Longstreet's only reply each time was: "General Lee's orders are to attack up the Emmittsburg Road."

Longstreet even came himself to Hood to give him the last answer. Some of Longstreet's own officers claim that Longstreet was sullen because he did not approve of Lee's policy of the offensive here; and Longstreet, in his own book, throws all the blame on Lee for not riding with him and personally directing his attack.

But by this time Longstreet, having ignored Hood's plan to encircle Big Round Top and so get into Meade's rear, had decided to attempt the same result in a different way. That is to say, beside the direct frontal attack up the Emmittsburg Road on Birney's whole line. Hood was also to pass beyond Birney's left at the Devil's Den, go up the ravine between the two Round Tops, and so, by a shorter line, outflank Meade's entire position on the left and attack him in the rear.

Little Round Top, as we have seen, terminated Cemetery Ridge, at the extreme southern end of Meade's original lines. It is a bold, rocky hill, probably 150 to 200 feet high. Its western side towards the main valley is rough and steep. Its southern side, toward Big Round Top, is even rougher and steeper, and covered with great rocks and boulders, but sloping more gradually at the bottom to the swale which separates Little Round Top from Big Round Top. This latter hill is probably 300 or 400 feet high. The apexes of the two hills are probably 1,000 feet apart. The sides of Big Round Top slope more gradually. So that there was room enough, to be sure, between the two hills for a very considerable body of Confederate troops to pass up the swale. But, on the other hand, this was also extremely difficult on account of the thick woods and the enormous number of rocks and boulders covering the

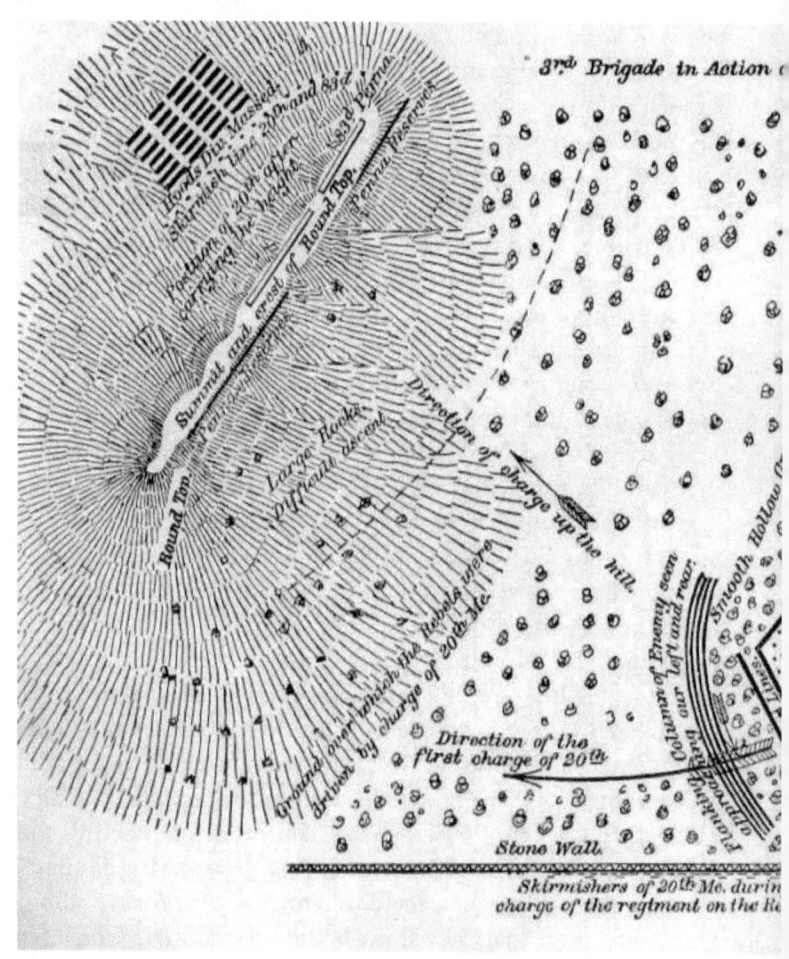

MAP OF LITTLE ROUND TOP BY

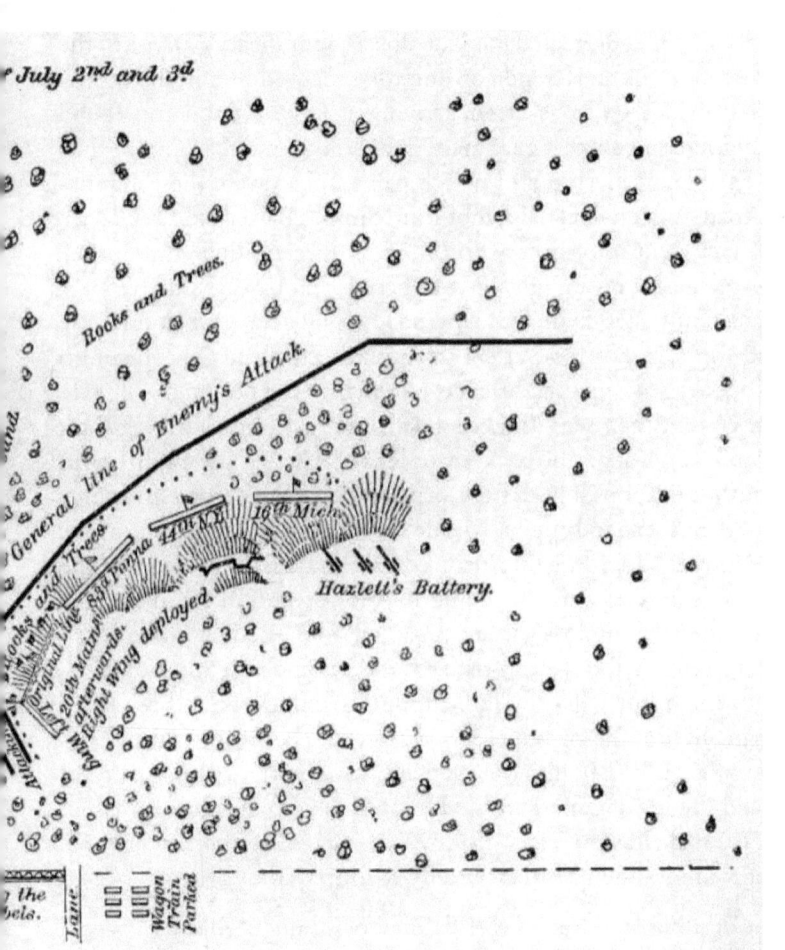

COLONEL JAMES C. RICE 44TH N.Y.

whole ground, even out so far as the Devil's Den—and beyond it.

Let us now turn to the other side of our story. Along in the early afternoon of this same day, July 2nd, Meade, finding that Sickles had abandoned his original position on Cemetery Ridge at the extreme left, sent General Warren, at Warren's own request, to see how things were there. For Meade, himself knew how carefully that part of his line needed to be protected; he had already sent Geary's Division the night before to Little Round Top and only relieved him in the morning with Sickles' Corps. Warren, arriving at Little Round Top, found nobody there but some signal men. They told him they thought they had seen troops in a clump of woods half a mile toward the Emmittsburg Road. Warren ordered a shot from Smith's Battery, located at the Devil's Den, sent into those woods; and, in the resulting commotion, caught the gleam of sunlight on gun barrels and bayonets there.

Warren instantly divined the intended Confederate attack on Little Round Top, which was as yet entirely unprotected, and sent one of his aides to Sickles asking for a brigade; but Sickles said he could not spare a man. Warren then sent another aide to Meade himself asking for a division; and Meade sent back an order to Sykes of the Fifth Corps to furnish the troops. The Fifth Corps, arriving early in the morning, had first been sent to support Meade's right; but on the arrival of the Sixth Corps, the Fifth, being relieved, was massed in the rear of the Federal left, until it was now being moved forward in the middle of the afternoon, to support Birney, already hard pressed by Longstreet.

What happened from this on, at Little Round Top, and how Vincent got there just when he did, are points about which the leading historians have hitherto hopelessly disagreed. Hardly any of them, as our present author points out, actually took part in this particular fight, and the leading men on the Union side who did were nearly all killed. We shall, however, hear from Warren and Chamberlain later on.

But to quote the historians briefly. Swinton says:

> The leading division of the Fifth Corps, under Barnes, was passing out to reinforce Sickles. Warren assumed the responsibility of detaching from this force the brigade of Vincent, and this he hurried up to hold the position.

Doubleday says:

> Warren, without losing a moment, rode over to Barnes, took the responsibility of detaching Vincent's brigade and hurried it back to take position on Little Round Top.

The Comte de Paris says:

> Sykes had immediately ordered Colonel Vincent, commanding Barnes' Third Brigade, to proceed to occupy the foot of Little Round Top.

Walker says:

> Warren takes the responsibility of detaching the foremost troops and hurries them forward to anticipate the Confederates.

Hunt says:

> The enemy was already advancing, when, noticing the approach of the Fifth Corps, Warren rode to meet it, caused Weed's and Vincent's Brigades and Hazlitt's Battery to be detached and hurried them to the summit.

De Trobriand says:

> Warren took upon himself to detach a brigade commanded by Colonel Vincent, and to hurry it on the run to the summit of Little Round Top."

Powell says:

> Sykes yielded to Warren's urgent request and Barnes directed Colonel Vincent to proceed to that point with his brigade.

Stine says:

> Warren, seeing Vincent's brigade approaching, rode up to Sykes and Barnes, and requested that Vincent be moved on Little Round Top and hold it.

Sykes, in his report at the time, says:

> In the meantime, Vincent's brigade, had seized the rocky height, closely followed by Weed's. These troops were posted under the direction of General Warren.

Barnes, in his report at the time, says:

> General Sykes yielded to General Warren's earnest request: and I (Barnes) immediately directed Colonel Vincent to proceed to that point with his brigade." (If Barnes did himself issue such an order to Vincent, it will be plain later on that it never reached Vincent.)

So much for the histories and the reports. They all seem to indicate that Vincent acted simply in obedience to orders; some say Warren's, some say Sykes', Barnes says his own.

Now let us hear next, however, from the personal letters of some of these same leaders, written later on. These letters are the new and first-class authorities found by our author, and which were mostly in the possession of Captain Farley, the historian of the 110th New York Regiment. In 186t Lieutenant Mackenzie, of Warren's Staff, wrote General Meade, saying:

> General Sickles, when called on by General Warren, through me, to furnish troops for the defence of that position, refused, stating his whole command was necessary to defend his front. General Sykes furnished troops as soon as called on.

But General Sykes himself, writing Captain Farley, in 1872, says:

> How Vincent got to Round Top, I do not know; unless hearing my *aide-de-camp* deliver the orders for the corps to take the left of the line, he made his way there, of his own soldierly instinct.

General Warren, also writing Captain Farley in 1872, says:

> I did not see Vincent's Brigade come up; but I suppose it was about this time they did, and, coming up behind me through the woods and taking post to the left (their proper place), I did not see them.

And again, also in 1872, Warren writes:

> If I detached Vincent's Brigade, I don't recollect it.

And again:

> You may be sure if I had given the account of my taking responsibility of detaching troops and hurrying them at the last moment to the hilltop, I should have said that it was O'Rorke and his regiment that I detached. (This was the case.)

These personal letters alone, then, would seem conclusive that neither Warren nor Sykes recollected having given Vincent orders.

But now let us hear the still more direct testimony of our author himself. It will be remembered that Sykes, with his Fifth Corps, was now moving forward to support Sickles; and Barnes, of the First Division, had gone ahead to select his position. Here Warren's *aide*, coming back with an order from Meade to Sykes to send troops to Little Round Top, met Sykes. I now quote the author's own words:

Sykes immediately sent one of his staff to direct Barnes to send one of his brigades. But Barnes had not returned to the division. Vincent was sitting on his horse at the head of the column, waiting orders. Seeing Sykes' *aide* approaching, he rode forward to meet him. I followed with the flag, and distinctly heard the following conversation: 'Captain, what are your orders.'
The captain replied: 'Where is General Barnes?'
Vincent said: 'What are your orders? Give me your orders!'
The captain answered: 'General Sykes told me to direct General Barnes to send one of his brigades to occupy that hill yonder,' pointing to Little Round Top.
Vincent said: 'I will take the responsibility of taking my brigade there.' Returning to the brigade, he directed Colonel Rice, the (next) senior colonel, to bring the brigade to the hill as rapidly as possible; then rode away to the northwest face of the hill. I followed him.

So much in the author's exact words.

He then says, substantially, that Vincent did not stop on the flat ridge of Little Round Top and post his troops there; for there they could have offered little resistance to the threatened attack, through the thick woods, up the ravine between the two hills. But, instead, Vincent led his column, out of sight, through the woods behind Little Round Top; then down the ravine, past the southern shoulder of this hill and around to and along its steep western slope, about half way up its face; so, fronting, at a considerable distance, the Devil's Den, which was Birney's extreme left.

Here, then, Vincent's Brigade (the Third, of the First Division, of the Fifth Corps), of about twelve hundred men, was posted, in the following order: On the western face of Little Round Top, on his extreme right, the 16th Michigan, with part of its own right running back up the hill, so guarding its own flank; next, to the left, on the same western face, the 44th New York; then the 83rd Pennsylvania (Vincent's own regiment), still partly on the western face, but also with its left bent well back on the southern slope, and so up the ravine; then, on the extreme left, the 20th Maine, continuing the line up the ravine along the southern slope of Little Round Top, and facing Big Round Top.

The forces selected by Hood to make the attack here were part of Law's Brigade, of five Alabama regiments, and part of Robertson's

Brigade of four regiments—three from Texas and one from Arkansas. Within ten minutes after Vincent's men were in position, the first attack, made by about half of this Confederate force, was along Vincent's whole line, and was desperately renewed again and again for at least half an hour. Finding this unsuccessful for the time being, the Confederates made two additional moves. For the rest of Hood's Division had meanwhile driven back Ward from his position near the Devil's Den, on Birney's extreme left.

The way being thus cleared, three more regiments of the attacking force were now thrown against Vincent's extreme right, hoping to break his line there and so outflank him. Soon that part of the 16th Michigan, *viz.*, about three companies of it, which were guarding this flank, overpowered by this terrific assault, gradually gave way and was driven back; and it was here that Vincent, trying to rally these men, fell mortally wounded. Just about this time Weed's Brigade, of Ayres' Division of the Fifth Corps, was moving forward to reinforce Sickles. Warren, who was still on the ridge of Little Round Top, seeing the newly threatened attack on Vincent's right and riding down off the ridge for reinforcements, promptly and unhesitatingly detached O'Rorke's 140th New York from Weed's Brigade (Warren's old command) and hurried it to the hill. O'Rorke told Warren that General Weed was ahead and expected the brigade to follow him.

"Never mind that," said Warren, "bring your regiment up here and I will take the responsibility." Soon the 140th came over the crest, on the run and with a yell, just as Vincent's right was driven back and the Confederates had got foothold on the steep western face of the hill. With no time to load guns, but with bayonets fixed, the 140th now dashed down upon the Confederates and quickly drove them back into the valley, pursuing them and taking many prisoners. But this great success cost this fine regiment its gallant and beloved Colonel O'Rorke, who fell dead close to where Vincent lay.

Shortly after, the rest of Weed's Brigade, sent back for the purpose, had come up and taken position in support of Lieutenant Hazlitt's battery on the hilltop. Soon Weed, too, was shot; and Hazlitt, stooping over him to take his last words, was also instantly killed, falling literally across Weed's body. Altogether it was a ghastly and costly harvest of splendid young Union leaders reaped, in so short a time, by the Confederate sharpshooters who were now at Devil's Den, only a quarter of a mile away, and concealed behind its great rocks as big as houses.

The other new move of the enemy, at almost the same time, was against Chamberlain's 20th Maine Regiment, on Vincent's extreme left. Chamberlain himself, writing only two years ago, in *Hearst's Magazine*, says:

> Reaching the southern face of Little Round Top, I found Vincent there, with intense poise and look. He said with a voice of awe, as if translating the tables of the eternal law, 'I place you here. This is the left of the Union line. You understand. You are to hold this ground at all costs.' I did understand full well; but had more to learn regarding the costs.

He had, indeed! For now, the two other Alabama regiments, not yet engaged, had made their way through the woods along the slope of Big Round Top. in order to outflank and enfilade the 20th Maine. To meet this attack Chamberlain refused his left wing to a position nearly at right angles to the rest of his regiment, and had to take long intervals to do it. Writers on both sides describe the fighting here as most desperate. The advancing and retreating lines, it is said, "surged back and forth like waves" over a space of a few hundred feet. A Confederate officer, surrendering his sword with one hand, fired his pistol at Chamberlain's head with the other.

At least five separate assaults were made and repulsed in the course of an hour or two. A third of Chamberlain's men were dead or disabled. Their ammunition was gone. The enemy was in no better shape. It was growing dark. At last Chamberlain ordered the bayonet; and the enemy was soon hopelessly and finally driven from the field here, as elsewhere, about Little Round Top. Five hundred prisoners were taken, including two colonels. Colonel Oates, commanding one of the Alabama regiments, says in his history:

> I found the undertaking to capture Little Round Top too great for my regiment. We were not driven from the field; I ordered the retreat; (but adds, like an honest man) When the signal was given, we ran like a herd of wild cattle!"

It was now nine o'clock. The fight in defence of Little Round Top had been made and won. The key of the Union position on that day's battlefield was still in our hands. There was little danger of a renewed attack at this point by the exhausted Confederate troops. But to guard against any such thing, the 20th Maine was moved higher up on Big Round Top; the lines of the 83rd Pennsylvania and 44th New York were straightened and extended to join it, and a fresh brigade

(Fisher's) was also moved up about midnight in support. So, closed the day of that fight on July 2nd.

Of the vital importance of this fight at Little Round Top to the Union cause there can be little doubt. There were other struggles during the war as great as that at Gettysburg. There were equal devotion and valour on that and other fields. But Gettysburg seems rightly regarded as the first real break in Lee's power, foretelling its end. The next day's final struggle there, with the repulse of Pickett's magnificent though hopeless charge against Meade's centre, was still to be made. But there can be no question that Little Round Top was the critical point of the battle on July 2nd.

As Colonel Powell says in his *History of the Fifth Corps*:

> Historians have exhausted themselves in describing the actions at the 'Peach Orchard.' . . . Great stress has been laid on the results of Pickett's charge . . . but the truth of history is, that the little brigade of Vincent, with the self-sacrificing valour of the 20th Maine, under the gallant leadership of Joshua L. Chamberlain, fighting among the rocks and scrub-oaks in the vale between the Round Tops and July 2, 1863, saved to the Union arms the historic field of Gettysburg. Had they faltered for one instant, there would have been no grand charge of Pickett; and Gettysburg would have been the mausoleum of departed hopes for the National cause; for Longstreet would have enveloped Little Round Top, capturing all on its crest from the rear and held the key of the whole position.

Lastly, our own author, Norton, declares that the one purpose of his seemingly belated book is, through the new information he furnishes, to secure the simple truth and justice of all the facts—and especially as they concern Vincent's part at Little Round Top. He does not hesitate to give Warren all the great primary credit he deserves in this fight, for his keen military eye and sound judgment, his prompt action in sending for reinforcements and his unhesitating assumption of responsibility in detaching and hurrying up O'Rorke's 140th New York at a critical moment. And with no less credit to Warren as a man; for Warren was himself the most modest and generous of men, never claiming credit for himself, always ready to give it to others.

O'Rorke's timely and successful charge is also seen to have been one of the saving factors in the fight. He was a fine officer, only recently graduated from West Point at the head of his class. Nor is there any less appreciation of the splendid part Chamberlain played here and for which indeed he was made brigadier-general shortly afterward. (He was finally brevetted Major-General of Volunteers, and was after the war Governor of Maine, and subsequently President of Bowdoin College.) But our author does insist that "hitherto, in two respects, justice has never been done to Vincent." First, as to Vincent's willingness, too, to take responsibility and his promptness in acting on it. he says:

> In spite of all that Warren, Sykes and Barnes did, it would have been too late, had not Vincent moved without waiting for an order from his immediate superior. The second respect, is in not having given Vincent the credit due him for his knowledge and skill in the choice of a position. (Vincent was not a trained soldier, but a civilian.) But the position chosen by Vincent, (he claims) was the best possible for preventing the Confederates from turning or capturing the hill. The event proved that his instinct for the point of vantage was of the highest order.

Hood himself said in his report to Longstreet:

> I found that by reason of the concavity of the enemy's (that is, Vincent's) line we would be subject to a destructive fire in flank and rear as well as in front; and that it was impossible ... under this number of cross-fires, to put the enemy to flight.

Even Longstreet wrote our author in 1901 as follows:

> It gives me pleasure to state, in reference to the worth of Little Round Top to the Union Army at Gettysburg, that it was everything to the success of the Union battle..... And, General Vincent's prompt action in moving to save that point held it and was the means of getting the battle to his side. Many minutes' delay would have given the Confederates the field.

And, finally, since the publication of Mr. Norton's book two years ago, a West Point professor has written him that he has cleared up confusion, made good his points, and that his book is now a text-book at West Point on *The Attack and Defense of Little Round Top*.

Colonel Vincent's appointment as brigadier-general was made the next day by President Lincoln, on General Meade's recommendation by telegraph. He died, however, five days afterward, on July 7th, just as the appointment reached him. A heroic-size bronze figure of General

Vincent, on a high pedestal, stands on the southern slope of Little Round Top.

The Attack and Defense of Little Round Top
by Oliver W Norton

1. Introduction

This is not a history of the Battle of Gettysburg, but an attempt to describe more fully and accurately than has heretofore been done that part of the battle which was fought on one corner of the field, where, more than in any other place, the fate of the contest between the two armies was decided. On July 1, 1863, the battle was between portions of each army only. On July 2 both armies had arrived on the field. The main attack of the Confederates was directed against the left of the Union line. Much has been written in regard to the battle on and about Little Round Top, with more contradictory statements by both Union and Confederate writers than about almost any other part of the battle.

The author, who was an eye-witness of the attack and took part in the defence on this part of the line, believes that it will serve to give a better idea of the fight on Little Round Top if in connection with what he saw and heard he presents the official reports of the Union and Confederate officers and extracts from the accounts of the leading historians which relate to this part of the battle, with his comparison and criticism of these documents, together with some important letters and papers not heretofore published.

It is nearly half a century since the battle was fought. The greater part of the armies which contended in this, the greatest battle of the war, have passed over the river. It should be possible for those who remain, and to whom this battle is a memory only, to recognise the sincerity and the valour of their foes, to put aside all hatred and prejudice, and, recognising that we are all Americans, proud of our country, treat all with fairness and impartiality. In what the author has to say he hopes to do this.

This attitude will not oblige him, in cases where writers have in his opinion deliberately misrepresented the facts to cover their own misconduct, to refrain from pointing this out. On the other hand, he believes that where writers make statements with which he cannot agree, but which have no relation to their own conduct, these statements have been made in good faith as the result of the best information obtainable at the time they were written.

One reason why such incorrect accounts appear is probably that the commanders of the two brigades and the battery which fought the battle for the defence of Little Round Top,—Vincent, Weed and Hazlett,—were killed or mortally wounded; O'Rorke, who commanded the One Hundred and Fortieth New York, was killed, and Rice, who succeeded Vincent in his command of the brigade, was killed in battle a few months later. Had any of these lived until they had time to write their reminiscences after the war the accounts might have been very different.

General Warren played a most important part in this battle. The historians have credited to him much that he never claimed for himself. He made no official report, and died in 1882, before any of the histories referred to in this book were published. A few months ago, the author was permitted to see and copy a number of personal letters from General Warren relating mostly to the battle on Little Round Top, which the officer to whom they were written has kindly permitted the author to publish. These letters were never intended for publication, but it is from just such letters that true history is written. They reveal so much of the character of General Warren, his patriotism and his love for the men who died on Little Round Top, that as a contribution to the history of that day they should be given to the public.

There is no part of the Battle of Gettysburg, the greatest battle of the Civil War, the facts in regard to which have been less understood, because more misrepresented, than the struggle for the possession of Little Round Top. Its capture by the Confederates during the battle of the second day would have forced Meade to abandon his strong position in disorderly retreat. Its retention by the Union army made that position secure. There is a general agreement among historians and writers that this statement is true; but here the agreement ends. No two writers agree in their statements of what actually took place.

In order to give the reader a basis for a better understanding of the facts, I purpose to give all the official reports of the Union and Confederate officers engaged on this part of the field, extracts from the writings of leading historians and others, with my own account and some hitherto unpublished letters and papers, which I think will convince a careful reader that in many respects the generally accepted accounts are erroneous.

I have no doubt that it will seem presumptuous in a private soldier to come forward nearly half a century after the battle and contradict the statements of so many writers much abler than himself. There is some justification for this attempt in the fact that these writers contradict one another. Although a private soldier, I was at the time of the Battle of Gettysburg, and for some time before and after, on detached service at the Headquarters of the Third Brigade, First Division, Fifth Army Corps, commanded when the battle began by Colonel Strong Vincent. I was brigade bugler, mounted, and bearer of the brigade headquarters flag. As such, it was my duty to keep near the brigade commander, following him closely where ever he went, when the army was on the march or moving about a battlefield.

Each brigade in the army had a distinctive headquarters flag, bearing the corps badge, and by a different arrangement of its red, white, and blue colours enabling a staff officer or any other person familiar with the system to tell from any distance at which it could be clearly seen the organisation to which it belonged and where he could find its commander. This duty gave me a better opportunity than even the officers of the brigade staff enjoyed, to see what occurred and hear verbal orders given or received. The officers of the staff were frequently absent at intervals, conveying orders or seeking information, while I remained constantly with the brigade commander.

My recollection of what I saw and heard that day is as clear and distinct as that of any event in my life. Since the discovery by me, about a year since, of a large number of letters from General Warren, General Sykes, that Comte de Paris, and others never before published, throwing a new light on the subject, which the recipient has kindly given me permission to publish, I have been making a careful examination of all the literature which I have been able to find relating to this part of the battle, with the purpose of collecting and presenting these various accounts to the public in convenient form for comparison and reference, in connection with my own recollections. The official reports are necessarily fragmentary. This is especially true of the Confederate reports. I have not been able to find any reports made at the time by the division commanders of either Hood's or McLaws' divisions. In my account of their movements it is necessary to depend on the few brigade and regimental reports which are available.

2. The Historians

In addition to my own account, with the official reports of the commanders of Union and Confederate troops which were engaged in this part of the battle, and letters and papers not heretofore published, I have made extracts from the following books:

William Swinton, *Campaigns of the Army of the Potomac*; Abner Doubleday, *Chancellorsville and Gettysburg*; Comte de Paris, *The Civil War in America*; Francis A. Walker, *History of the Second Army Corps*; Henry J. Hunt, in *Battles and Leaders of the Civil War*; Regis de Trobriand, *Four Years with the Army of the Potomac*; William H. Powell, *The Fifth Army Corps*; J. M. Vanderslice, *Gettysburg Then and Now*; J. H. Stine, *History of the Army of the Potomac*; R. K. Beecham, *Gettysburg, the Pivotal Battle of the Civil War*; William C. Dates, *The War Between the Union and the Confederacy*; Edward M. Law, C. S. A., in *Battles and Leaders of the Civil War*.

A comparison of the accounts in these books shows that no two of them agree in their description of what took place on Little Round Top. With such differences, they cannot all be right. With due deference and crediting the authors with the intention to state the facts, I think that in important particulars not one has succeeded. No one can deny the importance of the part which General Warren performed in the emergency, but nearly all the writers, excluding, of course, the Confederates, have attributed to him things which he did not do and which he never claimed to have done, as I will show later by direct statements from Warren himself.

Not one of them credits Colonel Vincent with his action in taking the responsibility—when he knew that General Sykes had ordered a brigade of Barnes' division to be sent to Little Round Top—of taking his brigade there without waiting for an order from his division commander, who was not present. Had Vincent waited to be detached, or to receive his order through the usual channel, he would have arrived at his position on Little Round Top too late. The enemy would have been in possession and the men who arrived almost as soon as Vincent was in position could not have been driven off. However, let the historians speak for themselves.

William Swinton, *Campaigns of the Army of the Potomac:*

> Fortunately, at the time Hood made his attack. General Warren, chief engineer, happened to reach Little Round Top. The summit of this hill had been used as a signal station, and at the moment of his arrival the signal officers suddenly seeing that the enemy had penetrated between Round Top and the left of Sickles' line, and was approaching their position, were folding up their flags to leave; but Warren, commanding them to continue waving them so as to make at least a show on the hill, hastened to seek some force wherewith to occupy this important point. It happened at this pregnant moment that the head of Sykes' column, which had been ordered over to the left, reached this vicinity, and the leading division of this corps under General Barnes was then passing out to reinforce Sickles. General Warren assumed the responsibility of detaching from this force the brigade of Vincent, and this he hurried up to hold the position, while Hazlett's battery was by enormous labour dragged and lifted by hand up the rocky brow of the hill and planted on its summit. As these events followed in quick succession, it resulted that while that part of Hood's force that had penetrated to the left of the line was approaching the front slope of the Little Round Top, which in a few moments would have been seized by it, other claimants were hurrying up its rear. Vincent's men, thrown forward at the *pas de course*, and without time to load, reached the crest just as Hood's Texans, advancing in column and without skirmishers, were running to gain it.
> Little Round Top—the prize so eagerly coveted by both combatants—is a bold and rocky spur of the lofty and peaked hill Round Top. It is impossible to conceive a scene of greater wildness and desolation than is presented by its bare and mottled figure, up-piled with granite ledges and masses of rock and strewn with mighty boulders that might be the debris of some antique combat of the Titans.
> Here there ensued one of those mortal struggles rare in war,

when the hostile 'forces, clenching in close contest, illustrate whatever there is of savage and terrible in battle. Vincent's brigade, composed of the Sixteenth Michigan (Lieutenant-Colonel Welsh), the Forty-Fourth New York (Colonel Rice), the Eighty-Third Pennsylvania, (Captain Woodward), and the Twentieth Maine (Colonel Chamberlain), coming quickly into position, engaged Hood's troops in a hand-to-hand conflict, in which bayonets were crossed and muskets clubbed; and officers, seizing the rifles dropped from dead hands, joined in the fray. After half an hour of this desperate work the position was secured. Meantime, Weed's brigade of Ayres' division of the Fifth corps took part on Vincent's right on Little Round Top.

The One Hundred and Fortieth New York of this brigade had gone up simultaneously with Hazlett's battery and participated in the engagement. Hood's men, however, clung fast to the rocky glen at the base of the hill, and, working their way up the ravine between the Round Tops, succeeded in turning the left flank. The ammunition of Vincent's troops was already exhausted.

It therefore became necessary to use the steel, and the enemy was driven from this point by a charge with the bayonet by Colonel Chamberlain's Maine regiment. Yet this rocky bulwark was not secured without a heavy sacrifice. Colonel Vincent, who had so heroically met the first shock, laid down his life in defence of the position; O'Rorke and the much-beloved General Weed were killed; Hazlett, who commanded the battery, also fell at his perilous post; and among the ledges of rocks lay many hundred dead soldiers in blue.

The onset of Hood and McLaws upon Birney's front was made with great vigour, compelling General Sickles immediately to call for reinforcements; and it was in response to this request that General Barnes' division of the Fifth corps had been thrown out in support at the time General Warren detached from this division the brigade of Vincent to hold Little Round Top. Its other two brigades, under Colonels Tilton and Sweitzer, hastened to the support of Birney's hard-pressed troops on the advanced line; and General Humphreys, who held the right of the Third corps, but had not yet been attacked, sent one of his own brigades under Colonel Burling to still further help.

Swinton appears to have obtained his account of this part of the battle from various sources. He has confused the time and order of events and the movements of troops, so much as to give a wrong impression. He attributes to Vincent's brigade the timely arrival on the crest of the hill and the charge down the western slope which drove the Confederates from this part of the line. This was the work of Colonel O'Rorke and his regiment, the One Hundred and Fortieth New York. This was not the first attack on the Union position, but was the last. The first attack was made by the Fourth and Forty-Eighth Alabama of Law's brigade and the Fourth and Fifth Texas of Robertson's brigade, which came up the swale on the north side of Big Round Top and attacked the centre of Vincent's brigade posted on the southern slope of the hill.

A desperate fight had taken place there, lasting half an hour. During this time the other brigades of Hood's division had been assaulting Ward's brigade and Smith's battery at the Devil's Den. Ward maintained his position for some time, and it was not until he had been forced back that the way was open for the Confederates, who had been driven back by Vincent, to make their way northward along the Plum Run valley east of the Devil's Den to a point from which they could ascend the west front of Little Round Top, outflanking the Sixteenth Michigan on Vincent's right and driving it in. The timely arrival of O'Rorke and his men repelled this attack and saved the day on that part of our line. Meantime the Fifteenth and Forty-Seventh Alabama, which had come over the top of Big Round Top, attacked Vincent's left flank, held by the Twentieth Maine under Chamberlain.

Warren did not arrive on Little Round Top at the time Hood's division made this attack. He arrived at least an hour before this. When he arrived, the enemy was not in sight. Warren, having been informed by the signal officer that he thought he had seen the enemy in the woods between Plum Run and the Emmittsburg road, directed Smith's battery to fire a shot in that direction. The involuntary movement of the men concealed in the woods as this shot whistled over them, and the reflection of the sunlight on their bright bayonets and gun barrels, revealed to Warren a long line of the enemy in position far outflanking Birney's line.

Soon after this the batteries of Hood's and McLaws' divisions opened fire on Birney, whose batteries responded, and this cannonade continued, according to different accounts, for from fifteen minutes to half an hour before the infantry advanced. Warren did not leave the

AT CLOSE QUARTERS ON THE FIRST DAY AT GETTYSBURG.

hill, but sent Lieutenant Mackenzie, one of the three young engineer officers on his staff, asking for a brigade to occupy Little Round Top. Sickles replied that he could not spare any, but Sykes promised to send a brigade. A long time after Barnes' division went to the front Weed's brigade of Ayres' division came along. Seeing the imminent danger, Warren left the hill and, detaching the One Hundred and Fortieth New York from the rear of this brigade, sent it to the crest of Little Round Top under the guidance of Lieutenant Roebling, another one of his staff. Warren did not return to the hill, but rode away to report to General Meade.

The reader of Swinton's account cannot gather from it the proper sequence of events. It would appear that Weed's brigade took part in this engagement. Except the One Hundred and Fortieth New York, it did not get into position on the hill until all the close fighting was done. Weed and Hazlett were killed by sharpshooters firing at long range after the Confederates had abandoned the hill, to return no more. For confirmation of my statements, see letters of Warren, Roebling, and Mackenzie in chapter 7, and Sykes' official report in chapter 3.

General Abner Doubleday: *Chancellorsville and Gettysburg*

> General Warren, who was on Meade's staff as chief engineer, had ridden ... to the signal station on Little Round Top to get a better view of the field. He saw the long line of the enemy approaching and about to overlap Ward's left, and perceived that Unless prompt succour arrived Little Round Top would fall into their hands. Once in their possession they would flank our whole line and post guns there to drive our troops from the ridge; so that this eminence was in reality the key of the battlefield and must be held at all hazards. He saw Barnes' division, which Sykes had ordered forward, formed for a charge and about to go to the relief of De Trobriand, who held the centre of Birney's line and who was sorely beset. Without losing a moment he rode down the slope, over to Barnes, took the responsibility of detaching Vincent's brigade, and hurried it back to take post on Little Round Top. He then sent a staff officer to inform General Meade of what he had done and to represent the immense importance of holding this commanding point. The victorious column of the enemy was subjected to the fire of a battery on Little Round Top and to another farther to the

right, but it kept on, went around Ward's brigade and rushed eagerly up the ravine between the two Round Tops to seize Little Round Top, which seemed to be defenceless. Vincent's brigade rapidly formed on the crest of a small spur which juts out from the hill, and, not having time to load, advanced with the bayonets in time to save the height. The contest soon became furious and the rocks were alive with musketry. General Vincent sent word to Barnes that the enemy were on him in overwhelming numbers, and Hazlett's regular battery, supported by the One Hundred and Fortieth New York, under Colonel O'Rorke of Weed's brigade, was sent as a reinforcement.

The battery was dragged with great labour to the crest of Little Round Top, and the One Hundred and Fortieth were posted on the slope on Vincent's right. They came upon the field just as the rebels, after failing to penetrate the centre, had driven back the right. In advancing to this exposed position Colonel O'Rorke, a brilliant young officer who had just graduated at the head of his class at West Point, was killed and his men thrown into some confusion; but Vincent rallied the line and repulsed the assault. In doing so he exposed himself very much, and was soon killed by a rebel sharpshooter. General Weed, who was on the crest with the battery, was mortally wounded in the same way, and as Hazlett leaned over to hear his last message a fatal bullet struck him also, and he dropped dead on the body of his chief.

Colonel Rice, of the Forty-Fourth New York, now took command in place of Vincent. The enemy, having been foiled at the centre and right, stole around through the woods and turned the left of the line, but Chamberlain's regiment, the Twentieth Maine, was folded back by him around the rear of the mountain to resist the attack. The rebels came on like wolves, with deafening yells and forced Chamberlain's men over the crest, but they rallied and drove their assailants back in their turn. This was twice repeated, and then a brigade of the Pennsylvania Reserves and one of the Fifth corps dashed over the hill. The Twentieth Maine made a grand final charge and drove the rebels from the valley between the Round Tops, capturing a large number of prisoners. Not a moment too soon, for Chamberlain had lost a third of his command and was entirely out of ammunition. Vincent's men in this affair took two colonels, fifteen officers, and five hundred men prisoners, and a thousand stand of arms. Hill in his official report says, 'Hood's right was held as in a vise.'

Doubleday's account is more nearly correct than some of the others, but he makes one error, when he says that:

> General Warren, who was on Meade's staff as chief engineer, had ridden about this time to the signal station on Little Round Top to get a better view of the field. He saw the long line of the enemy approaching and about to overlap Ward's left, and perceived that unless prompt succour arrived Little Round Top would fall into their hands. Once in their possession, they would flank our whole line and post guns there to drive our troops from the ridge; so that this eminence was in reality the key of the battlefield and must be held at all hazards. He saw Barnes' division, which Sykes had ordered forward, formed for a charge and about to go to the relief of De Trobriand, who held the centre of Birney's line and who was sorely beset. Without losing a moment he rode down the slope, over to Barnes, took the responsibility of detaching Vincent's brigade and hurried it back to take post on Little Round Top. He then sent a staff officer to inform General Meade of what he had done and to represent the immense importance of holding this commanding point.

This statement about his taking the responsibility of detaching Vincent's brigade and hurrying it back to take post on Little Round Top is imaginary. (See Warren's letters to Captain Farley, and Lieutenant Mackenzie's letter to General Meade.) Doubleday may have been well informed about the first day's battle, but he makes no claim to have been with the troops on the left during the second day, and apparently got his information of what took place there, at least to some extent, from rumours sent in by what was called in the war time "the grapevine telegraph."

Comte de Paris: *The Civil War in America*, Vol. iii

> About a quarter to four o'clock Warren, following Meade's instructions, had reached this hill (Little Round Top), and was climbing it for the purpose of surveying the country. The officers of the signal corps stationed on the top having informed him that they thought they had seen the enemy's lines in the

woods between Plum Run and the Emmittsburg road, he had ordered Smith's battery to fire a shot in that direction. Just as the projectile passed whistling above the trees all the Confederate soldiers had instinctively raised their heads, and this simultaneous movement being communicated to the polished arms they held in their hands, Warren had caught their reflection like a streak of lightning, winding with a long trail among the leaves. This momentary apparition had been a revelation to him; he had divined the danger which menaced Little Round Top, and understood by the same token the importance of this position. It was necessary to hasten in order to find defenders for it. Following in the wake of Sykes, who had just crossed the hill on foot with Barnes' division, he had found him near the wheatfield completing the reconnaissance of which we have spoken. The commander of the Fifth corps had immediately ordered Colonel Vincent, who was in command of Barnes' Third brigade, to proceed to occupy the foot of Little Round Top; Hazlett's battery was to co-operate with him. Warren, going in advance of them, had reached his post of observation to witness the first attack of Law against the four regiments which alone are defending the gorge of Plum Run.

One moment later the bulk of these troops was falling back upon the flank of the Devil's Den hill, while a party of sharpshooters was trying to find shelter among the rocks scattered along the western flank of Little Round Top. The Confederates were hastening in pursuit of them; their projectiles already reached the elevated post whence Warren was watching this exciting scene. He could not, however, see Vincent's brigade, which, encompassing the hill at the west, had disappeared in the woods.

This position, easy to defend and impossible to recapture, whose importance Warren alone seems to have then understood, was therefore about to fall into the hands of the enemy, without striking a blow. The young general of engineers makes a last effort to save it. He directs the officers of the signal corps, who are preparing to abandon a post without defenders, to continue waving their flags, in spite of the enemy's fire, in order to deceive him and detain him for a few moments while he is going to ask for assistance from a body of troops whose column he sees moving along the road followed a short time since by

Barnes. It is the Third brigade of Ayres' division of the Fifth corps, under command of General Weed, and is preceding the rest of the division at a considerable distance.

Weed has gone forward in advance to ask for instructions from Sickles; but the first regiment that Warren encounters is commanded by Colonel O'Rorke, his friend and during a certain period of time his subordinate, who does not hesitate to respond to the pressing demands of his former chief. While the rest of the brigade is continuing its march, O'Rorke causes the column of the One Hundred and Fortieth New York, which, fortunately, is of considerable strength, to scale directly the acclivities of Little Round Top.

During this time, Vincent, hastening the pace of his soldiers, has reached the southern extremity of this same hill. On this side, it is not so steep as on the other sides, being prolonged by a ridge which about halfway presents a horizontal stretch of nearly one hundred yards in length, descending thence by gentle gradations as far as the foot of the large Round Top. This ridge affords an excellent position to Vincent for barring the passage to Law's soldiers, who are rapidly advancing in his direction. He posts himself along the western slope, with the Sixteenth Michigan on the right, below the very summit of the hill, the Forty-Fourth New York and the Eighty-Third Pennsylvania in the centre, and the Twentieth Maine, under Colonel Chamberlain, on the left, along the extremity of the ridge. These troops could not have arrived more opportunely.

Hood, after being for some time held stationary by the difficulty of keeping his soldiers in the ranks under the fire of a Federal battery posted at the bottom of the gorge, has at last reached the foot of Little Round Top, which he points out to them as a prey thenceforth easily captured. A great yell goes up from the ranks of the assailants, who rush with impetuosity upon the centre of Vincent's brigade. But upon this ground all the advantages are in favour of the defence, while the fire of the Unionists, sheltered among its inaccessible recesses, stops the. Confederates, who stumble at every step they take in their efforts to reach them. They do not turn back on that account, but, posting themselves in their turn behind the rocks, engage in a murderous encounter with Vincent's brigade, which defends itself almost at the point of the muzzle.

Law, seeing the resistance which this small band makes in front of him, determines to turn it. He extends his left for the purpose of outflanking the Sixteenth Michigan, and attacks it with so much vigour that it cannot resist the onslaught. The situation is becoming serious for the Federals; Vincent is entirely isolated from the rest of the army, and no longer protects the principal point of the position, the summit of Little Round Top, on which the officers of the signal corps are bravely continuing to wave their colours.

At the very moment when the Sixteenth Michigan is succumbing, O'Rorke's soldiers, by a really providential coincidence, reach at a full run this summit which Warren points out to them as the citadel to be preserved at any cost.

At their feet lies the vast battlefield, whence are heard vague noises and savage cries, the rattling of musketry, the cannon's roar, and where all the incidents of the combat are seen through a cloud of smoke; but they have no leisure to contemplate this spectacle, for they find themselves face to face with Law's soldiers, who are climbing the hill on the opposite side. A few minutes' delay among the Federals would have sufficed to put the Confederates in possession of the summit. Never perhaps was seen the winner of a race secure such a prize at so little cost. The Unionists, although surprised, do not, however, hesitate. They have time neither to form in line of battle nor even to load their guns or fix bayonets. O'Rorke calls them and pushes them forward.

A large number of them fall at the fire of the enemy; the rest rush down upon the latter at a run, brandishing their muskets aloft; and this movement suffices to stop the Confederates. The Federals take prisoners those among the assailants who had been foremost in the race, and open a brisk fire of musketry upon the others. Vincent's right, having recovered from its check, comes to their assistance. Hazlett's battery has scaled Little Round Top, with the One Hundred and Fortieth New York; the most extraordinary efforts, together with the co-operation of a portion of the regiment, have been required to haul the pieces of artillery as far as the summit.

Although the position is very dangerous, for showers of bullets are falling around the guns, which cannot be depressed enough to reach the enemy along the slope which he is scaling, Hazlett boldly takes his position and directs his fire against the Confederate reserve in the valley; he knows that the presence of his guns encourages the Union infantry. The Federal line, thus strengthened, presents an impregnable front to Hood's assaults; the position of Little Round Top is safe for the present. But this advantage has been dearly bought; in a few minutes the One Hundred and Fortieth New York has lost more than one hundred men, a large number of officers being wounded. The valiant O'Rorke has paid with his life for the example of bravery which he set to his soldiers. Having left West Point two years previously with the highest honours, he had been destined, in the judgment of all his comrades, for the most elevated positions in the army.

A personal and desperate struggle takes place along the whole front of the two bodies of troops. They watch each other, and aim from behind the rocks and bushes; some of the combatants are seen here and there climbing trees in order to secure a better shot; the balls whistle in every direction; two pieces of Smith's Federal battery take the line of the assailants obliquely, throwing shells into their midst. The dead and wounded disappear among the rocks. On both sides the officers perform prodigies of valour, for they feel the importance of the disputed position. Law is not satisfied with musketry-fire, which may be prolonged without any decisive success; he wishes to pierce the enemy's line, and brings back against the One Hundred and Fortieth New York the soldiers of his command who had been stopped by the unexpected arrival of this regiment; but Vincent, who had assumed command of the whole line, hastens with a few reinforcements and the attack is repulsed.

The combatants are beginning to be exhausted on both sides; the Federals have seen Vincent fall gloriously with a large number of his men; the losses of the Confederates are also heavy; the most serious one is that of Hood, who, being always at the post of danger, has been badly wounded in the arm. . . .

Reinforcements, equally needful, arrive about the same time on the extreme Federal left, in front of Little Round Top. Before the combat had begun at this point Sykes had directed Ayres' division toward this position; Weed's brigade, which preceded the other two at a considerable distance, had been turned aside, without the knowledge of the commander of the Fifth corps, by a pressing call from Sickles, and it was going to the assistance of the Third corps when Warren went to seek O'Rorke and his regiment. As soon as Sykes was informed of this fact, he ordered Weed, who had not yet fallen into line, to return with all possible haste to take the position already occupied by the One Hundred and Fortieth New York. This order was promptly executed.

Weed reached Little Round Top at the moment when Vincent was mortally wounded and when both sides were preparing to renew the struggle which had been temporarily suspended. He takes position on the right of Vincent's brigade, of which Colonel Rice has assumed the command, thus enabling him to reinforce his left. Chamberlain, on his part, in order to keep the enemy in check, has been obliged to place a portion of the Twentieth Maine *en potence* above the defile which separates the two summits. It is, in fact, against this point that Law directs all his efforts, and the combat is resumed with fresh vigour, without allowing Weed time to deploy his battalions.

His soldiers, having speedily recovered, rush to the assault with the earnestness of men who have never encountered an obstacle without breaking it down. He strives to outflank the Federal line in order to reach Little Round Top by way of the eastern side of the ridge; his troops have been under less fire on this side, but they have to do with the Twentieth Maine, which defends its position with all the vigour of the strong race of backwoodsmen among whom it has been recruited; again they fight hand to hand, the assailants still trying to turn their adversaries during the combat, the latter prolonging their line and bringing it more and more to the rear, in order to frustrate this manoeuvre. . . .

About an hour since we left the two parties in conflict along the flank opposite to this elevated position, and Law's soldiers, in spite of their reduced number, rushing against the Twentieth Maine. The firing of musketry is again heard along the whole line. Weed, who sets an example to all around him, is mortally wounded near Hazlett's battery, whose commander, stooping to receive his last words, is struck in his turn, and falls lifeless upon the body of his chief; nearly all the superior officers are either killed or wounded. But the enemy is also exhausted: in order to surround the left of the Federals he has prolonged his line to

too great an extent. Colonel Chamberlain takes advantage of it to charge the enemy in his turn. The Confederates, surprised by this attack, are repulsed, leaving behind them more than three hundred wounded and prisoners. . . .
Chamberlain has scaled the slopes of the Great Round Top with a few soldiers and captured a squad of the enemy which had come to reconnoitre. Fisher's brigade joins him in occupying this commanding position, thus closing all access to the Confederates at this point.

The Civil War in America, by the Comte de Paris, is generally conceded to be one of the best, if not the best history yet written. It was written in French, apparently as a study for military students. It has the merit of being impartial. Other histories, whether Union or Confederate, almost invariably show a preference for one side or the other in the conflict. The Comte de Paris and two other French noblemen, the Prince de Joinville and the Duc de Chartres, came to the United States and tendered their services to the Government. The Duc de Chartres was a younger brother of the Comte de Paris. They were grandsons of Louis Philippe. These three served as volunteer *aides-de-camp* on the staff of General McClellan in 1862. The Comte de Paris was the legitimate heir to the French throne as next in succession in the Bourbon dynasty. He was a trained soldier, and gave many years of careful and painstaking work to this history, but died before he had finished it.

While he was writing, our government gave him or his authorised agent every facility for inspecting and copying official records and documents. He had many acquaintances among military men, especially Union officers, who gladly gave him all the assistance in their power. (See the Warren letters and the letters to Captain Farley, which will give an idea of his earnest desire to ascertain the facts and his method of obtaining information.) The work in French was published in six volumes, which are consolidated into four volumes in the English translation. The work ends with the close of the campaigns of 1863. In view of its importance and general accuracy I have quoted at greater length from his account of the battle at Little Round Top than I have from some other writers. With some hesitation, I venture to question a few of his statements which I think are not quite in accordance with the facts. They are very few, and the wonder is that, writing on the other side of the Atlantic, he could have written an account so free from faults. He has done better than some of our own historians who were officers of high rank and present in the battle.

He says that Warren, following Meade's instructions, reached Little Round Top about a quarter to four o'clock, and by a shot which he ordered Smith's battery to fire into the woods between Plum Run and the Emmittsburg road, he discovered a long line of the enemy concealed in those woods. I think the time of Warren's arrival on Little Round Top was somewhat earlier. There is a general agreement among the Confederate authorities that the divisions of Hood and McLaws were in position by 3 p.m., or shortly after, each with four batteries of artillery massed on its left. At 3:30 p. m., these batteries had opened a heavy cannonade on the Union line, which was replied to by the Union batteries between Little Round Top and the Peach Orchard.

The Comte de Paris says, as quoted above:

> Following in the wake of Sykes, who had just crossed the hill on foot with Barnes' division, he (Warren) had found him near the wheat-field completing the reconnaissance of which we have spoken. The commander of the Fifth corps had immediately ordered Colonel Vincent, who was in command of Barnes' Third brigade, to proceed to occupy the foot of Little Round Top.

This statement is incredible in some respects; part of it has been repeated by another writer, who says that Sykes and Barnes preceded on foot Barnes' division. No private soldier in the Fifth corps, knowing the distances that Sykes and Barnes had to traverse that day, would believe that they went about on foot. My own recollection is that both were well mounted and accompanied by the mounted officers of their respective staffs and a number of mounted orderlies. A corps or division commander in the immediate presence of the enemy, wishing to get a better view, might temporarily dismount to be less conspicuous; but he could not properly handle his corps or division by going about on foot. This erroneous statement is traceable to one of the few incorrect translations of the French edition of Comte de Paris' book. The original reads that Sykes had just crossed *"au pied de la colline,"* meaning the foot of the hill, referring to the ridge extending north from Little Round Top.

I believe that Warren did not leave the hill after he reached the signal station until he went down and detached O'Rorke's regiment.

(See Warren's letters and Sykes' letter to Captain Farley.) Warren had with him that day three lieutenants of engineers serving on his staff, Mackenzie, Reese, and Roebling, also some mounted orderlies. Meade sent Warren to Little Round Top to observe the battle from that elevation and keep him, Meade, informed of its progress. Warren used these officers of his staff to keep in touch with Meade and take such measures as in his judgment seemed necessary. He sent Mackenzie to Sickles and Sykes asking for troops to be sent to Little Round Top, explaining the necessity. Sickles refused, but Sykes promised a brigade. (See Mackenzie's letter to Meade, March, 1864).

I believe that neither Sykes nor Barnes detached Vincent's brigade and directed it to take position on the foot of Little Round Top. I find no evidence that Sykes saw the position where Vincent's brigade fought, at any time during the battle. What actually happened in this connection I relate in my own statement.

The Comte de Paris' narration then continues:

> Warren, going in advance of them (Vincent's brigade), had reached his post of observation to witness the first attack of Law against the four regiments which alone are defending the gorge of Plum Run. One moment later the bulk of these troops are falling back upon the flank of the Devil's Den hill, while a party of sharpshooters was trying to find shelter among the rocks scattered along the western flank of Little Round Top. The Confederates were hastening in pursuit of them; their projectiles already reached the elevated post whence Warren was watching this exciting scene. He could not, however, see Vincent's brigade, which, encompassing the hill at the west, had disappeared in the woods.

This implies that Warren did not wait to conduct Vincent to his position on the south foot of Little Round Top, but returned to his place at the signal station. I think, as previously stated, that Warren had not left the hill. If, by the first attack of Law on the four regiments (Ward's brigade) defending the gorge of Plum Run is meant Law's brigade, it is a mistake. The Comte de Paris seems to have thought, as appears later in his account, that Hood was still in command of his division; but Hood was wounded near his batteries during the cannonading which preceded the advance of the infantry, and was carried off the field, leaving Law, the senior brigade commander, in command of the four brigades of Hood's division.

No regiment of Law's brigade, with the possible exception of the Forty-Fourth Alabama, took part in this attack on Ward. Ward's brigade was not driven back in a moment, but held its position for nearly an hour. The first attack on Ward was made by the First Texas and Third Arkansas of Robertson's brigade. They were not strong enough to drive back Ward's men. They were soon joined by Benning's Georgia brigade, and later by Anderson's Georgia brigade, on the left of Robertson and Benning. The Fourth and Fifth Texas of Robertson's brigade went with Law's regiments up the swale on the north side of Big Round Top to attack Vincent. They did not rejoin the other regiments of Robertson's brigade until night, when the brigade was reassembled near the western foot of Big Round Top. (See Confederate official reports.)

The statement that Warren could not see Vincent's brigade "which, encompassing the hill on the west, disappeared in the woods," is a surprising error. If Vincent had tried to reach his position by passing along the west front of Little Round Top, he would have been in full view from Warren's post at the signal station; but would have been stopped by the Confederates then swarming around Devil's Den. This is the statement of the English translation; but examining the original French, I find that it reads encompassing the hill "à l'est," meaning on the east. This is in accordance with the facts. (See Warren's letters.)

Vincent's brigade reached its position without serious interference from the enemy. A few shells burst near the column as it crossed the Plum Run valley. It passed the northern end of Little Round Top, then, turning to the right, made its way through the woods along the eastern slope until it passed the high rock, and was formed on the lower ground between the two Round Tops. The brigade was all in position there and had thrown out skirmishers toward the southeast and the west before a single Confederate made his appearance.

Comte de Paris continues:

> During this time, Vincent, hastening the pace of his soldiers, has reached the southern extremity of this same hill. On this side, it is not so steep as on the other sides, being prolonged by a ridge which about halfway presents a horizontal stretch of nearly one hundred yards in length, descending thence by gentle gradations as far as the foot of the large Round Top. This ridge affords an excellent position to Vincent for barring the passage to Law's soldiers, who are rapidly advancing in his direction.

I think that "during this time" refers to the time in which Warren was watching the fight at the Devil's Den and not to the time which Vincent took in reaching his position after leaving Barnes' division. Some have thought that Warren, as soon as he returned to the hill and saw the probability of Confederate success in driving Ward back,—thus opening a way for the enemy to reach the summit of the hill,—also saw Weed's brigade approaching, and rode to meet it to secure reinforcements for this part of the hill. Vincent had been fighting in his position at least half an hour before the Confederates drove Ward back and opened the way for their advance to the summit. After Vincent left the division, Sykes spent some time in posting the other two brigades in the position which he had selected for them, and then rode back to the vicinity of Rock Creek to bring up the other two divisions of the corps. On the way, he met Weed's brigade, and ordered Weed to place it on Little Round Top.

It must have been at least half an hour after Vincent got into position before Weed's brigade arrived where Warren could see them. During this half hour Vincent, had been fighting Law's brigade and the Fourth and Fifth Texas regiments. These troops did not abandon their attempt to break the centre of Vincent's brigade without a desperate struggle. They did not make the movement to turn Vincent's right flank until their assaults on the centre seemed hopeless. So long as Ward held his position at the Devil's Den they could not have made this flank movement by the Plum Run valley; but when Ward was driven back the way was open and they took advantage of it.

Then, Warren, seeing the danger, left the hill for the first time and, detaching O'Rorke's regiment from Weed's brigade, sent his aide—Lieutenant Roebling—to conduct it to the crest of the hill, where it arrived just in time to drive back the Confederates. Warren did not return to the hill, but rode away to meet General Meade. (For Sykes' movement see his official report.)

Narrative continues:

> Hood, after being for some time held stationary by the difficulty of keeping his soldiers in the ranks under the fire of a Federal battery posted at the bottom of the gorge, has at last reached the foot of Little Round Top, which he points out to them as a prey thenceforth easily captured.

Later, in speaking of the losses at this point, the relation says:

> The losses of the Confederates are also heavy; the most serious

one is that of Hood, who, being always at the post of danger, has been badly wounded in the arm.

Neither Law nor Hood made any official report of his part in the Battle of Gettysburg. Several years after the battle Law explains why, in a paper contributed to the *Century Magazine*, and published in *Battles and Leaders of the Civil War*. There is no evidence that Hood was present with his division at any time after the infantry advanced to the attack. He was wounded by a shell while near the batteries of his division soon after the artillery opened fire, and was carried from the field. Law, as senior brigade commander, assumed command of the division, leaving the command of the brigade to Colonel Sheffield, of the Forty-Eighth Alabama. Sheffield's official report mentions the fact, but has nothing to say of what he did as brigade commander, confining his statement to the action of his own regiment. (See Law's paper, quoted elsewhere, and Hood's letter to Longstreet, quoted in Oates' book, *The War Between the Union and the Confederacy*.)

The statement that Law brought back his soldiers for a second assault on the One Hundred and Fortieth New York, and that Vincent assumed command of the whole line, is incorrect. The Confederates who made the flank movement against the right of the Sixteenth Michigan, and succeeded in driving back the greater part of three companies on the right of this regiment, with the regimental colours, were right among the Union men. Vincent fell while endeavouring to rally the men of the Sixteenth.

Just at this moment O'Rorke with his men came over the crest of the hill and, charging down the hill, drove back the enemy, capturing some and killing and wounding many others. They formed on the right of the remainder of the Michigan regiment, and remained there, sheltering themselves as well as they could among the rocks on the western slope, and no further advance was made by the Confederates against this position. Weed did not arrive with the other regiments of his brigade until sometime after Vincent fell, and after the Confederate assault had been repulsed.

In this account, too little credit is given to O'Rorke and his regiment. Vincent had fallen, and the Confederates, who had been baffled in all their previous attempts to break his line, had succeeded at last in driving in the right flank. Those of the enemy who had already entered our line were followed closely by a crowd of their comrades swarming up the hill. Nothing could have stopped them from doubling up our broken line except the timely arrival of O'Rorke and his men. It was a hand-to-hand conflict, but the Confederates were forced to yield. It lasted only a short time, but in that time more than a hundred men of the One Hundred and Fortieth had fallen. This regiment alone bore the brunt of the attack. Their gallant young colonel was instantly killed, within a few feet of where Vincent lay. The other regiments of Weed's brigade did not arrive until the close fighting at that point was finished. The losses of these three regiments combined were much less than those of the One Hundred and Fortieth alone.

General Francis A. Walker: *History of the Second Army Corps*

The position of Little Round Top, not less important upon the left than Cemetery Hill upon the centre, or Culp's Hill upon the right, had been strangely neglected ever since Geary, sent thither by Hancock upon his first arrival on the field, had been withdrawn to join the Twelfth corps at Culp's. The vast extension involved in Sickles' advance had left no troops available to occupy the hill, and thousands of Confederates, fierce and eager, were advancing to seize it while defended solely by a signal officer and his two assistants. No, not by these alone.

One other was there—a slender, graceful young officer of engineers, Warren, who had climbed the slope to scan the western horizon, where his prescient mind had descried the signs of danger. Perceiving the yet distant approach of Law's brigade, Warren commands the signal officers to continue their work to the last moment, in order to create the impression that the hill is occupied, and darting northward seeks some casual force that may anticipate the fatal occupation of Little Round Top by the enemy.

It is the head of the column of the Fifth corps which he meets, hastening to the support of De Trobriand. He takes the responsibility of detaching the foremost troops, and hurries them forward to anticipate the arrival of the Confederate line of battle. There is not a minute to spare. The opposing forces meet on the crest; the contest is close, fierce, and deadly. The rocky slopes and narrow wooded passes resound with infernal clamour. Vincent falls at the head of his men. Weed also is struck down with a mortal wound, and as Hazlett bends over him to catch the last message, he, too, is thrown lifeless upon the body of his friend. But our line is now complete, and the valour of the men of Maine, Michigan, New York, and Pennsylvania has made it secure. Well did General Abbott say that but for the wonderful *coup d'oeil* of Warren and his prompt acceptance of responsibility the name of Gettysburg might only have been known in history as that of the place where the Union cause made its grave.

One wonders where General Walker obtained this information about Warren detaching Vincent's brigade. He certainly did not get it from Warren. His opportunities for learning the facts about the Second corps were ample, and his history of that corps is an admirable book. But Warren's statements in his own letters show that for once Walker was mistaken.

General Henry J. Hunt: *Battles and Leaders of the Civil War*, Vol. iii.

As soon as Longstreet's attack commenced, General Warren was sent by General Meade to see to the condition of the extreme left. The duty could not have been intrusted to better hands. Passing along the lines, he found Little Round Top, the key of the position, unoccupied except by a signal station. The enemy at the time lay concealed, awaiting the signal for assault, when a shot fired in their direction caused a sudden movement on their part which, by the gleam of reflected sunlight from their bayonets, revealed their long lines outflanking the position.

Fully comprehending the imminent danger, Warren sent to General Meade for a division. The enemy was already advancing when, noticing the approach of the Fifth corps, Warren rode to meet it, caused Weed's and Vincent's brigades and Hazlett's battery to be detached from the latter, and hurried them to the summit.

The passage of the six guns through the roadless woods and amongst the rocks was marvellous. Under ordinary circumstances it would have been considered an impossible feat, but the eagerness of the men to get into action with their comrades of the infantry, and the skilful driving, brought them without delay to the very summit, where they went immediately into battle. They were barely in time, for the enemy were also climbing the hill. A close and bloody hand-to-hand struggle ensued, which left both Round Tops in our possession. Weed and Hazlett were killed, and Vincent was mortally wounded—all young men of great promise.

Weed had served with much distinction as an artillerist in the Peninsular, Second Bull Run, and Antietam campaigns, had become chief of artillery of his army corps, and at Chancellorsville showed such special aptitude and fitness for large artillery commands that he was immediately promoted from captain to brigadier-general and transferred to the infantry. Hazlett was killed whilst bending over his former chief to receive his last message. Lieutenant Rittenhouse efficiently commanded the battery during the remainder of the battle.

One would infer from the order of the names that Weed's brigade came first, followed by Vincent, and that Warren detached or caused to be detached both brigades and hurried them to the summit of Round Top with Hazlett's battery. This is a mistake. Vincent's brigade did not go to the summit, and Weed's brigade, except the One Hundred and Fortieth New York, did not reach there until the infantry fighting was finished, except the desultory, long-distance firing of the sharpshooters.

General Hunt was chief of artillery, and his statements about the batteries are made with authority; but he had no direct connection with the movements of the infantry.

General Regis De Trobriand: *Four Years with the Army of the Potomac*

When the enemy had turned Ward's left, that was but the first step towards getting possession of Little Round Top. He pushed his forces on rapidly from that point, and began to climb the steep hill with so much the greater impunity that the summit had not as yet been occupied by us except by a squad of the signal service. Fortune willed, at that moment, that Warren, chief engineer on the staff, should arrive on this point, whence the view embraced the attack in its whole extent. A glance told him the imminence of the danger, and he ran to Barnes' division of the Fifth corps, on its way to reinforce us. He took upon himself to detach from it a brigade commanded by Colonel Vincent, and to hurry it, on the run, to the summit of Little Round Top, which Hood's Texans were also endeavouring to reach from the other side.

Both of the parties arrived at the crest at nearly the same time. They both understood the vital importance of the position. So, without stopping to fire, they rushed upon each other with the bayonet. In that hand-to-hand contest, with equal courage, the solid muscles of the North prevailed over the hot blood of the

Lieut.-General John B. Hood

Brevet Major-General Henry J. Hunt,
chief of artillery of the Army of the Potomac

South. Our men were victorious, and the position was saved; not without, however, a continuation of a deadly fire from the assailants against General Weed's brigade, which had joined that of Colonel Vincent, and on Hazlett's battery, which the men had succeeded, with unheard-of efforts, in dragging up to the top, through woods and over rocks. Finally, a bayonet charge of the Twentieth Maine, under the lead of Colonel Chamberlain, swept the ground of the enemy. The possession of Little Round Top cost us dearly. Weed, Vincent, and Hazlett paid their lives for it. And how many more!

This is another example of erroneous statements by a writer who was not present. Warren arrived at the signal station some time before any attack was made on Ward. The first attack on Little Round Top was made on Vincent's brigade, which was not on the summit, but was posted on the southern slope in front of Big Round Top. The attack from the Plum Run Valley was directed against Vincent's right flank. It was the last of several assaults on Vincent, and was repulsed by the One Hundred and Fortieth New York. Warren did not detach Vincent, and Vincent did not go to the summit.

Lieutenant-Colonel William H. Powell: *The Fifth Army Corps*

Soon after 6 a.m., July 2, General Meade directed his son and *aide*. Captain George Meade, to ride down to General Sickles, explain where headquarters of the army were located, find out if his troops were in position, and ask if he had anything to report. Captain Meade, returning, reported that his mission had been made known to General Sickles, who was resting in his tent, by Captain Randolph, chief of artillery. Third Army Corps, who had brought in reply the statement that his troops were not yet in position, and that he was in some doubt as to where he was to go.

General Meade directed his son to ride back to General Sickles as quickly as possible and urge on him the necessity of getting his troops in position immediately. Captain Meade returned at once to Third corps headquarters, where he found the tent previously occupied by General Sickles struck, the staff mounted and on duty, and General Sickles himself about to mount.

In reply to General Meade's message. General Sickles reported that his troops were then moving and would soon be in position. General Meade sent no order by his son with regard to the line to be occupied. It could not have been far from 7 a.m. when Captain Meade found General Sickles preparing to mount.

In his official report General Geary says:

> At 5 a.m. on the second, having been relieved by the Third Army Corps, in obedience to orders from Major-General Slocum, the division was placed on the right of the centre of the main line of battle east of the turnpike.'

General Geary afterward explained to General Meade that, upon receiving notice that he would be relieved by General Sickles, he sent to him a staff officer instructed to explain the importance of the position he held, and to ask that, if troops could not be sent at once to relieve him, at least a staff officer might be sent to acquaint himself with the position and be ready to post the troops when they arrived. He received for answer that 'General Sickles would attend to it in due time,' and after waiting some time in vain for either troops or officers, he withdrew, considering himself relieved.

In his official report, General D. B. Birney says:

> At 7 a.m., under orders from Major-General Sickles, I relieved Geary's division and formed a line, resting its left on the Sugar-Loaf Mountain (Little Round Top), and the right thrown in a direct line toward the cemetery, connecting on the right with the Second division of this corps. My picket line was in the Emmittsburg road, with sharpshooters some three hundred yards in advance.'

General A. A. Humphreys, in his report, says:

> At an early hour of the morning my division was massed in the vicinity of its bivouac, facing the Emmittsburg road, near the crest of the ridge running from the cemetery of Gettysburg in a southerly direction to a rugged, conical-shaped hill, which I find goes by the name of Round Top, about two miles from Gettysburg.

Manifestly, General Sickles at or about 7 a.m. formed his line where General Meade, upon reaching the field, had instructed him to post it. If further proof could be needed, it is amply furnished by General Sickles' criticisms of the line. The order, however, was repeated to General Sickles by General Meade in person, just before noon of July 2:

General Humphreys reports:

Shortly after midday I was ordered to form my division in line of battle, my left joining the right of the First division of the Third corps, Major-General Birney commanding, and my right resting opposite the left of General Caldwell's division of the Second corps, which was massed on the crest near my place of bivouac. The line I was directed to occupy was near the foot of the westerly slope of the ridge I have already mentioned.

'Shortly after midday' was shortly after General Meade had repeated his' order to General Sickles, and the line occupied in disregard of that order was that styled by General Hunt 'the Plum Run line,' and declared by him 'not an eligible line to occupy.' It was some five hundred yards in front of the position assigned to the Third corps by General Meade.

The Sixth Army Corps reached Gettysburg about 2 p.m., July 2. Upon its arrival being reported to him. General Meade directed the Fifth corps to move at once to the left of his line, and the Sixth to occupy the position vacated by the Fifth. Shortly after 2 p.m. he rode to the left to await the arrival of the troops. He then found that General Sickles had advanced his line still farther, taking a position with his First division in front of Little Round Top, from the Devil's Den to the peach orchard, and was about advancing his Second division up to the Emmittsburg road.

Up to this time, with the exception of a reconnaissance sent out at General Hunt's suggestion, just before noon, little more than picket firing had occurred along the Third corps front; but now the brief discussion of the situation by the army and corps commanders was interrupted by the advance of the Confederate lines in force. To General Meade's remark that he had moved out too far. General Sickles had just rejoined: 'Very well, sir, I'll withdraw then,' when Longstreet's artillery opened. Saying, 'I wish to God you could, sir, but you see those people do not intend to let you,' General Meade left him and rode out upon the line.

General Sickles then ordered his Second division, General A. A. Humphreys commanding, to advance to the Emmittsburg road. As this movement was commencing. General Humphreys received an order directly from General Meade, instructing him to move his division at once to Little Round Top. The division was immediately started by the left flank toward that point, but had only started when the order was recalled by General Meade; the troops retraced the steps taken and moved out to the Emmittsburg road.

At General Warren's suggestion, General Meade had previously sent that officer to ascertain the exact condition of affairs upon the extreme left, and beyond doubt it was his confidence in General Warren, and his knowledge that the Fifth corps must soon appear upon the ground, and would be aided by Caldwell's division of the Second corps, which he had ordered to report to General Sykes at Little Round Top, that induced the recall of his order to General Humphreys, which would have left the right of the Third corps temporarily unguarded, while securing the far more important and more imperilled left.

Attended by Lieutenants W. A. Roebling and Ranald S. Mackenzie, General Warren reached the summit of Little Round Top and found it held only by a signal officer and his assistants. It is an injustice to General Warren to assert that he discovered Little Round Top to be the key to the Federal position when he reached the lookout on its summit on July 2. It is not to be supposed that the fact escaped his quick eye on July 1, when General Hancock noted it and took possession. General Geary had not failed to recognise the importance of the position assigned to him that night, and General Meade, in ordering the Third corps into position, relieving Geary's division on July 2, or in directing the movement of Humphreys' division from the right of the Third corps line to the unguarded point, had not acted ignorantly.

General Humphreys was not blind, and General Sykes' dispositions as the Fifth corps reached the field evince his comprehension of the evident facts, and even General Sickles admits knowledge of the importance of the trust he disregarded. While Warren, standing upon the rocky summit, undoubtedly Realised better than any other officer on the field the full importance of the position, his notable service lay in his instant comprehension of how utterly it had been abandoned, and in his characteristic promptness in securing the dispositions that held it safe. He was the saviour, not the discoverer, of Little Round Top.

General Warren at once sent Lieutenant Mackenzie to General

Sickles with a request that troops should be sent to occupy it. General Sickles refused, saying that his whole command was necessary to defend his front. General Warren sent, by the same messenger, a note to General Meade requesting him to send at least a division to him. But the emergency grew more urgent with every moment. The whole Confederate line was sweeping from out the woods in which it had formed, far outflanking the left of the Third corps line where Smith's battery, in air and almost unsupported on the rocks of the Devil's Den, gallantly waited its doom,—and between that left and Round Top the way to the death of the nation lay invitingly open to the confidently advancing enemy.

To Warren's quick eye and clear mind the fate of the Third corps line was manifest, and at that moment this was the only eye that saw, the only mind that comprehended, the full gravity of the situation. But with him to see and know was to act. Noticing troops moving out the Peach Orchard road to join in the hopeless struggle in front, bidding the signal officer to continue waving his flags in defiance, he spurred down the steep hillside. In the meantime, General Meade had sent orders to Sykes to send a brigade to report to Sickles. The corps was then waiting orders on the bank of Pipe Creek. Weed started promptly, and after going a little distance, he turned to Colonel O'Rorke and said that he would go on and find General Sickles, and would leave O'Rorke in command of the brigade. He left all the brigade staff—except Lieutenant E. N. Warren—and brigade flag with O'Rorke. Weed and his *aide* rode forward at a rapid gait and found General Sickles, and then sent Lieutenant Warren back to pilot the brigade to him. The lieutenant rode back rapidly, and when he got to Little Round Top found the brigade going up the slope. He told O'Rorke that the brigade was expected to go to General Sickles. General Warren was there also, and he said he would keep O'Rorke's regiment.

General Warren, in descending from Little Round Top, where he had been scanning the field, having observed the approach of Weed's brigade, rode straight toward the head of the column. He called out to O'Rorke, beginning to speak while some eight or ten rods from him, that he wanted him to go up there; that the enemy was advancing unopposed up the opposite side of the hill down which he had come, and he wanted one regiment to meet him. He was apparently greatly excited, and spoke in his usually impulsive style. O'Rorke told him that General Weed was ahead and expected the brigade to follow him. 'Never mind that,' said General Warren. 'Bring your regiment up here, and I will take the responsibility.' It was at this time that Lieutenant Warren put in an appearance.

O'Rorke, without hesitation, turned to the left and followed the officer who had accompanied General Warren, while Warren himself rode rapidly down the hillside. The remainder of the brigade started to join General Weed, under the guidance of Lieutenant Warren. It had gone but a short distance before General Sykes sent a staff officer to know where the brigade was going. Being told, 'To report to General Sickles,' and although the brigade was not stopped, the staff officer requested Lieutenant Warren to go with him to General Weed. They rode as fast as they could,—the distance was not great,—and he told General Weed that he would have to return, as no troops could be spared by General Sykes, and that he would have to return and rejoin his brigade.

General Weed informed General Sickles of the message and hurried back to the troops, and on rejoining was ordered to double-quick them and hurry to Little Round Top, where the One Hundred and Fortieth was hotly engaged. General Warren had ridden to the head of the column in quest of General Weed, and, finding that he was still absent, halted the brigade to await his return. In the meantime, he had met Hazlett's battery and started it after the One Hundred and Fortieth New York. Upon Weed's return, he having received the orders from General Sykes, the brigade countermarched and followed the One Hundred and Fortieth into position.

Guided by Lieutenant Roebling, O'Rorke had dashed up the eastern slope of Little Round Top to gain the face beyond the summit; some of the guns of Hazlett's battery plunging through his line, as, with horses urged to frantic efforts and cannoneers aiding at the wheels, it made for the pinnacle it gained—and holds in history. As they reached the crest the very jaws of hell yawned before them. Upon their right the Third corps line was completely outflanked by Longstreet's impetuous advance, and up the ravine at their feet in front Hood's brigades were panting in their effort to gain the vantage ground that would enable them to add the ignominy of a rout to the disaster of the day. The One Hundred and Fortieth was moving right in front, and not a musket was loaded or a bayonet fixed. The emergency, however, called for action far more than for tactics or precaution.' Springing from his horse, with a shout, 'Down this way, men!' O'Rorke, followed by his command, rushed down the rocky slope, with at least the impetus of a charge.

It took such order as was possible and opened fire upon the enemy. The firing for a few moments was rapid and deadly on both sides, and, standing erect and unsheltered to urge on and encourage his men, O'Rorke, shot through the neck, fell dead without a word. But the Confederate rush was checked, and before it could be urged on again Weed had closed the Ninety-first Pennsylvania upon the One Hundred and Fortieth New York, while the One Hundred and Forty-sixth New York and the One Hundred and Fifty-Fifth Pennsylvania had formed line upon the right of Hazlett's battery, which now crowned the crest. Then Weed and Hazlett fell upon that rocky crest, martyrs to the cause of the Union.

Immediately after starting Weed's brigade from where the corps was lying at Pipe Creek, General Sykes received General Meade's order to take position upon the left. Sykes started his corps upon the road, and, accompanied by General Barnes, commanding the First division, preceded it for the purpose of examining the position he was to occupy. Discovering the undefended left of the Third corps line and the inadequacy of the support given to Smith's battery, he suggested to General Birney to close his division line upon the battery, while he (Sykes) would fill the gap which would be made by the movement with troops from the Fifth corps. Barnes was about being placed in position when General Warren rode rapidly up to General Sykes, with whom Barnes was riding, and, pointing out the position of Round Top, urged the importance of assistance in that direction.

General Sykes yielded to his urgent request, and General Barnes directed Colonel Vincent, commanding the Third brigade, to proceed to that point with his brigade, consisting of the Sixteenth Michigan, Colonel Vincent; Forty-Fourth New York, Colonel Rice; Eighty-Third Pennsylvania, Captain Woodward; and Twentieth Maine, Colonel Chamberlain. Vincent moved with great promptness to the post assigned him. Passing an open field in the hollow ground, in which some Union batteries were going into position, Vincent reached the skirt of a piece of woods, in the farther edge of which there was a heavy musketry fire (O'Rorke's), and when about to go forward into line Colonel Chamberlain received from Colonel Vincent orders to move to the left at the double-quick, taking a farm road crossing Plum Run, in order to gain a rugged mountain spur, called Granite Spur, or Little Round Top.

The enemy's artillery got range of the column as it was climbing the spur, and the crashing of the shells among the rocks and tree-tops made the men move lively along the crest. One or two shells burst in the ranks. Passing to the southern slope of Little Round Top, Colonel Vincent indicated to Colonel Chamberlain the ground his regiment was to occupy, informing him that this was the extreme left of the general line, which he was to hold at all hazards. These were the last words Chamberlain ever heard from Vincent, as it was only a few moments afterwards the latter met his death.

The line faced generally toward a more conspicuous eminence to the southwest, which is known as Sugar Loaf, or Round Top. Between this and Chamberlain's position intervened a smooth and thinly wooded hollow. His line formed, he immediately detached Company B, Captain Morrill commanding, to extend from the left flank across this hollow as a line of skirmishers, with directions to act as occasion might dictate, to prevent a surprise in the exposed flank and rear.

The artillery fire on the position had meanwhile been constant and heavy, but his formation was scarcely complete when the artillery was replaced by a vigorous infantry assault upon the centre of the brigade to Chamberlain's right. This very soon involved the right of the Twentieth Maine, and gradually extended along res entire front. The action was quite sharp and at close quarters. In the midst of this, an officer from the centre informed Chamberlain that some important movement of the enemy was going on in his front, beyond that of the line with which they were engaged. Mounting a large rock. Chamberlain saw a considerable body of the enemy moving by the flank in rear of their engaged line and passing from the direction of the foot of Great Round Top through the valley toward the front of his left. The close engagement not permitting any change of front, he immediately stretched his regiment to the left, by taking intervals, at the same time refusing his left wing, so that it was nearly at right angles with his right, thus occupying about twice the extent of his ordinary front, some of the companies being brought into single rank when the nature of the ground gave sufficient strength or shelter.

The officers and men understood Chamberlain's wishes so well that this movement was executed under fire, the right wing keeping up fire without giving the enemy any occasion to seize or suspect their advantage. But they were not a moment too soon; the enemy's flanking column, having gained its desired direction, burst upon the left with great demonstration, where they evidently had expected an unguarded flank.

A brisk fire was opened at close range, which was so sudden and effective that the Confederates soon fell back among the rocks and low trees in the valley, only to burst forth again with a shout, and rapidly advanced, firing as they came. They pushed up to within a dozen yards of the Union line before the terrible effectiveness of its fire compelled them to break and take shelter.

They renewed the assault on the whole front, and for an hour the fighting was severe. Squads of the enemy broke through the line in several places, and the fight was literally hand-to-hand. The edge of the fight rolled backward and forward like a wave. The dead and wounded were now in front and then in rear. Forced from its position, the regiment desperately recovered it and pushed the enemy down to the foot of the slope. The intervals of the struggle were seized to remove the wounded of both sides, to gather ammunition from the cartridge-boxes of disabled friend or foe on the field, and even to secure better muskets than the Enfields, which were found not to stand service so well. Rude shelters were thrown up of the loose rocks that covered the ground.

The Confederates gathered all their energies for a final assault. Chamberlain had gotten his thin line into as good shape as possible, when a strong force emerged from the scrub-wood in the valley, in two lines in echelon by the right, and, opening a heavy fire, the first line pressed forward as if it meant to sweep everything before it. Fire was opened on it as well as could be with the scant ammunition snatched from the fallen. It did not seem possible to withstand another shock like the one coming on. The loss had been severe. One-half of Chamberlain's left wing had fallen, and a third of the regiment lay just behind it dead or badly wounded.

At this moment, the anxiety was increased by a great roar of musketry in the rear, on the farther or northerly slope of Little Round Top, apparently on the flank of Weed's brigade, then on the crest, in support of Hazlett's battery. The bullets from this attack struck in the left rear of the Twentieth Maine, and it was feared that the enemy had nearly surrounded Little Round Top, and therefore only a desperate chance was left for the small force in the valley. Chamberlain's ammunition was soon exhausted. His men were firing their last shots, and getting ready to club their muskets.

Chamberlain deemed it imperative to strike before he was struck by the overwhelming force in a hand-to-hand fight, which he could not possibly have withstood or survived. At that crisis, he ordered the bayonet. The word was enough. It ran like fire along the line from man to man, and rose into a shout, with which they sprang forward upon the enemy, now not thirty yards distant. Like greyhounds they bounded over shelter, from rock to rock, and launched their fury on the advancing foe. It was veritably 'a forlorn hope.' The effect was surprising; many of the enemy's first line threw down their arms and surrendered.

An officer fired his pistol at Chamberlain's head with one hand, while he handed him his sword with the other. Holding fast by the right and swinging toward the left, the Twentieth Maine made an extended right wheel before which the enemy's second line broke and fell back, fighting from tree to tree, many being captured, until the devoted little Union band had swept the valley of the enemy and cleared the front of nearly the entire brigade.

Four hundred prisoners, including two field and several line officers from the Fifteenth and Forty-Seventh Alabama, with some of the Fourth and Fifth Texas, were sent to the rear, while one hundred and fifty Confederates were found killed and wounded in the front. These troops could not be reinforced at the critical period, as Ayres had been thrown to the front and

Crawford was only arriving.

Historians have exhausted themselves in describing the actions of the 'Peach Orchard' and the events of the third day at Gettysburg. Great stress has been laid upon the results of Pickett's charge, while famous pictures have presented that scene to the gaze of the American public; but the truth of history is, that the little brigade of Vincent's, with the self-sacrificing valour of the Twentieth Maine, under the gallant leadership of Joshua L. Chamberlain, fighting amidst the scrub-oak and rocks in that vale between the Round Tops on the second of July, 1863, saved to the Union arms the historic field of Gettysburg.

Had they faltered for one instant—had they not exceeded their actual duty—while the left of the Third corps was swung in the air half a mile to the right and front of Little Round Top, there would have been no grand charge of Pickett, and 'Gettysburg' would have been the mausoleum of departed hopes for the national cause; for Longstreet would have enveloped Little Round Top, captured all on its crest from the rear, and held the key of the whole position.

In view of such possibilities, it is no wonder that General Meade said to General Sickles, 'I wish to God you could, sir, but you see those people do not intend to let you,' when that officer desired to withdraw his line.

Lieutenant-Colonel Powell at the Battle of Gettysburg was a first lieutenant and *aide-de-camp* on the staff of General Romeyn B. Ayres, commanding the Second division of the Fifth corps. His duty kept him near his chief except for short absences in conveying orders or reporting movements. Ayres makes no mention in his official report of having been on Little Round Top at any time during the battle. Sykes had commanded this division previous to June 28, when Meade was assigned to the command of the army and Sykes succeeded him in the command of the corps. Sykes in his official report says that after posting the two brigades of Barnes' division he returned to order up the remainder of the corps from the vicinity of the Baltimore Pike near the Rock Creek bridge.

On the way, he met Weed's brigade, and ordered it to take position on Little Round Top, then continued on his way to the brigades of Ayres' division. Having started these, he returned to the front, found Weed's brigade, which had not stopped at Little Round Top, moving out to reinforce Sickles. He ordered it to return to the post which he had previously assigned to it. Ayres came up with the other brigades and took position on the ridge north of Little Round Top. Later these brigades under Ayres went forward to a position near the Devil's Den. In all probability, Powell accompanied his chief and had no personal knowledge of the fight on Little Round Top. His book was published in 1896, thirty-three years after the battle.

One would think that an officer of the regular army who served in one of the divisions which participated in the battle on and near Little Round Top, to whom the official records were open, might have been able, in the lapse of a third of a century, to get nearer the facts. He states that Weed's brigade was the first organisation of the Fifth corps to leave the corps near Pipe Creek and proceed to the left under an order to reinforce Sickles. He gets first O'Rorke's regiment, then the remainder of Weed's brigade under Warren's direction posted on Little Round Top and receiving the Confederate assault on the crest of the hill, as the beginning of operations on that part of the field. When this is well started, Warren rides down the hill again and, intercepting Barnes' division, detaches Vincent's brigade and hurries it off to the south slope of the hill where it fought.

A perusal of the official report of his corps commander would have shown him that Barnes' division was the first of the corps to arrive, that Vincent's brigade had gone to its position on Little Round Top before Sykes posted the First and Second brigades on Birney's line; that Sykes then rode to the rear and, meeting Weed's brigade, ordered it to take position on Little Round Top, and continued until he met the other two brigades of Ayres' division; after starting them to the front he returned and found Weed's brigade, except the One Hundred and Fortieth New York, moving out to reinforce Sickles, recalled it, and finally got it in position on Little Round Top after all the close fighting was done. (See Sykes' official report; Captain Farley's *Number Nine*; and the Warren letters.)

Powell says that Vincent, while *en route*, reached the skirt of a piece of woods, in the farther edge of which there was a heavy musketry fire (O'Rorke's). This indicates that Powell supposed that O'Rorke was already engaged before Vincent reached his position. The fact is, that Vincent had been engaged for half an hour before Warren left the hill and detached O'Rorke. Vincent, commanding the brigade, was colonel of the Eighty-Third Pennsylvania, not of the Sixteenth Michigan, as stated by Powell. Vincent's brigade did not move along the crest of the hill, but through the woods in rear of it. A few shells burst in the midst of them as they were crossing Plum Run Valley, but once behind the hill they were screened from observation and their line was formed, guns loaded, and everything ready before they were discovered by the enemy.

Powell speaks twice of Pipe Creek, meaning Rock Creek; but this is evidently a slip of the pen, as Pipe Creek was in Maryland, miles away from Gettysburg.

Notwithstanding the many inaccuracies in this account, I can forgive him in consideration of his splendid tribute to the gallantry of Vincent's brigade and its decisive effect on the result of the battle. I would have made the praise include O'Rorke and the One Hundred and Fortieth New York.

J. M. Vanderslice: *Gettysburg Then and Now*

... In the meantime, Law's brigade,—Fifteenth, Forty-Seventh, Fourth, Forty-Fourth, and Forty-Eighth Alabama Infantry,—with the Fourth and Fifth Texas, of Robertson's brigade, the two latter regiments following Law by a misunderstanding of orders, moved forward over as rough ground as was ever passed over by troops, to seize Round Top, and were, after skirmishing with the Second United States Sharpshooters, met by the Fourth Maine, Fortieth New York, and Sixth New Jersey Infantry, the latter being of Burling's brigade, which had been hurried into position to oppose them. Though making brave resistance, these regiments were forced back, and the position of Round Top and Ward's left endangered.

During this time, General Warren, chief engineer on Meade's staff, had ascended Little Round Top, and not only saw the importance of holding it, but saw the columns of the enemy under Law, of Hood's division, advancing to seize it, driving before them the regiments at its base. He hastened to the road where Ayres' division of the Fifth corps was passing to the front, detached the One Hundred and Fortieth New York Infantry from Weed's brigade and hurried it up the steep hill.

Before the One Hundred and Fortieth reached its position, Vincent's brigade of Barnes' division, which had been sent to hold Round Top, arrived upon the summit and went into position upon a ledge just below, the Sixteenth Michigan Infantry on the right, the Forty-Fourth New York and Eighty-Third

Pennsylvania in the centre, and the Twentieth Maine on the left. Hood's troops were already charging up the hill, and a desperate encounter ensued. At last Law, believing he could not force the front, attempted a flank movement upon the Sixteenth Michigan with the Forty-Eighth and the Forty-Fourth Alabama Infantry, while the Fourth Alabama, Fifth and Fourth Texas attacked the Sixteenth Michigan, Forty-Fourth New York, and Eighty-Third Pennsylvania in front.

At the same time the Forty-Seventh Alabama engaged the Twentieth Maine farther to the left in front, and the Fifteenth Alabama endeavoured to turn its left. The movement upon the flank of the Sixteenth Michigan was proving successful when O'Rorke reached the right of the Sixteenth with his One Hundred and Fortieth New York. The enemy were within a few feet of the top, and O'Rorke had no time to form, but charged his regiment down the opposite slope. Hazlett's Battery D, Fifth United States, had by great effort scaled the heights and opened upon the Confederates.

The youthful O'Rorke, who had but two years before left West Point, was among the killed.

For nearly an hour the terrible conflict went on upon the crest of Little Round Top, the fighting continuing desperate (especially on the front of the Eighty-Third Pennsylvania and the Twentieth Maine), where at times the enemy broke through, and hand-to-hand encounters occurred. At last a charge of the Twentieth, when its ammunition was exhausted, led by Colonel Chamberlain, drove the enemy from the hill with a loss of many prisoners. The balance of Weed's brigade—Ninety-First and One Hundred and Fifty-Fifth Pennsylvania, and One Hundred and Forty-Sixth New York—had taken position on Vincent's right, and the rocky summit of the Federal left was secured, but at the cost of the lives of Generals Vincent and Weed, Colonel O'Rorke, Lieutenant Hazlett, and many others. General Vincent was killed while urging on his men. He had just been promoted from the colonelcy of the Eighty-Third Pennsylvania, by which regiment, and by his whole brigade, he was greatly beloved, being a cultured and gallant young officer. "General Weed was slain at his former battery, Hazlett's, on the summit of Little Round Top. Seeing his commander fall. Lieutenant Hazlett hastened to his side. The general seemed desirous of telling something, and while Hazlett was bending over him the bullet of a sharpshooter killed the lieutenant, and he fell upon the body of his dead comrade. The Confederate General Hood was also wounded here.

The statement that the five Alabama regiments of Law's brigade and the Fourth and Fifth Texas of Robertson's attacked Ward's brigade at the Devil's Den is not corroborated by any evidence that I have been able to find. The Confederate official reports show that all these regiments, with the exception of the Forty-Fourth Alabama, went up the swale on the north side of Big Round Top, two of them going over the top of the mountain, and their attack was directed against Vincent's brigade and the One Hundred and Fortieth New York on Little Round Top. The attack on the Devil's Den was made, according to the official reports, by the Forty-Fourth Alabama, the other two regiments of Robertson's brigade, Benning's and Anderson's Georgia brigades, all of Hood's division.

Vincent's brigade did not go to the summit of Little Round Top, but passed behind the ridge its whole length and to a position on the slope south of it. (See Union and Confederate official reports.)

General Hood was not wounded here. According to his own statement, he was wounded while standing near the batteries of his division before the infantry advanced. He was carried off the field and General Law assumed command of Hood's division, and retained it during the battle and until Hood's recovery and return to duty, sometime later. (See Law's paper on the *Struggle for Round Top* and Hood's letter to Longstreet, quoted in Dates' book, *The War Between the Union and the Confederacy*.)

★★★★★★

The reader should understand that in this paper where "Law" is mentioned the reference is to Hood's division, after Hood was wounded at the beginning of the artillery battle and before the infantry was engaged. When Hood was disabled Law assumed command of the division, leaving the immediate command of his brigade to Colonel Sheffield, of the Forty-Eighth Alabama regiment. Law directed the early movements of his brigade, including their advance up the valley to attack the position held by Vincent, but later took charge of Robertson's, Benning's, and Anderson's brigades.—O. W. N.

★★★★★★

J. H. Stine: *History of the Army of the Potomac:*

But another reason other than his concealed movement influenced the delay of the attack by Longstreet, namely. Law's brigade of Hood's division, for which he was waiting, had not yet arrived. Law arrived a little before twelve o'clock, and was at once directed to move to the extreme right of the Confederate line, which was to sweep up Plum Run. When Law moved to the place assigned him his right rested at the base of Big Round Top. Taking a hasty survey of the country around him, he saw no cavalry occupying the country south of that bold mountain and wondered at its absence, and then queried if the Union soldiers occupied that great natural fortification; but as none were visible he decided to send a scouting party up its steep side to discover, if possible, the location and strength of the Union force there, if any. In a short time one of them returned to him with the information that they had ascended to the summit and found that it was not held by the Federals.

Law made haste to communicate this important information to Hood, who speedily sent it to Longstreet. As no attention was paid to it, Law again called Hood's attention to the fact, and added that he (Law) had captured some Union soldiers, who claimed to be going to the rear in the direction of Emmittsburg on surgeon's certificates. Law questioned them as to the position of the reserve hospital and reserve artillery, which they located, and said a road east of Round Top led there. Again, Longstreet was urged to move farther to the right and at least occupy Big Round Top, but he sent word to Hood that Lee's orders were positive to make an attack where he (Longstreet) had posted the two divisions, and that they must be obeyed.

On the receipt of that order from Longstreet, Hood directed his division to prepare for action and directed his artillery to open on the Union left at the Devil's Den and to the right of it. The cannonading did not continue long before Hood was wounded in the arm, when Law succeeded to the command of the division. Law commanded an Alabama brigade, composed of the Fourth, Fifteenth, Forty-Fourth, Forty-Seventh, and Forty-Eighth Alabama. Colonel Sheffield, of the latter regiment, assumed command of the brigade when Law was assigned to the division. On the left of the Alabama brigade was Robertson's

Texas brigade. This line was supported by the Georgia brigades commanded by Benning and G. T. Anderson.

McLaws' line on the left was formed with Kershaw on the left of Robertson, and Barksdale on Kershaw's left, supported by Semmes and Wofford. Thus, the Confederate line was prepared to advance on Sickles, who was awaiting the assault. Each division had four batteries. Law says he had twenty guns in action. If this is true, it is fair to presume that McLaws had twenty, and thus Longstreet opened the battle on the afternoon of the 2nd with at least forty guns.

Law advanced up the Valley of Death, through which Plum Run flows, with his brigade on the right, which, instead of following in the valley, veered to the right to avoid the heavy and well-aimed fire of Smith's battery, stationed on the rocks of Devil's Den. An interval was thus left between that brigade and the right of Robertson's Texas brigade. Benning's brigade was ordered forward to fill the interval. At the same time, Anderson's brigade was directed to move to the left of Robertson, and Law hurled his whole division on the left of Birney's division with great force.

Captain Smith had posted four of his guns at Devil's Den while he left the other section 150 yards in the rear. The Fourth Maine supported his battery. General Hunt, chief of artillery, had just ridden along inspecting especially the position of batteries. As he passed Smith, and saw his cannon on that advanced position, he remarked that the guns were well posted, but would be difficult to remove in case the enemy forced back our infantry. Smith knew it was a desperate fight, and worked his guns with great effect.

In the council of war, held about three o'clock, Meade directed Sykes to Little Round Top, with the Fifth corps. Longstreet began his attack while it was in session, and Sickles merely reported, and immediately returned to the front. When Sykes arrived at the base of Little Round Top he had been preceded by Warren, for the council had been speedily closed, and the generals prepared for action.

When Warren arrived on the summit of Little Round Top the soldiers of the signal station were rolling up their flags to retire, as the enemy under Law were pressing so closely that their lives were already in great danger, and it was always understood that the signal stations were not to be exposed to the enemy's fire. Warren directed them to unfurl their flags and continue their work of signalling with Meade's headquarters. Seeing Vincent's brigade, of Barnes' division, of the Fifth corps, approaching, Warren rode up to Sykes and Barnes and requested that Vincent be moved on Little Round Top and hold it, as the Alabama brigade was hurrying up its side from the direction of Plum Run to take possession of the summit. Vincent's men seized two guns of Hazlett's battery and dragged them to the crest, where they were placed in position to bear on Law near the Devil's Den. . . . While the Union forces had been compelled to yield ground under Ayres and Caldwell, yet Law saw that he could not get possession of Little Round Top by following these two generals, as he would have to advance over an open space where he would be exposed to a fire that would greatly deplete his ranks before he could arrive where Ayres and Caldwell were posted, who would then in turn charge him back over the wheat-field, and perhaps break his weakened lines. Before the action began, he wanted to take possession of Big Round Top, but was compelled to follow up the Valley of Death according to Lee's orders.

He then thought he saw a chance to drive our troops from Little Round Top by sending a force up the secluded depression between the Round Tops, which was only a few rods wide and covered with woods, which would shield his movements; but again his efforts were foiled, for Vincent had formed his brigade in a semicircle, with the right of the Sixteenth Michigan resting not far from Hazlett's battery; the Forty-Fourth New York, on its left, tracing along the side of the mountain; the Eighty-Third Pennsylvania, on its left, stretching down to the depression between the two mountains; and the Twentieth Maine, under Colonel Chamberlain, was on the left of the brigade, and occupying a position between the two mountains. Law attacked vigorously the whole front of Vincent.

The Forty-Fourth New York and Eighty-Third Pennsylvania repulsed several assaults; when the Sixteenth Michigan on the right was attacked a part of that regiment gave way; but Patrick H. O'Rorke, commanding the One Hundred and Fortieth New York, at once threw his regiment in and saved that point. General Weed had been mortally wounded and Lieutenant Hazlett, while stooping over him to receive what he supposed was his last command, was shot and died with his arms around him. As O'Rorke charged, Vincent was mortally wounded, and soon Patrick O'Rorke heroically surrendered up his life. Thus Weed, Vincent, O'Rorke, and Hazlett lay near each other, silent in death, on Little Round Top.

The battle still waged with great ferocity, for as yet the enemy had not given up the hope of carrying Little Round Top, the key to the situation. Failing in the effort to break through the right and capture Hazlett's guns, and possess the summit, Law moved his troops back and again attacked the centre and the left. While the assault on Vincent's centre was made with great determination, the left, under Chamberlain, was assailed with desperation.

Vincent having fallen mortally wounded, Colonel James C. Rice, of the Forty-Fourth New York, assumed command of the brigade. Of the last attack, he says:

> Now occurred the most critical time of the action. For above half an hour the struggle was desperate. At length, the enemy pressed so strongly upon the left flank of Colonel Chamberlain's regiment that he wisely determined to change the order of battle, and commanded his left wing to fall back at right angles to his right. He then ordered a charge, and repulsed the enemy at every point.

General Crawford having arrived with two brigades of the Pennsylvania Reserves, Fisher's brigade was directed to support Vincent's brigade on Round Top, and was posted in the rear. At dusk Colonels Rice, Chamberlain, and Fisher held a consultation and decided that it would be unwise to permit the enemy to hold the crest of Big Round Top, as it would be fortified during the night and would compel Little Round Top to be evacuated in the morning, if artillery were posted on it. It was therefore decided that Fisher, with two of his regiments, and Chamberlain, with his regiment, should charge up the mountain at once and dislodge Law's force there.

Accordingly, these two officers, with the Twentieth Maine and Fifth and Twelfth Pennsylvania Reserves, ascended the mountain and drove the enemy before them, capturing some thirty prisoners, including one of General Law's staff. Chamberlain in the darkness was unable to tell whether he was near a heavy body of the enemy or not, and sent back for the Eighty-Third Pennsylvania and Forty-Fourth New York. Fisher had moved to the right of Chamberlain and occupied a position on the side of Big Round Top, but in the night sent two regiments to Chamberlain's left. Thus, ended the conflict on the Round Tops, leaving both in possession of the Union troops, but which had cost so many precious lives.

This is an interesting account, but differs in some respects from all the others. There are some statements not corroborated by any evidence which I have been able to find, either in official reports or elsewhere. Stine ignores the fact made clear by Robertson's report, that two of his regiments, the Fourth and Fifth Texas, became separated from the other two on their left and did not attack the Devil's Den, but went up the swale with Law's brigade to attack Vincent. He states that Warren arrived on Little Round Top at the time when the enemy's infantry was attacking Ward's brigade at the Devil's Den. Warren arrived before any advance of the Confederate infantry was made. He directed Smith's battery at the Devil's Den to fire a shot into the woods to the south, between Plum Run and the Emmittsburg road, and discovered a long line of the enemy's infantry there.

The Confederate batteries had not yet opened fire on Birney's line. Warren did not go to Sykes and Barnes to ask for Vincent's brigade. Vincent did not assist in getting Hazlett's guns up the hill. Warren says that he, with some stragglers from the Third corps, assisted in getting up the first two of Hazlett's guns. The other two sections came up later, breaking through the column of the One Hundred and Fortieth New York. The reader should bear in mind the distinction between Law as brigade commander and division commander. Law assumed command of the division before the infantry became engaged. I find no record that he gave any orders to his own brigade after starting it up the swale on the north side of Big Round Top. He was fully occupied in directing the attack against Birney's line. The reports of regimental commanders making the attack on Little Round Top contain no mention of receiving any orders from Law or Sheffield. The statement about the action of Fisher and his brigade will be noticed in another place.

Captain R. K. Beecham: *Gettysburg, The Pivotal Battle of the Civil War.*

The Third corps, commanded by General Sickles, 12,000 strong, also arrived on the field at an early hour in the morning. This gave Meade a force of 46,000 men all told, to meet Lee's army, very early on the morning of July 2. Thus, it appeared that General Meade had employed the night to great advantage, and had made every effort in his power to unite his army so that he might in his first battle meet his great antagonist on somewhere near equal terms. Still the Fifth corps, commanded by General Sykes, 12,500 strong, and the Sixth corps, commanded by General Sedgwick, 15,500 (28,000 in all, or more than one-third of Meade's whole army), were many weary miles away.

General Meade was extremely cautious, too cautious to be apt to win a great victory like the capture or annihilation of the army opposed to him, and in this instance, he had every reason to be cautious, from the fact that a third of his army was still far away from the field. Meade reasoned that as Lee had marched his army far from his base, and had actually carried the war into a locality unknown to him, it would be the proper thing to encourage him to fight a truly offensive battle on grounds of Meade's own choosing; and certainly, he did not wish to assume a position, if he could possibly avoid it, that would occasion the renewal of the contest before the arrival of the Fifth and Sixth corps. The longer Lee delayed his attack, assuming that he would certainly attack Meade's chosen position, the more advantageous the situation became.

By extending Hancock's line southward along Cemetery Ridge to Round Top, Meade would have a strong, compact position, with his left absolutely secure. The Fifth corps was approaching the field by the Taneytown Road, and would arrive in the exact locality to reinforce readily any part of his west front, as the Taneytown Road runs the whole length of Cemetery Ridge and only three or four hundred yards in rear of the crest. Sickles' corps, nearly 12,000 strong, was ample to form an invincible battle-line from Hancock's left to that impregnable bastion to the southward.

Because of the absence of the Fifth and Sixth corps, but for no other reason, was Meade justified in placing his army in such a purely defensive position; for, to abandon the Emmittsburg Road to Longstreet was in itself a victory for Lee.

But the Fifth and Sixth corps were not there, and the preparation for battle was obliged to go on without them. Therefore, in the absence of twenty-eight thousand infantry and artillery, and until they should arrive, it may have been good generalship on Meade's part to assume the strongest defensive position possible and manoeuvre to delay rather than facilitate and invite attack. Meade's idea was to watch the enemy, and retreat hastily if he started to move away from his front. Sickles' idea was to shove his lines into the enemy's teeth.

At twenty minutes past six o'clock the situation of the Union army was desperate. If Lee did not support Longstreet with reinforcements from his centre and left, as Longstreet complained bitterly that he did not, what can be said of Meade? What did the commander-in-chief of the Union army do to relieve the tension? If it is true that Lee was asleep, or had forgotten his 'old war horse,' as he sometimes called Longstreet, in the stress of the mightiest effort of his life, is it not also true that Meade came very near forgetting Hancock in his desperate struggle to maintain his position? To the right of Hancock's line many batteries, and three divisions, or seven brigades of Union infantry defended the west front of Cemetery Hill; and two of those brigades had hardly pulled a trigger in the battle of the previous day.

They were not under Hancock's command, and Meade did not feel warranted in weakening the line by a single regiment, although the position was naturally so rugged and strong that a skirmish line could have held it against a line of battle. At least he did not. It was not Longstreet against the Army of the Potomac; but up to that moment and until half an hour later, it was Longstreet's three divisions, comprising thirteen brigades, against Hancock's and Birney's three divisions, comprising eleven brigades, so that the weight of the *battalia* was with Longstreet.

But now the time had arrived when it became necessary for Meade, the commanding general of the Union army, to make some movement on the chessboard of war; for surely and certainly it was the danger hour, not alone for the Army of the Potomac, but for the American Republic as well. Since the birth of the nation there was never an hour fraught with danger more imminent. The life of the nation was in the balance. Two hours before, Meade had received a despatch from Sedgwick informing him that the Sixth corps was on the march and doing its utmost to reach the field. About the same time a despatch from Sykes informed him that the Fifth corps was nearer by several miles than the Sixth; the men of the Fifth corps were not made of asbestos, but what humanity could they would do. It is not recorded of Meade that, as he watched and waited during those anxious hours, he was heard to murmur, 'Sykes or night!' but more than likely that prayer was in his heart.

At twenty minutes past six o'clock the vanguard of the Fifth corps was not yet in sight, and Meade could wait no longer for their coming. Then he sent a despatch to Slocum that imperilled the right, but did not relieve the left. It showed Meade's good intentions, however, which were worth something, and if he did more than mean well, history has failed to make a record of it.

The despatch to Slocum called for reinforcements. Slocum sent him Lockwood's brigade of his First division, but as the call was most urgent, Slocum concluded to take some chances; so, hastily turning his whole line over to the care of General Greene and his Third brigade of the Second division, with instructions to extend a skirmish line to replace his line of battle from the crest of Culp's Hill to Rock Greek, and, if attacked, to hold the whole line as long as possible, and when the battle became too heavy, to retire to the crest and hold that citadel forever, Slocum marched away to the left with the balance of the Twelfth corps, leaving one brigade—a mere skirmish line—to hold Culp's Hill and its important slopes against Johnson's division of four brigades. It was a daring and perilous movement, one of the mighty risks of war that sometimes must be taken.

General G. K. Warren, chief of engineers on General Meade's staff, may truthfully be called the saviour of Little Round Top; and for his work that day he earned the everlasting gratitude of his country; but without a heroic effort on the part of others, no man could have saved it; and the key to our left, as Little Round Top certainly was, would have fallen into the hands of the Confederates.

Along in the afternoon, when the battle was raging fiercely to the westward, General Warren rode far down Cemetery Ridge ascended that knob of boulders, and established on the summit thereof a signal station. The eastern and northern faces of Little

Round Top, though steep and rocky, are not nearly so high and difficult of ascent as the western face from Death Valley. Warren soon made the discovery that the bold knob on which he stood was a most important position—not for the Union Army while it remained unoccupied by the Confederates, as it then was; but if it were once in their possession and crowned with their artillery, they could enfilade the entire length of Cemetery Ridge and take Meade's position in reverse from Cemetery Hill to Rock Creek.

Yet there was not a Union soldier there to defend it, except Warren and two or three men of the signal corps. Then, as the afternoon wore away and the battle drew nearer, increasing in fury around the wheat-field, Warren made the further discovery that Law had his eye on Little Round Top; and as he looked he saw a flanking column moving out from Devil's Den across Plum Run valley, headed directly for the knob of boulders on which he stood.

A message to signal headquarters at Cemetery Hill could bring no timely relief, even if a regiment could be spared for that purpose, as the distance was more than two miles, and within half an hour the advancing Confederates would be in possession without firing a gun. But there were defenders nearer; at that moment Warren's ears caught the sound of marching troops, and the vanguard of the Fifth corps, so anxiously looked for by Meade and Hancock, appeared on the Taneytown Road not four hundred yards in rear of the threatened position.

Never in the history of war was arrival more timely. The advent of Blucher's army on the field of Waterloo was not more opportune to the exhausted English than was Sykes' corps to Warren and the exhausted troops of Hancock and Birney. A further delay of half an hour for any cause and Sykes would have found Little Round Top in Law's possession and Cemetery Ridge occupied by Longstreet and his Confederates. The Army of the Potomac would have been split into two fragments, the Fifth and Sixth corps out of the battle, and Lee master of the situation.

Had Longstreet begun his battle two hours earlier,—at two rather than at four o'clock,—it would have been over before Sykes' arrival, and the battle of Gettysburg would have been counted as the most terrible defeat of the Union cause. Lee's unaccountable hesitation and unreadiness in the morning; Sickles' daring and defiant salient, that puzzled Longstreet and delayed his attack; the stubborn resistance and endurance of the Third corps—all combined to bring a far-reaching victory to the Union cause at the bloody sunset hour.

Warren hurried down over the rocks to the point where he had left his horse, and rode in haste to the marching column, detaching Vincent's brigade of the First division, which he hurried to the summit of Little Round Top just in time to meet Law's brigade of Alabamans climbing its western face, and they drove back the Southern men into the valley. In this struggle the valiant Vincent was mortally wounded. Tilton's and Sweitzer's brigades of Sykes' corps were hurried to the front to reinforce the Second and Third corps.

Then out of the former chaos the battle along the eastern verge of the wheat-field began to assume form and regularity. The First and Second brigades of the Second division, and also the Third division of two brigades of the Fifth corps, followed in support of the main battle, meeting with a withering fire Longstreet's temporarily victorious brigades that had won the wheat-field and were advancing toward the crest of Cemetery Ridge.

But Law had not yet abandoned his design on Little Round Top; and Benning's brigade of Georgians having reinforced the Alabamans, they tried again to carry the hill of boulders. General Weed, with the Third brigade of the Second division of the Fifth, was then ordered to reinforce and hold Little Round Top. Colonel O'Rorke, with the One Hundred and Fortieth New York Infantry, was the first to reach the firing line in support of Vincent's brigade, and a hand-to-hand conflict raged again on the slippery rocks and declivities. By order of Weed, Hazlett's battery (D of the Fifth United States Artillery) was by hand and with ropes dragged to the summit; but the Confederate sharpshooters, located behind the boulders of Devil's Den, picked off the Union artillerymen so rapidly as to render their guns of little or no service for a time. General Weed was mortally wounded, and while Hazlett was leaning over him, receiving his dying message, he also was hit, and fell dead across Weed's body.

We have had occasion heretofore to speak of the expert marksmanship of the Confederate soldiers, but on no field of the war did they exhibit greater skill in that capacity than at this time and place. The rocks of Devil's Den are certainly five hundred yards, and probably more, from the summit of Little Round Top; but across the yawning chasm of Plum Run they made life uncertain for the Union soldiers who guarded it. The Confederates, however, had one great advantage over their opponents. They were shooting upward, and the boulders of Little Round Top were aglow with the rays of the setting sun. The Union soldiers stood out against the sky clear and distinct to their eyes, a shining mark for their dexterity; while the superior quality of their powder must also be taken into consideration.

On the other hand, the Union soldiers were looking downward into an abyss, as it were, with the dazzling sunshine in their eyes, and the marks at which they directed their shots indistinct, within the shadow of overhanging rocks. Nevertheless, a company or two of Berdan's sharpshooters were hastily distributed among the rocks and crevices, and they soon returned the Confederate fire with satisfactory effect; and as the sun went down behind the South mountain, giving to each party of distant combatants a fair and equal chance, the Union artillery was brought into play upon their rocky stronghold, with the result that, when the battle was over, many a Georgian and many an Alabaman was found among the rocks of Devil's Den who never retreated, not a few bearing no mark of ball or shell, but killed by the concussion of shell or solid-shot against the rocks upon which they depended for protection.

So, Little Round Top was held and made secure, but the battle did not cease with the going down of the sun; for half an hour later it was raging terrifically in Death Valley and along the wheat-field plateau. The stone walls and rocky defences on the east side of the wheat-field were recaptured, as was also Devil's Den, and held by the Union forces. At eight o'clock the battle ceased. Longstreet says: 'While Meade's lines were growing, my men were dropping; we had no others to call to their aid, and the weight against us was too heavy to carry. The sun was down, and with it went down the severe battle.' That statement is true. During the sunset hour the weight of *battalia* was against Longstreet.

The Fifth corps entered the arena at about seven o'clock. It comprised eight brigades and numbered twelve thousand five hundred men; but as the afternoon was terribly hot and the corps had marched steadily and rapidly, if it went into the battle with twelve thousand men it made a splendid record. A reinforcement of twelve thousand fresh soldiers (for although weary enough with marching and nearly exhausted with excessive heat, they were fresh in comparison with the men who had been hours in battle) to a battle-line originally but eighteen thousand strong, and that had lost thousands, is a great addition to its battle strength. Thus, the Union army, starting in with Sickles' corps of twelve thousand, was reinforced after the first hour with six thousand, and again at seven o'clock with twelve thousand, making its battle strength at the finish nineteen brigades and thirty thousand men, less the loss of the day; while Longstreet made the battle without reinforcements, but from start to finish with thirteen brigades and twenty-six thousand. On the whole it was not so very unequal. Longstreet says: 'My loss was about six thousand; Meade's between twelve and fourteen thousand.' It is useless at this point to discuss the Confederate losses; but Longstreet's estimate of the Union losses is greatly exaggerated. Assuming that the Third corps' entire loss of four thousand one hundred and ninety-eight was sustained on the second of July, and also the Fifth corps' entire loss of two thousand one hundred and eighty-six, to the sum of which we add half the entire loss of the Second corps, which cannot be far from a correct estimate, and it brings the aggregate loss of the Union army on July 2 up to about nine thousand, which is more than forty *per cent*, in excess of Longstreet's loss as he estimates it.

But whatever the battle losses of the second of July may have been, it was the decisive battle of the series, and bloody enough to satisfy any votary of war and carnage.

It must have been about seven o'clock when the first shots were fired by Vincent's brigade of the Fifth corps on Little Round Top. Within a few minutes thereafter every brigade and every regiment of that twelve thousand men were in the fire and fury of battle, where they remained to the end of the struggle. One hour only, one hour at the going down of the sun, and until darkness overshadowed the earth, and yet in that short space of time the Fifth corps sustained a loss of more than two thousand men. Was there ever a bloodier sunset hour?

After dark Meade ordered the withdrawal of his lines from all points westward to the ridge, extending an unbroken line from Cemetery Hill to Round Top; and Sickles made no objection, being content to let his 'salient' go with his leg.

Before seeking his couch that night, it is said that Lee on bended knees offered up thanks to God on high for what Longstreet had so dearly won; and Meade returned thanks to the same wise Providence for what Longstreet had failed to win; while the whole Army of the Potomac thanked God indeed for the timely arrival of the Fifth corps; and all the people of the United States thanked Him, and the boys of the Third, Second, and Fifth corps for their heroic fighting, done all along the line.

Beecham's *Gettysburg*, etc., published in 1911, is not worthy of serious consideration. My reason for introducing extracts from it is, that as the latest account of the battle of Gettysburg, it will be read by many readers who have never seen the earlier accounts, who may accept it as a truthful history of the battle. It is no more history than is Victor Hugo's account of the battle of Waterloo. It may be poetry or romance, but cannot have any standing as a relation of facts, especially in regard to the battle of the second day. It is amazing that a writer who has access to the official records, and the many valuable books which have been published on the subject, could have invented such a tale. He does not hesitate to reveal the most secret thoughts and purposes of both Meade and Lee, which are here made known for the first time. He gives no heed to what these officers have said for themselves.

The Fifth corps came from Hanover. By midnight of July 1 the advance of the corps halted within two or three miles of the battlefield. At daylight, it was again on the march, and by seven o'clock in the morning was (with the exception of two brigades of Crawford's division, which arrived a little later) in position on the right of the Twelfth corps. By two o'clock in the afternoon the Sixth corps began to arrive by the Baltimore Pike. By Meade's order it relieved the Fifth corps on the right. Sykes then massed his corps near the crossing of the Baltimore Pike over Rock Creek, in rear of the centre of the Union line of battle, where it was in good position to move to any part of the line which needed reinforcements.

What shall we say of the historian who says that at 6:20 p.m. the Fifth and Sixth corps were many weary miles away, and that at 7 p.m.

the head of the Fifth corps began to arrive by the Taneytown road, and who makes no further mention of the presence of the Sixth corps on the field that day? Further comment is unnecessary. If the reader will compare the extracts which I have quoted with the official reports and the accounts of other writers, it will not be difficult to form a correct opinion of the value of this book as history.

The War Between the Union and the Confederacy, by William C. Oates, Colonel Fifteenth Alabama Infantry.

> When we arrived Generals Lee and Longstreet were together on an eminence in our front, on Seminary Ridge, and appeared to be inspecting with field-glasses the position of the Federals. We were allowed but a few minutes' rest, when the divisions of McLaws and Hood were moved in line by the right flank around to the south of the Federal position. There was a good deal of delay on the march, which was quite circuitous, for the purpose of covering the movement from the enemy. Finally Hood marched across the rear of McLaws and went into line on the crest of the little ridge across the Emmittsburg road, with Benning's brigade in rear of his centre, constituting a second line, his battalion of artillery, sixteen pieces, in position on his left. McLaws then formed his division of four brigades in two lines of battle on Hood's left, with sixteen pieces of artillery in position on McLaws' left.
>
> This line crossed the Emmittsburg road and was partially parallel with it. The extreme right of Hood's line was considerably in advance and north of that road, and its right directly opposite to the centre of the Great Round Top Mountain. Law's brigade constituted the right of Hood's line, and was formed at first in single line, as follows:
>
> My regiment, the Fifteenth Alabama, in the centre, the Forty-Fourth and Forty-Eighth Alabama regiments to my right, and the Forty-Seventh and Fourth Alabama regiments to my left. Thus formed, about *3:30 o'clock p.m.* (italics are mine.—O. W. N.) both battalions of artillery opened fire. The Federals replied from their guns on and near Little Round Top, and within a few minutes our line advanced in quick time under the fire of our guns, through an open field about three or four hundred yards and then down a gentle slope for a quarter of a mile, through the open valley of Plum Run, a small, muddy,

meandering stream running through it near the base of the mountains.

******

Footnote to Oates' work.—The advance was not skilfully made in all respects. Five companies from two of the regiments of the brigade covered its front as skirmishers. The two from the Forty-Eighth on the right were under the command of a captain, the three from: the Forty-Seventh likewise commanded by a captain, and in the advance were soon disconnected from each other, but all moved directly toward the centre, and bore to the right of the southern front of Great Round Top, and passed around it to the right on the eastern side. Captain A. O. Dickson, then first lieutenant of Company A, one of the skirmish companies of the Forty-Eighth regiment, now lives in Brooksville, Blount County, Alabama, and is an intelligent, reliable man. He says that these companies passed entirely around to the northern side of the mountain without encountering any Union troops, and in this way these companies were not in the battle of July 2. Captain J. Q. Burton, of the Forty-Seventh, who lives at Opelika, and is a reliable gentleman, says that three companies from that regiment went the same way, never encountered the enemy, and were not in the battle.

Had these five companies gone farther and joined my column on the north side of Great Round Top, I could have captured the ordnance train, and it would have enabled me, in all probability, to have captured Little Round Top. The Forty-Eighth regiment was ordered across the rear to the left early in the advance. The attack, instead of being straight forward, as the skirmishers doubtless believed it would be, was a left half-wheel, but of which the skirmishers were not informed, so they went to the right and the line of battle to the left. On such an occasion a competent field officer should have been in command of the skirmish line of the brigade and before he begun the advance have received definite instructions from the brigade commander. There was no such arrangement on this occasion, and as a consequence five companies of the brigade were not in the battle.

"No communication as to what was intended to be done was made to the regimental commanders until after the advance began. This was a common practice in those days; but it was wrong. The colonels of the regiments about to engage in battle should always be informed of what is to be done before the advance begins, and it is the duty of the staff officers to see the orders carried out.

******

Law's brigade was the first to move, but the two regiments to my right were dropped back a short distance, and as we entered the valley the Forty-Fourth Alabama was directed to the left to attack the Devil's Den, and the Forty-Eighth continued as a reserve or second line, which made the Fifteenth a little in advance and on the extreme right of Longstreet's column of attack. Benning's—the Texas—and Anderson's brigades moved in echelon into the action, so that our division was spread out like the outer edge of a half-open fan, and as the right drove the enemy from the base of the mountain each brigade in succession would strike the enemy's line on the flank or quartering, so that as we drove them our line would shorten and hence strengthen; but General Sickles had changed his line after the first formation, so that Birney's division, with Ward's brigade on its left at the Devil's Den and extending along a ridge to the Emmittsburg road, was facing us, instead of the other way, as General Lee thought. Sickles thus gave us an unexpected and very warm reception. He constantly received reinforcements, which made his line hard to drive.

Sickles' apprehension of another flank movement on Lee's part, as at Chancellorsville, was well founded; but the same man was not there to conduct it as at that place two months before. To guard against a similar surprise, Sickles changed his first formation and placed Birney's fine division, well supported, on his flank and facing to the rear, which thwarted Lee's plan of attack made two hours before, which was a masterly piece of strategy when made. Rapid change of conditions in all human affairs bring unexpected results. As the most authentic account of Longstreet's attack and the spirit in which he made it, I quote from Major-General Hood's report to him long after the battle, as follows:

> General Lee was, seemingly, anxious you should attack that morning. He remarked to me, "The enemy is here, and if we do not whip him, he will whip us." You thought it better to await the arrival of Pickett's division, at that time still in the rear, in order to make the attack; and you said to me, subsequently, whilst we were seated together near the trunk of a tree:
>
> "The General is a little nervous this morning; he wishes me to attack; I do not wish to do so without Pickett. I

never like to go into battle with one boot off."

Thus, passed the forenoon of that eventful day, when in the afternoon, about three o'clock, it was decided to await no longer Pickett's division, but to proceed to our extreme right and attack up the Emmittsburg road. McLaws moved off, and I followed with my division. In a short time, I was ordered to quicken the march of my troops and to pass to the front of McLaws.

This movement was accomplished by throwing out an advanced force to tear down fences and clear the way. The instructions I received were to place my division across the Emmittsburg road, form line of battle, and attack. Before reaching this road, however, I had sent forward some of my picked Texas scouts to ascertain the position of the enemy's extreme left flank. They soon reported to me that it rested upon Round Top Mountain (meaning Little Round Top); that the country was open, and that I could march through an open woodland pasture around Round Top (meaning Great Round Top), and assault the enemy in flank and rear; that their wagon trains were parked in rear of their lines and were badly exposed to our attack in that direction.

As soon as I arrived upon the Emmittsburg road I placed one or two batteries in position and opened fire. A reply from the enemy's guns soon developed his lines. His left rested on or near Round Top (meaning Little Round Top) with line bending back and again forward, forming, as it were, a concave line, as approached by the Emmittsburg road. A considerable body of troops was posted in front of their main line, between the Emmittsburg Road and Round Top Mountain. This force was in line of battle upon an eminence near a peach orchard. (This was Birney's division of Sickles' corps.)

I found that in making the attack according to orders, *viz.*, up the Emmittsburg road, I should have first to encounter and drive off this advanced line of battle; secondly, at the base and along the slope of the mountain, to confront immense boulders of stone so massed together as to form narrow openings, which would break our ranks and cause the men to scatter whilst climbing up the rocky precipice.

I found, moreover, that my division would be exposed to a heavy fire from the main line of the enemy in position on the crest of the high range, of which Round Top was the extreme left; and, by reason of the concavity of the enemy's line, that we would be subject to a destructive fire in flank and rear, as well as in front; and deemed it almost an impossibility to clamber along the boulders up this steep and rugged mountain, and, under this number of crossfires, put the enemy to flight. I knew that if the feat was accomplished, it must be at a fearful sacrifice of as brave and gallant soldiers as ever engaged in battle.

The reconnaissance of my Texas scouts and the development of the Federal lines were effected in a very short space of time; in truth, shorter than I have taken to recall and jot down these facts, although the scenes and events of that day are as clear to my mind as if the great battle had been fought yesterday. I was in possession of these important facts so shortly after reaching the Emmittsburg road, as ordered, and to urge that you allow me to turn Round Top, and attack the enemy in flank and rear. Accordingly, I despatched a staff officer, bearing to you my request to be allowed to make the proposed movement on account of the above-stated reasons. Your reply was quickly received: "General Lee's orders are to attack up the Emmittsburg road." I sent another officer, saying I feared nothing could be accomplished by such an attack, and renewed my request to turn Round Top. Again, your answer was, "General Lee's orders are to attack up the Emmittsburg road."

During this interim I had continued the use of the batteries upon the enemy, and had become more and more convinced that the Federal line extended to Round Top, and that I could not reasonably hope to accomplish much by the attack as ordered. In fact, it seemed to me that the enemy occupied a position by nature so strong,—I may say impregnable,—that, independently of their flank fire, they could easily repel our attack by merely throwing and rolling stones down the mountain side as we approached.

A third time I despatched one of my staff to explain fully in regard to the situation and suggest that you had better come and look for yourself. I selected, in this instance, my adjutant-general, Colonel Harry Sellers, whom you know to be not only an officer of great courage, but also of marked ability. Colonel Sellers returned with the same message: "General Lee's orders are to attack up the Emmittsburg road." Almost simultaneously. Colonel Fairfax, of your staff, rode up and repeated the above orders.

After this urgent protest against entering the battle at Gettysburg according to instructions, which protest is the first and only one I ever made during my entire military career, I ordered my line to advance and make the assault.

As my troops were moving forward you rode up in person; a brief conversation passed between us, during which I again expressed the fears above mentioned, and regret at not being allowed to attack in flank around Round Top. You answered to this effect: "We must obey the orders of General Lee." I then rode forward with my line under a heavy fire. In about twenty minutes, after reaching the peach orchard, I was severely wounded in the arm, and borne from the field.

With this wound terminated my participation in this great battle. As I was borne off on a litter to the rear I could but experience deep distress of mind and heart at the thought of the inevitable fate of my brave fellow-soldiers, who formed one of the grandest divisions of that world-renowned army; and I shall ever believe had I been permitted to turn Round Top Mountain, we would not only have gained that position, but have been able finally to rout the enemy.'

Skirmishers from Law's brigade, who passed around Great Round Top on its east side, confirm the statement of Hood's scouts, that no Union troops were there.

General Law rode up to me as we were advancing, and informed me that I was then on the extreme right of our line and for me to hug the base of Great Round Top and go up the valley between the two mountains, (italics are mine,—O. W. N.), until I found the left of the Union line, to turn it and do all the damage I could, and that Lieutenant-Colonel Bulger would be instructed to keep the Forty-Seventh closed to my regiment, and if separated from the brigade he would act under my orders. Just after we crossed Plum Run we received the first fire from the enemy's infantry. It was Stoughton's Second Regiment United States Sharpshooters, posted behind a fence at or near the southern foot of Great Round Top. They reached that position as we advanced through the old field. No other troops were there, nor on that mountain at that time. I did not halt at the first fire, but looked to the rear for the Forty-Eighth Alabama, and saw it going, under General Law's order, across the rear of our line to the left, it was said, to reinforce the Texas brigade, which was hotly engaged.

That left no one in my rear or on my right to meet this foe. They were in the woods, and I did not know the number of them. I received the second fire. Lieutenant-Colonel Feagin and one or two of the men fell. I knew it would not do to go on and leave that force, I knew not how strong, in our rear with no troops of ours to take care of them; so, I gave the command to change direction to the right. The seven companies of the Forty-Seventh swung around with the Fifteenth and kept in line with it. The other three companies of that regiment were sent forward as skirmishers before the advance began. The sharpshooters retreated up the south front of the mountain, pursued by my command.

In places the men had to climb up, catching to the rocks and bushes and crawling over the boulders in the face of the fire of the enemy, who kept retreating, taking shelter and firing down on us from behind the rocks and crags which covered the side of the mountain thicker than gravestones in a city cemetery. Fortunately, they usually overshot us. We could see our foe only as they dodged back from one boulder to another, hence our fire was scattering. As we advanced up the mountain they ceased firing about halfway up, divided, and a battalion went around the mountain on each side.

Those who went up to the right fired a few shots at my flank. To meet this I deployed Company A, and moved it by the left flank to protect my right, and continued my rugged ascent until we reached the top. Some of my men fainted from heat, exhaustion, and thirst. I halted and let them lie down and rest a few minutes. My right lay exactly where the observatory now stands, and the line extended down the slope westward. I saw Gettysburg through the foliage of the trees. Saw the smoke and heard the roar of battle which was then raging at the Devil's Den, in the peach orchard, up the Emmittsburg road, and on the west and south of the Little Round Top. I saw from the highest point of rocks that we were then on the most commanding elevation in that neighbourhood. I knew that my men were too much exhausted to make a good fight without a few minutes' rest.

To show their condition, I quote from General Longstreet, who says in his book:

> Law completed his march of twenty-eight miles in eleven hours, the best marching in either army, to reach the field of Gettysburg.

In addition to this, we had ascended that mountain in pursuit of the sharpshooters, which but few men at this day are able to climb without the accoutrements, rifles, and knapsacks carried by those heroic men. Greater heroes never shouldered muskets than those Alabamans.

When we formed line of battle before the advance began, a detail was made of two men from each of the eleven companies of my regiment to take all the canteens to a well about one hundred yards in our rear and fill them with cool water before we went into the fight. Before this detail could fill the canteens, the advance was ordered. It would have been infinitely better to have waited five minutes for those twenty-two men and the canteens of water, but generals never ask a colonel if his regiment is ready to move. The order was given and away we went. The water detail followed with the canteens of water, but when they got into the woods they missed us, walked right into the Yankee lines, and were captured, canteens and all. My men in the ranks, in the intense heat, suffered greatly for water.

The loss of those twenty-two men and lack of water contributed largely to our failure to take Little Round Top a few minutes later. About five minutes after I halted, Captain Terrell, assistant adjutant-general to General Law, rode up by the only pathway on the southeast side of the mountain, and inquired why I had halted. I told him. He then informed me that General Hood was wounded. Law was in command of the division, and sent me his compliments, said for me to press on, turn the Union left, and capture Little Round Top, if possible, and to lose no time.

I then called his attention to my position. A precipice on the east and north, right at my feet; a very steep, stony, and wooded mountain-side on the west. The only approach to it by our enemy, a long-wooded slope on the northwest, where the pathway to the observatory now is. Within half an hour I could convert it into a Gibraltar that I could hold against ten times the number of men that I had, hence in my judgment it should be held and occupied by artillery as soon as possible, as it was higher than the other mountain and would command the entire field. Terrell replied that probably I was right, but that he had no authority to change or originate orders, which I very well knew; but with his sanction I would have remained at that point until I could have heard from Law or some superior in rank. I inquired for Law. Terrell said that as senior brigadier he was commanding the division, and along the line to the left. He then repeated that General Law had sent him to tell me to lose no time, but to press forward and drive everything before me as far as possible.

General Meade did not then know the importance of the Round Tops. He admitted before the Committee of Congress on the Conduct of the War that it was the key-point to his position. He soon discovered its importance, and at the very moment we occupied it he sent couriers to General Sykes to occupy it with his division as speedily as possible. I felt confident that Law did not know my position, or he would not order me from it. I had not seen him or any other general officer after I received Stoughton's fire, and did not see any general or staff officer, other than Terrell, until the morning of July 3; and I am confident that no general and but the one staff officer ascended Great Round Top.

From an examination of the reports of the generals on each side and the testimony taken by the joint committee of Congress, there appears to have been confusion and inaccuracy of statement about Round Top Mountain, and a failure to discriminate between them. There are two mountains, Great, or Big Round Top, and Little Round Top. They are from apex to apex 1,000 yards apart, and Big Round Top is southeast of Little Round Top and 120 feet higher. Many of the generals in their reports speak of 'Round Top,' without indicating which. A reader who is familiar with the field or was in the fight can understand pretty well which is referred to, but one unacquainted with the topography of the field will find some difficulty in understanding which of these twin mountains is meant.

For the benefit of such, I will say from my knowledge of it that Little Round Top is in most cases the one referred to in reports. Notwithstanding my conviction of the importance of holding and occupying Big Round Top with artillery, which I endeavoured to communicate to Law through Terrell (he never reached General Law until near the close of the battle), I considered it my duty to obey the order communicated to me by Terrell, whom I knew to be a trustworthy and gallant officer, but it was against my judgment to leave that strong position. It looked to me to be the key-point of the field, as artillery on it would have commanded the other Round Top and the Federal line toward Gettysburg as far as it extended along Cemetery Ridge; but the order was to find and turn the left of the Union line, and that was on Little Round Top; the battle was raging below. I therefore caused both regiments to face to the left and moved to the left, so as to avoid the precipice in our front, and then ordered the line by the right flank forward and passed to the left-oblique entirely down the northern side of the mountain without encountering any opposition whatever.

While descending in rear of Vincent's Spur, in plain view was the Federal wagon-trains, and less than three hundred yards distant was an extensive park of Federal ordnance wagons, which satisfied me that we were then in their rear. I ordered Captain Shaaf to deploy his Company A, surround and capture the ordnance wagons, have them driven in under a spur of the mountain, and detached his company for the purpose. Advancing rapidly, without any skirmishers in front, the woods being open without undergrowth, I saw no enemy until within forty or fifty steps of an irregular ledge of rocks, a splendid line of natural breastworks running about parallel with the front of the Forty-Seventh regiment and my four left companies, and then sloping back in front of my centre and right at an angle of about thirty-five or forty degrees.

Vincent's brigade, consisting of the Sixteenth Michigan on the right. Forty-Fourth New York, Eighty-Third Pennsylvania, and Twentieth Maine regiments, reached this position ten minutes before my arrival, and they piled a few rocks from boulder to boulder, making the zigzag line more complete, and were concealed behind it ready to receive us. From behind this ledge, unexpectedly to us, because concealed, they poured into us the most destructive fire I ever saw. Our line halted, but did not break. The enemy were formed in line as named from their right to left. We received the fire of the three left regiments. As men fell their comrades closed the gap, returning the fire most spiritedly. I could see through the smoke men of the Twentieth Maine in front of my right wing running from tree to tree back westward toward the main body, and I advanced my right, swinging it around, overlapping and turning their left.

At the dedication of the monument on Little Round Top to the Forty-Fourth New York regiment on July 3, 1893, in delivering the oration. Captain Nash, describing the assaults made upon Vincent's brigade, which held that spur of the mountain during the battle of the afternoon of July 2, 1863, among other things said:

> In the meantime, the enemy sent a strong flanking column to envelop and turn the left of the brigade held by the Twentieth Maine. Success there opened to him vantage ground from which to operate on the flank and rear of our entire army. While his regiment was under a heavy fire, with great presence of mind Colonel Chamberlain changed direction of his left wing and took intervals to the left to meet the new emergency. For an hour, the terrible contest at this point ensued, the edge of the fight rolling backward and forward like a wave.

The flanking column referred to by Captain Nash was mine. At the erection of monuments to the Twentieth Maine regiment on Little Round Top, October 3, 1889, Captain Howard L. Prince, the historian of that regiment, said in his oration, among other things, that:

> Again, and again was this mad rush repeated, each time to be beaten off by the ever-thinning line that desperately clung to its ledge of rock, refusing to yield except

as it involuntarily shrunk for a pace or two at a time from the storm of lead which swept its front. Colonel Oates himself advanced close to our line at the head of his men, and at times the hostile forces were actually at hand-to-hand distance. Twice the rebels were followed down the slope so sharply that they were obliged to use the bayonet, and in places small squads of their men in their charges reached our actual front.

The reports of both commanders are authority for these statements. The front surged backward and forward like a wave. At times our dead and wounded were in front of our line, and then by a superhuman effort our gallant lads would carry the combat forward beyond their prostrate forms. Continually the gray lines crept up by squads under protecting trees and boulders, and the firing became at closer and closer range.

And even the enemy's line essayed to reach around the then front of blue that stretched out in places in single rank and could not go much farther without breaking. So far had they extended, that their bullets passed beyond and into the ranks of the other regiments farther up the hill, and Captain Woodward, commanding the Eighty-Third, sent his adjutant to ask if the Twentieth had been turned. Colonel Chamberlain assured him that he was holding his ground, but would like a company, if possible, to extend his line. Captain Woodward was unable to do this, but by shortening his line somewhat he was able to cover the right of the Twentieth and enable it to take a little more ground to the left.

Meanwhile the brigade in front of the hill was hard pushed to hold its own, and the heavy roar of musketry in the fitful lulls of our guns came to the anxious ears of our commander and told too plainly what would be the result if our line gave way. Not a man in that devoted band but knew that the safety of the brigade, and perhaps of the army, depended on the steadfastness with which that point was held, and so fought on and on, with no hope of assistance, but not a thought of giving up. Already nearly half of the little force is prostrate. The dead and the wounded clog the footsteps of the living.

General Chamberlain, who was colonel of the Twentieth Maine, afterwards made general for his conduct on that occasion, and after the war Governor of Maine, in his address, delivered on the same occasion, said:

> All can see what would have become of our brigade swallowed up; of Weed's struck in the rear; of Hazlett's guns taken in the flank and turned to launch their thunderbolts upon our troops, already sore pressed in the gorge at our feet, and the fields upon the great front and right. Round Top lost, the day lost, Gettysburg lost, who can tell what for loss thence would follow!

Captain Prince of the Twentieth Maine, in his oration above referred to, claims that 'fifty dead bodies of the Fifteenth Alabama men were buried in the front of his regiment and about one hundred of the badly wounded were left behind to become prisoners.' His is an overestimate of the number of the dead from the Fifteenth Alabama. There were present in the seven companies of the Forty-Seventh, as shown by the muster roll, an aggregate of but 154 men. Only four or five of these were killed and about twenty wounded. If they buried fifty dead, that included those from the Forty-Seventh companies with the Fifteenth dead. He was certainly mistaken as to the number badly wounded, including both regiments, for several of these, fully one-half, went to the Confederate rear.

Prince also said: 'Four hundred prisoners, mostly from the Fifteenth and Forty-Seventh Alabama, were sent to the rear.' This is an egregiously mistaken statement. I have examined the muster rolls of the companies of the Fifteenth, made soon after the battle, in which the names were given of the captured without wounds, and there was a total of but 84, most of them being with Adjutant Waddell when the retreat was ordered, which they did not hear. If every man in the seven companies of the Forty-Seventh which went into the action (only 154) were included, it would make but 238, and we know that at least one hundred and twenty-odd of the Forty-Seventh escaped and were afterwards in line all night. Deduct the killed and wounded from those companies, and Captain Prince has but little over half the number of prisoners which he says were taken from those regiments and sent to the rear. General Chamberlain fell into the same error. All of us, on both sides, who were in such hot places as that were made to see double, and are disposed to exaggerate in favour of our respective sides, and do it honestly in most cases.

If I had had one more regiment we would have completely turned the flank and have won Little Round Top, which would have forced Meade's whole left wing to retire. Had the Forty-Eighth Alabama not been transferred to the left it would have driven the sharpshooters, and then following my advance we would have gotten in the rear of the Federal line and have completely turned the tide of battle in favour of the Confederates. With the five companies of skirmishers which had gone to the east of the mountain, they might have made my assault successful. Another lost opportunity.

I knew that the left of the Forty-Seventh was disconnected, I knew not how far from the right of the Fourth Alabama, and consequently was outflanked on its left and without support. The seven companies of that regiment present confronted the Eighty-Third Pennsylvania and was enfiladed by the left-oblique fire of the left wing of the Forty-Fourth New York, which was very destructive, and drove the men from the obstructions behind which they were sheltering. Lieutenant-Colonel Bulger, in command of the Forty-Seventh Alabama companies, a most gallant old gentleman over sixty years of age, fell severely wounded, and soon afterward his seven companies, after behaving most gallantly, broke, and in confusion retreated southward toward the position of the other regiments of the brigade and reached their right.

I aided their gallant Major Campbell in his efforts to hold them, but, having no support on the left, they could not be rallied and held to the position. When the Fifteenth was driven back. Colonel Bulger was left sitting by a tree, sword in hand, shot through one lung and bleeding profusely. A captain in the Forty-Fourth New York approached and demanded his sword. The old colonel said, 'What is your rank?' The reply was, 'I am a captain.' Bulger said, 'Well, I am a lieutenant-colonel, and I will not surrender my sword except to an officer of equal rank.' The captain then said, 'Surrender your sword, or I will kill you.' Colonel Bulger promptly replied, 'You may kill and be d——d! I shall never surrender my sword to an officer of lower rank.'

The captain was so amused at the old colonel's high notions of military etiquette that he went for his colonel, Rice, to whom the sword was gracefully surrendered. Rice's statement of the circumstance caused Colonel Bulger to be better cared for than he would otherwise have been, which probably saved his life.'

✶✶✶✶✶✶

(*Footnote to Oates' work.*—General Chamberlain denies this statement, and says that Bulger surrendered to him. Rice and Bulger are both dead and there is now no living witness to verify the statement. The writer derived his information from Colonel Bulger.)

✶✶✶✶✶✶

When exchanged in the summer of 1864 he was promoted to the colonelcy of his regiment, went to the front, and served with it for a short time, and was then honourably retired. He was not made a brigadier-general, as reported in vol. vii of *Confederate Military History*, but returned to his home in Dadeville, Alabama, and was elected to the State Senate in August, 1864, where he served until the surrender. He was in the Secession Convention in 1861, voted against secession, and refused to sign the ordinance. But when the war came as a consequence, he raised a company and fought heroically through the struggle. He was unskilled in tactics and lacking in disciplinary power, but he possessed such a high order of courage that he was greatly respected by his men, who stood bravely with him until he fell. He died in 1900, about ninety-five years of age.

Just as the Forty-Seventh companies were being driven back, I ordered my regiment to change direction to the left, swing around, and drive the Federals from the ledge of rocks, for the purpose of enfilading their line, relieving the Forty-Seventh, gain the enemy's rear, and drive him from the hill. My men obeyed and advanced about halfway to the enemy's position, but the fire was so destructive that my line wavered like a man trying to walk against a strong wind, and then slowly, doggedly, gave back a little; then with no one upon the left or right of me, my regiment exposed, while the enemy was still under cover, to stand there and die was sheer folly; either to retreat or advance became a necessity.

The Lieutenant-Colonel, I. B. Feagin, had lost his leg at Plum Run; the heroic Captain Ellison had fallen; while Captain

Brainard, one of the bravest and best officers in the regiment, in leading his company forward, fell, exclaiming, 'Oh, God! that I could see my mother!' and instantly expired. Lieutenant John A. Oates, my dear brother, succeeded to the command of the company, but was pierced through by a number of bullets, and fell mortally wounded. Lieutenant Cody fell mortally wounded. Captain Bethune and several other officers were seriously wounded, while the carnage in the ranks was appalling.

I again ordered the advance, and, knowing the officers and men of that gallant old regiment, I felt sure that they would follow their commander anywhere in the line of duty. I passed through the line waving my sword, shouting, 'Forward, men, to the ledge!' and was promptly followed by the command in splendid style. We drove the Federals from their strong defensive position; five times they rallied and charged us, twice coming so near that some of my men had to use the bayonet, but in vain was their effort. It was our time now to deal death and destruction to a gallant foe, and the account was speedily settled. I led this charge and sprang upon the ledge of rock, using my pistol within musket length, when the rush of my men drove the Maine men from the ledge along the line now indicated by stone markers on the east end of Vincent's Spur.

I have seen a statement from General Chamberlain that his right was not forced back beyond the point or angle of the rocky ledge where the right marker of his regiment stands. My recollection is quite different. At this angle and to the southwest of it is where I lost the greatest number of my men. The Twentieth Maine was driven back from this ledge, but not farther than to the next ledge on the mountain-side. I recall a circumstance which I recollect. I, with my regiment, made a rush forward from the ledge. About forty steps up the slope there is a large boulder about midway the Spur. The Maine regiment charged my line, coming right up in a hand-to-hand encounter. My regimental colours were just a step or two to the right of that boulder, and I was within ten feet. A Maine man reached to grasp the staff of the colours when Ensign Archibald stepped back and Sergeant Pat O'Connor stove his bayonet through the head of the Yankee, who fell dead. I witnessed that incident, which impressed me beyond the point of being forgotten. There never were harder fighters than the Twentieth Maine men and their gallant colonel. His skill and persistency and the great bravery of his men saved Little Round Top and the Army of the Potomac from defeat.

Great events sometimes turn on comparatively small affairs. My position rapidly became untenable. The Federal infantry were reported to be coming down on my right, and certainly were closing in on my rear, while some dismounted cavalry were closing the only avenue of escape on my left rear. I sent my sergeant-major with a request to Colonel Bowles, of the Fourth Alabama, the next in line to the left, to come to my relief. He returned within a minute and reported that none of our troops were in sight, the enemy to be between us and the Fourth Alabama, and swarming in the woods south of Little Round Top. The lamented Captain Park, who was afterwards killed at Knoxville, and Captain Hill, killed near Richmond in 1864, came and informed me that the enemy were closing in on our rear.

I sent Park to ascertain their number. He soon returned and reported that two regiments were coming up behind us, and just then I saw them halt behind a fence, some two hundred yards distant, from which they opened fire on us. These, I have since learned from him, were the battalions of Stoughton's sharpshooters, each of which carried a flag, hence the impression that there were two regiments. They had been lost in the woods, but, guided by the firing, came up in our rear. At Balaklava Captain Nolan's six hundred had cannon to the right of them, cannon to the left of them, cannon in front of them, which volleyed and thundered. But at this moment the Fifteenth Alabama had infantry in front of them, to the right of them, dismounted cavalry to the left of them, and infantry in the rear of them. With a withering and deadly fire pouring in upon us from every direction, it seemed that the regiment was doomed to destruction. While one man was shot in the face, his right-hand or left-hand comrade was shot in the side or back. Some were struck simultaneously with two or three balls from different directions.

Captains Hill and Park suggested that I should order a retreat; but this seemed impracticable. My dead and wounded were then nearly as great in number as those still on duty. They literally covered the ground. The blood stood in puddles in some places on the rocks; the ground was soaked with the blood of as brave men as ever fell on the red field of battle. I still hoped for reinforcements or for the tide of success to turn my way. It seemed impossible to retreat, and I therefore replied to my captains, 'Return to your companies; we will sell out as dearly as possible.' Hill made no reply, but Park smiled pleasantly, gave me the military salute, and said, 'All right, sir.'

On reflection, a few moments later I saw no hope of success, and did order a retreat, but did not undertake to retire in order. I sent Sergeant-Major Norris (who is now a physician residing in Brazil) and had the officers and men advised the best I could that when the signal was given that we would not try to retreat in order, but everyone should run in the direction from whence we came, and halt on be top of the Big Round Top Mountain. I found the undertaking to capture Little Round Top too great for my regiment unsupported. I waited until the next charge of the Twentieth Maine was repulsed, as it would give my men a better chance to get out unhurt, and then ordered the retreat.

"The historian of that regiment claims that its charge drove us from the field. This is not true; *I ordered the retreat*. (Italics are Oates'.—O. W. N.) He was, I believe, the chaplain, and not present to see it. Doubtless he was at prayer a safe distance in the rear. Colonel Chamberlain also reported it, and doubtless believed it; but it was just as I state, I ordered the retreat.

When the signal was given, we ran like a herd of wild cattle, right through the line of dismounted cavalrymen. Some of the men as they ran through seized three of the cavalrymen by the collars and carried them out prisoners. As we ran, a man named Keils, of Company H, from Henry County, who was to my right and rear, had his throat cut by a bullet, and he ran past me breathing at his throat and the blood spattering. His windpipe was entirely severed, but notwithstanding he crossed the mountain and died in the field hospital that night or the next morning.

Captain De B. Waddell, who was then adjutant of the regiment, when we had reached our most advanced position, about one hundred and fifty yards from the top of Little Round Top, where the New York monument now stands, came and asked me to let him take forty or fifty men from the right wing of the regiment and advance to some rocks from which to enfilade the Union line, the Twentieth Maine and Eighty-Third Pennsylvania. I authorised it, and he had about fifty men behind a ledge of rocks or ridge of ground, and doing effective work when I ordered the retreat. The firing was so heavy that he did not hear the order, but said he saw me and the men near me start, and knew that it was a retreat. Sergeant-Major Norris, when communicating to commanders of companies that I would order a retreat, did not so inform Waddell. He gave the order and broke to run. He saw two of his men fall. He escaped, but his men were captured.

When he reached the foot of the mountain he there met Company A coming out of the woods to the east of the position from which we had just retreated. This was the company whose captain I had ordered, as we advanced down the north side of Great Round Top, to deploy his company in open order to surround and capture the train of ordnance wagons. Captain Shaaf claimed that there were Union troops in the woods east of the wagons and he feared capture of his company if he attempted to capture the wagons, and desisted in consequence. He should then have rejoined the regiment at once, but did not.

The troops in the woods were Stoughton's sharpshooters, and perhaps Morrell's company of the Twentieth Maine. Waddell caused the company to take a stand a short distance up the mountain-side, where by their fire they checked and turned back the Maine men who were pursuing my regiment. When I visited the battlefield after the war, I could not understand how the trees on that side of Round Top near its base were scarred on each side by bullets, and why monuments or markers were set up there, as I thought no battle occurred there. Afterwards Captain Waddell (now an Episcopal clergyman at Meridian, Mississippi) explained it.

The absence of Company A from the assault on Little Round Top, the capture of the water detail, and the number overcome by heat who had fallen out on scaling the rugged mountain, reduced my regiment to less than four hundred officers and men who made that assault. All these facts I did not know when I made my report, nor when I wrote the article for the Southern Historical Society papers in 1878, but close investigation since the war revealed them to me. In the hasty manner of writing my report, I took as a basis of the strength of my regiment its last muster before we began the march to Pennsylvania. I also wrote the article after the war on the same basis, which was a mistake. When approaching the top of the mountain in retreat, I made an attempt to halt and re-form the regiment; but the men were helping wounded and disabled comrades, and scattered in the woods and among the rocks, so that it could not then be done.

I was so overcome by heat and exertion that I fainted and fell, and would have been captured but for two stalwart, powerful men of the regiment, who carried me to the top of the mountain, where Dr. Reeves, the assistant surgeon, poured water on my head from a canteen, until it revived me. I never can forget those two men, for I dreaded a prison more than death. When I revived, I turned over the command of the regiment to Captain Hill temporarily, with directions to retire to the open field at the foot of the mountain on the line of our advance. This was between sunset and dark; the fighting along our line had pretty well ceased. It had been terrific all along Longstreet's front. His seventeen thousand men had done the best fighting of any equal number of troops during the war, but had not accomplished anything in the way of substantial results.

Lee's plan for Longstreet's attack was up the Emmittsburg road, beginning with the right brigade, which was Law's, where I was. Had General Longstreet been where the attack began, he would have seen the necessity of protecting my flank from the assault of United States sharpshooters. Had that been done, I would, with the six hundred veterans I had, have reached Little Round Top before Vincent's brigade did, and would easily have captured that place, which would have won the battle. Or had he seen the Fifteenth and Forty-Seventh regiments when they reached the top of Great Round Top, and ordered a battery and another regiment to aid me in holding that mountain, it would have been held—which Meade admitted, in his testimony on the conduct of the war, was the key to his position. With that in our possession he could not have held any of the ground which he subsequently held to the last, for it was the key-point of his position. Instead of this, General Longstreet was near the other end of his line, more than a mile away from his right, and never knew that those regiments passed over the top of Big Round Top until years after the battle, when he saw it in print.

Though he may not have approved Lee's plan, it was his duty to have loyally and to the best of his ability executed that plan. Had he done so, I have no doubt of the success of the attack. General Lee was at fault for failing to have Longstreet's two divisions, then on the field (except Law's brigade), seize the Round Tops in the forenoon, when there were no Union troops on them. When the assault was made at 3:30 p. m. neither of these mountains was occupied in force, but Sickles' corps was advanced beyond and obstructed a direct attack on Little Round Top. Longstreet was responsible and at fault for the negligent and bungling manner in which it was done.

The change made in his line by General Sickles, which was unknown to General Lee, greatly impaired his plan; but notwithstanding his shrewd change and its tendency to thwart the plan, yet had Longstreet skilfully and loyally, instead of sullenly and disapprovingly, executed it, he would have won the battle. When he found the change in Sickles' lines—of which he knew that General Lee was not aware—he should have adopted General Hood's suggestion to turn the flank and attack in the rear; but because Lee had ordered him to attack in a particular way, he would not change, though he knew that if Lee himself had been present he would have changed the order of attack when he discovered the change in Sickles' line which made it necessary.

General Longstreet in his book throws all the blame on Lee for not riding with him and personally directing his attack, as follows:

> We were left to our own resources in finding ground upon which to organise for battle. The enemy had changed position somewhat after the march was ordered, but, as we were not informed of his position before the march, we could not know of the change. The Confederate commander did not care to ride near us, to give information of a change to assist in preparing for attack, nor to inquire if new and better combinations might be made.

General Lee mistakenly supposed that Longstreet understood the situation, position of the enemy, etc., and possessed the ability and patriotism sufficient to make that attack wisely without his presence.

General Longstreet disapproved the plan of attack because Lee was departing from the policy, declared by him before he moved from Virginia, of an aggressive defensive campaign, which Longstreet approved. He may have been right; it may have been best for Lee to have flanked Meade out of his strong position and have forced him to attack and thus to have acted on the defensive. Lee gave his reasons why he did not pursue that course, which were well-nigh conclusive. Longstreet had no right to sulk because of this change of policy. Sulking was disloyalty to his chief. If his conduct was not half-hearted and wilful, then the only explanation of it is that he was a failure as a general, and no one believes that.

Hood saw the necessity, and insisted on a change of the plan of attack, but because Lee had ordered it, without a knowledge of Sickles' change of lines, Longstreet obeyed Lee's order literally, although Hood showed him the necessity of a change, and by his mulishness lost the greatest battle of the war. General Law fully concurred in Hood's views. A supposition that Hood's request would be granted may account for Law's skirmishers passing around Big Round Top to the east and thus missing the battle.

Early on the morning of the 2nd General Meade expected Lee to attack him on his right, and determined to attack Lee before the latter moved against him. At 9:30 a.m., he ordered Slocum, who commanded the Twelfth and Fifth corps, constituting the right wing of the Union army, to get ready to attack, and that he would give the signal as soon as the Sixth corps arrived within supporting distance. Slocum, whom General Sherman afterwards said was as capable of commanding 80,000 men as he was, carefully examined the ground in his front, with its uneven surface, woods, hills, and streams, and reported to Meade adversely and advised against making the attack.

General Meade then surveyed the field with the view of attacking by his front, or left, and then summoned his corps commanders to a conference. Sickles did not come, but sent word that his corps, on the extreme left, was threatened with an attack and that he could not leave. Thereupon Meade sent him a peremptory order to attend the conference at once. Sickles then went, and as he rode up Longstreet's guns opened upon his line. Meade told him not to dismount, but return to his command. Meade reinforced him heavily and saved him from utter rout.

The assault of Longstreet was the opening of the battle of that day. Slocum's decision and advice were wise. Had Slocum made that attack it would have been on Swell's corps, which would have allowed Longstreet's and Hill's corps to advance against the Third and Second, Sickles' and Hancock's corps, which were inferior numerically, and they would have been driven back against Meade's attacking column, which Ewell could have held at bay for a time. Lee would have thus gained the advantage of position and Meade would inevitably have lost the battle. Slocum's advice and Sickles' wise disposition of his corps saved Meade from dishonour and the Army of the Potomac from defeat—two New York Union Democrats.

Inasmuch as General Lee did not have Longstreet seize the Round Tops in the forenoon, he had better have awaited the results of that conference; and had it been to attack him it would have been to his advantage, for, as Stonewall Jackson said on his deathbed, 'My troops sometimes fail to drive the enemy from their position, but theirs always fail to drive my men from their position.' But of. course Lee was not aware of that conference.

The Yankees did not occupy the top of Big Round Top until after dark. It was dark when my regiment reached the valley, and here we bivouacked for the night. After all had gotten up, I ordered the roll of the companies to be called. When the battle commenced, four hours previously, mine was the strongest and finest regiment in Hood's division. Its effectives numbered about five hundred officers and men. Now two hundred and twenty-three enlisted men answered at roll-call, and more than one-half of the officers had been left on the field, only nineteen answering to their names; but some of the officers and men came up in the course of the night and next morning, who had been overcome by the heat during the advance the previous evening.

Some of the men that night voluntarily went back across the mountain, and in the darkness penetrated the Federal lines for the purpose of removing some of our wounded. They reached the scene and started out with some of the wounded officers, but were discovered and shot at by the Federal pickets, and had in consequence to leave the wounded, but succeeded in getting back to the regiment, and brought to me Lieutenant Cody's knife and pocketbook. These men reported to me that Big Round Top was, even at that late hour, occupied by only a thin skirmish line. I am sorry that I do not remember the names of those brave men who voluntarily went within the enemy's lines to relieve and save from capture wounded comrades.

Soon after the advance began the gallant Lieutenant-Colonel Isaac B. Feagin was shot through the knee, which necessitated amputation of the limb. The major was voluntarily with the wagon-train, and consequently I had no field officer to assist me. I discovered some time before we reached Gettysburg that my brother, Lieutenant John A. Oates, had fallen behind some distance, and was reported sick. I sent back a horse for him and he came up. Just before we advanced I went to him where he was lying on the ground in rear of his company, and saw at once that he was sick.

I thereupon told him not to go into the action, but when we advanced to remain where he was, because he was unable to bear the fatigue. He replied, with the most dogged and fiery determination, 'Brother, I will not do it. If I were to remain here people would say that I did it through cowardice. No, sir, I am an officer, and will never disgrace the uniform I wear; I shall go through, unless I am killed, which I think is quite likely.' These were the last words ever passed between us. When he fell, struck by several balls, Lieutenant Isaac H. Parks, who had been his schoolfellow, ran to him and dragged him behind a large stone, and just as Parks let him down another ball struck one of his hands and carried away his little finger. Parks was for many years after the war a prominent lawyer at Rutledge, Crenshaw County, Alabama, and represented his county in both branches of the legislature, and in the Constitutional Convention of 1875, and died in 1900. Lieutenant Cody, a boy about eighteen years old, the best officer I ever saw of his age, except Major Latimer of the artillery, fell near my brother, mortally wounded. When we retreated, they, with most of our wounded and eighty-four men who were not, were taken prisoners, and the wounded were removed to the Federal field hospital, where they were as well cared for as wounded soldiers in the hands of an enemy ever are. Cody lived twenty-one and my brother twenty-three days. A Miss Lightner, a Virginia lady and Southern sympathizer, nursed them to the last, and Doctor Reid, of the One Hundred and Fifty-Fifth Pennsylvania Regiment, did all that he could for them and had them decently buried when they died. He sent to me by flag of truce my brother's old gold watch, his pocketbook and money. I endeavoured for years after the war to find Doctor Reid, without success, but finally obtained his address, Lancaster, Pennsylvania, and had a very pleasant and satisfactory correspondence with him. I had theretofore never had an opportunity of expressing to him the full measure of my gratitude for his attention to my brother and Lieutenant Cody.

The dear, good ministering angel. Miss Lightner, has long since passed beyond the arena of bloody battles and grim death, to reap that priceless reward which is promised to the charitable and the good. Some of our wounded were not treated so well. Some were not removed from the places where they fell for two or three days. Sergeant Johns, of Company B, had one of his thighs broken, and lay where he fell, in all the hard rain of the third and fourth days of July, and was not removed until the battle was over and Lee on his way back to Virginia. He lay on his back, could not turn, and kept from drowning by putting his hat over his face. He recovered, and was alive several years after the war, and living in Texas.

Captain J. Henry Ellison was a son of the Rev. Dr. Ellison, a distinguished Methodist divine. When I gave the order to change direction to the left to drive the Twentieth Maine Regiment, he did not hear it with distinctness. He stepped toward me, and placing his hand behind his ear inquired, 'What is the order, Colonel?' I repeated it. He turned to his company and cried out, 'Forward, my men, forward!' and fell shot through the head. I saw the ball strike him; that is, I was looking at him when it did. He fell upon his left shoulder, turned upon his back, raised his arms, clenched his fists, gave one shudder, his arms fell, and he was dead. He wore that day a very fine captain's uniform which I had presented to him after my promotion, and I thought at the moment of his death that he was the handsomest and finest specimen of manhood that ever went down upon a field of carnage.

There was no better regiment in the Confederate Army than

the Fifteenth Alabama, and when properly commanded, if it failed to carry any point against which it was thrown, no other single regiment need try it. The long and rapid march, the climb of Great Round Top's rugged front without water, impaired its power of endurance, but it fought hard and persistently until ordered to retreat. The other regiments of the brigade did their duty at Gettysburg, but the Fifteenth struck the hardest knot.

The following from the pen of Colonel W. F. Perry describes 'The Devil's Den' and the assault of his regiment, the Forty-Fourth Alabama, upon it:

> Large rocks, from six to fifteen feet high, are thrown together in confusion over a considerable area, and yet so disposed as to leave everywhere among them winding passages carpeted with moss. Many of its recesses are never visited by the sunshine, and a cavernous coolness pervades the air within it.
>
> A short distance to the east the frowning bastions of Little Round Top rise two hundred feet above the level of the plain. An abrupt elevation, thirty or forty feet high, itself buttressed with rocks, constitutes the western boundary of this strange formation.
>
> The view was imposing. Little Round Top, crowned with artillery, resembled a volcano in eruption; while the hillock near the Devil's Den resembled a small one. The distance between them, diminished by the view in perspective, appeared as a secondary crater near its base. It was evident that a formidable task was before us.
>
> The enemy was as invisible to us as we were to them. The presence of a battery of artillery of course implied the presence of a strong supporting force of infantry. Of its strength, its position, and the nature of its defences we were in total ignorance. We were soon to learn. As the line emerged from the woods into the open space mentioned above, a sheet of flame burst from the rocks less than fifty yards away. A few scattering shots in the beginning gave warning in time for my men to fall down, and thus largely to escape the effect of the main volley. They doubtless seemed to the enemy to be all dead, but the volley of the fire which they immediately returned proved that they were very much alive.

No language can express the intensity of the solicitude with which I surveyed the strange, wild situation which had suddenly burst upon my view. Upon the decision of a moment depended the honour of my command, and perhaps the lives of many brave men. I knew that, if called upon, they would follow me, and felt confident that the place could be carried by an impetuous charge. But then what? There were no supporting troops in sight. A heavy force of the enemy might envelop and overpower us. It was certain that we should be exposed to a plunging, enfilading fire from Little Round Top. And yet the demoralisation and shame of a retreat, and an exposure to be shot in the back, were not to be thought of. Before the enemy had time to load their guns a decision was made. Leaping over the prostrate line before me, I shouted the order, "Forward!" and started for the rocks. The response was a bound, a yell, and a rush, and in ten seconds my men were pouring into the Den, and the enemy were escaping from the opposite side. A few prisoners were taken. Two soldiers of the Fourth Maine regiment surrendered to me in person at the edge of the rocks as my line overtook and passed me.

In the charge the left wing of the regiment struck the hill on which the artillery were stationed, and the centre and the right swept into the rocks east of it. Maj. George W. Carey led the left wing up the hill and, bounding over the rocks on its crest, landed among the artillerymen ahead of the line, and received their surrender. One of the officers of the battery whom I met soon after complimented his gallantry and that of his men in the highest terms. The major a few moments later found me near the foot of the hill, completely prostrated by heat and excessive exertion. He exhibited several swords as an evidence that the artillery had surrendered, and complained that guns from both sides were playing upon the position. This I knew to be true as to the Federal side. At the very entrance of the labyrinth a spherical case-shot from Round Top had exploded very near my head and thrown its deadly contents against a rock almost within my reach. He was ordered to hurry back and withdraw the men from the crest so that they could find shelter on the side of the hill.

In a very short time he came back in great haste and informed me that a force of the enemy large enough to envelop our position was moving down upon us. I sprang to my feet with the intention of climbing the hill to see the situation and determine what to do; but found myself unable to stand without support. While we were anxiously discussing the situation, a line of battle, moving in splendid style, swept in from Seminary Ridge upon the left, and met the threatening force. One of us remarked, "There is Benning; we are all right now." Benning's march was so directed that his right lapped upon my left, and poured over the hill upon which were the abandoned guns.

A furious battle now began along his entire line, as well as my own, which had pressed through to the north side of the rocks. It has always been to me a source of sincere regret that my disability, which continued until after nightfall, prevented me from seeing anything that occurred after the arrival of Benning's line.

My loss was comparatively light, considering the desperate character of the fighting. This was due to three causes: The happy dodge given the first volley of the enemy, the rush made upon them before they had time to reload, and the protection afterwards afforded by the rocks. The killed and wounded numbered ninety-two, a little over one-fourth of those who went into action.

Thus, ended the second day's fighting.

Many books about the Civil War have been published, histories of the armies, of corps, divisions, brigades, and regiments, enough to make a large library. Comparatively few are from the Confederate side. *The War Between the Union and the Confederacy*, by General Oates, is the only one which I have found which treats of the battle for the possession of Little Round Top; for this reason, I have quoted from it at greater length than I have from any other publication. Its author was a gallant Confederate soldier, who fought through the war, and afterward was prominent in his State in politics, having received the highest honours at the disposal of its grateful people.

At the Battle of Gettysburg, he was the colonel of the Fifteenth Alabama regiment in Law's brigade. He says that at this time his regiment was the largest and best in Hood's division. His book was published in 1905, forty-two years after the battle of Gettysburg. He seems to have been well acquainted with all the officers and enlisted men of his regiment, and throughout the book says more about its individual members than I have seen in any other regimental history, for while he criticises freely the conduct of the Confederate generals and their campaigns, it is essentially the history of Colonel Oates and his men. There are many statements in his account of their part in the attack on Little Round Top which do not agree with statements of others, both Union and Confederate officers, which I do not feel competent to criticise, but I must mention a few of a different character.

Military etiquette requires that official reports shall be confined to the part taken by the organisation under the command of the officer reporting, without alluding to the other organisations unless the action of the latter modifies that of his own. Colonel Oates' report of the Fifteenth Alabama, dated August 8, 1863, complies with this requirement; but it differs materially from the account in his book. He and his regiment, with the Forty-Seventh Alabama, which, according to his account, was temporarily under his command, did as much to break up Vincent's brigade as any equal number of well trained and disciplined soldiers either Union or Confederate could have done under the circumstances.

It seems ungenerous, to say the least, that he should claim that parts of these two regiments alone comprised all of the Confederates engaged on this part of the field. He ignores the presence of the Fourth and Fifth Texas of Robertson's brigade, and the remaining regiments of Law's brigade. If, as he states, the force which attacked Vincent consisted of 154 men of the Forty-Seventh Alabama, and less than 400 of the Fifteenth Alabama, it reflects very little credit on Vincent's brigade, which entered the fight with about 1,100 men, that any of the Confederates escaped death or capture.

I have found no evidence anywhere confirming his statement that just before his retreat there were two battalions of sharpshooters on his right, dismounted cavalry on his left, and infantry in his rear. Stoughton's battalion of the Second United States Sharpshooters consisted of eight small companies. The First battalion, under Colonel Berdan, which also belonged to Ward's brigade, was sent out to the west of the Peach Orchard early in the day and did not return to

Ward's brigade that day. The Second battalion was sent out by Ward as a skirmish line to cover his front. Stoughton says that the five companies on his right were outflanked and, being forced to retire, fell back to the main line of the brigade.

The other three companies retreated before the Fifteenth and Forty-Seventh Alabama, going up the western slope of Big Round Top before these regiments, and divided before reaching the summit. The greater part of them went around the left of the Forty-Seventh, and after they passed made their way down the slope to the northwest and rejoined their brigade. The remainder of this line, about a dozen men, kept to the right of the Fifteenth Alabama.

Oates deployed his Company A, and they followed these few sharpshooters until they drove them off the hill at the eastern end; there they joined with Captain Morrill's company of the Twentieth Maine, which Chamberlain had sent out as skirmishers in that direction. When Chamberlain made his final charge, Morrill's company, with this dozen sharpshooters, came up and joined in the charge. If there were any dismounted cavalry in that vicinity it is a mystery where they came from. All accounts except this agree that there were no Union cavalry on the left during the engagement on July 2. Law says that he sent out scouts in every direction and failed to discover even a cavalry picket. It seems incredible that there could have been any Union infantry in the rear of Oates' line while his attack on the Twentieth Maine and Eighty-Third Pennsylvania was in progress.

The incident of the surrender of the punctilious Lieutenant-Colonel Bulger is not of great importance. I notice it only because of Oates' discredit of Chamberlain's account. It seems to have taken place while Chamberlain was conducting the charge of the Twentieth Maine, which cleared the valley of the Confederates. Colonel Rice did not go forward with this charge. The other regiments of the brigade remained in position and Rice properly remained with them. Chamberlain's report is dated July 6, and was in the hands of Rice within a day or two. If Rice had received this surrender he would naturally have asked Chamberlain to modify his report. I was at brigade headquarters until sometime after Colonel Rice received his commission as brigadier-general, and was transferred to the command of a brigade in another corps. The incidents of the battle were the subject of frequent conversation among the men and officers at brigade headquarters, and if Bulger's surrender had been made as Oates describes it I am sure I should have heard of it.

In questioning the accuracy of the statement of Captain Prince about the number of prisoners taken, he is not quite fair.

Captain Prince says the prisoners were mostly from the Fifteenth and Forty-Seventh Alabama. As these regiments made the fight against the Twentieth Maine, and the fighting there was long continued and very desperate. Prince's attention was naturally directed there. He says that the four hundred prisoners were "mostly" from the Fifteenth and Forty-Seventh Alabama; but many prisoners belonging to the Fourth and Forty-Eighth Alabama and the Fourth and Fifth Texas were also taken. Vincent's other regiments took their full share, and a total of four hundred for the brigade does not seem excessive.

General E. M. Law, C. S. A.: *The Struggle for Round Top, Battles and Leaders of the Civil War,* Vol. iii

More has been written concerning the Battle of Gettysburg than any other 'passage of arms' between the Federal and Confederate troops during the Civil War. The engagement of the first of July, brought on by accident, on the part of the Confederates at least, in which two corps of the Federal army under General Reynolds were defeated and driven through Gettysburg by portions of Hill's and Ewell's corps, has been often and fully described by the officers on both sides. Ewell's attack on the Federal right in the vicinity of Culp's Hill on the second of July, and Longstreet's advance upon the Federal left on the same day, so far as relates to one division of the latter's command (McLaws'), have been detailed with equal minuteness by those engaged.

The magnificent charge of Pickett's division on the third day has been the theme of a host of writers who deemed it an honour to have stood in the lines of blue by which that charge was repelled, and those who, on the other hand, thought it no less an honour to have shared the fortunes of the torn and shattered columns of gray which only failed to accomplish impossibilities.

But concerning the operations of Lee's extreme right wing, extending to the foot of Round Top, little or nothing has been written on the Confederate side. This part of the line was held by Hood's division of Longstreet's corps, and was really the key to the whole position of Gettysburg. Here some of the most stubborn fighting of that desperate battle was done, and here a determined effort of the Federal cavalry to reach the right rear of the Confederate army on the third of July was frustrated—an attempt which, if successful, must have resulted disastrously to that army.

The meagreness of the details of the operations referred to may be accounted for by the fact that General Longstreet personally superintended the left of his line, consisting of McLaws' division of his own corps, supported by B. H. Anderson's division of Hill's corps, and hence knew comparatively little from personal observation of the movements of Hood's division; and, also, that General Hood was wounded early in the engagement on the second of July, and, relinquishing the command of the division, could not report its subsequent operations.

As senior brigadier, I succeeded to the command of Hood's division, and directed its movements during the engagements of the second and third of July. But owing to the active and constant movements of our army for some weeks after the battle, I was able to obtain the reports of brigade commanders only a very short time previous to being ordered to the army of General Bragg at Chickamauga. This prevented me from making a report at the time, and it was afterward neglected.

The facts stated in this paper are therefore many of them published for the first time. It remains for the impartial reader to decide whether they do not constitute an important part of the history of the most memorable battle of the war; for Gettysburg was the turning-point in the great struggle. Together with the fall of Vicksburg, which occurred simultaneously with the retreat of Lee's army toward the Potomac, it inspired the armies and people of the North with fresh courage and stimulated anew the hopes of ultimate success, which were visibly flagging under an almost uninterrupted series of reverses to the Federal armies in Virginia, extending over a period of nearly two years. On the other hand, it was at Gettysburg that the right arm of the South was broken, and it must always stand out in Confederate annals as in the history of a brave and kindred people stands

Flodden's fatal field,
Where shivered was fair Scotland's spear,
And broken was her shield.

It was now past four o'clock in the afternoon, and our troops were in position for the attack. The flank movement by which they came into position is referred to in the following dispatch from the Federal signal station on Little Round Top: 'To General Meade—four o'clock p. m. The only infantry of the enemy visible is on the extreme (Federal) left; it has been moving toward Emmittsburg.' It will thus be seen that the movement, in spite of our precautions, was not unobserved.

The Confederate line of battle occupied a ridge, partly wooded, with a valley intervening between it and the heights held by the Federal troops in front. The position occupied by the Federal left wing in front of us was now fully disclosed to view, and it was certainly one of the most formidable it had ever been the fortune of any troops to confront. Round Top rose like a huge sentinel guarding the Federal left flank, while the spurs and ridges trending off to the north of it afforded unrivaled positions for the use of artillery.

The puffs of smoke rising at intervals along the line of hills, as the Federal batteries fired upon such portions of our line as became exposed to view, clearly showed that these advantages had not been neglected. The thick woods that in great part covered the sides of Round Top and the adjacent hills concealed from view the rugged nature of the ground, which increased fourfold the difficulties of the attack.

How far up the slope of Round Top the Federal left extended we could not tell, as the woods effectually concealed from view everything in that quarter.

In order to gain information upon this important point, I sent out a detail of six picked men as scouts, with instructions to move as rapidly as possible to the summit of Round Top, making a detour to their right, and 'feeling' down from that point, to locate the left of the Federal line. The entire absence of Federal cavalry on our right, as well as other indications leading to the same conclusion, convinced me that the Federals, relying upon the protection of the mountain, considered their flank secure; and it was therefore their most vulnerable point. Impressed with this view, I further instructed the scouts when they reached the summit to observe carefully the state of affairs on the other side, and to send a 'runner' back to me with such intelligence as they might be able to gain. They moved off at a trot.

A few moments after they had started I saw in the valley, some distance to our right, several dark figures moving across the fields from the rear of Round Top in the direction of the Emmittsburg road. These, on being captured, proved to be Federal soldiers, who seemed surprised at our sudden appearance in that quarter, and who, on being questioned, stated that they had surgeon's certificates and were going 'to the rear.' They indicated 'the rear' by pointing toward Emmittsburg, and in reply to the question where they came from, they said from the 'medical train behind the mountain'—referring to Round Top. They also stated that the medical and ordnance trains 'around the mountain' were insecurely guarded, no attack being expected at that point; and that the other side of the mountain could be easily reached by a good farm road, along which they had just travelled, the distance being little more than a mile.

On my way to convey this information to General Hood, I met a messenger from my scouts, who had reached the crest of Round Top. He reported that there was no Federal force on the summit, and confirmed in every particular the statements of the prisoners I had just captured. If there had previously been any question in regard to the policy of a front attack, there now remained not a shadow of a doubt that our true *point d'appui* was Round Top, from which the Confederate right wing could be extended toward the Taneytown and Baltimore roads on the Federal left and rear.

I found General Hood on the ridge where his line had been formed, communicated to him the information I had obtained, and pointed out the ease with which a movement by the right flank might be made. He coincided fully with my views, but said that his orders were positive to attack in front, as soon as the left of the corps should get into position. I therefore entered a formal protest against a direct attack, on the grounds:

1. That the great natural strength of the enemy's position in our front rendered the result of a direct assault extremely uncertain.

2. That, even if successful, the victory would be purchased at too great a sacrifice of life, and our troops would be in no condition to improve it.

3. That a front attack was unnecessary—the occupation of Round Top during the night by moving upon it from the south,

and the extension of our right wing from that point across the enemy's left and rear, being not only practicable, but easy.

4. That such a movement would compel a change of front on the part of the enemy, the abandonment of his strong position on the heights, and force him to attack us in position.

General Hood called up Captain Hamilton, of his staff, and requested me to repeat the protest to him, and the grounds on which it was made. He then directed Captain Hamilton to find General Longstreet as quickly as possible and deliver the protest, and to say to him that he (Hood) indorsed it fully. Hamilton rode off at once, but in about ten minutes returned, accompanied by a staff officer of General Longstreet, who said to General Hood, in my hearing, 'General Longstreet orders that you begin the attack at once.' Hood turned to me and merely said, 'You hear the order?' I at once moved my brigade to the assault. . . .

Our order of attack—issued as soon as the two divisions of Longstreet's corps came into position on the line already described—was, that the movement should begin on the right, my brigade on that flank leading, the other commands taking it up successively toward the left. It was near 5 o'clock p. m. when we advanced to the attack. The artillery on both sides had been warmly engaged for about fifteen minutes, and continued to fire heavily until we became engaged with the Federal infantry, when the Confederate batteries ceased firing to avoid injury to our own troops, who were then, for the most part, concealed by the woods about the base of Round Top and the spurs to the north of it. General Hood was severely wounded in the arm by a shot from the Federal artillery as we moved into action.

Advancing rapidly across the valley which separated the opposing lines,—all the time under a heavy fire from the batteries,—our front line struck the enemy's skirmishers posted along the farther edge of the valley. Brushing these quickly away, we soon came upon their first line of battle, running along the lower slopes of the hills known as Devil's Den, to our left of Round Top, and separated from the latter by Plum Run valley. The fighting soon became close and severe. Exposed to the artillery fire from the heights in front and on our left, as well as to the musketry of the infantry, it required all the courage and steadiness of the veterans who composed the army of Northern

Virginia—whose spirit was never higher than then—to face the storm. Not one moment was lost. With rapidly thinning ranks the gray line swept on, until the blue line in front wavered, broke, and seemed to dissolve in the woods and rocks on the mountain-side. The advance continued steadily, the centre of the division moving directly upon the guns on the hill adjoining Devil's Den on the north, from which we had been suffering so severely.

In order to secure my right flank, I extended it well up on the side of Round Top, and my brigade, in closing to the right, left a considerable interval between its left and the right of the Texas brigade of Robertson. Into this interval, I threw Benning's Georgia brigade, which had up to that time occupied the second line. At the same time, seeing a heavy Federal force on Robertson's left, and no Confederate troops having come up to extend our line in that direction, Anderson's Georgia brigade, till then also in the second line, was thrown out on that flank.

Thus disposed, the division continued to move forward, encountering, as it ascended the heights around the battery on the spur and to the right and left of it, a most determined resistance from the Federal troops, who seemed to be continually reinforced. The ground was rough and difficult, broken by rocks and boulders, which rendered an orderly advance impossible.

Sometimes the Federals would hold one side of the huge boulders on the slope until the Confederates occupied the other. In some cases my men with reckless daring mounted to the top of the large rocks in order to get a better view and to deliver their fire with greater effect. One of these, Sergeant Barber of the Texas brigade, having reached a rock a little in advance of the line, stood erect on the top of it, loading and firing as coolly as if unconscious of danger, while the air around him was fairly swarming with bullets. He soon fell helpless from several wounds; but he held his rock, lying upon the top of it until the litter-bearers carried him off.

In less than an hour from the time we advanced to the attack the hill by Devil's Den opposite our centre was taken, with three pieces of the artillery that had occupied it. The remaining piece was run down the opposite slope by the gunners, and escaped capture.

In the meantime, my brigade, on the right, had swept over the northern slope of Round Top, cleared it of the enemy, and then, making a partial change of front to the left, advanced upon Little Round Top, which lay in rear of the spur on which the battery had been taken. This change of direction soon exposed it to a flank attack on the right by fresh troops (Vincent's brigade), rendering it necessary to retire it to the general line.

While our centre and right wing were engaged as I have described, Anderson's brigade, on the left, was subjected to great annoyance and loss by movements of the enemy upon its left flank, being frequently compelled to change the front of the regiments on that flank to repel attacks from that direction.

Up to this time I had seen nothing of McLaws' division, which was to have extended our left and to have moved to the attack at the same time. I therefore halted my line, which had become broken and disorganised by the roughness of the ground over which it had been fighting, and, placing it in as advantageous a position as possible for receiving any attack that the Federals might be disposed to make, I hurried back to the ridge from which we had originally advanced. I found McLaws still in position there, his troops suffering considerably from a severe fire of artillery from the opposite hills.

I was informed by General Kershaw, who held the right of this division, that although he understood the general instructions that the forward movement was to be taken up from the right, he had not yet received the order to move, from his division commander. I pointed out the position of Hood's division, and urged the necessity of immediate support on its left. General Kershaw requested me to designate the point on which his right flank should be directed, and promptly moved to the attack, the movement being taken up by the whole division.

When Hood's division first attacked, General Meade, alarmed for the safety of his left wing, and doubtless fully alive to the importance of holding so vital a point as Round Top and its adjacent spurs, commenced sending reinforcements to the threatened points. We encountered some of these in our first advance, and others were arriving as McLaws came up on our left. In its advance this division extended from the 'Peach Orchard' near the Emmittsburg road, on its left, to the 'wheat-field' north of the hill on which we had captured the Federal battery, where its right wing connected with my left. As McLaws advanced, we again moved forward on his right, and the fighting continued in 'see-saw' style—first one side and then the other gaining ground or losing it, with small advantage to either, until dark.

At the close of the engagement Hood's division held the hill where the battery had been taken and the ridge to its left—our right extending across Devil's Den and well up on the northwestern slope of Round Top. During the night, this line was strengthened by the construction of a breastwork of the loose stones that abounded all along the positions occupied by the troops, and the light of the next morning disclosed the fact that the Federal troops in front of us had improved their time in the same way. In fact, all through the night we could hear them at work as the rocks were dropped in place on the works, and no doubt they heard us just as distinctly while we were engaged in the same life-preserving operation.

Though the losses had been severe on both sides, comparatively few prisoners had been taken. But early in the night, in the confusion resulting from the fight over such rugged ground, and the darkness of the wooded mountainside, men of both armies, in search of their commands, occasionally wandered into the opposing picket-lines and were captured. Many of the Federal wounded were left in our lines, on the ground from which their troops had been forced back, and some of ours remained in their hands in the most advanced positions which we had reached and had been compelled to abandon. Among these latter was Colonel Powell of the Fifth Texas regiment, who was shot through the body and afterward died.

Powell was a stout, portly man, with a full beard, resembling, in many respects. General Longstreet, and the first impression of his captors was that they had taken that officer. Indeed, it was asserted positively by some of the prisoners we picked up during the night that Longstreet was badly wounded and a prisoner in their hands, and they obstinately refused to credit our statements to the contrary. . . .

This paper by General Law, written for the *Century Magazine* many years after the battle, is an able discussion of the strategy of Meade and Lee, and is well worth reading whether or not one agrees with his opinion of the reasons for the defeat of the Confederates. I have made extracts of the portions which relate to the fight for the possession of Little Round Top. As Hood was wounded before the Confederate infantry reached the Union lines, and Law succeeded him in the command of the division, it appears that, after starting his brigade on its way to attack Vincent, he devoted his time to the direction of the other brigades of the division in their attack on Birney's line.

We are obliged to depend for information from Confederate sources on the reports of their regimental commanders, with an explanation in Robertson's report of his brigade, of the reason for the participation by two of his regiments—the Fourth and Fifth Texas—in the attack on Little Round Top. These Alabama and Texas men were magnificent soldiers, and they made desperate attempts to gain the coveted position. Whether they would have succeeded had Hood or Law been present to direct them is a question which we need not raise, since they have not. The regimental commanders, according to their reports, acted generally on their own initiative. Colonel Sheffield, who assumed command of Law's brigade when Law took the division, merely mentions the fact in his report, but says nothing of any orders given by him to any regiments except his own.

The scouts which Law sent to the top of Round Top evidently examined the ground to the north of it, and saw no Union troops in position. They must have seen the narrow valley leading up from Plum Run along the north side of Round Top, and reported that. Law was prepared by this information to start his brigade up this valley as soon as he had cleared the western slope of Round Top. Whether he had reported this to Hood and was directed by him to send a part of his forces in that direction, is not stated; but believing the way was clear to reach and occupy or turn little Round Top, we must suppose that experienced officers like Hood or Law would not neglect to take advantage of it. If Vincent had not reached that point and prepared to receive them, the attempt would have succeeded; but Vincent was there first, and it failed.

It is evident from this statement by Law, and Hood's letter to Longstreet written sometime after the war (quoted in Oates' book), that both of these officers protested against making a direct attack on the front of Birney's line. Longstreet also had pleaded with Lee to be allowed to move around the east end of Big Round Top to get in the rear of Meade's left, threatening his communications and forcing him to abandon his strong position on the right. It may be that the hope that Longstreet would yield to their repeated importunities caused Hood's division to go so far to the east that when it faced to the front

Law's brigade so far over-lapped Big Round Top that it was necessary to move the two regiments on its right to its left, and even to the left of the Fourth and Fifth Texas, which under orders had kept closed on the Fourth Alabama, the left of Law's brigade. For some reason not explained by Law, his brigade in advancing obliqued to the right. After moving two regiments to the left, the Fifteenth and Forty-Seventh Alabama were still so far to the east that they struck the south side of the western slope and, following the sharpshooters of Stoughton's skirmish line, wheeled to the right and went up over the top of the mountain. (See Gates' account in his book, Robertson's official report, and reports of regimental commanders in Law's and Robertson's brigades.)

******

The following paper, although not published in book form, belongs with the accounts by other historians. It is one of a series of papers written by Captain Farley describing the history of the One Hundred and Fortieth New York Volunteers, published at intervals in a Rochester newspaper, and is Number Nine of that series. This regiment was raised in Rochester, New York, and was commanded by Colonel Patrick H. O'Rorke from its organisation until his death in the Battle of Gettysburg. As shown by the Warren letters, Captain Farley's Number Nine had been submitted to General Warren and, after some suggestions made by him, the final revised draft met Warren's approval. Warren was so impressed with its value that he requested that a copy of it should be sent to the Comte de Paris, who was then writing his *History of the Civil War in America*. This request was complied with, and the information obtained from this paper may be plainly seen in the chapter on Gettysburg in the Comte de Paris' work. Captain Farley has kindly permitted me to publish the paper in this book.

******

Captain Farley's "Number Nine" Reminiscences by Porter Farley.

On Wednesday July 1, 1863, the Fifth corps, of which our regiment formed a part, having that morning crossed the line dividing the States of Maryland and Pennsylvania, halted about the middle of the afternoon within sight of the town of Hanover. All the country through which we that day passed had been overrun by the rebel cavalry. The inhabitants hailed the army of the Potomac as their deliverers from a threatened wholesale desolation. The day before our arrival there had been quite a lively cavalry fight at Hanover. We came in sight of the town at about 3 p.m. and halted in an open field just beyond its suburbs. Our rest, however, was but short. News soon reached us of heavy fighting which had that day taken place some fourteen miles to the westward, at the town then insignificant, but now known to fame as Gettysburg. The only particulars of the action which we could learn were that the First corps had been engaged and that General Reynolds, its commander, had been killed.

At six o'clock that evening we were in motion again, making all possible speed toward Gettysburg, the point upon which the entire army was then concentrating.

This was campaigning under circumstances entirely different from any of our former experiences. We were on the soil of a loyal State and were hastening to meet a presumptuous foe who had audaciously invaded it. The kindly anxious interest with which the country women and children gazed upon us as they stood at their gates while we marched by, and the alacrity with which they furnished water and food to those who needed it, were incentives to better feelings than those engendered by the sulky faces and contemptuous treatment with which we had been so familiar in our Virginia marches.

I have heard and read many stories of the meanness with which the Pennsylvanians treated the Union soldiers during the Gettysburg campaign, of the parsimony which prompted them to charge and take money for water and outrageous prices for food furnished to men whose wants were extreme, but justice compels me to say that I never saw anything of it. On the contrary, I witnessed the exhibition of a great deal of liberality and was the recipient of it in my own person. Doubtless some of the shameful stories we have heard were true, but I feel very certain that the miscreants who were guilty of such meanness were exceptions among the many, and that a few poor, shrivelled souls were able by thus abusing common decency to bring a reproach upon a kind-hearted and grateful community.

We pushed on till one o'clock in the morning of Thursday, July 2, and then halted and lay down to rest in the road. Overcome by fatigue, the men were asleep almost as soon as they touched the ground. To how many of the poor fellows did this prove the last sleep from which they were ever to arise!

Captain Porter Farley

At about four o'clock we were roused again, and shaking off as best we could the terrible drowsines which oppressed us, moved still further westward. After marching about two hours we halted and the regiments of our brigade formed in column by divisions in the rear of other troops that were deployed in lines of battle, with all dispositions made as if in the presence of the enemy.

It was while waiting here that an orderly brought to Colonel O'Rorke a circular addressed by General Meade to the army. O'Rorke and I were both mounted and standing in front of the column. He glanced over the paper, handed it to me and told me to read it to the regiment. It was as follows:

Circular.
Headquarters Army of the Potomac,
June 30, 1863.

The commanding general requests that previous to the engagement soon expected with the enemy, corps and all other commanding officers will address their troops, explaining to them briefly the immense issues involved in this struggle. The enemy are on our soil. The whole country now looks anxiously to this army to deliver it from the presence of the foe. Our failure to do so will leave us no such welcome as the swelling of millions of hearts with pride and joy at our success would give to every soldier in the army. Homes, firesides, and domestic altars are involved. The army has fought well heretofore. It is believed that it will fight more desperately and bravely than ever if it is addressed in fitting terms.

Corps and other commanders are authorised to order the instant death of any soldier who fails in his duty at this hour.

By command of Major-General Meade.

S. Williams, Ass't Adj't Gen'l.

West Pointers are not habitual speechmakers, and our colonel was no exception to the ride; but the order just read explicitly directed all commanding officers to 'address their troops, explaining to them briefly the immense issues involved in this struggle,' and in obedience to it, then and there, sitting on his little brown horse in front of the regimental colours, dressed as we all so well remember him in his soft felt hat, long white leather gloves, and military cape, Pat O'Rorke made the first and only speech which he ever addressed to his regiment. It was short and to the point, and I regret that I cannot repeat the whole of it, but his closing words I remember very well, when he said, 'I call on the file-closers to do their duty, and if there is a man this day base enough to leave his company, let him die in his tracks—shoot him down like a dog.'

Those were the words of a man who meant to do his duty, and was resolved that everyone under his command should do the same. The episode was dramatic to the highest degree. The sentiment and the occasion were not such as to elicit boisterous applause; but a low murmur of approval throughout his audience showed that as a body they were ready to follow wherever a brave man would lead.

The whole army, with the exception of the Sixth corps, had by this time arrived upon the field. In the disposition of the troops our corps was held as a reserve within the curved range of hills whose crests formed our chosen line of battle. During the day we were moved from place to place, according as different parts of the grand line seemed more exposed or threatened. Thus early in the morning we were behind the extreme right; later in the day we were massed on Rock Creek, near the point where it is crossed by the Baltimore pike. This position was in rear of our main line, which has generally been described as shaped like a horseshoe, with its convexity turned toward the enemy, but which may more properly be compared to a fish-hook, its shank beginning on the northern slope of Round Top and running almost due north along the crests of Little Round Top and Cemetery Ridge, its curve beginning at the cemetery and its barb and point represented by Culp's Hill.

Late in the afternoon we were ordered to move to the left of the line where the booming of artillery admonished us that the bloody work of the day had begun in right earnest.

We soon reached the sloping ground where the ascent began on our side up the ridge, beyond which the battle at that time was raging. I have said that we could hear the artillery, though it still had a distant sound; but now the rifle balls coming over the hill began to whistle through the air high above us, and in the woods to our left on the hillside we saw the surgeons at work over the wounded; and yet, strange to say, we could but very indistinctly hear the sound of musketry. It must have been owing to the intervening hill or the direction of the wind, or both causes combined, for we were even then upon the very verge of the battle, and when we mounted the ridge two or three minutes later its full fury burst upon us.

The First division of our corps, commanded by Brigadier-General Barnes, had preceded us. Our division, the Second, under Brigadier-General R. B. Ayres, followed it. Our brigade, under Brigadier-General Stephen H. Weed, led the division, and though my recollection of the order in which the regiments were marching does not agree with that of other officers present, I think that our regiment was the rear one of the brigade, and that the leading regiments of our brigade were just passing over that slightly elevated ground north of Little Round Top when down its slope on our left, accompanied by a single mounted officer and an orderly, rode General G. K. Warren, our former brigade commander, then acting as General Meade's chief engineer.

Warren came straight toward the head of the regiment, where I was riding with the colonel. He called out to O'Rorke, beginning to speak while still some eight or ten rods from us, that he wanted us to come up there; that the enemy were advancing unopposed up the opposite side of the hill, down which he had just come, and he wanted our regiment to meet them. He was evidently greatly excited and spoke in his usual impulsive style. O'Rorke answered, 'General Weed is ahead and expects me to follow him.' 'Never mind that,' said Warren, 'bring your regiment up here and I will take the responsibility.'

It was a perplexing situation, but without hesitating O'Rorke turned to the left and followed the officer who had been riding with Warren, while Warren himself rode rapidly down the stony hill, whether in the direction from which we had just come or to overtake the rest of our brigade, I cannot say, but evidently to find and order up more troops. The cause for this haste is graphically described by General Warren himself in a letter which he kindly wrote me under date of July 13, 1872, from which I here take the liberty to quote. He says:

> Just before the action began in earnest on July 2, I was with General Meade near General Sickles, whose troops

seemed very badly disposed on that part of the field. At my suggestion. General Meade sent me to the left to examine the condition of affairs, and I continued on till I reached Little Round Top. There were no troops on it, and it was used as a signal station. I saw that this was the key of the whole position, and that our troops in the woods in front of it could not see the ground, in front of them, so that the enemy would come upon them before they would be aware of it.

The long line of woods on the west side of the Emmittsburg road (which road was along a ridge) furnished an excellent place for the enemy to form out of sight, so I requested the captain of a rifle battery just in front of Little Round Top to fire a shot into these woods. He did so, and as the shot went whistling through the air the sound of it reached the enemy's troops and caused everyone to look in the direction of it. This motion revealed to me the glistening of gun barrels and bayonets of the enemy's line of battle, already formed and far outflanking the position of any of our troops, so that the line of his advance from his right to Little Round Top was unopposed.

I have been particular in telling this, as the discovery was intensely thrilling to my feelings and almost appalling. I immediately sent a hastily written dispatch to General Meade, to send a division at least to me, and General Meade directed the Fifth Army Corps to take position there. The battle was already beginning to rage at the peach orchard, and before a single man reached Round Top the whole line of the enemy moved on us in splendid array, shouting in the most confident tones. While I was still all alone with the signal officer, the musket balls began to fly around us, and he was about to fold up his flags and withdraw, but remained at my request and kept waving them in defiance.

Seeing troops going out on the peach orchard road, I rode down the hill and fortunately met my old brigade. General Weed, commanding it, had already passed the point, and I took the responsibility to detach Colonel O'Rorke, the head of whose regiment I struck, who on hearing my few words of explanation about the position moved at once to the hilltop. About this time First-Lieutenant Charles E. Hazlett, of the Fifth Artillery, with his battery of rifled cannon arrived. He comprehended the situation instantly, and planted a gun on the summit of the hill. He spoke to the effect that though he could do little execution on the enemy with his guns, he could aid in giving confidence to the infantry, and that his battery was of no consequence whatever compared with holding the position. He stayed there till he was killed.

I did not see Vincent's brigade come up, but I suppose it was about this time they did, and, coming up behind me through the woods and taking post to the left, their proper place, I did not see them. The full force of the enemy was now sweeping the Third Army Corps from its untenable position, and no troops nor any reinforcements could maintain it. It was the dreadful misfortune of the day that any reinforcements went to that line, for all alike. Third corps. Second corps, and Fifth corps, were driven from it with great loss. The earnest appeals for support drew, I suppose, the troops of the Fifth corps away from their intended position, that is, Little Round Top, out on the road to the peach orchard, and so it was that the Fifth corps reached this vital point in such small detachments.

I was wounded with a musket ball while talking with Lieutenant Hazlett on the hill, but not seriously, and seeing the position saved, while the whole line to the right and front of us was yielding and melting away under the enemy's fire and advance, I left the hill to rejoin General Meade, near the centre of the field, where a new crisis was at hand.

So much as explaining what Warren had seen when he came riding down on the head of our regiment and detached us so unexpectedly from the rest of our brigade, and now to resume the narrative of the part we took in the struggle which ensued for the possession of Little Round Top.

We turned off the road to our left and rushed along the wooded, rocky eastern slope of Little Round Top, ascending it while at the same time moving toward its southern extremity. It was just here that some of the guns of Hazlett's battery came rapidly up and plunged directly through our ranks, the horses being urged to frantic efforts by the whips of their drivers and the cannoneers assisting at the wheels, so great was the effort necessary to drag the guns and caissons up the ragged hillside.

As we reached the crest a never to be forgotten scene burst upon us. A great basin lay before us full of smoke and fire, and literally swarming with riderless horses and fighting, fleeing, and pursuing men. The air was saturated with the sulphurous fumes of battle and was ringing with the shouts and groans of the combatants. The wild cries of charging lines, the rattle of musketry, the booming of artillery, and the shrieks of the wounded were the orchestral accompaniments of a scene like very hell itself—as terrific as the warring of Milton's fiends in Pandemonium. The whole of Sickles' corps, and many other troops which had been sent to its support in that ill-chosen hollow, were being slaughtered and driven before the impetuous advance of Longstreet. But fascinating as was this terrible scene, we had no time to spend upon it. Bloody work was ready for us at our very feet.

Round Top, a conical hill several hundred feet in height, lay just to the south of us, and was separated from Little Round Top, on whose crest we were now moving, by a broad ravine leading down into the basin where the great fight was raging. Right up this ravine, which offered the easiest place of ascent, a rebel force, outflanking all our troops in the plain below, was advancing at the very moment when we reached the crest of the hill. Vincent's brigade of the First division of our corps had come up through the woods on the eastern slope of the hill, had deployed and taken position on its southern slope, and were at the moment of our arrival hotly engaged with a superior and aggressive force of the enemy. As soon as we reached the crest bullets came flying in among us. We were moving with the right in front and not a musket was loaded, a fact which Warren of course knew nothing about when he rushed us up there. The enemy were coming from our right, and to face them would bring our file-closers in front. The order, 'On the right, by file into line,' would have brought us into proper position; but there was no time to execute it, not even time to allow the natural impulse which manifested itself on the part of the men to halt and load the instant we received the enemy's fire. O'Rorke did not hesitate a moment. 'Dismount,' said he to me, for the ground before us was too rough to ride over. We sprang from our horses and gave them to the sergeant-major. O'Rorke shouted, 'Down this way, boys!' and following him we rushed down the rocky slope with all the same moral effect upon the rebels, who saw us coming, as if our bayonets had been fixed and we ready to charge upon them.

Coming abreast of Vincent's brigade, and taking advantage of such shelter as the huge rocks lying about there afforded, the men loaded and fired, and in less time than it takes to write it the onslaught of the rebels was fairly checked, and in a few minutes the woods in front of us were cleared except of the dead and wounded. Such of the rebels as had approached so near as to make escape almost impossible dropped their guns, threw up their hands, and upon a slight slackening of our fire rushed in upon us and gave themselves up as prisoners, while those not so near took advantage of the chance left them and retreated in disorder.

The firing for a few minutes was very rapid, and the execution on both sides was fearful. Captain Starks, of the leading company, received four wounds, but with splendid pluck stayed by his men till the affair was over. Captain Sibley, of the second company, was shot through both legs and lay perfectly helpless till carried off. O'Rorke exposed himself with the greatest gallantry, not taking the least advantage of the partial shelter which the rocks afforded. He was shot in the neck and dropped instantly dead without a word. Captain Spies, of Company B, was shot through the body and desperately hurt. Lieutenant Charles Klein, of the same company, and Lieutenant Hugh McGraw, of Company K, were both wounded in the leg, and both died in consequence.

Of the enlisted men, there were twenty-five killed and about eighty-four wounded. Klein and McGraw died, Spies and Sibley were so badly hurt that they never could rejoin us, and Starks with his four wounds, all of which were slight, fully recovered, and after a few weeks rejoined us, to meet a soldier's death the following spring in the fight near Spottsylvania Court-House. Our losses were much more severe than they would have been if our muskets had been loaded and if the regiment had been formed in proper line of battle before it rushed over the crest of the hill. This remark must not be construed as reflecting on any one. Warren did not know that our guns were empty, and if he had known it, or if he or O'Rorke had halted the column for the purpose of loading, it would have caused a delay which might, and probably would, have been disastrous beyond all calculation.

In a word, Gettysburg might have been the greatest disaster of the war, and might have turned the scales in favour of the rebellion. This may seem an extravagant statement; but everyone who was there will corroborate the assertion that the One Hundred and Fortieth regiment reached the crest of Little Round Top in the very nick of time, and before any other troops were there except a part of Hazlett's rifled battery, and that if we had not reached it first, thirty or sixty seconds later Hood's Texas brigade, which was the force we met, would have seized the hill which was the key to the whole Union line. The disorganised remnant of Sickles' routed corps would have been surrounded on three sides. Hazlett's battery would have been taken and its guns turned upon the Union troops in the field below.

The principal ammunition train, which was parked about half a mile in the rear, would have been lost, the general line of battle would have been doubled up, and a disastrous defeat would have been almost inevitable. Vincent's brigade of the First division of our corps might have done something to avert this disaster; but to do it they would have had to change their front under fire and on ground the most unsuitable for such an evolution. We of the One Hundred and Fortieth regiment are so self-gratulatory as to think that the arrival of the *Monitor* in Hampton Roads just when and as she did, was a circumstance no more fortunate for the Union cause than was our timely arrival to fill the gap just when and as we did on Little Round Top at Gettysburg.

That was our first really bloody engagement, and in all the subsequent experiences of the regiment upon many other desperate fields, the service there rendered upon Little Round Top must be regarded as the supreme event in its existence.

Vincent's brigade on our left fought splendidly and lost heavily. Vincent himself was killed. Hazlett's battery, which was stationed on the crest above and behind us, had not been able to do any execution upon the force which actually assailed us, but it played upon the rebel masses who were driving Sickles' corps in the plain below, and after our engagement was over it still kept firing upon any considerable body of rebels that remained in sight. What their losses had been during the heat of the engagement I cannot say, but after our fight was over and we had secured pretty good shelter behind the rocks on the western slope, their cannoneers were much exposed, and many fell by the bullets of the sharpshooters, who seemed swarming in the tree-tops and behind the rocks over in the direction of the peach orchard.

Man, after man fell under this murderous sharpshooting while those thus exposed were serving their guns directed upon an enemy not engaged in an attack upon our immediate front. For the better understanding of the part which this battery took in the action of that afternoon, it may be remarked that they did little or nothing in repelling the assault of the Texan brigade which fell upon us. Our men and the enemy were at too close quarters for that, and the nature of the ground did not permit the artillery to be of any immediate service to us. But Hazlett got his guns into position just at the time when Sickles' corps was falling back in great disorder before an overwhelming force, and it was against these advancing and for the moment victorious lines that he poured in an effective fire. Here, too, he met his death in a manner dramatic to the last degree, and yet to be described.

When Warren detached and sent us up the hill, word was sent to our brigade commander, General Stephen H. Weed, notifying him of the fact, he having gone at the head of the brigade directly to the front to the support of Sickles' corps. Upon receiving this word, Weed brought back the regiments with him as hastily as possible and put them in position to our right along the crest of Little Round Top, not, however, arriving till our bloody affair was over. But the sharpshooters were still doing their best against Hazlett's gunners, and it was while standing among them that Weed received a mortal wound. Believing that he was about to die, he was in the very act of committing his last messages to his friend Hazlett, who stooped over him, when there came the whiz and thud of another bullet as it sunk into Hazlett's brain, and that brave artilleryman fell a corpse across the body of his dying friend.

Thus, had fallen our brigadier, the commander of the battery which we supported, and our gallant young colonel.

The general was carried at once behind the shelter of a rock, and was soon taken in an ambulance to the farmhouse of Louis A. Bushman, which, as well as his barns and outhouses, had been taken possession of and was being used as our division hospital. Weed suffered intensely, but for some time after he was hurt was entirely conscious and able to communicate the messages which he had begun to give to Hazlett. This he did to Lieutenant William H. Crennell, quartermaster of our regiment, who, with the other quartermasters of our brigade, had served during this campaign as Weed's aides. Among other things. Weed asked that when he was dead the ring which he wore might be taken from his finger and, with the pocketbook containing his private letters, be carried to the young lady to whom he was engaged to be married. As the father of that young lady has for many years been a public character, it may not be inappropriate to state that she was the daughter of Simon Cameron of Pennsylvania.

Weed's bravery even unto death, and his bluff, outspoken manner, were well exemplified by the clearness with which he made his dying requests, well knowing they were such, and by the emphasis with which he spoke, particularly in a reply which almost epitomises the character of the man, made to Crennell when he said to him, 'General, I hope you are not so very badly hurt.' Said Weed, 'I'm as dead a man as Julius Caesar.' He soon became delirious, and died at about nine o'clock that evening. During the fight our surgeons, Drs. Dean and Lord, had been stationed but a few rods in rear of the regiment, just over the crest of the hill. Here they gave the wounded such immediate attention as they needed before being sent to the division hospital at Bushman's farm. To this place, when the fight was over, Sergeant Wright and three other men of Company A carried our young colonel, and there laid him on the ground. I went with them. He had fallen instantly dead. A bloody froth on each side of his neck showed the fatal track of the bullet.

Up to that time in my life I had never felt a grief so sharply, nor Realised the significance of death so well, as then, when the wild excitement of our fight was over and I saw O'Rorke lying there so pale and peaceful. To me and all of us he had seemed so near the beau ideal of a soldier and a gentleman, all that he had been and the bright promise of what he was to be, was so fresh in our minds, and now, in an instant, the fatal bullet had cut short the chapter of that fair life. I choked with grief as I stood beside his lifeless form. I had known and loved him well, and in these last few weeks better than ever, my position as his adjutant naturally leading to intercourse of the most familiar kind, as day by day we ate our soldier's fare together and often at night slept with the same blanket covering us.

For him to die was to me like losing a brother, and that brother almost the perfection of the manly graces. What a blow was such a death to the young wife and loving family who far away waited for the news from Gettysburg; what was it to us of that regiment whose fortunes he had shared, whose wants and welfare he had watched over, and who had been the witnesses of the last gallant effort of his life when inspiring everyone who heard him with an enthusiasm which only master minds can impart, he started his men with their empty muskets full in the face of a withering fire and springing to their front in the wild 'rapture of the strife' fell dead among them.

It was only natural that his so sudden death should most deeply affect us. But time and place alike forbade the comfort which comes to the heart when it yields to its grief.

I took from his pockets his watch and some trifles, pulled from his hands the long gloves which he had worn and slipped them in his belt, helped compose his supple form in fitting way, collected the men who had brought him and others to the surgeon's station, and taking a last look at poor O'Rorke went back to the regiment.

At the Battle of Gettysburg Captain Farley was a first lieutenant and acting as the adjutant of the regiment. I see nothing to criticise in his account. It was written before any of the histories from which I have quoted were published, and was not influenced by any of the statements contained in them. It is the simple story of an intelligent soldier who was present in the battle, and related what he saw and heard. There is no attempt at fine writing; there was no need for that. I have read it many times, and never without emotion. His grief at O'Rorke's death was like mine for Vincent's. Many other heroes in blue and gray died on Little Round Top that day, and the grief over their loss was felt in many homes from Maine to Texas. Let us believe that the men on both sides who died there did not die in vain.

3. The Official Reports
(*Rebellion Records*, Series i. Vol. xxvii, part 2)

CONFEDERATE
LAW'S BRIGADE

Report of Col. James L. Sheffield, Forty-Eighth Alabama Infantry. (Commanding Law's Alabama Brigade after Gen. Hood was wounded.)

August 7, 1863.

I have the honour herewith to give a statement of the part taken by the Forty-Eighth Alabama in the battle of Gettysburg, on July 2 and 3.

On the morning of the 2nd *ultimo* this regiment, with the brigade, marched from New Guilford to the field, a distance of 20 miles, where we were placed in line of battle in the open field, where Companies A and H were ordered on picket. After lying in line of battle a half hour we were ordered forward, and advanced a distance of 1 mile over a very rough and rugged road, the worst cliffs of rocks there could have been travelled over.

On reaching the enemy's lines, where they were well and strongly situated, I ordered my regiment forward, which was gallantly obeyed until within about 20 paces of their line. Here the fire of the enemy was severe. Here the men opened fire on the enemy, and for some time continued, until the left, from the loss of men and their exposed position to a fire from the front and from the mountain on the right, were forced to fall back. The right steadily maintained its position for some time, forcing the enemy to withdraw from their first line and establish their line a short distance to their rear, where they continued their fire.

After the contest had continued for an hour and a half, and my whole regiment had been brought to the front the third time, only to be driven back, I ordered them to re-form in the rear of their advanced position. While doing this, I was ordered to take command of the brigade. After this, the regiment was commanded by Capt. T. J. Eubanks, who re-formed and carried it to the front, where the battleground was held during the night, bringing off our wounded.

In this battle the regiment had 275 men engaged. There were 102 killed, wounded, and missing.

On the 3rd *ultimo* the regiment was withdrawn a short distance, where we remained during the day, excepting while engaged in a short fight with cavalry.

At night, we were still farther withdrawn to the rear. The men and officers acted very well.

I cannot close without speaking of those who acted most conspicuously during the hottest of the conflict. Lieutenants (F. M.) Burk and (R. T.) Ewing and Captains Eubanks and (Jeremiah) Edwards are especially noticed for their gallantry in leading their men forward and remaining in front of their commands, encouraging their men.

Lieutenant-Colonel (W. M.) Hardwick and Major (C. B.) St. John were very efficient in performing their part until wounded.

It is proper to state that in the account of missing, 24 men were taken prisoners, with Captain Edwards and Lieutenant (T. L.) Christian (of General Law's staff), while posting pickets after night on the 2nd *ultimo*.

Report of Lieut.-Col. L. H. Scruggs, Fourth Alabama Infantry.

August 8, 1863.

In accordance with orders of the 6th instant, I have the honour to submit the following report of the operations of the regiment during the engagement of July 2 and 3, at Gettysburg, Pa. On the morning of the 2nd we took up the line of march from New Guilford in the direction of Gettysburg. After a rapid and fatiguing march of about 24 miles, arrived at the scene of action at 3:30 p.m., immediately taking our assigned position on the left of the brigade.

The order was then given to move forward, which we did at

a double-quick across a ploughed field for half a mile, the enemy's batteries playing upon us with great effect until we arrived at a stone fence, behind which the enemy's first line of infantry was posted, which position we soon succeeded in carrying with the bayonet. Then, having reached the foot of the mountain, the command halted a few minutes to re-form the line. We advanced up the mountain under a galling fire, driving the enemy before us until we arrived at a second line, where a strong force was posted behind another stone fence. Owing to the exhausted condition of the men and the roughness of the mountain-side, we found it impossible to carry this position. We retired in good order, though not until we had expended our ammunition. Having received a fresh supply of cartridges about dark, we remained in the enemy's front, some 200 yards distant, during the night.

Early on the next morning we threw up a line of breastworks composed of rock, and assumed the defensive, which position we held during the day until late in the afternoon, when the regiment was ordered some distance to the right, to meet the enemy's cavalry, which we soon dispersed. Then we remained in position until dark, when the remainder of the brigade moved to our rear, and were ordered to connect with it on the right, where we remained until the morning of the 4th.

Both officers and men behaved with much coolness and gallantry, and many brave and good soldiers fell, a noble sacrifice to their country's cause. The official list of casualties handed in will show the total of our casualties to be 87.

Report of Col. William C. Oates, Fifteenth Alabama Infantry.

August 8, 1863.

I have the honour to report, in obedience to orders from brigade headquarters, the participation of my regiment in the battle near Gettysburg on the 2nd *ultimo*.

My regiment occupied the centre of the brigade when the line of battle was formed. During the advance, the two regiments on my right (Forty-Eighth and Forty-Fourth Alabama.—O. W. N.) were moved by the left flank across my rear, which threw me on the extreme right of the whole line. I encountered the enemy's sharpshooters posted behind a stone fence, and sustained some loss thereby. It was here that Lieut.-Col. Isaac B.

Col. William C. Oates

General James Longstreet

Feagin, a most excellent and gallant officer, received a severe wound in the right knee, which caused him to lose his leg. Privates (A.) Kennedy, of Company B, and (William) Trimmer, of Company G, were killed at this point and Private (G. E.) Spencer, Company D, severely wounded.

After crossing the fence, I received an order from Brigadier-General Law to left-wheel my regiment and move in the direction of the heights upon my left, which order I failed to obey, for the reason that when I received it I was rapidly advancing up the mountain, and in my front I discovered a heavy force of the enemy. Besides this, there was great difficulty in accomplishing the manoeuvre at that moment, as the regiment on my left (Forty-Seventh Alabama) was crowding me on the left and running into my regiment, which had already created considerable confusion. In the event that I had obeyed the order I should have come in contact with the regiment on my left, and also have exposed my right flank to an enfilading fire from the enemy. I therefore continued to press forward, my right passing over the top of the mountain, on the right of the line.

On reaching the foot of the mountain below I found the enemy in heavy force, posted in rear of large rocks upon a slight elevation beyond a depression of some 300 yards in width between the base of the mountain and the open plain beyond. I engaged them, my right meeting the left of their line exactly. Here I lost several gallant officers and men.

After firing two or three rounds, I discovered that the enemy were giving way in my front. I ordered a charge, and the enemy in my front fled; but that portion of his line confronting the two companies on my left held their ground, and continued a most galling fire upon my left.

Just at this moment I discovered the regiment on my left (Forty-Seventh Alabama) retiring. I halted my regiment as its left reached a very large rock, and ordered a left-wheel of the regiment, which was executed in good order under fire, thus taking advantage of a ledge of rocks running off in a line perpendicular to the one I had just abandoned, and affording very good protection to my men. This position enabled me to keep up a constant flank and cross fire upon the enemy, which in less than five minutes caused him to change front. Receiving reinforcements, he charged me five times, and was as often repulsed with heavy loss. Finally, I discovered that the enemy had flanked me on the right, and two regiments were moving rapidly upon my rear and not 200 yards distant, when, to save my regiment from capture or destruction, I ordered a retreat.

Having become exhausted from fatigue and the excessive heat of the day, I turned the command of the regiment over to Capt. B. A. Hill, and instructed him to take the men off the field and re-form the regiment and report to the brigade.

My loss was, as near as can now be ascertained, as follows, to-wit: 17 killed upon the field, 54 wounded and brought off the field, and 90 missing, most of whom are either killed or wounded. Among the killed and wounded are 8 officers, most of whom were very gallant and efficient men.

Recapitulation: Killed, 17; wounded, 54; missing, 90; total, 161.

Report of Col. William F. Perry, Forty-Fourth Alabama Infantry.

Near Fredericksburg, Va.,
August 8, 1863.

I have the honour to submit the following report of the part taken by the regiment under my command in the Battle of Gettysburg, Pa., on July 2:

It occupied the place of the second battalion in the line formed by the brigade on the heights, which ran parallel with and fronting the enemy's position. Having advanced with the brigade down the long slope and through the intervening meadow, it was detached from its place in the line by order of General Law, and by a flank movement was brought to the extreme left of the brigade.

When at a short distance from the stone fence near the base of the mountain, General Law informed me that he expected my regiment to take a battery which had been playing on our line from the moment the advance began. This battery was situated, not on the mountain itself, but on a rugged cliff which formed the abrupt termination of a ridge that proceeded from the mountain, and ran in a direction somewhat parallel with it, leaving a valley destitute of trees and filled with immense boulders between them. This valley, not more than 300 paces in breadth, and the cliff on which their artillery was stationed were occupied by two regiments of the enemy's infantry.

The direction of the regiment after crossing the stone fence was such that a march to the front would have carried it to the right of the enemy's position. It was therefore wheeled to the left, so as to confront that position, its left opposite the battery, and its right extending toward the base of the mountain. This movement was executed under fire, and within 200 yards of the enemy. The forward movement was immediately ordered, and was responded to with an alacrity and courage seldom, if ever, excelled on the battlefield.

As the men emerged from the forest into the valley before mentioned, they received a deadly volley at short range, which in a few seconds killed or disabled one-fourth their number. Halting without an order from me, and availing themselves of the shelter which the rocks afforded, they returned the fire. Such was their extreme exhaustion, having marched without interruption 24 miles to reach the battlefield, and advanced at a doublequick step fully a mile to engage the enemy, that I hesitated for an instant to order them immediately forward. Perceiving very soon, however, that the enemy were giving way, I rushed forward, shouting to them to advance. It was with the greatest difficulty that I could make myself heard or understood above the din of battle. The order was, however, extended along the line, and was promptly obeyed. The men sprang forward over the rocks, swept the position, and took possession of the heights, capturing 40 or 50 prisoners around the battery and among the cliffs.

Meanwhile the enemy had put a battery in position on a terrace of the mountain to our right, which opened upon us an enfilading fire of grape and spherical case-shot. A sharp fire of small-arms was also opened from the same direction. This was not destructive, however, owing to the protection afforded by the rocks. Soon the enemy appeared moving down upon our front in heavy force. At this critical moment, General Benning's brigade of Georgians advanced gallantly into action. His extreme right, lapping upon my left, swarmed over the cliffs and mingled with my men. It was now past 5 p.m. The conflict continued to rage with great fury until dark. Again, and again the enemy in great force attempted to dislodge us from the position and retake the battery, in each case with signal failure and heavy loss.

Lieutenant-Colonel (John A.J Jones, Major (George W.) Gary,

and Lieutenant (W. P.) Becker, acting adjutant, behaved with great coolness and courage. I abstain from mentioning by name others who deserve special commendation, because the list would be so long as to confer little distinction on any single individual, and because injustice might be done to others whose good conduct escaped my observation.

The regiment lost: Killed, 24; wounded, 66; missing, 4.

Report of Maj. James M. Campbell, Forty-Seventh Alabama Infantry.

August 7, 1863.

A report of the part my regiment took in the fight at Gettysburg:

Before our line was formed three companies were detached from my regiment and placed in rear of our right, to guard a road. These companies remained on this part of the field, almost constantly skirmishing with the enemy, until we fell back on the morning of the 4th, when they rejoined their command. The other seven companies went into the fight in line with the brigade. There was some confusion in these companies, owing to the fact that in the charge the lieutenant-colonel expected the colonel to give all the necessary commands, and the colonel remained so far behind that his presence on the field was but a trammel on the lieutenant-colonel.

The colonel having been left behind, and the lieutenant-colonel (fighting most nobly) killed, I took command of the regiment, and, after the first repulse of the brigade, in obedience to orders I deployed a part of my men on the right of the brigade, where they remained until the close of the fight. (Lieut. Col. M. J. Bulger was not killed. On July 16, 1863, he became colonel, *vice* James W. Jackson, resigned.—Footnote in *Rebellion Records*.) After the firing ceased, in obedience to orders from Colonel (James L.) Sheffield, commanding brigade, I threw my regiment out as skirmishers on our right, where they remained until morning.

Out of the 21 officers, 4 were killed on the field. All of these (the 21) acted well. The colonel and adjutant are not included in this number.

About one-third of the whole number of men were killed and wounded.

Robertson's Brigade

Report of Brig.-Gen. J. B. Robertson, C. S. Army, Commanding Brigade.

Headquarters Texas Brigade,
Near Bunker Hill, Va., July 17, 1863.

I have the honour to submit through you my report of the action of my brigade in the battle of Gettysburg, on July 2 and 3. I have been too much occupied with the duties imposed by the marches and manoeuvres we have gone through to allow me to make this report at an earlier time.

The division arrived on the ground in front of the position of the enemy that we were to attack but a few minutes before we were ordered to advance. I therefore got but a glance at the field on which we had to operate before we entered upon it. I was ordered to keep my right well closed on Brigadier-General Law's left, and to let my left rest on the Emmittsburg pike. I had advanced but a short distance when I discovered that my brigade would not fill the space between General Law's left and the pike named, and that I must leave the pike, or disconnect myself from General Law, on my right.

Understanding before the action commenced that the attack on our part was to be general, and that the force of General McLaws was to advance simultaneously with us on my immediate left, and seeing at once that a mountain held by the enemy in heavy force with artillery to the right of General Law's centre was the key to the enemy's left, I abandoned the pike and closed on General Law's left. This caused some separation of my regiments, which was remedied as promptly as the numerous stone and rail fences that intersected the field through which we were advancing would allow.

As we advanced through this field, for half a mile we were exposed to a heavy and destructive fire of canister, grape, and shell from six pieces of their artillery on the mountain alluded to, and the same number on a commanding hill but a short distance to the left of the mountain, and from the enemy's sharpshooters from behind the numerous rocks, fences, and houses in the field.

As we approached the base of the mountain General Law moved to the right, and I was moving obliquely to the right to close on him when my whole line encountered the fire of the enemy's main line, posted behind rocks and a stone fence. The Fourth and Fifth Texas regiments, under the direction of their gallant commanders (Colonels Powell and Key), while returning the fire and driving the enemy before them, continued to close on General Law, to their right. At the same time the First Texas and Third Arkansas, under their gallant commanders (Lieutenant-Colonel (P. A.) Work and Colonel Manning) were hotly engaged with a greatly superior force, while at the same time a heavy force appeared and opened fire on Colonel Manning's left, seriously threatening his left flank, to meet which he threw two or three companies with their front to his left flank, and protected his left.

On discovering this heavy force on my left flank, and seeing that no attack was being made by any of our forces on my left, I at once sent a courier to Major-General Hood, stating that I was hard pressed on my left; that General McLaws' forces were not engaging the enemy to my left (which enabled him to move fresh troops from that part of his line down on me) , and that I must have reinforcements.

Lieutenant-Colonel Work, with the First Texas regiment, having pressed forward to the crest of the hill and driven the enemy from his battery, I ordered him to the left, to the relief and support of Colonel Manning, directing Major (F. S.) Bass with two companies to hold the hill, while Colonel Work with the rest of the regiment went to Colonel Manning's relief. With this assistance, Colonel Manning drove the enemy back and entered the woods after him, when the enemy reoccupied the hill and his batteries in Colonel Work's front, from which Colonel Work again drove him.

For an hour and upward these two regiments maintained one of the hottest contests, against five or six times their number, that I have witnessed. The moving of Colonel Work to the left, to relieve Colonel Manning while the Fourth and Fifth Texas were closing to the right on General Law's brigade, separated these two regiments from the others. They were steadily moving to the right and front, driving the enemy before them, when they passed the woods or ravine to my right. After finding that I could not move the First and Third to the right to join them, I sent to recall them, ordering them to move to the left until the left of the Fourth should rest on the right of the First; but my messenger found two of General Law's regiments on the left of my two (the Fourth and Fifth Texas), and did not find these regiments at all.

About this time my *aide,* Lieutenant Scott, reported my two regiments (the Fourth and Fifth Texas) in the centre of General Law's brigade, and that they could not be moved without greatly injuring his line. I sent a request to General Law to look to them.

At this point my assistant adjutant and inspector-general reported from the Fourth and Fifth that they were hotly engaged, and wanted reinforcements. My courier, sent to General Hood, returned, and reported him wounded and carried from the field. I sent a messenger to Lieutenant-General Longstreet for reinforcements, and at the same time sent to Generals (George T.) Anderson and Benning, urging them to hurry up to my support. They came up, joined us, and fought gallantly; but as fast as we would break one line of the enemy another fresh one would present itself, the enemy reinforcing his lines in our front from his reserves at the base of the mountain to our right and front, and from his lines to our left. Having no attack from us in his front, he threw his forces from there, on us.

Before the arrival of Generals Anderson and Benning, Col. J. C. G. Key, who gallantly led the Fourth Texas regiment in, up to the time of receiving a severe wound, passed me, being led to the rear. About the same time, I learned of the fall and dangerous wounding of Col. R. M. Powell, of the Fifth, who fell while gallantly leading his regiment in one of the impetuous charges of the Fourth and Fifth Texas on the strongly fortified mountain.

"Just after the arrival of General Anderson on my left I learned that the gallant Col.Van. H. Manning, of the Third Arkansas, had been wounded and carried from the field, and about the same time I received intelligence of the wounding and being carried from the field of those two able and efficient officers, Lieut. Cols. K. Bryan, of the Fifth, and B. F. Carter, of the Fourth, both of whom were wounded while bravely discharging their duty. Captain (J. R.) Woodward, acting major of the First Texas, was wounded near me, while gallantly discharging his duty.

The Fourth and Fifth Texas, under the command of Majors (J.

P.) Bane and (J. C) Rogers, continued to hold the ground of their original line, leaving the space over which they had made their successive charges strewn with their wounded and dead comrades, many of whom could not be removed, and were left upon the field.

The First Texas, under Lieutenant-Colonel Work, with a portion of Benning's brigade, held the field and the batteries taken by the First Texas. Three of the guns were brought off the field and secured; the other three, from the nature of the ground and their proximity to the enemy, were left. The Third Arkansas, under the command of Lieutenant-Colonel (R. S.J Taylor, ably assisted by Major (J. W.) Reedy, after Colonel Manning was borne from the field, sustained well the high character it made in the earlier part of the action.

When night closed the conflict, late in the evening, I was struck above the knee, which deprived me of the use of my leg, and prevented me from getting about the field. I retired some 200 yards to the rear, leaving the immediate command with Lieutenant-Colonel Work, the senior officer present, under whose supervision our wounded were brought out and guns secured, and our dead on that part of the field were buried the next day. About two o'clock that night the First Texas and Third Arkansas were moved by the right to the position occupied by the Fourth and Fifth, and formed on their left, where the brigade remained during the day of the 3rd, keeping up a continuous skirmishing with the enemy's sharpshooters, in which we had a number of our men severely wounded. I sent my assistant adjutant-general, Capt. F. L. Price, at daybreak to examine the position of the brigade and report to me as soon as he could, and, while in the discharge of that duty, was either killed or fell into the hands of the enemy, as he has not been seen or heard of since.

About dark on the evening of the 3rd the brigade, with the division, fell back to the hill and formed in line, where it remained during the 4th.

Lieutenant (J. R.) Loughridge, commanding Company I, Fourth Texas, who commanded the skirmishers in front of the Fourth, and who was left when; that regiment moved to the right, joined the First Texas, and did gallant service during the engagement.

In this, the hardest fought battle of the war in which I have been engaged, all, both officers and men, as far as my observation extended, fully sustained the high character they have heretofore made. Where all behaved so nobly individual distinction cannot with propriety be made.

I cannot close this report without expressing my thanks to my personal staff for the able and satisfactory manner in which they discharged their duties. The wounding of so many commanding officers, among them the division commander, rendered their duties peculiarly arduous. They were discharged with zeal and promptness. Capt. F. L. Price, my assistant adjutant-general, whose loss on the morning of the 3rd I have to deplore, was an active, efficient officer, and did his duty nobly. My *aide-de-camp*, Lieut. John G. Scott, my assistant adjutant and inspector general, Lieut. John W. Kerr, and Lieut. John Grace, volunteer *aide*, discharged their duties with a promptness and ability that merit special notice.

A list of the casualties in the several regiments, together with the reports from each of the regimental commanders is herewith submitted.

Report of Col. Van H. Manning, Third Arkansas Infantry

> Near Hagerstown, Md.,
> July 8, 1863.

I have the honour to report the part taken by this command in the recent battle near Gettysburg, Pa.

About four o'clock in the evening of July 2 I was ordered to move against the enemy, keeping my right well connected with the left of the First Texas regiment, and hold my left on the Emmittsburg road, then some 200 yards in my front and out of view.

Upon reaching this road I discovered, from the direction the directing regiment was taking, that I could not with the length of my line carry out the latter order; hence I decided to keep my command on a prolongation of the line formed by the troops on my right. After marching in line of battle at a brisk gait (part of the way at a double-quick) for about 1,000 yards, all the time exposed to a destructive fire from artillery, we engaged the enemy at short range, strongly posted behind a rock fence at the edge of woods. We drove him back with but little loss for a distance of 150 yards, when I ascertained that I was suffering from a fire to my left and rear. Thereupon I ordered a change of front to the rear on first company, but the noise consequent upon the heavy firing then going on swallowed up my command, and I contented myself with the irregular drawing back of the left wing, giving it an excellent fire, which pressed the enemy back in a very short while, whereupon the whole line advanced, the enemy fighting stubbornly, but retiring.

Soon I was again admonished that my left was seriously threatened, when I ordered the command back 50 or 75 yards to meet this contingency. He was again driven back, and I stretched out my front twice its legitimate length, guarding well my left, and advanced to the ledge of rocks from which we had previously been dislodged by the enemy's movement upon my flank. I experienced some annoyance from the exposure of this flank up to this moment, when Colonel (F. H.) Little, of the Eleventh Georgia regiment, joined to my left. The Fifty-Ninth Georgia regiment, coming also at this time, occupied the line with my command. Some little time after this I was disabled by concussion and wound on my nose and forehead. The command then devolved upon Lieutenant-Colonel Taylor, who will report its operations subsequent to this time.

It would be invidious to make special mention of gallantry with either officers or men when all did so well, fighting greatly superior numbers and at great disadvantage. I might safely assume that the bearing of the entire command was of the highest creditable character.

No guns or colours were captured, and but few (some 25) prisoners, a number of whom were sent to the rear with wounded men.

Below I submit a list of killed, wounded, and missing. The wounded include only those disabled indefinitely. Quite a number were temporarily disabled by slight wounds, but resumed their duties in a few days; hence I make no mention of them in this report.

Report of Lieut. Col. P. A. Work, First Texas Infantry

July 9, 1863.

The following is submitted as a report of the part sustained by the First Texas regiment in the engagement of Thursday, July 2, near Gettysburg, Pa., to-wit:

The regiment, together with the brigade, having been ordered forward to the attack about 4 p.m., continued to advance by the front for a distance exceeding half a mile, the Fourth Texas upon the right and the Third Arkansas upon the left, when Company I, commanded by Lieut. J. H. Wooters, and thrown out as skirmishers, engaged the skirmishers of the enemy, driving them back upon a regiment supporting the enemy's battery, and then, aided by volunteers from this (First Texas) regiment, engaging the regiment and artillery, succeeded in driving back the regiment and silencing the enemy's guns, taking and holding possession of the latter.

While this regiment was closely following our skirmishers, and had reached to within about 125 yards of the enemy's artillery, the Third Arkansas regiment, upon my left, became hotly engaged with a strong force of the enemy upon its front and left, and, to preserve and protect its left flank, was forced to retire to a point some 75 or 100 yards to my rear and left, thus leaving my left flank uncovered and exposed, to protect which I halted and threw out upon my left and rear Company G, commanded by Lieut. B. A. Campbell (some 40 men), which soon engaged the enemy and drove them from their threatening position to my left and the front of the Third Arkansas. It was while in the execution of this order that Lieutenant Campbell, a brave and gallant officer, fell, pierced through the heart.

Owing to the failure (as informed by Brigadier-General Robertson) of the troops that were assigned to the position on the left of this (Robertson's) brigade to arrive promptly, neither this nor the Third Arkansas regiment was able to advance, without advancing against a vastly superior force and with the left flank of the Third Arkansas (protecting my left) exposed to attack.

After the lapse of several minutes Benning's brigade made its appearance, but instead of occupying the ground to the left of Robertson's brigade so as to enable the latter to move forward with its left flank secured from attack, it occupied the ground still occupied by a portion, at least, of this brigade, the Fifteenth Georgia regiment falling in and remaining with the First Texas regiment. After several ineffectual efforts upon the part of both the commanders of the Fifteenth Georgia and myself to separate the men of the two regiments, we gave the order to move forward, when both regiments, thus commingled, moved forward and occupied the crest of the hill, some 1oo yards or more to the front, and where the enemy's artillery was stationed, where we remained until the close of the day and until two o'clock on Friday morning.

During the evening of the 2nd an incessant fire was kept up by this regiment, and the enemy was several times repulsed in their efforts to retake the hill. My position was such that I was enabled to pour a deadly enfilading fire into the enemy as they advanced through a wheat-field to attack the troops in position on my left, and I have not a doubt that this fire contributed greatly to the repulse of the forces of the enemy attacking our forces some 300 to 500 yards on my left.

Once during the evening the troops upon my left were driven back, and my left was exposed, when, directing Capt. H. E. Moss, Company D, to take charge of the colours, and retaining them there with a few men to hold the hill until the regiment could safely retire, I ordered the regiment to fall back to a stone fence about 100 yards in rear.

The major portion of the regiment and the Fifteenth Georgia fell back as ordered; but quite a large number, having noticed that the colours were not moving to the rear, refused to withdraw, and, remaining upon the crest of the hill, succeeded in holding the enemy in check in their immediate front, and obliquely upon their front and left, until the troops upon my left had been re-formed and were again advanced, when I directed Maj. F. S. Bass to return to the crest of the hill with the body of the regiment, and, with Capt. D. K. Rice, of Company C, proceeded myself to collect together all fugitives, slightly wounded, and exhausted men, and placed them so as to protect my right and rear from an attack from that quarter, one of my advanced scouts in that direction having reported to me that a column of the enemy was moving down a ravine or hollow and threatening me in that quarter.

Having made every disposition to guard my right and rear, I placed Capt. D. K. Rice in charge of such defence, and proceeded to the Third Arkansas regiment, of which General Robertson had ordered me to take charge. After the loss of some half hour in searching for the Third Arkansas. I found Lieut.-Col. Taylor and Major Reedy, of that regiment, both alive and uninjured, and in charge of the regiment, which was doing its duty nobly and well.

Late in the evening a terrific fire of artillery was concentrated against the hill occupied by this (the First) regiment, and many were killed and wounded, some losing their heads and others so horribly mutilated and mangled that their identity could scarcely be established; but, notwithstanding this, all the men continued heroically and unflinchingly to maintain their position.

Immediately after dark, having detailed Companies E and I for the purpose, I sent three pieces of the artillery captured to the rear. There were three other pieces, two at one point and one at another, that I was unable to remove, for the reason that they were located between the lines of the enemy and our own, and were so much exposed that they could not be approached excepting under a murderous fire. While they could not be removed by me, neither could they be approached by the enemy, for the same fire that drove the artillerists from their guns and the infantry from their support was ever in readiness to keep them in check and drive them back.

With but two exceptions, to-wit, Private (Richard) Childers, of Company E, and Private (W. F.) Brooks, Company K, each and every man of the regiment proved himself a hero. Hundreds might be mentioned, each of whom with reason and propriety might point to his gallant acts and daring deeds, and the lieutenant-colonel commanding feels that he cannot call attention to the bearing of a few only of these without doing some share of injustice to those not mentioned; and though he is urged to mention the names of Privates (W.Y.) Salter, Company I, (J. N.J Kirksey and (G.) Barfield, Company B, and (W.J.) Barbee, Company L, for great and striking gallantry, and does mention them, he feels that he is neglecting others of equal merit. Private Barbee, though a mounted courier, acting for Major-General Hood, entered the ranks of his Company (L), and fought through the engagement. At one time, he mounted a rock upon the highest pinnacle of the hill, and there, exposed to a raking, deadly fire from artillery and musketry, stood until he had fired twenty-five shots, when he received a minie ball wound in the right thigh, and fell.

Having exhausted their original supply of ammunition, the men supplied themselves from the cartridge-boxes of their dead and disabled comrades and from the dead and wounded of the enemy, frequently going in front of the hill to secure a cartridge-box. Many of the officers threw aside their swords, seized a rifle, and, going into the ranks, fought bravely and nobly.

The regiment lost in killed, 25; in wounded, 48; and missing, 20; a list of the names of whom, giving the company and character of wound of those wounded, is hereto annexed as part of this report.

I would state that Capt. John R. Woodward, of Company G, entered the engagement as acting major in charge of the left wing early in the engagement. He was wounded in the head by the fragment of a shell, and was borne from the field.

In addition to the above report I have the following to submit: During the evening of Friday, July 2, Company I, commanded by Lieutenant (J. R.) Loughridge, having become separated from the Fourth Texas regiment, of which it was a part, attached itself to the First Texas regiment, and remained with it throughout the evening and night, until the latter was moved to the position occupied by the brigade on July 3, doing its full duty and battling bravely.

Report of Major John P. Bane, Fourth Texas Infantry.

July 9, 1863.

I have the honour to submit the following report of the part taken by my regiment in the action near Gettysburg, Pa., July 2 and 3:

About 4:30 p. m. the 2nd instant we were ordered to advance on the enemy, who occupied the heights about 1¼ miles distant, the Fifth Texas, the directing battalion, on my right, and the First Texas on my left. Advancing at double-quick, we soon met the enemy's skirmishers, who occupied a skirt of thick undergrowth about one-quarter of a mile from the base of the cliffs, upon which the enemy had a battery playing upon us with the most deadly effect.

After a short pause while repelling his skirmishers, I was ordered by General Robertson to move by the right flank, so as to cover all the ground between us and the directing battalion. Moving about 200 yards, I met the enemy in full force in a heavy, wooded ground, sheltering themselves behind rocks, from which, after a sharp contest, he was driven to the heights beyond in our front and in close proximity to the mountain, and there, I was pained to learn that the gallant Lieutenant-Colonel B. F. Carter was severely wounded while crossing a stone wall near the base of the mountain. I was also informed that Col. John C. G. Key, while gallantly urging the men to the front, was severely wounded. The command then devolved upon me. Many of the officers and men had been killed and wounded up to this time.

Finding it impossible to carry the heights by assault with my thinned ranks, I ordered my command to fall back in the skirt of timber, the position then occupied being enfiladed by the batteries on the left and exposed to heavy fire of musketry in my immediate front. Being joined by the Fifth Texas on my right, I again attempted to drive the enemy from the heights by assaults, but with like results. Again, being reinforced by the Forty-Eighth Alabama, commanded by the gallant Colonel (James L.) Sheffield, and the Forty-Fourth Alabama, whose commander I did not learn, we again charged their works, but were repulsed, and then, under the order of General Law, I ordered my command to fall back under cover of the timber, on a slight elevation within short range of the enemy. I formed my regiment in line of battle, leaving the battlefield contested ground.

At the dawn of day, I had a stone wall about two feet high thrown up, which afforded some protection to the men occupying the position from which we had driven the enemy, until sunset of the 3rd instant, at which time I was ordered to move my command, in conjunction with the remainder of the brigade, by the right flank, to occupy the ground from which we first advanced upon the enemy.

I accord to each and all of my officers and men my warmest congratulations for their continued and unceasing gallantry during the entire engagement.

The following list of casualties is appended.

All of which is respectfully submitted.

Report of Lieut. Col. K. Bryan, Fifth Texas Infantry.

Near Hagerstown, Md.,
July 8, 1863.

Col. R. M. Powell having fallen into the hands of the enemy, it devolves upon me, as lieutenant-colonel of the regiment, to report the part taken by it as far as came under my observation in the action of (July) 2 and 3, near Gettysburg, Pa.

About 4 p.m. on the 2nd instant General Hood's division was drawn up in line of battle fronting the heights occupied by the enemy. The Fifth Texas regiment occupied the right of the brigade, resting on General Law's left, whose brigade was the one of direction. At the word 'Forward!' the regiment moved forward in good order. The enemy had a line of sharpshooters at the foot of the first height, behind a stone fence, about three-fourths of a mile from our starting point, which distance was passed over by our line at a double-quick and a run.

At our approach the enemy retired to the top of the first height, protected by a ledge of rocks. A short halt was made at the stone fence, to enable those who had fallen behind to regain their places. When the command 'Forward!' again fell from the lips of our gallant colonel, every man leaped the fence and advanced rapidly up the hillside. The enemy again fled at our approach, sheltering himself behind his fortified position on the top of the second height, about 200 yards distant from the first.

From this position, we failed to drive them. Our failure was owing to the rocky nature of the ground over which we had to pass, the huge rocks forming defiles through which not more than 3 or 4 men could pass abreast, thus breaking up our alignment and rendering its reformation impossible. Notwithstanding the difficulties to overcome, the men pressed on to the pass of the precipitous stronghold, forming and securing the enemy's second position, many of our officers and men falling in passing the open space between the heights. Here we halted, there being small clusters of rocks far below the elevated position of the enemy, which gave us partial protection. From this position, we were enabled to deliver our fire for the first time with accuracy.

Seeing that the men were in the best obtainable position and deeming a farther advance without reinforcements impracticable (a great many of the regiment having been already disabled), I looked for Colonel Powell, to know his next order. Failing to see him, I concluded at once that he, like many of his gallant officers and men, had fallen a victim to the deadly missiles of the enemy, which were being showered like hail upon us. I moved toward the centre, passing many officers and men who had fallen, having discharged their whole duty like true soldiers. I had not proceeded far when I discovered the prostrate form of our noble colonel, who had fallen at his post, his face to the foe. I hastened toward him, when I received a wound in my left arm. On reaching the colonel, I found that he was not dead; but seeing the rent in his coat where the ball had passed out, my fears were excited that his wound would prove mortal. The haemorrhage from my own wound forced me from the field, leaving the command upon Major Rogers.

The officers and men of my wing of the regiment continued to discharge their duties in a manner worthy of our cause so long as I remained upon the field, and from their conduct heretofore I would not hesitate to vouch for them during the remainder of the battle.

Captain (John S.) Cleveland, of Company H, was on the right. His skilful management of his own company aided me vastly in the direction of my wing.

Report of Maj. J. C. Rogers, Fifth Texas Infantry.

Near Hagerstown, Md.,
July5, 1863.

I have the honour to forward a continuation of the report of the part taken by the Fifth Texas regiment in the action of the 2nd and 3rd instant, after the wounding of Colonels Powell and Bryan, when the command devolved upon me, the regiment still holding the position as left by Colonel Bryan, firing with accuracy and deadly effect.

The order to fall back came from some unknown source, and, finding that the regiments on our right and left had retired, it became necessary to follow. I therefore gave the order for the regiment to about-face and retire to the rear, which they did in good order until they reached the position mentioned in Colonel Bryan's report as the second position of the enemy, and here we halted and re-formed, in connection with the other regiments. From the exhausted condition of the men it was deemed necessary to remain here for a few moments.

The regiments were again ordered forward, which they did in the most gallant manner, and regained their first position, which they held as long as it was tenable; and a farther advance being impracticable, owing to the nature of the ground, as expressed in Colonel Bryan's report, they again retired in good order to an open space about 50 yards in rear, when here it was discovered for the first time that nearly two-thirds of our officers and men had been killed and wounded.

Only a few moments were here consumed to allow the men to recover their breath, when, in obedience to orders, I again moved the regiment forward to attack the enemy in their impregnable position. The coolness and determination of the men and officers were equal to the occasion. They advanced boldly over the ground strewn with the bodies of their dead and dying comrades to the base of what they knew to be an impregnable fortification. We held this position until it was discovered that we had no supports either on the right or left and were about to be flanked, and therefore were again compelled to retire, which the regiment did in good order to the point mentioned in Colonel Bryan's report as the second position of the enemy, which place we were ordered to hold at all hazards, which we did.

Just before day on the morning of the 3rd orders reached me that breastworks must be thrown up, and the position held. The order was obeyed. During the day, constant skirmishing was kept up with the enemy, which resulted in the loss to us of many of our best scouts. Late in the evening, in obedience to orders, I about-faced my regiment and marched three-quarters of a mile to the crest of the ridge from which the charge of the day previous commenced. Here we threw up breastworks, behind which we remained during the night.

I would respectfully beg leave to call attention to the valuable assistance I received from Capt. John S. Cleveland in the management of the right wing of my regiment, and Capt. T. T. Clay on the left; also to the heroic conduct of T. W. Fitzgerald, of Company A, who was colour-bearer. He pressed gallantly forward, and was badly wounded far in front. J. A. Howard, of Company B, colour corporal, then took the flag and remained firmly at his post. He was almost instantly killed. The colours were then taken by Sergeant W. S. Evans, of Company F, who planted them defiantly in the face of the foe during the remainder of the fight, always advancing promptly to the front when the order was given.

The general conduct of officers and men was beyond all praise.

BENNING'S BRIGADE

Report of Brig-Gen. Henry L. Benning, C. S. Army, Commanding Brigade.

Headquarters Benning's Brigade,
August 3, 1863.

In obedience to an order from the headquarters of this division, I have the honour to submit to you the following report of the operations of this brigade since it left Culpeper Court House for the other side of the Potomac:

About 2 or 3 p.m. on July 2, *ultimo*, I was informed by Major-General Hood that his division, as the right of Lieutenant-General Longstreet's corps, was about to attack the left of the enemy's line, and that in the attack my brigade would follow Law's brigade at the distance of about 400 yards. In order to get to the place, they assigned me, in the rear of General Law, it was necessary to move the brigade 500 or 600 yards farther to the right. Having done this, I advanced in line of battle. A wood intervened between us and the enemy, which, though it did not prevent their shells from reaching us and producing some casualties, yet completely hid them from our view. On emerging from the woods their position became visible. Before us, at the distance of 600 or 800 yards, was an oblong mountain peak, or spur, presenting to us a steep face, much roughened by rocks. To the right, 400 or 500 yards from the peak, was the main mountain itself, with a side that looked almost perpendicular. Its summit overlooked the peak just sufficiently to command it well. On the summit of the peak were three pieces of artillery, and a little in advance of them, on a sort of uneven, irregular shelf, were three others. To the right and left of the battery, as well as immediately in its rear, were lines of infantry, as we afterward ascertained. This formed the enemy's first line of battle. On the top of the mountain itself, and a little to the right of the peak, were five other guns. These commanded our approaches to the peak for nearly the whole way. To the right and left of these guns extended the enemy's second line of infantry. Where that line crossed the gorge running between the peak and the mountain, a point 500 or 600 yards in the rear of the peak, were two other guns. This we ascertained when the right of the brigade reached the gorge, by the terrible fire from them which swept down the gorge.

Thus, what we had to encounter were thirteen guns, and two, if not more, lines of infantry posted on mountain heights. The intervening spur over which we had to march to reach the first line was nearly all open. Our own first line also became visible, advancing about 400 yards in our front. The part of it in our front I took to be Law's brigade, and so I followed it. In truth, it was Robertson's, Law's being farther to the right. This I did not discover until late in the fight, a wood on the right concealing from me most of Law's brigade. My line continued to follow the first line, halting once or twice to preserve its interval. At length, I saw that the first line would not be able alone to carry the peak, so I advanced without halting again.

When my line reached the foot of the peak I found there a part of the First Texas, struggling to make the ascent, the rest of the brigade having gone to the right and left, the Fourth and Fifth Texas to the right, and the Third Arkansas to the left. The part of the First Texas referred to falling in with my brigade, the whole line commenced ascending the rugged steep and (on the right) crossing the gorge. The ground was difficult, rocks in many places presenting, by their precipitous sides, insurmountable obstacles, while the fire of the enemy was very heavy and very deadly. The progress was therefore not very rapid; but it was regular and uninterrupted.

After a while the enemy were driven from their three front guns. The advance continued, and at length they were driven completely from the peak, but they carried with them the three rear guns on its summit, its sudden descent on the other side favouring the operation, so that we captured only the three front guns. These were 10-pounder Parrotts. A number of prisoners also were taken—more, I suppose, than 100.

The peak being thus taken and the enemy's first line driven behind his second, I made my dispositions to hold the ground gained, which was all that I could do, as I was then much in advance of every other part of our line of battle, and the second line of the enemy on the mountain itself was in a position which seemed to me almost impregnable to any merely front attack, even with fresh men. Indeed, to hold the ground we had, appeared a difficult task. The shells of the enemy from the adjacent mountain were incessantly bursting along the summit of the peak, and every head that showed itself was the target of a minie ball. Several attempts by flank movements were made to dislodge us, but by the gallantry of the regiments on the right and left they all failed. We held the position until late next day, when we were ordered back to the crest of the wooded hill from which we first saw the enemy on the day before.

Our loss was heavy, not less than 400 in killed, wounded, and missing. Of this number an unusually large proportion were killed and badly wounded. Among the killed were Col. John A. Jones, of the Twentieth Georgia, and Lieut.-Col. William T. Harris, commanding the Second Georgia. Colonel Jones was killed late in the action, not far from the captured guns, after the enemy's forces were driven from the position and they had themselves opened upon it with shell from their other batteries, a fragment of one of which, glancing from a rock, passed through his brain. He had behaved with great coolness and gallantry. He fell just as success came in sight. Colonel Harris was farther to the right, where he and his regiment were exposed to the terrible fire of the two pieces which swept the gorge, as well as to the infantry fire of the enemy's left. A ball passed through his heart, killing him instantly. His gallantry had been most conspicuous.

I had no means of ascertaining the precise loss of the enemy. In killed and wounded it must have been large. Dead and wounded lay scattered over the ground of the conflict and of the retreat. From the latter, they were removed by the enemy during the night. We took about 300 prisoners in all.

The conduct of both officers and men was generally, as far as I could observe it, excellent. Under a fire from so many cannon and toward the last from so much musketry, they advanced steadily over ground for the most part open, mounted a difficult height, drove back from it the enemy, occupied his line, took three guns, captured a number of prisoners, and against his utmost efforts held all they had gained. The captured guns were taken by the Twentieth Georgia (Colonel Jones and, after his death, Lieutenant-Colonel Waddell), the part of the First Texas above referred to (Colonel Work), and the Seventeenth Georgia (Colonel Hodges); but the honour of the capture was not exclusively theirs. They could not have taken—certainly could not have held—the guns if Lieutenant-Colonel Harris and, after his death, Major (William S.) Shepherd, on the left with the Second Georgia, and Colonel Du Bose, with the Fifteenth Georgia, on the right, had not by the hardest kind of fighting and at great loss protected their flanks. Colonel Du Bose not only drove back the enemy's line, but repulsed repeated attacks made to recover it, taking over 100 prisoners. The same may be said of the Second, excepting that it did not take so many prisoners.

General Hood was severely wounded during the cannonade which preceded the advance of the infantry and was carried to the rear. General Law was not informed of this until the infantry was in close proximity to the Union line, when as senior brigade commander he assumed command of the four brigades of Hood's division. For reasons explained in Law's admirable paper published many years after the war, in the *Century Magazine,* from which I have quoted extracts, no report of the part taken by Hood's division was made, either by Hood or Law. As Anderson's brigade was too far to the left to have had any influence in the attack on Little Round Top, I have omitted its report. Benning's report of his brigade, which attacked Ward at the Devil's Den, is so complete that I have omitted the regimental reports.

I have given in full the regimental reports of Law's and Robertson's brigades and the brigade report by Robertson. The Confederates left the scene of their attack almost immediately. At the time of writing these reports they knew nothing of the nomenclature of this part of the battlefield, which since has become so familiar. The names Devil's Den, Little Round Top, and Big Round Top do not appear; instead, they speak of high peaks, rocky ridges, mountains, gorges, and valleys in a way which makes it difficult in some cases to trace their movements exactly.

However, from other indications I think I have been able to locate them correctly in stating that the attack on the Devil's Den was made by the First Texas and Third Arkansas of Robertson's brigade, the four regiments of Benning's and Law's Forty-Fourth Alabama, and that the attack on Little Round Top was made by Robertson's Fourth and Fifth Texas, Law's Fourth, Fifteenth, Forty-Seventh, and Forty-Eighth Alabama, with a possibility that the Forty-Fourth Alabama joined on the left of the Forty-Eighth Alabama in the last assault on Little

Round Top, as shown on the Government map mentioned elsewhere.

Forty-Eighth Alabama

I have placed this report out of its numerical order because there is no other report of Law's brigade, and Sheffield states that, having learned that Hood was wounded and Law had assumed command of the division, he was ordered to assume command of the brigade. He did not learn this fact, however, until his regiment had been fighting one hour and a half and been three times repulsed. So far as this part of the battle is concerned, it is in no sense a report of the brigade. He makes no mention of having given any orders to any other regiments during the attack on Vincent, and none of the regimental reports mention the receipt of any orders from him. He says that when he took command of the brigade Captain T. J. Eubanks took command of the regiment and re-formed it, and gallantly led it to the front. This change of commanders appears to have taken place after the brigade had been three times repulsed and had retired in some disorder out of range.

I have been unable to find any record of the order which moved the Forty-Eighth Alabama and the Fourth and Fifth Texas to the Confederate left to make the attack on Vincent's right flank. As soon as I could get a musket after the first attack on Vincent's centre began, I took my place in the line between the right of the Forty-Fourth New York and the left of the Sixteenth Michigan, and remained there until the last assault was repulsed. I am sure that these three Confederate regiments did not move to the left directly in front of our line.

Marching by the flank immediately in front of our position, without opportunity to make any resistance, they would have been cut to pieces before they had covered half the ground necessary to reach the place from which they made the assault. They must have gone north in the Plum Run valley behind the big rocks which separated that valley from the western foot of Little Round Top. By this time, Ward's brigade had been driven back from its position at the Devil's Den and the way was open in that direction. May it not be possible that Colonel Sheffield ordered this movement after the troops of his brigade had recovered from the disorder of their last repulse and had got into reasonable order again? The officers and men were plucky and determined. Having failed in a direct assault on Vincent's front, they evidently hoped for better results from a flank attack on Vincent's right, while the Fifteenth, Forty-Seventh and Fourth Alabama were attacking Vincent's left. Sheffield's report, like the others, leaves many gaps to be filled. If the above explanation is not correct, a better one will be gladly received.

Fourth Alabama

This report is certainly not a history of the Battle of Gettysburg. Without violating the military rule which requires official reports to be confined to the operations of the organisation reported, it might with propriety have given a more extended account of the operations of this regiment. On the first reading one would suppose that this regiment did not participate in the attack on Vincent, but was engaged on the western front of Big Round Top. Its first position in line was the left one of the five Alabama regiments of Law's brigade. Robertson's brigade of one Arkansas and three Texas regiments was ordered to keep in connection with the left of Law's brigade.

In advancing, Law's men obliqued to the right and Robertson's Fourth and Fifth Texas followed this movement. Ward's brigade at the Devil's Den was the objective. Seeing that his brigade had gone too far to the right and was facing the south side of Big Round Top, Law directed the two regiments on his right, the Forty-Eighth and Forty-Fourth Alabama, to halt and then move by the flank to the left of his brigade. While the Fourth and Fifth Texas had followed this oblique movement, Robertson's other two regiments had gone straight on to the Devil's Den, leaving a considerable interval between the two parts of his brigade. The Forty-Eighth and Forty-Fourth Alabama continued their flank movement to the left until they had passed the Fourth and Fifth Texas, then came to the front with the Forty-Eighth on the left of the Fourth Texas and the Forty-Fourth on the extreme left of Law's line. Near the foot of the hill from which they advanced they struck the left of Stoughton's sharpshooters stationed behind a stone wall facing south near the west front of Big Round Top.

After a stubborn resistance, the sharpshooters retired, three companies of them going up the west front of Big Round Top in the woods, closely followed by the right two regiments of Law's brigade, the Fifteenth and Forty-Seventh Alabama. The remainder of Law's men crossed the western slope and the low ground to the west of it until they came to the narrow valley which runs along the north side of Big Round Top. Here by Law's orders the Forty-Fourth Alabama wheeled to the left and advanced against Smith's battery on the Devil's Den.

The Fourth and Forty-Eighth Alabama, with the Fourth and Fifth

Texas, marched in columns up this valley to seize the Little Round Top or turn it. The Fourth Alabama was one of these regiments. Meeting Vincent's skirmishers, they quickly formed in line of battle in the following order from right to left: Fourth Alabama, Fifth Texas, Fourth Texas, and Forty-Eighth Alabama. The Fourth Alabama swung around to attack the Eighty-Third Pennsylvania from the south. The other regiments faced the right wing of the Eighty-Third, Forty-Fourth, and the left of the Sixteenth Michigan.

After a few minutes of desperate fighting this line retired a short distance and took shelter behind the rocks, but soon re-formed the line and advanced again. I think the Fourth Alabama retired and returned with the others. In any event, they were there when Oates' column, consisting of the Fifteenth and Forty-Seventh Alabama, was seen advancing along the foot of Big Round Top in rear of the Fourth Alabama, which remained there until sometime after Oates' men had come to close quarters with the Twentieth Maine. When the Fourth Alabama finally retired, with the troops which it had accompanied, it took shelter on the western slope of Big Round Top and did no more fighting that day.

Fifteenth Alabama

As Colonel Oates, has made a long and elaborate account in his book, *The War Between the Union and the Confederacy*, which I have quoted elsewhere, with my comments, I have nothing further to add here. The reader is referred to this paper among my extracts from the histories.

Forty-Fourth Alabama

This regiment appears to have advanced into the Plum Run valley on the flank of the battery on the Devil's Den and to have fought the infantry posted in the rear of the battery to support it. When Benning's brigade advanced, its line more than covered the front of the Devil's Den, one regiment at least being in the Plum Run valley, and joining the left of the Forty-Fourth Alabama. The Union line retreated from the three front guns of the battery. The remaining three were taken to the rear. With Benning's brigade and part of Robertson's holding this position, the Forty-Fourth was left free to join the Forty-Eighth in the advance against the crest of Little Round Top if it wished to do so. Colonel Perry does not mention any such movement. In a letter written to Colonel Oates by Colonel Perry several years after the war, which I have quoted in my extracts from Oates' book, Perry speaks of his exhaustion and of his having been stunned by the explosion of a shell near him. He was not in condition to know much about what happened at the end of the fight about the Devil's Den. He makes no mention in his report of the withdrawal of his regiment nor where it went when withdrawn.

Forty-Seventh Alabama

This report is very incomplete. It makes no mention of the fact that the regiment went with the Fifteenth Alabama to the summit of Big Round Top. From Major Campbell's statement in commendation of the conduct of the officers of the regiment, not including the colonel and adjutant, and from Oates' statement that Law told him that in case the Fifteenth and Forty-Seventh were separated from the brigade, the Forty-Seventh would be under his command, it is evident there was considerable demoralization among the field and staff of the Forty-Seventh. The resignation of the colonel and the promotion of the lieutenant-colonel, Bulger, to be colonel to date from July 16, is conclusive. Oates' statement that the lieutenant-colonel, although very courageous, was unfitted to command the regiment by reason of his age and his inexperience and ignorance of tactics, may explain Law's reason for placing the direction of the regiment under certain contingencies in the hands of Colonel Oates. The note in the official report which states that Bulger was not killed in the action was made by the editor or compiler of the *Rebellion Records*.

Bulger was the officer who surrendered to Colonel Chamberlain by handing him his sword with one hand and firing his pistol at him with the other. He was well cared for by the Union surgeons and lived for many years after the war. Major Campbell's statement that after the first repulse of the brigade he deployed a part of his men on the right of the brigade, where they remained until the close of the fight, is not very probable, if it refers to the repulse by Vincent's brigade. The Fifteenth Alabama was on the right of the Forty-Seventh, and under the circumstances it is not likely that a detachment of the Forty-Seventh would have been sent to the right of the Fifteenth. Possibly he refers to a movement made after his regiment had returned to the woods on the western foot of Big Round Top. The first repulse of the brigade occurred before the Fifteenth and Forty-Seventh Alabama came down from the mountain.

Robertson's Brigade Report

This is an excellent report. If all the official reports were like it in careful and intelligible description, there would be little trouble in forming a correct idea of the movements. It explains clearly how two of his regiments, the Fourth and Fifth Texas, became separated from the other two regiments of his brigade and fought with Law's brigade in the attack on Little Round Top. His regimental reports give more details.

Third Arkansas

As the attack of this regiment in connection with Anderson's brigade was made against De Trobriand's line on the west of the Devil's Den, and it had little if any effect on the fight for possession of Little Round Top, I see no occasion for comment. I mention it only as a part of Robertson's brigade.

First Texas

This regiment was principally engaged on the left of the line in front of Smith's battery at the Devil's Den. One company of the Fourth Texas which had been thrown out as skirmishers in the advance went straight forward while its regiment moved to the right to maintain its connection with Law's brigade. This company fought through the day with the First Texas. Benning's brigade, following closely Robertson's advance, came up and its left mingled with the First Texas in the assault and capture of three guns of this battery.

Fourth Texas

This report, like that of the Fifth Texas and some others, is wanting in definiteness of detail about positions. What he calls the first position of the enemy is evidently the stone wall behind which Stoughton's sharpshooters were posted. One might suppose from his statement that Stoughton retreated and was followed to his second position at the base of the mountain, but he evidently means the position of Vincent's brigade, against which repeated assaults were made and repulsed. The lieutenant-colonel, Carter, was severely wounded in the fight with Stoughton at the stone wall. This was followed by the wounding of Colonel Key in the assault on Vincent, leaving Major Bane in command. Colonel Key was able to walk, as Robertson in his report mentions seeing him as he was led to the rear. In addition to the fight with Stoughton at the stone wall, he speaks of three assaults, in the first of which the enemy was driven to the heights beyond, in close proximity to the mountain.

This evidently refers to the falling back of Vincent's skirmishers to the main line, followed by the Confederates, who retreated after a few minutes of close fighting. The second assault was made in connection with the Fifth Texas, with like results. He does not mention the Fourth Alabama on the right of the Fifth Texas, nor the Forty-Eighth Alabama on the left of the Fourth Texas, but I think the four regiments were there and continued their desperate fighting for some time. I think the third assault was that made against Vincent's right flank which was repulsed by the One Hundred and Fortieth New York. This is the only instance in which the Forty-Fourth Alabama is mentioned as participating in the assaults on Little Round Top.

During the first part of the battle the Forty-Fourth Alabama was, according to the report of its commander, fighting at the Devil's Den. As I have stated elsewhere, this position was carried by the Confederates before the assault on Vincent's right flank, and the Forty-Fourth may have joined in this assault with the Texas regiments and the Forty-Eighth Alabama on the left of the latter, as represented in the Government map showing the position of troops. In this assault the Forty-Eighth was commanded by Captain Eubanks, not by Colonel Sheffield, as stated by Major Bane.

Fifth Texas

This report is in two parts, the first by Lieutenant-Colonel K. Bryan, who took command when Colonel Powell was wounded in front of Vincent's brigade, the second by Major J. C. Rogers, who succeeded to the command when Lieutenant-Colonel Bryan was wounded. Like the report of the Fourth Texas by Major Bane, it is very difficult to follow; but there is no doubt the place mentioned in both as the second position of the enemy is the position of Vincent's brigade, as Colonel Powell was wounded in front of Vincent's line and was made a prisoner there. As they speak about following the enemy to their second position, about two hundred yards distant, from which they drove them, they appear to have supposed that their first encounter at the stone wall was with Vincent's men, who retreated to their second position near the base of the mountain.

This cannot be true, for two reasons: Vincent's men were not at the stone wall where the first encounter occurred. They did not follow Stoughton, because three regiments of Law's brigade on their right took care of Stoughton, who retreated up the west front of Big Round Top. Their statement that they drove the enemy from their second position into their fortified line near the base of the mountain, from which they failed to drive them, must refer to the falling back of Vincent's skirmishers. This would not be so clear if it were not certain that their main attack was against Vincent.

There Colonel Powell was wounded and made prisoner by the Eighty-Third Pennsylvania, as were a large number of his men. I think there is no question that after driving the sharpshooters from the stone fence, the Fourth Alabama, Fifth Texas, Fourth Texas, and Forty-Eighth Alabama kept straight on in more or less regular line of battle until they reached the little valley extending along the north side of Big Round Top, and then, by Law's direction, moved by the right flank up this valley until they reached and attacked Vincent.

Benning's Brigade Report

As Benning did not attack Little Round Top, but fought his battle against Ward's brigade. Smith's battery, and the reinforcements sent to their support, I have not thought it necessary to include his regimental reports. As there were several claimants for the honour of the capture of the three guns of Smith's battery, I shall not attempt to decide between them. There was glory enough for all.

Union

(*Rebellion Records*, Series I, Vol. xxvii, part i)

Report of Maj.-Gen. George Sykes, U. S. Army, commanding Fifth Army Corps.

> Headquarters Fifth Army Corps,
> Camp Near Warrenton, Va., July 31, 1863.
> On the 28th *ultimo*, by the assignment of General Meade to the command of the Army of the Potomac, I became the senior general of this corps.
> On June 29 and 30 and on July 1 and 2 I made long, rapid, and fatiguing marches, starting at Frederick, Md., and reaching the field of Gettysburg, *via* Liberty, Union Mills, Hanover, etc., about 8 a. m., on the latter date. My troops took position on the right of our line, but it being thought too extended, they were subsequently massed near the bridge over Rock Creek, on the

Baltimore and Gettysburg pike and within reach of the Twelfth Army Corps. While thus situated, I was directed to support the Third corps, General Sickles commanding, with a brigade, should it be required.

At 3 p.m., General Meade sent for me, and while myself and other corps commanders were conversing with him, the enemy formed, opened the battle, and developed his attack on our left. I was at once ordered to throw my whole corps to that point and hold it at all hazards. This, of course, relieved my troops from any call from the commander of the Third Corps. *En route* to the position thus assigned the Fifth corps, various staff officers from General Sickles met me, and, in the name of that officer, asked for assistance. I explained to them that it was impossible for me to give it; the key of the battlefield was intrusted to my keeping, and I could not and would not jeopardize it by a division of my forces.

A rocky ridge, commanding almost an entire view of the plateau held by our army, was on our extreme left. Between it and the position occupied by Birney's division, Third corps, was a narrow gorge filled with immense boulders and flanked on either side by dense woods. It afforded excellent cover and an excellent approach for the enemy, both of which he promptly made use of. The rocky ridge commanded and controlled this gorge. In examining it and the ground adjacent previous to posting my troops, I found a battery at its outer edge and without adequate support. I galloped to General Birney, whose troops were nearest, explained to him the necessity of protecting the guns, and suggested that he should close his division on the battery, and hold the edge of the woods on its right. I promised to fill the gap he opened, which I did with Sweitzer's and Tilton's brigades, of my First division, posting them myself. In the meantime, Vincent's brigade, of this division, had seized the rocky height, closely followed by Weed's brigade, Second division. These troops were posted under the direction of General Warren, chief engineer of this army. After closing the interval made by Birney with the brigades of General Barnes, I rode rapidly to the Taneytown pike to bring up the remaining troops of the corps, and on my return with them found the greater part of Weed's brigade moving away from the height where it had been stationed, and where its presence was vital.

I dispatched a staff officer to know of the general why he had vacated the ground assigned him. His reply was, 'By order of General Sickles.' I at once directed him to re-occupy it, which was done at the double-quick step. Hardly had he reached it before the enemy came on in tremendous force. Vincent's brigade and O'Rorke's regiment (Weed's brigade) were and had been sorely pressed. Both those heroic commanders had fallen; but Weed again in position, Hazlett working his guns superbly, and the timely arrival of Ayres' brigades of Regulars, who were at once ordered to attack, stemmed the tide, and rolled away the foe in our front.

At a later hour, by the withdrawal or retreat of the troops on his right, first, a division of the Third corps, and next, Caldwell's command, of the Second corps, a large body of the enemy gained his right and rear, and Ayres was compelled to fight his way, front and flank, to the heel of the gorge. This he did steadily, in excellent order, and connected with his left brigade (Weed's) on the general line of battle. But his loss was fearful; some of the regiments left sixty *per cent*, of their number on the ground. As Ayres assumed this new position. General Crawford's command (my Third division) was ordered to the front, and, entering the woods, became briskly engaged with the enemy. This combat lasted till dusk, and resulted in General Crawford's gaining considerable ground, capturing many prisoners, and a flag of a Georgia regiment.

Night closed the fight. The key of the battlefield was in our possession intact. Vincent, Weed, and Hazlett, chiefs lamented throughout the corps and army, sealed with their lives the spot intrusted to their keeping, and on which so much depended. The general line of battle on the left was shortened, strengthened, firm. Pickets were established, and the troops slept on their arms. Sedgwick (Sixth corps) had moved up to my aid.

On the 3rd Crawford held his ground in front, sustained by Bartlett's division of Sedgwick's corps. The troops remained as the day before. Desultory firing from the pickets continued along our front. At 1 p.m. the enemy commenced a furious cannonade from more than one hundred guns, and occasionally a part of it was bestowed on the Fifth and Sixth corps. It was the prelude to his attack, which soon followed and raged to our right; but, beaten, baffled, and discomfited, he returned to the shelter of the forests west of the Emmittsburg and Gettysburg pike. My artillery on the rocky ridge helped to shatter and disorganise his troops.

On the 4th reconnaissances were made, but developed nothing save a line of skirmishers covering his troops, and artillery on the slope falling away from the turnpike to the west.

"On the 5th I began the march to Williamsport.

I respectfully call the attention of the major-general commanding, to the services of the artillery of this corps, under its chief, Capt. A. P. Martin, and the subordinate battery commanders, as detailed in his report.

The regular batteries were the greatest sufferers. Hazlett's battery (D, Fifth U. S. Artillery) was especially distinguished, and Watson's battery (I, same regiment) though unfortunately taken away by General Sickles, without my consent or knowledge, after falling into the hands of the enemy, was recaptured by Lieutenant Peeples, of the battery, heading the Garibaldi Guard, in the most heroic and gallant manner. Lieutenant Peeples richly deserves promotion for his conduct, and I trust the government will not withhold it.

I am happy to say the Fifth corps sustained its reputation. An important duty was confided to it, which was faithfully and gallantly performed. Other brave men helped them in its execution, among whom the Sixth corps was the most prominent.

I respectfully beg leave to call attention to the reports of division and brigade commanders, herewith enclosed.

The division commanders, Generals Barnes, Ayres, and Crawford, aided me in every particular with the utmost zeal and heartiness. I most urgently unite in their recommendations of the various gentlemen who distinguished themselves in and around the field of Gettysburg.

Colonel Rice, who succeeded to the command of the Third brigade, First division, on the fall of Colonel Vincent, deserves great credit for the management of his troops. His position on our extreme left was one of the most important held by the corps, and the unflinching tenacity with which he maintained it, and his subsequent forcible occupation of the ground possessed by the enemy, with Chamberlain's regiment (Twentieth Maine) and two regiments of Fisher's brigade. Third division, are worthy of the highest praise.

The medical department, under Surgeon J. J. Milhau and Asst. Surg. C. P. Russell, was organised in the most effective and satisfactory manner.

My personal staff and the chiefs of departments were zealous, indefatigable, and ready for any emergency. I name them in the order of rank, and respectfully recommend them to the notice of the Department of War: Lieut.-Col. Fred. T. Locke, assistant adjutant-general; Lieut.-Col. William H. Owen, chief quartermaster; Capt. D. L. Smith, acting chief commissary of subsistence; Surg. J. J. Milhau, U. S. Army, medical director; Asst. Surg. C. P. Russell, U. S. Army, medical inspector; Capt. John W. Williams, assistant adjutant-general and acting *aide-de-camp*; Capt. William Jay, *aide-de-camp*, and First Lieut. George T. Ingham, Eleventh U. S. Infantry, *aide-de-camp*.

The signal officers, Capt. W. H. Hill and Lieut. I. S. Lyon, performed their duties creditably.

General Weed and Colonel Vincent, officers of rare promise, gave their lives to their country. The former had been conspicuous during the war, won and adorned his promotion, and surrendered it and his life on the spot he was called upon to defend.

In this campaign of the Army of the Potomac, consequent upon Lee's second invasion of Maryland, troops never endured more, marched more in the same length of time, suffered more, deserved more, or fought better than they. Prompt response and obedience to all orders characterized them. Their record up to July 24, with its incalculable results, is a study, and has few parallels in this history of the rebellion.

Tabular and nominal lists have preceded this report.

I enclose the reports of division and other commanders, and with them a list of casualties in the corps.

Report of Brig.-Gen. Charles Griffin, U. S. Army, commanding First Division.

> Hdqrs. First Division, Fifth Army Corps,
> Near Beverly Ford, Va., August 14, 1863.

In compliance with circular from headquarters Army of the Potomac, dated August 12, 1863, I have the honour to report that I arrived at Gettysburg on July 3 last, and relieved General Barnes, in command of the Division, on the 4th. . . . (As the remainder of this report relates to movements of the division after the Battle of Gettysburg, it is omitted).

Report of Brig.-Gen. James Barnes, U. S. Army, commanding First Division.

Headquarters First Division, Fifth Corps,
Beverly Ford, Va., August 24, 1863.

I have the honour to submit the following report of the operations of the First division of the Fifth corps from June 28 to July 9, including the Battle of Gettysburg and the movements of the command during the few days previous and subsequent thereto, in conformity with instructions from headquarters:

On June 28, after a succession of rapid marches from Virginia, the division encamped about two miles south of Frederick City, Md.

On the 29th, the command of the Army of the Potomac having devolved upon Major-General Meade, until then commanding the Fifth corps, Major-General Sykes, who had succeeded to the command of the corps, directed an early movement forward. The First division, under my command, moved accordingly through Frederick City toward the town of Liberty, and, passing beyond that place about two miles, bivouacked for the night.

On the 30th, at 4 a.m., the march was resumed and continued toward Union Mills, approaching the place with proper precautions, on account of a heavy body of cavalry of the enemy, some 8,000 or 10,000 in number, as reported, then occupying it. Upon reaching the town, we found that this cavalry force had left it some three or four hours before our arrival, and had gone in the direction of Hanover.

The division halted here for the night, and on the following morning, July 1, left at an early hour for Hanover, where it arrived at about 4 o'clock in the afternoon. Orders were here received to halt for the night, but scarcely had arms been stacked when news was received that an engagement had that day taken place between the enemy and a portion of the army at Gettysburg. Orders were received for an immediate resumption of the march toward Gettysburg, and, notwithstanding a long march had already been accomplished, the orders were received by the troops with the utmost enthusiasm. The division was soon on the road, and continued its march toward Gettysburg, halting after midnight about 2 miles from that place. Resuming its march, after a brief rest of two or three hours, the division reached Gettysburg at about 7 o'clock in the morning of July 2. The Eighteenth Massachusetts, Colonel Hayes commanding, was immediately detached to support a battery upon the left of the road, and the remaining portion of the command was placed in position, by direction of General Sykes, on the right of the Second division of the corps, south of and facing toward the village.

The Ninth Massachusetts, Colonel Guiney commanding, was here detailed from the Second brigade, as skirmishers, and deployed at some distance in front of the line.

The command here rested for further instructions. After the lapse of an hour or more the division received orders to change its position, moving some distance to the rear and toward the left of this first line, but it remained in this new position for a short period only. Orders were again received to move still farther to the left, and, subsequently crossing the creek over a small bridge, we were held in reserve in an orchard on the left of the road, with instructions to wait there for further orders. Here the Eighteenth Massachusetts, detached as above stated early in the morning, rejoined the command, and was posted on the opposite side of the road. These various movements occupied the time until long after midday. The sound of the enemy's artillery still indicated a movement toward the left of the point where we were then halted.

Between 4 and 5 o'clock in the afternoon orders were received from General Sykes to move toward the left and to the front. The column was immediately formed, and moved rapidly up by the Taneytown road to the ground assigned to the division. General Sykes and myself, preceding the advance of the column upon the ground upon which it was to take position, reconnoitred the field, and the position to be held by the command was determined upon by him.

Soon after, the head of the column entered upon the field. At the same time, General Warren, of the staff of General Meade, came up, riding rapidly from the left, and, pointing out the position of the elevation known as the Round Top, not far off and toward the left, urged the importance of assistance in that direction. General Sykes yielded to his earnest request, and I immediately directed Colonel Vincent, commanding the Third brigade, to proceed to that point with his brigade. Colonel Vincent moved with great promptness to the post assigned to him. The brigade consisted of the Sixteenth Michigan, the Forty-Fourth New York, the Eighty-Third Pennsylvania, and the Twentieth Maine regiments.

The Second brigade, commanded by Colonel Sweitzer, arrived next upon the ground. This brigade consisted of the Fourth Michigan, the Sixty-Second Pennsylvania, the Ninth Massachusetts, and the Thirty-Second Massachusetts. The Ninth Massachusetts, however, was absent, being upon the special duty for which it had been detailed in the morning. Upon receiving his instructions Colonel Sweitzer placed his command promptly in position.

The First brigade, under the command of Colonel Tilton, arrived next. This brigade was composed of the Eighteenth Massachusetts, the Twenty-Second Massachusetts, the One Hundred and Eighteenth Pennsylvania, and the First Michigan regiments. The position assigned to it was on the right of the ground occupied by the Second brigade, and was immediately placed by Colonel Tilton, in conformity with the instruction given to him.

The division thus in position constituted the right of the Fifth corps, and its place in line was on the left of the ground assigned to the Third corps. The line was on the edge of a thick wood, the ground to the front being cleared of timber, but interspersed with rocks and some straggling trees. As the two brigades entered the wood they passed over a line of troops, understood to be a portion of a brigade of the Third corps; they were lying down upon the ground.

Upon the right of our position an open space, apparently unprotected, extended to some distance. Upon calling the attention of General Sykes to it, he remarked, referring to the part of the Third corps over which we had passed and then lying down in our rear, that those troops were to be removed. The remaining portion of the Third corps was understood to be at some distance to the right, and much in advance of what seemed to be their natural and true position. This unguarded space was watched with great anxiety. There was little time, however, for deliberation. General Sykes, called by his duty to the left of the line, went toward that portion of his command. The attack of the enemy commenced almost immediately along my front. It was very severe, but was gallantly withstood.

After some time, during which the firing was very heavy, the enemy showed itself in great force upon our right flank. He had penetrated through the unguarded space there, and commenced pouring in a destructive fire from the advantageous position he had gained, and without changing my front there were no means of checking his advance toward my rear. Colonel Tilton, commanding the First brigade, which was on the right, was immediately directed to change his front to the right, and the order was at once executed, deliberately, yet promptly, and in good order. Colonel Sweitzer, commanding the Second brigade, on the left of the First, was immediately notified of this change upon his right, and directed to fall back in good order, and to take up a new position a short distance in his rear, for the purpose of co-operating in opposing this heavy attack upon the flank. This brigade, consisting at that time of only three regiments, numbering in all, officers and men, 1,010, was placed promptly and in good order as directed. The First brigade numbered in all, officers and men, 654.

Affairs being in this position. General Caldwell, commanding a brigade of the Second corps, came up in great haste and stated to me that his brigade, then in the woods a short distance to the left, was driving the enemy in his front, and urgently requested assistance. I immediately directed Colonel Sweitzer to go to his relief. He moved his brigade forward in line, to the front and left, his men giving cheers as they advanced across an open field to the edge of the wood; but the progress of the enemy upon our flank still continued, and this brigade was compelled again to change its front to repel his advance, and soon found itself in close conflict with him. The Fourth Michigan and the Sixty-second Pennsylvania were in actual contact with him. Colonel Jeffords, commanding the Fourth Michigan, was thrust through with a bayonet while gallantly attempting to rescue his colours from the grasp of the enemy.

Finding himself unable to compete with numbers far superior to his own, and that the enemy was gaining ground to his rear, Colonel Sweitzer directed his command to retire slowly, but orderly, halting and firing as they retired, and took position on elevated ground a short distance to his rear, and succeeded in preventing the enemy from making any further progress in that direction.

In the meantime, the movements of the First brigade, under similar circumstances, corresponded with those of the Second. This brigade, small in numbers, fired, and retired in good order, and succeeded in reaching the ground on the opposite side of the open field toward the left, and there halted. The darkness put an end to the conflict, and the enemy was foiled in his effort to get in the rear of the command. The Ninth Massachusetts shortly afterward rejoined the Second brigade, having been relieved from the duty upon which it had been detailed early in the morning. In this position the two brigades remained during the night.

On the following day, the First brigade was directed to relieve the Third brigade at Little Round Top, where it also had succeeded in maintaining the position assigned to it, as will appear in the sequel.

I cannot speak in terms too commendatory of the bearing of the officers and men of these two brigades during the progress of this conflict. Skilfully directed by the two brigade commanders, they obeyed with cool intrepidity every order issued to them, under the most trying circumstances, and long resisted superior numbers with firmness. Partly surrounded by the enemy, they succeeded in preventing the left of the line from being taken in reverse, resisting an attack not exceeded, I am, sure, in violence in any contest hitherto occurring. The exposure of their flank, arising from whatever cause, placed them in a most dangerous position, and their heroic conduct alone saved the command, at least, if not the entire left of the army, from disaster. The statement of the casualties of the contest is sufficient evidence of their gallant resistance, and it is alike due to those who have survived and to the memory of the gallant dead that this record should be made of their valour and devotion.

The Third brigade, as above related, was detached from the division upon its arrival upon the ground and was consequently removed from my immediate oversight. The record of its service, however, drawn principally from the report of its commander, belongs to this record of the service of the division.

Colonel Vincent, commanding the brigade, upon being detached, as above mentioned, proceeded promptly to the position assigned him. It was upon an elevated and rocky hill known as the Little Round Top. It was situated at some distance to our left, and near the extreme left of the line of battle. Its defence was of the utmost importance. When the brigade was placed in position the Twentieth Maine occupied the left of the line, the Sixteenth Michigan the right, the Eighty-Third Pennsylvania and the Forty-Fourth New York the centre. The Third division of the Fifth corps was posted on the right of the brigade. The enemy had concentrated a heavy force in front of the line, and began a fierce attack immediately after the troops were in position. Repeated charges were made upon the centre of the brigade, but the line was unbroken. A vigorous attack upon the right caused a temporary wavering there, but, the One Hundred and Fortieth New York coming promptly to its support, it was re-established at once.

It was at this time that Colonel Vincent, commanding the brigade, while rallying this part of his command, fell mortally wounded. He was a gallant officer, beloved and respected by his command and by all who knew him. His death is a serious loss to the army and the country.

Upon the removal of Colonel Vincent from the field, the command of the brigade devolved upon Colonel Rice, of the Forty-Fourth New York Volunteers. The enemy, as stated, having in vain attempted to break the right of the brigade, renewed his attack upon the centre and left. The Twentieth Maine, Colonel Chamberlain commanding, was posted on the left. It consisted of 380 men and officers. While the enemy in its front was making a fierce attack, a brigade was observed in the rear of their lines moving by its right flank and passing through a slight ravine on our left, with the evident purpose of gaining a position on the left flank of this regiment.

Colonel Chamberlain at once threw back his left wing, and extended his right wing by intervals toward the left, in order to avoid diminishing the extent of his front. The brigade of the enemy alluded to reaching a proper position, attacked him furiously on the left flank, advancing within 10 paces and rapidly firing. They were first checked and then repulsed by the left wing of the regiment, thrown back for that purpose.

A second, third, and fourth time the enemy renewed their attempt to break this line, and each time they were successfully repelled by that handful of men. Four times that little interval of 10 paces was the scene of a desperate conflict. The ground was strewn with dead and wounded men of both sides, promiscuously mingled. Their ammunition was exhausted; they replenished it from the cartridge-boxes of the men lying around them, whether friends or foes, but even this resource soon failed them; the enemy in greatly superior numbers pressed hard; men and officers began to look to the rear for safety, but the gallant commander of the regiment ordered the bayonets to be fixed, and, at the command, 'Forward!' that wearied and worn body of men rushed onward with a shout.

The enemy fell back. Pressing on and wheeling to the right in open intervals, the left wing came again in line with the right wing, and then the whole regiment deployed at intervals of 5 paces, followed up the advantage they had gained. The enemy threw down their arms and surrendered in large numbers; the others fled rapidly from the contest; 368 prisoners, including 1colonel, 1 lieutenant-colonel, and a dozen other officers of lesser rank, were sent to the rear; 50 of their dead lay upon the field, and large numbers of their wounded; 30 of this gallant regiment were killed, over 100 were wounded, but not one was taken a prisoner, and none were missing.

It was now nearly dark. A portion of the enemy appeared to have occupied the summit of the rocky hill to the left. The men of this brave regiment, exhausted by their labours, had thrown themselves upon the ground, and many of them sunk at once in sleep. Colonel Rice, now in command of the brigade, directed Colonel Chamberlain to drive the enemy from this height. The order was at once given. Roused again to action, and advancing with fixed bayonets and without firing, lest the smallness of their numbers might be suspected, they rushed up the hill.

Twenty-five more prisoners, including some staff officers, were added to the number previously taken, with a loss to the regiment of 1 officer mortally wounded and 1 man taken prisoner by the enemy. It was ascertained that these troops occupying the hill had been sent from Hood's division, which was then massed a few hundred yards distant, and that their object was to reconnoitre the position, as a preliminary to taking possession of the height.

In addition to the prisoners above mentioned as taken by this regiment, 300 stand of arms were also captured by them. It is due to this regiment and to its commander that their service should be thus recorded in some detail.

Upon receiving a reinforcement of five regiments of the Third division, under command of Colonel Fisher, Colonel Rice detached two of them to the aid of Colonel Chamberlain, in order to maintain the position, he had gained, and he was thus enabled to hold it, and the enemy, having been repelled upon every point of his attack and night coming on, withdrew from the conflict.

Colonel Rice directed the Forty-Fourth New York and the Eighty-Third Pennsylvania to move to the front and gather up the wounded, who, including those of the enemy who had been left upon the field, were carefully brought in. The total results of the service of this brigade are stated by Colonel Rice to be 500 prisoners captured, including 2 colonels and 15 other commissioned officers, and 1,000 stand of arms. The brigade numbered about 1,000 men.

The following day was principally occupied in burying the dead. The Third brigade was relieved by the First brigade, and held the position occupied by it.

It would be a grateful task to relate in detail the services of many who deserve a more particular mention, but the limits of this report will not permit. No one failed in his duty.

A tribute is due to the memory of Colonel Vincent, who fell, mortally wounded, early in the engagement. He lingered a few days after the engagement. His promotion as a brigadier-general was sent to him at once as an appreciation of his services by the government, but it reached him too late for his own recognition. He expired soon after its receipt.

A special mention should also be made of Colonel Jeffords, of the Fourth Michigan Volunteers, who sealed his devotion to his country with his blood while contending hand-to-hand with overpowering numbers, in endeavouring to rescue the colours of his regiment from the hands of the enemy.

To Colonels Tilton, Sweitzer, and Rice, the commanders of brigades, great credit is due for the successful and skilful management of their commands under the very trying circumstances in which they were placed. Colonel Chamberlain, of the Twentieth Maine Volunteers, whose service I have endeavoured briefly to describe, deserves especial mention.

To the officers of my staff I am indebted for efficient and prompt attention to their arduous duties, namely: Captain (Catharinus B.) Mervine, assistant adjutant-general; Lieuts. (Charles H.) Ross and (T. Corwin) Case, *aides*; Captain (George M.) Barnard, assistant inspector-general of the division, and Dr. (Charles) Shippen, the medical director of the division.

The command remained in the same position the two following days.

Being disabled for further actual command of the division, the opportune arrival of General Griffin enabled me to relinquish it to him, and the division moved toward Middletown, where it arrived on July 8.

A tabular and a nominal return of casualties have been duly forwarded. The total strength of the division upon entering the engagement was, in the three brigades, 2664, and the aggregate of killed, wounded, and missing 897.

Report of Col. William S. Tilton, Twenty-second Massachusetts, commanding First Brigade.

Hdqrs. First Brig., First Div., Fifth Army Corps,
Middletown, Md., July 9, 1863.

I have the honour to report the part taken by this brigade in the battles of the 2nd and 3rd instant.

At 4:30 p.m., on July 2, the brigade under my command advanced to the front, and was placed, by order of General Barnes, in order of battle in a piece of woods at the south of Mr. Rose's house. The Second brigade was on our left, but there being no infantry upon our right I made a crotchet by refusing the right wing of my right battalion (One Hundred and Eighteenth Pennsylvania Volunteers, Colonel Gwyn).

No sooner was the line formed than the foe attacked our front. The onslaught was terrible and my losses heavy, so much so that I was somewhat doubtful if our line could withstand it. This fact I communicated to the general commanding division, who ordered me to fall back in good order if unable to hold the position; but my men behaved nobly, and twice repulsed the assailants. My colonels wished to advance. Being anxious about my right, however, I reconnoitred in person, and discovered the enemy in large force coming from the direction of Rose's house, with the evident design of outflanking me. I immediately retired and took up a new position (in two lines) at the left and rear of a battery which had been posted about three hundred yards to my right and rear.

The battery soon commenced to retreat, firing, followed by the rebels, who were now again upon my right flank. To avoid this flank movement, I retired, firing, a short distance in the timber, and then moved across an open field, took up a new position upon the right of the Second division, and reported to General Sykes. In this last movement, I was greatly embarrassed by squads of men and parts of regiments who, hurrying from the front, broke into and through my line. I think, however, that I saved my brigade from great disaster after it could no longer do any good in front, and succeeded in forming a new line, which was retained through the night.

All of my officers and men did their duty, their whole duty, and showed the greatest coolness and courage, and where all did so well it were invidious to mention names.

On the 3rd we relieved the Third brigade, on duty, holding the rocky hill upon the extreme left.

On the 4th I advanced the brigade to the edge of the woods in our front, and sent out a strong line of skirmishers to feel the enemy. The report of this reconnaissance has been made by order directly to Major-General Sykes.

My loss on the 2nd instant was 12 killed, 80 wounded, and 17 missing; total, 109.

Owing to forced marches we had remaining on the 2nd only 474 men, and as part of these were not actually engaged, it will be seen that the percentage of loss is very great.

Report of Col. Jacob B. Sweitzer, Sixty-second Pennsylvania, commanding Second Brigade.

Headquarters Second Brigade,
Camp Near Warrenton, Va., July 31, 1863.

In obedience to orders I respectfully submit the following report of the operations of this brigade during the recent Battle of Gettysburg:

After a hard march on the day previous, July 1, from Unionville,

Md., by way of Hanover, the brigade bivouacked after 12 p. m., with the division in the woods by the roadside, 4 or 5 miles distant from the battlefield.

Next morning by daylight we were on the march again, the Second brigade leading. Having arrived near what I supposed to be the right of our line, and near a farmhouse and barn, the division was massed, the brigades occupying positions in the order of their numbers from right to left. General Sykes' division being on our left. Here a call was made for a regiment from this brigade for picket duty by General Barnes, and Colonel Guiney, with the Ninth Massachusetts, was directed to report to him for instructions, and did so.

Shortly after this the division changed front to the left, at nearly a right angle with its former position, and formed in line of battalions in close column by division.

We had been in this position but a few moments before we were again moved a considerable distance to the left; then moved by the front across the creek, and massed in an orchard on the hill above the bridge on the Gettysburg turnpike. There we remained until late in the afternoon (the precise time I do not remember), and the command had a few hours quiet and rest.

Meanwhile there had been very little firing along the line, and I came to the conclusion the day would pass without the division being called into action. But soon after cannonading was heard on the left, and we were moved quite a distance farther to the left, and diagonally to the front skirting in our march the woods in rear of or in which our lines were formed. When we moved off from the orchard, the Third brigade, being on the left of the division, moved first, the Second and First brigades following in the inverted order.

The Second brigade was placed in position in a wood fronting an open field, the woods bordering two sides of the field, the side in which we were and also that extending at right angles from our left toward the enemy, and in the last-mentioned wood the First brigade was posted, connecting with our left. Having formed the three regiments of this brigade in line of battle (the Ninth Massachusetts being still absent on picket duty) in their regular order from right to left, and finding this formation threw the Thirty-Second Massachusetts, which was on the left, into an exposed position beyond the woods in low, cleared ground, I directed Colonel Prescott to change his front to the rear, so as to give him the benefit of the elevated ground and the cover of the woods, which movement he executed.

We had not remained long in this position before an attack commenced by the enemy in front of the First brigade and Thirty-Second Massachusetts. As there was no appearance of the enemy in front of the line formed by the Sixty-Second Pennsylvania and Fourth Michigan, I directed them to change front to the left, and form lines in rear 'of the Thirty-Second Massachusetts, to strengthen that position. During the execution of this order the attack continued; the firing was very severe, and we lost many brave officers and men. Here fell Major Lowry, second to none in all the attributes of a soldier and a gentleman.

When the attack commenced, word was sent by General Barnes that when we retired we should fall back under cover of the woods. This order was communicated to Colonel Prescott, whose regiment was then under the hottest fire. Understanding it to be a peremptory order to retire then, he replied, ' I don't want to retire; I am not ready to retire; I can hold this place,' and he made good his assertion. Being informed that he misunderstood the order, which was only intended to inform him how to retire when it became necessary, he was satisfied, and he and his command held their ground manfully.

Some time after that word was sent that the First brigade was retiring, and General Barnes sent me word to fall back also, which I did in perfect good order, the regiments retaining their alignments and halting and firing as they came back. Having arrived at the road leading along the rear of the wheat-field, the brigade was formed in line in the woods in rear of the road, and parallel to it, the right resting at the corner of the woods toward the front. We had not remained here more than, say, fifteen minutes, when a general officer I had never seen before rode up to me, and said his command was driving the enemy in the woods in front of the wheat-field; that he needed the support of a brigade, and desired to know if I would give him mine.

I referred him to General Barnes, and said I would obey his directions with pleasure. He spoke to the general, who was not far off. General Barnes came and stated to me what had been said to him by General Caldwell (this I learned was the officer who had lately spoken to me), and asked me if I would take the brigade in. I told him I would if he wished me to do so. He said he did. The command was then called to attention. General Barnes got out in front of them and made a few patriotic remarks, to which they responded with a cheer, and we started off across the wheat-field in a line parallel to the road, our right flank resting on the woods. We advanced to the stone fence beyond the wheat-field next to the woods, and took position behind it to support, as we supposed, our friends in the woods in front. The Fourth Michigan, being on the right of the brigade, extended beyond the stone fence, and was, consequently, most exposed.

We had scarcely got to this position before I noticed regiments retiring from the woods on our right, which I supposed were relieved by others who had taken their places, and would protect us in that direction. I observed also that there was considerable firing diagonally toward our rear from these woods, which I then thought were shots from our troops aimed over us at the enemy in the woods beyond and falling short. They were, however, much too frequent to be pleasant, and my colour-bearer, Ed. Martin, remarked, 'Colonel, I'll be —— if I don't think we are faced the wrong way; the rebs are up there in the woods behind us, on the right.'

About this time, too, word was brought me from the Fourth Michigan and Sixty-Second Pennsylvania that the enemy was getting into our rear in the woods on the right. I directed these regiments to change front, to face in that direction and meet them, which they did, the firing in the meanwhile being rapid and severe. I at the same time dispatched Lieutenant Seitz, *aide-de-camp*, to communicate to General Barnes our situation. He reached the point where he had last seen General Barnes. He was not there. Lieutenant Seitz found the enemy had reached that point, and he came near falling into their hands himself; his horse was killed, and he made his way back to me on foot; reported that General Barnes was not to be found; that the enemy was in the woods on our right as far back as where we had started from, and along the road in rear of the wheat-field.

"Finding that we were surrounded; that our enemy was under cover, while we were in the open field exposed to their fire, I directed the command to fall back. This was done in order, the command halting and firing as it retired. The Fourth Michigan and Sixty-Second Pennsylvania had become mixed up with the enemy, and many hand-to-hand conflicts occurred. Colonel Jeffords, the gallant commander of the Fourth Michigan, was thrust through with a bayonet in a contest over his colours, and Sergt. William McFairman, Company I, and Private William McCarter, Company A, Sixty-Second Pennsylvania, receive honourable mention by Colonel Hull in his report, for their conduct during this part of the engagement.

Finding as we retired in the direction from which we advanced that the fire of the enemy grew more severe on our right, I took a diagonal direction toward the corner of the wheat-field on our left and rear. We crossed the stone fence on this side of the field, and retired to the rear of the battery on the elevation beyond, where the command was halted.

We had lost heavily in our passage across the field. The Fourth Michigan and Sixty-Second Pennsylvania had been surrounded, and a large proportion of those regiments were missing, either killed, wounded, or prisoners. What remained of the command formed in the rear of the battery and we were shortly afterward joined by the Ninth Massachusetts, which had been absent all day on detached duty.

It is difficult to conceive of a more trying situation than that in which three regiments of this command had lately found themselves, and from which they had just effected their escape; in fact, I have since understood that one of General Barnes' *aides* remarked to him shortly after we had advanced, when it was discovered the enemy was behind us on the flank, that he might bid goodbye to the Second brigade. I was also informed by General Barnes that, learning soon after we had advanced the situation on our right, he had dispatched an orderly to me with the information and a verbal order to withdraw, but the orderly never reached me.

Every officer and man in the command, so far as I am informed, did his whole duty. All stood their ground and fought unflinchingly until they were ordered by me to retire, and in falling back behaved with coolness and deliberation. We lost many of our best officers and men.

I subjoin a field report of the regiments engaged on the morning of July 2, and also a report of the same regiments on July 4. A nominal and tabular report of casualties in the command has already been forwarded.

About dark on the evening of the 2nd the acting assistant adjutant-general of the First brigade came to me and inquired for General Barnes; said he was directed by General Sykes to tell him to have the Second brigade form on the right of the First in the position they then were. As General Barnes was not present, I received the order, and put the Second brigade in the position indicated, where we remained until the evening of the 5th, when the division advanced toward Emmittsburg.

In conclusion, I desire to express my gratification at the conduct of my staff during the engagement; Captain (George) Monteith, acting assistant adjutant-general; Captain (Alvan C) Lamson, acting assistant inspector-general; Captain (John S.) Burdett, acting commissary of subsistence, and Lieutenant (John A. M.) Seitz, acting *aide-de-camp*. They were prompt and fearless in the discharge of their duty. We were all fortunate enough to escape being hit, though a number of horses in the party were shot, two of the orderlies', the bugler's. Lieutenant Seitz's, and my own.

Report of Colonel James C. Rice', Forty-Fourth New York, commanding Third Brigade.

July 31, 1863.

In compliance with orders from division headquarters, I have the honour to report the operations of this brigade during the battle near Gettysburg on the 2nd and 3rd inst.

The brigade, under the command of the late Colonel Vincent, was detached from the division and ordered into position at about 4 p.m. of the 2nd instant, on the extreme left of our line of battle. The Twentieth Maine occupied the extreme left of the brigade line, the Sixteenth Michigan the extreme right, connecting with the Third Division, under General Crawford, while the Eighty-Third Pennsylvania and Forty-Fourth New York occupied the centre. The muskets taken into action by the brigade numbered about one thousand.

The ground occupied by the brigade in line of battle was nearly that of a quarter circle, composed mostly of high rocks and cliffs in the centre and becoming more wooded and less rugged as you approached to the left. The right was thrown forward somewhat to the front of the ledge of rocks, and was much more exposed than other parts of the line. A comparatively smooth ravine extended along the entire front, perhaps 50 yards from our line, while on the left and beyond a high and jagged mountain rises, called Round Top hill. That the disposition of the forces and the nature of the ground may be better understood by the general commanding, I send with this report a diagram of the same.

The brigade had scarcely formed in line of battle and pushed forward its skirmishers when a division of the enemy's forces, under General Hood, made a desperate attack along the entire line of the brigade. He approached in three columns, with no skirmishers in advance. The object of the enemy was evident. If he could gain the vantage ground occupied by this brigade, the left flank of our line must give way, opening to him a vast field for successful operations in the rear of our entire army.

To effect this object the enemy made every effort. Massing two or three brigades of his force, he tried for an hour in vain to break the lines of the Forty-Fourth New York and Eighty-Third Pennsylvania, charging again and again within a few yards of these unflinching troops. At every charge, he was repulsed with terrible slaughter. Despairing of success at this point, he made a desperate attack upon the extreme right of the brigade, forcing back a part of the Sixteenth Michigan. This regiment was broken, and, through some misunderstanding of orders, explained in the official report of the commanding officer, it was thrown into confusion; but being immediately supported by the One Hundred and Fortieth New York Volunteers, the line became again firm and unbroken.

It was at this point of time that Colonel Vincent, commanding the brigade, fell mortally wounded. Of the character of this gallant and accomplished officer I will speak before I close this report.

The enemy again attacked the centre with great vigour, and the extreme left with desperation. Passing one brigade of his forces by the right flank in three columns, he pushed through the ravine toward the left of our brigade, came immediately to a 'front,' and charged upon the Twentieth Maine. Now occurred the most critical time of the action. For above half an hour the struggle was desperate. At length, the enemy pressed so strongly upon the left flank of Colonel Chamberlain's regiment that he wisely determined to change the order of battle, and commanded his left wing to fall back at right angles to his right. He then ordered a charge and repulsed the enemy at every point.

On assuming the command of the brigade during this attack upon the centre and left, I at once passed along the line, and notified the officers and men of my own regiment that I was about to take command of the brigade and that they must hold their position to the last. I did this that no panic might arise. I then notified all the commanders of the regiments in person, and assured them of my determination to hold the line to the last. Colonel Chamberlain and other officers immediately informed me that their commands were out of ammunition. I had at this time neither an *aide* nor an orderly even to bear a message. (See P. S.) The enemy was still pressing heavily upon the line. I immediately pressed into service every officer and man in the rear not engaged in the action, whether known or unknown, and made them pledge their honour that they would deliver in person every order that I should send by them. I sent four of them, one after another, with orders for ammunition. The ammunition came promptly, was distributed at once, and the fight went on.

The enemy was now attempting to take possession of Round Top hill, a commanding position overlooking our left. It was evident no time was to be lost, and I sent at once other officers, whom I pressed into my service, with messages to the general commanding the corps, asking for reinforcements to support the brigade. The messages were promptly delivered, and five regiments were at once sent to my support from the Third division, General Crawford, under command of Colonel Fisher.

Having, with the aid of this officer, properly disposed of three regiments of this force, I ordered Colonel Chamberlain, of the Twentieth Maine, to advance and take possession of the mountain. This order was promptly and gallantly executed by this brave and accomplished officer, who rapidly drove the enemy over the mountain, capturing many prisoners. Colonel Fisher at once ordered two regiments of his command to support Colonel Chamberlain, and the hill remained permanently in our possession.

The forces of the enemy being now repulsed on our left and front, I ordered a detachment from the Forty-Fourth New York Volunteers and the Eighty-Third Pennsylvania to push forward and secure all the fruits of this hard-earned victory.

It was now eight o'clock in the evening, and before nine o'clock we had entire possession of the enemy's ground, had gathered up and brought in all of our own wounded and those of the enemy, and had taken and sent to the rear over five hundred prisoners, including two colonels and fifteen commissioned officers, together with over one thousand stand of arms belonging to the enemy.

The following morning the prisoners of the brigade buried all of our own dead and a large number of those of the enemy. The fearful loss of the enemy during this struggle may be estimated from the fact that over fifty of his dead were counted in front of the Twentieth Maine regiment, and his loss was nearly in that proportion along our entire line.

Although this brigade has been engaged in nearly all of the great battles of the Army of the Potomac, and has always greatly distinguished itself for gallant behavior, yet in none has it fought so desperately or achieved for itself such imperishable honours as in this severe conflict of the 2nd instant.

A nominal and tabular list of the casualties of this brigade has already been forwarded to the major-general commanding, but it is fitting again to mention the names of the brave and faithful officers of the command who fell in this desperate struggle. Of the Forty-Fourth New York Volunteers, Captain L. S. Larrabee and Lieutenants Dunham and Thomas; of the Twentieth Maine, Lieutenant Kendall, and of the Sixteenth Michigan, Lieutenants Browne, Jewett, and Borden were killed.

The brigade was relieved during the forenoon of the 3rd instant by the First brigade, and ordered to the centre of the line, where it remained in reserve the balance of the day, exposed to a severe cannonading, but with no loss, from the security of its position.

The colonel commanding would commend to the favourable notice of the general commanding the following-named officers, for their gallant conduct in battle on the 2nd instant: Colonel Chamberlain and Adjutant Chamberlain, of the Twentieth Maine; Lieutenant-Colonel Connor and Major Knox, of the Forty-Fourth New York Volunteers; Captain Woodward and Adjutant Gifford, of the Eighty-Third Pennsylvania, and Captain Elliott and Adjutant Jacklin, of the Sixteenth Michigan. Especially would I call the attention of the general commanding to the distinguished services rendered by Colonel Chamberlain throughout the entire struggle.

To the loss sustained by this command in the death of Colonel Vincent I can refer in no more appropriate language than that used in the general order announcing it to this brigade, a copy of which I herewith annex.

P. S.—In justice to the officers composing the staff, it gives me satisfaction to state, in explanation of my report, that at the time I took command, Captain (Eugene A.) Nash, inspector-general of the brigade, was, in obedience to orders received from Colonel Vincent, at the front watching the movements of the enemy, to report the same if he should attempt a flank movement; that Captain (John M.) Clark, assistant adjutant-general, in obedience to orders, was absent for ammunition, and that Captain (Amos M.) Judson, by orders, was absent for reinforcements.

During the night, these officers rendered me the greatest service, and I desire to commend each of them to the most favourable notice of the commanding general for their gallant conduct both under Colonel Vincent's command as well as my own.

General Orders No. 5.
Headquarters Third Brigade, First Division, Fifth Corps,
July 12, 1863.

The colonel commanding hereby announces to the brigade the death of Brig-Gen. Strong Vincent. He died near Gettysburg, Pa., July 7, 1863, from the effects of a wound received on the 2nd instant, and within sight of that field which his bravery had so greatly assisted to win. A day hallowed with all the glory of success is thus sombered by the sorrow of our loss. Wreaths of victory give way to chaplets of Mourning, hearts exultant to feelings of grief. A soldier, a scholar, a friend, has fallen. For his country, struggling for its life, he willingly gave his own. Grateful for his services, the State which proudly claims him as her own will give him an honoured grave and a costly monument, but he ever will remain buried in our hearts, and our love for his memory will outlast the stone which shall bear the inscription of his bravery, his virtues, and his patriotism.

While we deplore his death, and remember with sorrow our loss, let us emulate the example of his fidelity and patriotism, feeling that he lives but in vain who lives not for his God and his country."

Report of Col. Joshua L. Chamberlain, Twentieth Maine Infantry.

Field Near Emmittsburg, July 6, 1863.
In compliance with the request of the colonel commanding the brigade, I have the honour to submit a somewhat detailed report of the operations of the Twentieth Regiment Maine Volunteers in the Battle of Gettysburg, on the 2nd and 3rd instant. Having acted as the advance guard, made necessary by the proximity of the enemy's cavalry, on the march of the day before, my command on reaching Hanover, Pa., just before sunset on that day, were much worn, and lost no time in getting ready for an expected bivouac. Rations were scarcely issued, and the men about preparing supper, when rumours that the enemy had been encountered that day near Gettysburg absorbed every other interest, and very soon orders came to march forthwith to Gettysburg.

My men moved out with a promptitude and spirit extraordinary, the cheers and welcome they received on the road adding to their enthusiasm. After an hour or two of sleep by the roadside just before daybreak we reached the heights southeasterly of Gettysburg at about 7 a.m., July 2.

Massed at first with the rest of the division on the right of the road, we were moved several times farther toward the left. Although expecting every moment to be put into action, and held strictly in line of battle, yet the men were able to take some rest and make the most of their rations.

Somewhere near 4 p.m. a sharp cannonade, at some distance to our left and front, was the signal for a sudden and rapid movement of our whole division in the direction of this firing, which grew warmer as we approached. Passing an open field in the hollow ground in which some of our batteries were going into position, our brigade reached the skirt of a piece of woods, in the farther edge of which there was a heavy musketry fire, and when about to go forward into line we received from

Colonel Vincent, commanding the brigade, orders to move to the left at the double-quick, when we took a farm road crossing Plum Run in order to gain a rugged mountain spur called Granite Spur, or Little Round Top.

The enemy's artillery got range of our column as we were climbing the spur, and the crashing of the shells among the rocks and the tree tops made us move lively along the crest. One or two shells burst in our ranks. Passing to the southern slope of Little Round Top, Colonel Vincent indicated to me the ground my regiment was to occupy, informing me that this was the extreme left of our general line, and that a desperate attack was expected in order to turn that position, concluding by telling me I was to 'hold that ground at all hazards.' This was the last word I heard from him.

In order to commence by making my right firm, I formed my regiment on the right into line, giving such direction to the line as should best secure the advantage of the rough, rocky, and stragglingly wooded ground.

The line faced generally toward a more conspicuous eminence southwest of ours, which is known as Sugar Loaf, or Round Top. Between this and my position intervened a smooth and thinly wooded hollow. My line formed, I immediately detached Company B, Captain Morrill commanding, to extend from my left flank across this hollow as a line of skirmishers, with directions to act as occasion might dictate, to prevent a surprise on my exposed flank and rear.

The artillery fire on our position had meanwhile been constant and heavy, but my formation was scarcely complete when the artillery was replaced by a vigorous infantry assault upon the centre of our brigade to my right, but it very soon involved the right of my regiment and gradually extended along my entire front. The action was quite sharp and at close quarters.

In the midst of this an officer from my centre informed me that some important movement of the enemy was going on in his front, beyond that of the line with which we were engaged. Mounting a large rock, I was able to see a considerable body of the enemy moving by the flank in rear of their line engaged, and passing from the direction of the foot of Great Round Top through the valley toward the front of my left. The close engagement not allowing any change of front, I immediately stretched my regiment to the left, by taking intervals by the left flank, and at the same time 'refusing' my left wing, so that it was nearly at right angles with my right, thus occupying about twice the extent of our ordinary front, some of the companies being brought into single rank when the nature of the ground gave sufficient strength or shelter. My officers and men understood my wishes so well that this movement was executed under fire, the right wing keeping up fire, without giving the enemy any occasion to seize or even to suspect their advantage. But we were not a moment too soon; the enemy's flanking column having gained their desired direction, burst upon my left, where they evidently had expected an unguarded flank, with great demonstration.

We opened a brisk fire at close range, which was so sudden and effective that they soon fell back among the rocks and low trees in the valley, only to burst forth again with a shout, and rapidly advanced, firing as they came. They pushed up to within a dozen yards of us before the terrible effectiveness of our fire compelled them to break and take shelter.

They renewed the assault on our whole front, and for an hour the fighting was severe. Squads of the enemy broke through our line in several places, and the fight was literally hand-to-hand. The edge of the fight rolled backward and forward like a wave. The dead and wounded were now in front and then in our rear. Forced from our position, we desperately recovered it, and pushed the enemy down to the foot of the slope. The intervals of the struggle were seized to remove our wounded (and those of the enemy also), to gather ammunition from the cartridge-boxes of disabled friend or foe on the field, and even to secure better muskets than the Enfields, which we found did not stand service well. Rude shelters were thrown up of the loose rocks that covered the ground.

Captain Woodward, commanding the Eighty-Third Pennsylvania Volunteers, on my right, gallantly maintaining his fight, judiciously and with hearty co-operation made his movements conform to my necessities, so that my right was at no time exposed to a flank attack.

The enemy seemed to have gathered all their energies for their final assault. We had gotten our thin line into as good a shape as possible, when a strong force emerged from the scrub wood in the valley, as well as I could judge, in two lines in echelon by the right, and, opening a heavy fire, the first line came on as if they meant to sweep everything before them. We opened on them as well as we could with our scanty ammunition snatched from the field.

It did not seem possible to withstand another shock like this now coming on. Our loss had been severe. One-half of my left wing had fallen and a third of my regiment lay just behind us dead or badly wounded. At this moment, my anxiety was increased by a great roar of musketry in my rear, on the farther or northerly slope of Little Round Top, apparently on the flank of the regular brigade, which was in support of Hazlett's battery on the crest behind us. The bullets from this attack struck into my left rear, and I feared that the enemy might have nearly surrounded the Little Round Top, and only a desperate chance was left for us. My ammunition was soon exhausted. My men were firing their last shot and getting ready to 'club' their muskets.

It was imperative to strike before we were struck by this overwhelming force in a hand-to-hand fight, which we could not probably have withstood or survived. At that crisis, I ordered the bayonet. The word was enough. It ran like fire along the line from man to man, and rose into a shout, with which they sprang forward upon the enemy, now not thirty yards away. The effect was surprising; many of the enemy's first line threw down their arms and surrendered. An officer fired his pistol at my head with one hand while he handed me his sword with the other. Holding fast by our right, and swinging forward our left, we made an extended 'right wheel,' before the enemy's second line broke, and fell back, fighting from tree to tree, many being captured, until we had swept the valley and cleared the front of nearly our entire brigade.

Meantime, Captain Morrill with his skirmishers (sent out from my left flank), with some dozen or fifteen of the U. S. Sharpshooters who had put themselves under his direction, fell upon the enemy as they were breaking, and by his demonstrations, as well as his well-directed fire, added much to the effect of the charge.

Having thus cleared the valley and driven the enemy up the western slope of the Great Round Top, not wishing to press so far out as to hazard the ground I was to hold by leaving it exposed to a sudden rush of the enemy, I succeeded (although with some effort to stop my men, who declared they were 'on the road to Richmond') in getting the regiment into good order and resuming our original position.

Four hundred prisoners, including two field and several line officers, were sent to the rear. These were mainly from the Fifteenth and Forty-Seventh Alabama regiments, with some of the Fourth and Fifth Texas. One hundred and fifty of the enemy were found killed and wounded in our front.

At dusk Colonel Rice informed me of the fall of Colonel Vincent, which had devolved the command of the brigade on him, and that Colonel Fisher had come up with a brigade to our support. These troops were massed in our rear. It was the understanding, as Colonel Rice informed me, that Colonel Fisher's brigade was to advance and seize the western slope of Great Round Top, where the enemy had shortly before been driven. But after considerable delay this intention for some reason was not carried into execution.

We were apprehensive that if the enemy were allowed to strengthen himself in that position he would have a great advantage in renewing the attack on us at daylight or before. Colonel Rice then directed me to make the movement to seize that crest.

It was now 9 p.m. Without waiting to get ammunition, but trusting in part to the very circumstance of not exposing our movement or our small front by firing, and with bayonets fixed, the little handful of 200 men pressed up the mountain side in every extended order, as the steep and jagged surface of the ground compelled. We heard squads of the enemy falling back before us, and, when near the crest, we met a scattering and uncertain fire, which caused us the great loss of the gallant Lieutenant Linscott, who fell, mortally wounded. In the silent advance in the darkness we laid hold of 25 prisoners, among them a staff officer of General (E. M.) Law, commanding the brigade immediately opposed to us during the fight. Reaching the crest, and reconnoitring the ground, I placed the men in a strong position among the rocks, and informed Colonel Rice, requesting also ammunition and some support to our right, which was very near the enemy, their movements and words even being now distinctly heard by us.

Some confusion soon after resulted from the attempt of some regiment of Colonel Fisher's brigade to come to our support. They had found a wood road up the mountain, which brought them on my right flank, and also in proximity to the enemy, massed a little before. Hearing their approach, and thinking a movement from that quarter could only be from the enemy, I made disposition to receive them as such. In the confusion, which attended the attempt to form them in support of my right, the enemy opened a brisk fire, which disconcerted my efforts to form them and disheartened the supports themselves, so that I saw no more of them that night.

Feeling somewhat insecure in this isolated position, I sent in for the Eighty-Third Pennsylvania, which came speedily, followed by the Forty-Fourth New York, and, having seen these well posted, I sent a strong picket to the front, with instructions to report to me every half hour during the night and allowed the rest of my men to sleep on their arms.

At some time about midnight two regiments of Colonel Fisher's brigade came up the mountain beyond my left, and took position near the summit; but as the enemy did not threaten from that direction I made no effort to connect with them.

"We went into the fight with 386, all told—358 guns. Every pioneer and musician who could carry a musket went into the ranks. Even the sick and footsore, who could not keep up in the march, came up as soon as they could find their regiments and took their places in line of battle, while it was battle, indeed. Some prisoners I had under guard under sentence of court-martial, I was obliged to put into the fight, and they bore their part well, for which I shall recommend a commutation of their sentence.

The loss, so far as I can ascertain it, is 136—30 of whom were killed, and among the wounded are many mortally.

Captain Billings, Lieutenant Kendall, and Lieutenant Linscott are officers whose loss we deeply mourn—efficient soldiers and pure and high-minded men.

In such an engagement, there were many incidents of heroism and noble character which should have place even in an official report; but, under present circumstances, I am unable to do justice to them. I will say of that regiment that the resolution, courage, and heroic fortitude which enabled us to withstand so formidable an attack have happily led to so conspicuous a result, that they may safely trust to history to record their merits. About noon on the 3rd of July we were withdrawn, and formed on the right of the brigade, in the front edge of a piece of woods near the left centre of our main line of battle, where we were held in readiness to support our troops, then receiving the severe attack of the afternoon of that day.

On the 4th we made a reconnaissance to the front, to ascertain the movements of the enemy, but finding that they had retired, at least beyond Willoughby's Run, we returned to Little Round Top, where we buried our dead in the place where we had laid them during the fight, marking each grave by a head-board made of ammunition boxes, with each soldier's name cut upon it. We also buried 50 of the enemy's dead in front of our position of July 2. We then looked after our wounded, whom I had taken the responsibility of putting into the houses of citizens in the vicinity of Little Round Top, and on the morning of the 5th took up our march on the Emmittsburg road.

Report of Lieut.-Col. Nerval E. Welch, Sixteenth Michigan Infantry.

Near Emmittsburg, Md., July 6, 1863.
In reply to circular of this date from brigade headquarters as to the part this regiment sustained in the action of July 2 and 3, I have the honour to report:

The regiment, under my command, lay with the Third brigade. First division. Fifth corps, closed in mass, near and in rear of Gettysburg, to the left of the main road, during most of the day. The brigade was commanded by Col. Strong Vincent, Eighty-Third Regiment, Pennsylvania Volunteers.

About 4 p.m. we moved rapidly to the extreme left of our line of battle, and went into position on the left of the brigade, at that time circling the crest of a high, rocky hill. After deploying two of my largest companies as skirmishers—Brady's Sharpshooters from the left and Company A from the right—I was ordered at double-quick to the right of the brigade, and to take my position on the right of the Forty-Fourth New York. Before this could be accomplished, however, we were under a heavy fire of the enemy's infantry. We succeeded, however, in securing our places after some loss.

We remained in this position nearly half an hour, when someone (supposed to be General Weed or Major-General Sykes) called from the extreme crest of the hill to fall back nearer the top, where a much less exposed line could be taken up. This order was not obeyed, except by single individuals. From some misconstruction of orders, and entirely unwarrantable assumption of authority, Lieutenant Kydd ordered the colours back. None left with them, however, but three of the colour-guard. They followed the brigade colours to where Colonel Vincent, after being wounded, had been carried, where they remained all night, joining the regiment in the morning with 45 men who had left the field during and after the fight. All the remainder of the regiment retained their position until relieved.

The two companies sent out as skirmishers numbered about 50. The number of muskets taken in line was about 150; the number killed and wounded 59—21 killed. Several wounded have since died.

On the 3rd we took up a new line farther to the right, at the left of the brigade, and remained on our arms for twenty-four hours.

Captain Elliott and Adjutant Jacklin behaved with their usual gallantry. Captain Partridge, Lieutenants Borgman (wounded), Woodruff, Forsyth, Cameron (wounded, with arm amputated), Swart, Graham, Salter, and Captain Chandler behaved nobly and handled their men with coolness and valour. Lieutenants Browne, Company E, Jewett, Company K, and Borden, Company F, died bravely defending the flag they had sworn to support and that they loved in their hearts, and emulating the bravest. I had no truer or purer officers, and their loss cannot be replaced.

Report of Lieut.-Col. Freeman Connor, Forty-Fourth New York Infantry.

July 6, 1863.

I have the honour to submit the following report of the action taken by this regiment in the engagement of July 2:

About 4 p. m. our regiment. Col. J. C. Rice commanding, was placed in position on Round Top Hill, with the Eighty-Third Pennsylvania on our left and the Sixteenth Michigan on our right. Company B was immediately thrown out as skirmishers.

When they had advanced about 200 yards they met the enemy advancing in three lines of battle.

Orders were immediately given by Capt. L. S. Larrabee, commanding the company, to fall back upon the battalion. It was while executing this order that that faithful and brave officer was shot through the body and instantly killed, being the first officer that this regiment had ever had killed in battle.

The enemy continued to advance until the first line came within about 40 yards of our line. Upon their first appearance, we opened a heavy fire upon them, which was continued until they were compelled to retreat. After they had disappeared in our immediate front we turned our fire upon those who had advanced in the hollow to our right, and continued it until we were out of ammunition.

After we had been engaged about one hour Colonel Vincent, commanding brigade, was wounded, and the command fell upon Col. J. C. Rice, and the command of the regiment upon myself.

We remained in our position until the next morning about 8 a.m., when we were relieved by Colonel Hayes, Eighteenth Massachusetts. We were then moved to the right about three-eighths of a mile, and formed in line of battle, the Sixteenth Michigan on our left and the Twentieth Maine on our right.

I regret to add that in addition to Captain Larrabee, whose death I have already noted, the officers are called upon to mourn the loss of First Lieutenant Eugene L. Dunham, Company D, a brave and efficient officer, who was instantly killed during the heavy firing from the enemy in our front; Capt. William R. Bourne, Company K; Capt. Bennett Munger, Company C; Adjt. George B. Herendeen; First Lieut. Charles H. Zeilman, commanding Company F, and Second Lieut. Benjamin N. Thomas, Company K, were wounded, the latter, it is feared, mortally.

It affords me great pleasure to be able to state that both officers and men behaved with the greatest coolness and bravery, not a single case of cowardice having come to my ear.

Report of Capt. Orpheus S. Woodward, Eighty-Third Pennsylvania Infantry.

Near Emmittsburg, Md., July 6, 1863.

In compliance with orders from headquarters Third brigade,

First division, Fifth corps, I have the honour to report the following as the operations of my command during the battle of the 2nd, 3rd, 4th, and 5th instant.

On the morning of the 2nd instant, moved to the front. At about 2:30 p. m. was ordered into position on our extreme left, the Forty-Fourth New York on my right, the Twentieth Maine on my left. At 3:15 p.m. the enemy advanced and engaged my skirmishers, pressing on in force, with bayonets fixed. They soon drove in my skirmishers and engaged my regiment, posted behind rocks and stones hastily thrown up for defence. The contest continued lively until nearly 6 p. m., when the enemy fell back. I instantly threw forward a strong line of skirmishers, who captured between 50 and 60 prisoners and 200 stand of arms.

My men and officers acted splendidly. Where all did so well, I cannot discriminate.

My loss amounted to 10 killed and 45 wounded.

At 1:30 a. m. on the 3rd moved to the support of the Twentieth Maine, which had succeeded in taking a high hill a little to the left of my former position. Remained here until 10 a. m., when, being relieved by a regiment of the Pennsylvania Reserves, rejoined my brigade, massed in the woods just at the right of General Sykes' headquarters. Here I remained until 12 m., the 4th, when the brigade was thrown forward on a reconnaissance. We moved out and occupied the position occupied by the enemy the previous day; threw forward skirmishers, but found no opposing force within two miles. I deem it but proper to state that but for the prompt and skilful disposition made by Colonel Vincent of the troops under his command (the Third brigade), the enemy would have succeeded in turning our left.

I regret to state that Colonel Vincent was severely wounded. My command (his regiment) esteemed him highly as a gentleman, scholar, and soldier, and bitterly avenged his injury."

Report of Brig.-Gen. Romeyn B. Ayers, U. S. Army, commanding Second Division.

> Hdqrs. Second Division, Fifth Army Corps,
> July 28, 1863.

I have the honour to submit a report of the operations of this division in the Battle of Gettysburg, Pa.

The division was marched forward on the night of July 1 and 2 on the Gettysburg and Hanover road, and was formed in line of battle in rear of and facing that road, the First division on its right. Later in the day it was marched to the left and centre, and massed there. In the afternoon, the enemy's attack on the left of our position being developed, the division, preceded by the First division, was marched to the support of our troops engaged, the Third brigade being placed in position on the general line of battle upon a rocky hill (usually called Round Top Hill) of great importance, facing the Emmittsburg and Gettysburg pike. This brigade was ordered to hold this hill, which duty it performed well and effectually.

******

(Note:—The succeeding paragraphs relating to the action of the First and Second brigades, and the commendation of staff and other officers, are omitted).

******

In the death of Brig. Gen. Stephen H. Weed, volunteers, and captain Fifth U. S. Artillery, the service lost a distinguished and gallant soldier. Col. P. H. O'Rorke, One Hundred and Fortieth New York Volunteers and First Lieutenant U. S. Engineers, was a brave and valuable officer.

I enclose reports of brigade commanders. The list of casualties is now in your hands.

Report of Col. Kenner Garrard, One Hundred and Forty-sixth New York Infantry, commanding Third Brigade.

Hdqrs. Third Brigade, Second Division, Fifth Army Corps,
Camp near Berlin, Md., July 16, 1863.

I have the honour to make the following report of the part taken by the Third brigade in the late battle near Gettysburg:

On the 2nd instant, after changing position several times in the early part of the morning, the brigade with the division remained idle, lying by their arms until about 4 p. m. At this time the brigade was moved rapidly forward (most of the time at the double-quick) nearly 1½ miles, when it came under the fire of the enemy's musketry.

At this point the leading regiment, under the direction of General Warren, chief engineer Army of the Potomac, was led to the left, up on what is known as Round Top ridge. Hazlett's battery ascended the ridge immediately in rear of this regiment (the One Hundred and Fortieth New York Volunteers, Col. P. H. O'Rorke commanding), and went into battery on the summit. The One Hundred and Fortieth was formed in line and was immediately closely engaged with the enemy at short musket-range on the left slope of the ridge.

A portion of the First division. Fifth Army corps, was engaged to the left of the ridge, and this regiment and Hazlett's battery were brought up to assist the First division in repelling a heavy assault of the enemy, with the evident design of gaining this ridge. Colonel O'Rorke was mortally wounded at the head of his regiment while leading it into action.

The other regiments. One Hundred and Forty-sixth New York Volunteers and the Ninety-first and the One Hundred and Fifty-fifth Pennsylvania Volunteers, were led to the right and front some distance, and formed in line in a narrow valley to support a portion of the Third corps and Watson's battery, then severely pressed by the enemy. Before becoming engaged, however, orders were received for these regiments to return at double-quick to Round Top Ridge, and secure and hold that position. The Ninety-First was posted on the left of the battery, connecting with the One Hundred and Fortieth. The One Hundred and Forty-sixth and One Hundred and Fifty-Fifth were posted on the right, extending from the battery on the summit, along the crest of the ridge, to the gorge on the right. As soon as the regiments had their positions, men from each regiment were advanced down the slope to the front, in among the rocks, and, together with those in line on the crest, actively engaged the enemy during the rest of that day. At night this ridge, naturally strong, was strengthened by building a stone wall about halfway down the slope, wherever the rocks offered no protection to the men.

The next day the brigade remained in the same position, and, though under the shells of the enemy and exposed to their sharpshooters, it was not engaged to any extent.

When the brigade and Hazlett's battery seized this ridge, it was done under a heavy musketry fire, and was entirely unoccupied, excepting by a part of the First division, on the extreme left, and I am gratified to report to the general commanding the division that the order to secure and hold this ridge was faithfully executed. At no time during July 2, 3, and 4, after its position was assigned it, did any regiment of the brigade leave its place, excepting at the time of heavy assault a portion of some of the regiments advanced to the front down the slope of the ridge, in order to have a better fire at the enemy.

A few moments after General Weed, the brigade commander, had placed his command in position on this ridge, he was mortally wounded, on the summit, near the battery. Lieutenant Hazlett, commanding the battery, while offering his assistance to General Weed, fell, mortally wounded.

I am pleased to report that all the regiments performed their duty well, and that during the two days' battle the officers and men conducted themselves in the most praiseworthy manner.

A report of the casualties has already been furnished.

Report of Brig. Gen. Samuel W. Crawford, U, S. Army, commanding Third Division.

Hdqrs. Pa. Reserves, Third Div., Fifth Corps.,
July 10, 1863.

I have the honour to submit the following report of the operations of this division in the recent Battle near Gettysburg, Pa.:

At daylight on the 2nd instant, while resting my command near McSherrystown, having marched nearly all the previous night, I received an order from the major-general commanding the corps to march immediately toward Gettysburg. The column was put in motion at once, and by noon had arrived at the position occupied by the First and Second divisions of the corps, near the Gettysburg and Hanover turnpike.

At 2 o'clock an order reached me to form my command at once and proceed toward the left flank of our line, when my position would be indicated by a staff officer. The First division of the corps, which I had been directed to follow, had taken a different road from that indicated to me. Under the guidance, however, of Captain Moore, an *aide* of the general commanding the army, who had come from the field for fresh troops, I pushed rapidly forward, and arrived in a short time upon the field, and reported to Major-General Sykes. I received orders at once to mass my troops upon the right of a road running through our line, near our left flank, and which, descending a rocky slope, crossed a low marshy ground in front to a wheat-field lying between two thick belts of woods beyond.

The position occupied by our troops on the left was naturally a strong one. A rocky ridge, wooded at the top, extended along the left of our position, ending in a high hill, called the Round Top, whose sides covered with timber terminated abruptly in the plain below, while the entire ridge sloped toward a small stream that traversed the marshy ground in front. Beyond this lay two thick masses of timber, separated by a large wheat-field, and skirting this timber a low stone wall ran from right to left. The movement indicated had not been completed when I received a subsequent order to cross the road to the slope of the rocky ridge opposite the woods, and to cover the troops then engaged in front, should it become necessary for them to fall back. In carrying out this order I received instructions to detach one brigade of my command, to go to the left of Barnes' division, on the crest of the ridge. The Third brigade, under Col. J. W. Fisher, was detailed, and moved at once. The firing in front was heavy and incessant. The enemy, concentrating his forces opposite the left of our line, was throwing them in heavy masses upon our troops, and was steadily advancing.

Our troops in front, after a determined resistance, unable to withstand the force of the enemy, fell back, and some finally gave way. The plain to my front was covered with fugitives from all divisions, who rushed through my lines and along the road to the rear. Fragments of regiments came back in disorder, and without their arms, and for a moment all seemed lost. The enemy's skirmishers had reached the foot of the rocky ridge; his columns were following rapidly.

My command was formed in two lines, the second massed on the first. The Sixth regiment, Lieutenant-Colonel Ent, on the right, the First regiment. Colonel Talley, on the left, and the Eleventh regiment, of Fisher's brigade, under Colonel Jackson, in the centre. The second line consisted of the First Rifles (Bucktails), Colonel Taylor, and the Second regiment, Lieutenant-Colonel Woodward. Colonel McCandless, the brigade commander, commanded the whole.

Not a moment was to be lost. Uncovering our front, I ordered an immediate advance. The command advanced gallantly with loud cheers. Two well-directed volleys were delivered upon the advancing masses of the enemy, when the whole column charged at a run down the slope, driving the enemy back across the space beyond and across the stone wall, for the possession of which there was a short but determined struggle. The enemy retired to the wheat-field and the woods.

The second line was immediately deployed to the left, the First Rifles (Bucktails), under their gallant leader, Colonel Taylor, gaining the flank and dashing upon the enemy, who, endeavouring for a moment to make a stand, finally broke and fled in disorder across the field, leaving his dead and wounded in our hands. As night was approaching and my flanks were unprotected, I directed Colonel McCandless to hold the line of the stone wall and the woods on the right. Heavy lines of skirmishers were thrown out, and the ground firmly and permanently held. I then rode to the left, toward Fisher's brigade. Upon ascending the crest of the ridge I found, from the report of that officer, as well as from Colonel Rice, of Barnes' division, that the Round Top was still in possession of the enemy's skirmishers, who were firing upon our men.

It was important to hold this hill, as from its position it commanded that part of our line. I directed Colonel Fisher to occupy it at once. He immediately detached the Twelfth regiment, under Colonel Hardin, the Fifth, under Lieutenant-Colonel Dare, and the Twentieth Maine regiment, under Colonel Chamberlain, who advanced promptly, driving the enemy before them, capturing over 30 prisoners.

During the night, the division commanded by Brigadier-General Bartlett, of the Sixth corps, was moved up to my support. At five o'clock on the 3rd I received orders from General Sykes, commanding the corps, to advance that portion of my command which was holding the ground retaken on the left, and which still held the line of the stone wall in front, to enter the woods, and, if possible, drive out the enemy. It was supposed that the enemy had evacuated the position.

I proceeded at once to the spot, and directed the movement to be made. McCandless' brigade, with the Eleventh regiment, under Colonel Jackson, was ordered to advance, throwing out skirmishers toward the right in the direction of a battery established by the enemy at noon, and which was plainly visible. I requested Brigadier-General Bartlett to move up one of his regiments to the stone wall from which I advanced, and also to throw a force toward my right, to protect that flank. The men of his command moved promptly into position, and rendered efficient service. The movement had hardly begun before this battery opened with grape and canister. The woods on the right were soon cleared; as soon as the skirmishers approached the battery it ceased firing and fled.

The line was then formed, and, under the immediate direction of Colonel McCandless, dashed across the wheat-field and into the upper end of the woods. The enemy's skirmishers were driven back as he advanced, and the upper end of the woods was now cleared. The command then changed front to rear, and charged through the entire length of woods. One brigade of the enemy, commanded by Brigadier-General (George T.) Anderson and composed of Georgia troops, was encountered. It had taken position behind a stone wall running through the woods, and which they had made stronger by rails and logs. We fell upon their flank, completely routing them, taking over 200 prisoners, one stand of colours belonging to the Fifteenth Georgia, and many arms. The colours were taken by Sergt. John B. Thompson, Company G, First Rifles. Another brigade, under General Robertson, and composed of Texas troops, which lay concealed beyond the woods and near the foot of the ridge, ran, as reported by the prisoners, without firing a shot.

The enemy's force at this point (his extreme right) consisted of the division of Major-General Hood, and was composed of three brigades, under the rebel Generals Anderson, (J. B.) Robertson, and (H. L.) Benning. They very greatly outnumbered us, but the rapidity of the movement and the gallant dash of my men completely surprised and routed them. They fell back nearly a mile to a second ridge, and entrenched themselves. By this charge of McCandless' brigade and the Eleventh regiment. Colonel Jackson, the whole of the ground lost the previous day was retaken, together with all of our wounded, who, mingled with those of the rebels, were lying uncared for.

The dead of both sides lay in lines in every direction, and the large number of our own men showed how fierce had been the struggle and how faithfully and how persistently they had contested for the field against the superior masses of the enemy. The result of this movement was the recovery of all the ground lost by our troops, one 12-pounder Napoleon gun and three caissons, and upward of 7000 stand of arms. Large piles of these arms were found on brush heaps ready to be burned.

Our wounded were at once cared for, and, under the able and prompt management of Surg. L. W. Read, surgeon-in-chief of this division, who came promptly upon the field, they were moved to hospitals in the rear and carefully provided for.

On the 4th the large number of arms were collected, under the immediate direction of Lieutenant Harding, the ordnance officer of the division, and the brigade, which had been on incessant duty for forty-eight hours, under an annoying picket fire for a great period of the time, was withdrawn to the rear.

My list in killed and wounded was 20 officers and 190 men, 3 only missing.

The nominal and tabular list is enclosed.

Col. Charles Fred. Taylor, the gallant and brave leader of the Bucktail Regiment, fell while leading his regiment to the charge. No braver soldier and patriot has given his life to the cause.

The gallant men of this division fought upon their own soil, some of them at their very homes; and there was not an officer or private soldier who did not realise that the very contingency to meet which the division was formed had now arisen. The result is evinced in the gallantry displayed by those who were fortunate enough to enter the field when our left was overpowered and the enemy was boldly advancing upon the key of our position.

Great credit is due to Col. William McCandless, commanding the First brigade, for his management of his brigade and the prompt and faithful execution of the order given to him in the face of a galling fire on the 2nd, and for the rapid and successful dash upon the enemy on the 3rd; and I recommended him especially to the notice of the major-general commanding the corps. To Colonel Fisher, commanding the Third brigade, great credit is also due in early realising the importance of the occupation of the Round Top and in promptly and successfully occupying it. The enemy would undoubtedly have occupied it during the night.

The prompt and efficient support given to me by Brigadier-General Bartlett, commanding division. Sixth corps, I desire here to acknowledge.

The officers of my staff accompanied me throughout the action. Captain (Louis) Livingston, my senior *aide*; Captain (Richard T.) Auchmuty, assistant adjutant-general; Major (James P.) Speer, inspector-general, and Lieutenant (Richard P.) Henderson, *aide-de-camp*, accompanied the command on the charge and were among the foremost.

Captain Livingston and Lieutenant Henderson are deserving of especial commendation for the prompt and fearless conveyance of orders intrusted to them on the 3rd, under the immediate fire of the enemy's battery.

Lieutenant (William) Harding, the ordnance officer, managed his department with great credit, and promptly moved from the field a large proportion of the small-arms secured. His report has already been submitted.

Report of Col. Joseph W. Fisher, Fifth Pennsylvania Reserves, Commanding Third Brigade.

Hdqrs. Third Brigade, Pennsylvania Reserve Corps,
July 9, 1863.

I have the honour to report that at the recent battle of Gettysburg I marched my brigade to the left of General Sykes' corps, being the extreme left of the Army of the Potomac, and at once engaged the enemy, although very shortly afterward he retired, leaving large numbers of his killed and wounded on the field.

Soon after the close of the fight of the 2nd I discovered in my immediate front a hill called Round Top, from the summit of which the enemy was doing us great damage. I thought it highly important that we should at once occupy it. I accordingly took two regiments of my brigade, *viz.*, the Fifth, Lieutenant-Colonel Dare, and the Twelfth, Colonel Hardin, and. the Twentieth Maine, commanded by Colonel Chamberlain, and at 10 p. m. ascended the hill, which was occupied by a full brigade of the enemy. We went up steadily in line of battle, taking over 30 prisoners in our ascent.

In the morning, I discovered that the hill was of immense importance to us, inasmuch as that, if we had not taken it, the enemy most undoubtedly would have done so, and in that event our left would have suffered very much, if, indeed, it could have held its position at all. I also discovered that our troops were not well posted for defence, so I changed my position, throwing the left flank of the two regiments which had not gone up the hill around so as to completely cover the ravine between the two hills, and at once threw up a stone wall across the entire ravine and up the hill, thus giving my men a sure protection against any advance which could possibly have been made by the enemy.

My officers and men behaved throughout with great coolness and bravery. Among others equally worthy of and deserving special mention, I beg leave to call your attention to the conduct of Colonel Hardin, of the Twelfth regiment, who, still suffering from wounds received at Bull Run, went gallantly up the mountain, leading his regiment to where hot work was expected; Lieutenant-Colonel Dare, of the Fifth regiment, who was also wounded at Fredericksburg, led his regiment up the hill, over rocks and ravines; Colonel Warner, of the Tenth regiment, who is still so lame from wounds received at Antietam as to be unable to walk without support, went into the engagement against my wishes, and behaved with great coolness and courage; Lieutenant-Colonel Snodgrass, of the Ninth, evinced all the elements of a soldier in his calm and dignified demeanour, while all the subordinate field officers are deserving of special mention, especially Maj. James H. Larrimer, of the Fifth regiment, who, suffering from acute rheumatism, refused to remain out of the battle, although, in my judgment, unfit for duty.

The members of my staff. Lieutenant (John L.) Wright, acting assistant adjutant-general; Captain (Hart ley) Howard, brigade inspector; Lieutenants (Charles K.) Chamberlain and (William H. H.) Kerns, *aides*, all rendered me efficient support. Sergt. Thomas M. Fisher, acting as one of my orderlies, deserves special mention as exhibiting most remarkable coolness and bravery.

My brigade captured and turned in to the proper officer over 1000 stand of arms, brought off over 200 wounded rebels, and buried 80 of their dead. Taking it all in all, I have no hesitation in saying that my brigade fulfilled their mission to Gettysburg.

Report of Maj. Homer R. Stoughton, Second U. S. Sharpshooters, Third Army Corps.

(*Rebellion Records*, Vol. xxvii, part i.)

Hdqrs. Second Regiment U. S. Sharpshooters,
July 27, 1863.

I have the honour to report the operations of the Second U. S.

Sharpshooters at Gettysburg, Pa., as follows:

On the morning of July 2 I was placed in line on the extreme left of the Third corps, remaining there for nearly one hour, when the colonel commanding instructed me to place my command in a position to cover a ravine near Sugar Loaf hill, which I did by putting Company H on the brow of the hill, with vedettes overlooking the ravine, and Company D in the ravine near the woods, to watch the enemy's movements in that direction. Companies A, E, G, and C formed a line perpendicular to the cross-road that intersects with the Emmittsburg pike. Companies B and F I held in reserve.

I remained in this position until about 2 p. m., when General Ward directed that I should deploy my regiment across the ravine and through the woods on the right, and advance. I moved forward to a brook some 200 yards beyond a second cross-road running perpendicular to the Emmittsburg pike, and intersecting with it in front of Sugar Loaf hill. I sent forward scouts to reconnoitre the ground. I then rode out perhaps the distance of half a mile, and discovered the enemy's skirmishers advancing on my right, which, being unsupported by any connection with skirmishers on my right, I was compelled to withdraw to protect my flank. In this position, we had but little time to wait. The enemy's skirmishers advanced to the top of the hill in our front, and immediately after they placed a battery directly in our front, and, being too far for our range, I sent forward a few men under cover of woods on the left, and silenced one piece nearest us.

The enemy then advanced a line of battle covering our entire front and flank. While they were advancing, the Second regiment did splendid execution, killing and wounding a great many. One regiment broke three times, and rallied, before it would advance. I held my position until their line of battle was within 100 yards of me and their skirmishers were pushing my right flank, when I ordered my men to fall back, firing as they retired. My left wing retreated up the hill and allowed the enemy to pass up the ravine, when they poured a destructive fire into his flank and rear.

Here Adjutant Norton, with about a dozen men, captured and sent to the rear 22 prisoners. Special mention should be made of this officer for his coolness and bravery during this day's engagement.

The right wing fell back gradually until they mingled with the regiments composing the Second brigade, and remained till night, when the brigade was relieved.

In this day's action were wounded Capts. E. T. Rowell, (acting major), J. McClure, and A. Buxton. Our loss was 28 killed, wounded, and missing. Among the missing was Lieut. D. B. Petti John, Company A.

On the 3rd instant the Second regiment was not engaged, with the exception of about a dozen volunteers, who went out to the front of the breastworks of the First Army corps, to silence one of the enemy's guns, which was accomplished, losing 1 killed and 1 wounded.

On the 4th instant I was ordered to move forward to the Emmittsburg pike, a few hundred yards to the left of the cemetery, and to deploy four companies to skirmish through the field to the woods in front. The enemy was driven back to his earthworks, about 150 or 200 yards from his first position. We held this position through the day, under a sharp fire from his sharpshooters.

The regiment sustained a loss this day of 3 killed and 8 wounded. Among the wounded was Lieutenant Law, Company E.

At 7:30 p.m. I was relieved by a New Jersey regiment, of the Sixth corps, and rejoined the brigade.

The reader will find in these reports, as well as in those of the Confederate officers, some omissions, discrepancies, and contradictory statements; but they are exact copies of the original documents published by authority of the War Department as the official records of the War of the Rebellion. In my comments, I shall assume that in general they present the facts according to the best knowledge and belief of the officers who made the reports at the time they were made, except in a few cases where I have good reason to believe that they contain deliberate misstatements made with the purpose of concealing misconduct or of unduly magnifying the importance of the service of the organisation under the command of the officer who makes the report. In justice to the truth of history, I think such misstatements should be exposed.

Sykes' Report of the Fifth Army Corps

General Sykes had been a soldier all his life since his boyhood.

He entered the Military Academy as a cadet in 1838, was graduated in 1842, and continued in the army until his death, in 1880, passing through all the grades from second lieutenant to major-general of Volunteers and brevet major-general in the Regular Army. He served in the war with Mexico, and was brevetted for gallant and meritorious conduct in the Battle of Cerro Gordo. He was made a brigadier-general of Volunteers September 28, 1861, and major-general of Volunteers November 29, 1862, and placed in command of the Second division of the Fifth Army Corps, which contained the two brigades of the Regular Army. On June 28, 1863, when General Meade, who had been in command of the Fifth Army Corps, was assigned to the command of the Army of the Potomac, Sykes succeeded him in command of the corps.

General Barnes, who commanded the First division of Sykes' corps, was graduated from the Military Academy in 1829 as second lieutenant. Having served in this grade about seven years, he was promoted to be first lieutenant, and within a month resigned and left the army. July 26, 1861, he was commissioned colonel of the Eighteenth Massachusetts, which became part of Porter's division, later the First division of the Fifth corps. The same day that Sykes was made major general of Volunteers, November 29, 1862, Barnes was made brigadier-general of Volunteers and assigned to the command of this brigade.

In the changes, which occurred, General Griffin became commander of this First division. After the battle of Chancellorsville General Griffin was absent temporarily on account of illness, and Barnes as senior brigadier assumed command of the division. He was one of the oldest officers in the army. If he entered the Academy at sixteen years of age, the lowest limit for cadets, he must have been born in 1809, or earlier. Although Sykes speaks kindly of him in his report, it is evident from his statement that he posted Barnes' brigades himself, that he had no great confidence in him as an officer to be trusted, on this day at least, to act on his own responsibility. This is confirmed by the statements of Tilton and Sweitzer, commanders of two brigades of which Barnes had charge during the battle, that when they reached their last position at the close of the action they reported to the corps commander and received orders from him, as Barnes was not present.

Griffin arrived on the field July 3, and relieved Barnes in the command of the division July 4. We hear no more of Barnes during the war, except as commander in charge of a camp of Confederate prisoners. I give these facts as the reason for my opinion that Barnes' statement cannot be received as entitled to full credence.

The reader will note that in Sykes' report there is no confirmation of Barnes' statement that while he and Sykes were together, Warren came to them asking for troops for Little Round Top; that Sykes yielded to his importunity and that he, Barnes, sent Vincent's brigade. The statement so often made that Barnes' division, preceded by Sykes and Barnes, moved out by the road which crosses the ridge at the north foot of Little Round Top and runs to the Emmittsburg road north of the wheat-field and the peach orchard is not correct. My recollection is that Barnes' division moved by the road which runs from the Baltimore Pike to the Taneytown road south of Cemetery hill, then turned south on the Taneytown road until they were in rear of the position which had been occupied by Humphreys' division in the morning, then left the road and marched across the fields to a point a little northeast of the wheat-field, where they halted, and Sykes and Barnes went forward into the woods west of the wheat-field. When Vincent's brigade moved to its position between Round Top and Little Round Top, it came by this road crossing the Plum Run valley just west of the north front of Little Round Top.

I think Sykes is mistaken in the statement that Vincent's and Weed's brigades were posted under the direction of Warren. Sykes had ordered Weed, when he met him before his brigade reached Little Round Top, to take position there. He knew that Warren was there at that time, and evidently supposed that he would take charge of troops sent there. Sykes says that when he returned he saw the greater part of Weed's brigade moving away from the position which he had assigned to it, and sent a staff officer to inquire why he had vacated the position. Learning that Weed's brigade was moving to the front by order of Sickles, he ordered him to return and reoccupy it. He could not reoccupy a position which he had not previously occupied.

All other accounts agree that no part of Weed's brigade except the One Hundred and Fortieth New York had previously been on Little Round Top, and when it finally arrived Warren was not there. When Warren detached the One Hundred and Fortieth New York and sent it to the crest of Little Round Top, he left Lieutenant Roebling, of his staff, to conduct it there and rode away to meet General Meade. He did not return to the hill, did not see Vincent's brigade come up, and had nothing to do with posting it. For confirmation of this statement see Warren's letters to Captain Farley, quoted Ch. 7.

Sykes' statement that Crawford's division moved to the front across the Plum Run Valley is only partly correct. Only two brigades of Crawford's division were present in the battle. One of Crawford's brigades under McCandless, with the Eleventh Pennsylvania Reserves, made this attack under Crawford's personal direction. The remaining four regiments of Fisher's brigade remained in reserve. About dusk Fisher was sent with these four regiments to support Vincent, but they did not arrive in time to take any part in the repulse of the enemy on that part of the field.

BARNES' REPORT FIRST DIVISION

This report was not made until August 24, nearly two months after the battle, and then only in conformity to instructions from headquarters. It is made up in great part by copying from the reports of his brigade commanders. This is excusable, so far as the report of Vincent's brigade is concerned, because it was removed from his personal observation. I wish to treat Barnes fairly. Concerning his statement that he detached Vincent's brigade and sent it to Little Round Top, I give him the benefit of supposing that the officer of Sykes' staff who told Vincent that Sykes had sent him to direct Barnes to send one of his brigades to that hill yonder, pointing to Little Round Top, found Barnes after Vincent had gone, and Barnes sent the order to Vincent. Barnes was not with his division, and did not return to the other two brigades until after Vincent had gone. If he had been with Sykes, as he states, Sykes would not have sent one of his staff with an order for him, but would have given it to him in person. Barnes' statement that Warren came to them, when he and Sykes were together, has no confirmation either from Warren, Sykes, or any other person entitled to know, so far as I have been able to ascertain.

On the contrary, the letter from Lieutenant Mackenzie to General Meade, which I have quoted elsewhere, shows clearly that Warren sent Mackenzie to Sickles and Sykes to ask for troops on Little Round Top. Sickles refused, but Sykes granted his request. This letter is short and formal, and is evidently in reply to an inquiry from General Meade; it should settle that question. I think Warren did not leave the vicinity of the signal station, after he arrived there some time before half past three o'clock, until Ward was driven back from the Devil's Den, when he went down to Weed's brigade, detached O'Rorke's regiment, and then rode away to find General Meade and report. By this time, Vincent's brigade had been fighting for half an hour.

It is evident from Sykes' statement that he posted the brigades of

Tilton and Sweitzer himself, and, from the reports of both these brigade commanders, that Barnes did not give them much assistance, and that when their stubborn fight ended by their occupation of the position which they held during the night, Barnes had disappeared; but Sykes was looking after them; he gave them orders and they reported to him. Where Barnes was at this time is not stated by himself or either of his brigade commanders.

Tilton's First Brigade

This report, as before stated, indicates very little assistance received from Barnes. The only order of Barnes which he mentions is one to fall back in good order if unable to hold the position. When he was flanked by overwhelming numbers he retired in as good order as the circumstances permitted and secured a position on a ridge not far from the Devil's Den, which he held during the night. He reported to General Sykes.

Sweitzer's Second Brigade

This report and that of the First Brigade show splendid fighting by the men and skilful management by the brigade commanders under trying circumstances. I think that nearly every division commander in the Army of the Potomac would have prevented the surprise which overwhelmed these brigades. The reader will note Sweitzer's statement that when his brigade reached its last position Barnes was not present, and he received and obeyed the order which Sykes had sent to Barnes.

Vincent's Third Brigade

This report was made by Colonel James C. Rice, who succeeded to the command when Vincent fell. As I have so fully described elsewhere the part taken by this brigade in the battle, I make no further comment on this report.

Twentieth Maine

Colonel Chamberlain wrote this report July 6, while the events were distinctly remembered. It was carefully prepared by an officer who knew the facts. His commendation of the character of his men is not, in my opinion, stronger than they deserve. His subsequent career in later campaigns, concluding with the surrender at Appomattox, shows his ability and the esteem and regard of his superior officers.

I have accepted his statements in this report as substantially correct. When he succeeded to the command of the brigade the officers and men of this organisation looked upon him as a worthy successor to Butterfield, Vincent, and Rice.

Sixteenth Michigan

It is with the deepest regret that I feel obliged to condemn this report as unworthy of its author and his gallant regiment, which formed a part of the Third brigade from Hall's Hill in front of Washington in the fall of 1861 to the surrender of the Confederate army at Appomattox, April 9, 1865, and on all other occasions I believe it performed its full duty with great credit. The greater part of the regiment fought with its usual valour at Gettysburg. The report is an effort to explain the misconduct of Lieutenant-Colonel Welch and a large portion of three companies on the right of the regiment. It is full of misstatements which were not accepted at the time by the brigade commander nor the commanders of the other regiments. It is not true that when the brigade reached its position the Sixteenth was on the left of the line, and that there two of its companies were thrown out as skirmishers. No skirmishers were thrown out by this regiment.

The Twentieth Maine was the left of the line when the brigade took its position and remained there. The Sixteenth came on the ground between the Forty-Fourth and Eighty-Third; and at Colonel Rice's request that these two regiments might fight side by side, as they had done in all their previous battles, Vincent ordered the Sixteenth to pass the Forty-Fourth, and placed it on the right of the line. The brigade was all in position and ready for the enemy before a shot was fired. There was no loss in the regiment before it reached its place in line. General Weed was not on the top of the high rock in rear of the regiment at any time during the battle; in fact, he did not reach Little Round Top until after the last assault of the enemy was repulsed. I have found no evidence that General Sykes was on that part of the field where Vincent's brigade fought during the battle of July 2.

The fact is that Welch was not in his proper place in rear of his regiment, where a competent officer, encouraging and sustaining his men, might have prevented the break which occurred. Vincent went up there and tried to restore order, but fell before he could do so. It is true that the enemy in great force had reached that part of the line, but the men of the Sixteenth had maintained their ground before, in face of determined assaults, and might have done so at this time if properly commanded; but they were seized with panic and ran for shelter behind the rocks. Colonel Rice in his report commends the commanders of each of the other regiments and some of their subordinate officers, but does not mention Lieutenant-Colonel Welch, commending only Captain Elliott and Adjutant Jacklin of the Sixteenth Michigan. These officers remained with that part of the regiment which held fast.

About dusk, after the fighting there had ceased. Colonel Rice directed me to take my flag, ride to the rear, and try to get some ambulances and stretcher bearers to care for our wounded. I found the whole country to the northeast of Little Round Top filled with field hospital tents, and ambulances coming and going, but all the ambulance officers that I appealed to replied that they were under orders and could not go where I asked without an order from the surgeon in charge. I was unable to find this officer, and continued on down the road running east from Little Round Top until I reached the last field hospital. Returning, I saw Colonel Welch sitting on his horse near the Bushman house, with his regimental colours and near him some forty or fifty of his men. I asked him where the brigade was. He replied that he did not know; that they had been driven from their position and he had followed my brigade flag, thinking they had gone in that direction.

I think Welch and these men had been skulking behind the high rocks and followed my flag when they saw me go down the hill. Welch told me that Colonel Vincent was in that house. This was the Bushman farmhouse, where Vincent had been carried after receiving his fatal wound. Dismounting, I left my horse and flag with one of the men of the Sixteenth. This man told me that he did not believe the brigade had left its position; neither did I. I entered the house, which was full of wounded men. I found Colonel Vincent in a room on the first floor. He was very pale and unable to speak, but he held out his hand to me. When I said to him, "The boys are still there, Colonel," his face lighted up with pleasure and he pressed my hand.

I tried to say a few words expressing my grief, but was too much overcome by the pathetic scene. He died in that house five days later. I hurriedly left the room and the house and returned to my post. I found the brigade there, as I expected. Some ambulances and stretchers had arrived and the surgeons were there. The men were gathering up the wounded men. Union and Confederate, and bringing them to the surgeons near the ambulances. The Confederate prisoners able to walk had been gathered in a squad under guard, and were soon sent to the rear.

Lieutenant-Colonel Welch in later campaigns and battles redeemed his reputation. He was made colonel of the regiment and was killed in one of the minor engagements on the lines south of Petersburg. He was leading a charge on the enemy's entrenchments and received a shot at close range from one of the Confederates, which killed him instantly.

Forty-Fourth New York

In view of the important part taken by the regiment in this battle, Lieutenant-Colonel Conner's report is very modest. One would suppose from reading it that the Confederates made only one attack on the front of this regiment, and that this lasted about an hour. This does not agree with the reports of the Confederate regiments which made this attack; but as a part of these men took shelter behind the large rocks within short range and continued firing, it seemed like a continuous battle. His remark about firing on the enemy in the hollow on the right evidently refers to the attack on the right of the brigade. Until Colonel Vincent fell Colonel Rice was in command of this regiment. He describes the attack in his brigade report. He overestimates the force of the enemy, as two or three brigades, but as prisoners taken were from Robertson's and Law's brigades, he is perhaps excusable. He says the enemy charged again and again within a few yards of these unflinching troops. As Connor, did not take command until the last of the assaults on the Forty-Fourth was repulsed, Colonel Rice's statement, in my opinion, is preferable.

Eighty-Third Pennsylvania

Captain Woodward is mistaken about the time of the engagement. The Fifth corps did not move from its position on the Baltimore Pike until sometime after three o'clock. The Confederate infantry was a mile distant from the Devil's Den when at four o'clock they began their advance against our line. The attack on Vincent's brigade must have commenced at some time between 4:30 and 5 p.m. Colonel and Brevet Brigadier-General Woodward is still living, or was a few months ago, at Neosho Falls, Kansas. He is seventy-seven years old, and, although minus one leg which he lost in battle in 1864, still enjoys fairly good health. In a letter, which I received from him, dated January 12, 1912, he admits his mistake in regard to the time, and authorises me to correct that statement to accord with the facts.

General Romeyn B. Ayres, Second Division

As the First and Second brigades, did not participate in the battle on Little Round Top, I make no comment on their gallant service elsewhere. The statement about the Third brigade (Weed's), that they were placed on Little Round Top and ordered to hold the hill,—which duty it performed well and effectually,—is technically true, although, with the exception of the One Hundred and Fortieth New York regiment, commanded by Colonel O'Rorke, it did not arrive on the hill until the last assault on that position had been repulsed.

Third Brigade,—Weed's

As General Weed was mortally wounded in the battle and died a few hours later, the report is made by Colonel Kenner Garrard, of the One Hundred and Forty-Sixth New York, who assumed command when Weed fell. There are no regimental reports of this brigade. Colonel Garrard makes no distinction between the different regiments of this brigade in regard to the importance of the part which each took in the action. The brigade was composed of good men, well officered. If they had been given the opportunity I have no doubt the other regiments would have maintained their reputation by the side of the One Hundred and Fortieth New York, but unfortunately, they did not arrive until this regiment had been fighting nearly or quite half an hour, had repulsed the last Confederate charge, and had lost a large number of its men and officers, including Colonel O'Rorke.

During this time the remainder of the brigade, which Sykes had ordered to Little Round Top, had marched by that position and under an order from Sickles had moved out toward the Emmittsburg road, to support the Third corps. By the time Sykes discovered this movement and ordered it back to Little Round Top, the attack by the Confederates had been repulsed by the One Hundred and Fortieth New York, and the battle had dwindled to long distance firing between the sharpshooters and individuals of both sides.

When Warren from his position near the signal corps saw the preparations for this attack, he rode down the hill and detaching the One Hundred and Fortieth New York from the rear of Weed's brigade, which was then moving out to the front, sent it up to the crest of the ridge, where it arrived just in time to prevent the success of the movement against the right flank of Vincent's brigade.

I regret that no regimental reports of this brigade in regard to the

Battle of Gettysburg are to be found in the *Official Records*. In the absence of these, for the part taken by the One Hundred and Fortieth New York I refer the reader to the admirable paper entitled Captain Farley's "Number Nine," which will be found in another part of this book. Captain Farley was acting as adjutant of the regiment at this time, and had an excellent opportunity to know what occurred.

It had been a mystery to me why Warren knew so little about the fight which Vincent was making on the southern slope of the ridge. In a visit to Little Round Top which I made last spring in company with Captain Farley and some other gentlemen, I discovered the reason. Near the middle of the ridge from north to south is its highest point; from there the crest slopes both to the north and to the south. There is also a more or less pronounced ridge running from this point toward the west, separating into two parts the western slope. With reference to the surroundings Vincent's position may be said to be almost in a hole. From this position the ground ascends sharply to the top of this ridge on the western slope, then descends quite rapidly from that point to the vicinity of the signal station where Warren stood. There was no artillery with Vincent, the wind was blowing toward the south, and, with the noise of the battle at the Devil's Den and beyond and the firing of Hazlett's battery near him, the musketry firing of Vincent's men and the Confederates attacking them could not be heard.

CRAWFORD, THIRD DIVISION

This division was composed exclusively of the "Pennsylvania Reserves." Only two brigades commanded by McCandless and Fisher were present at Gettysburg. As McCandless' brigade, with one regiment of Fisher's, was engaged on another part of the field, and this force with Bartlett's brigade of the Sixth corps, all under command of General Crawford, made the last attack which drove the Confederates from that part of the field, and this according to McCandless under the direct supervision of Crawford in the dusk after sunset, it is difficult to see how Crawford found time to visit Fisher's brigade, as stated by him. The reader will notice that Rice, Fisher, and Chamberlain make no mention of orders received from Crawford, or of his presence in that part of the field. Crawford's attack continued until dark, and finished the battle of July 2 on the left of our line. It was well planned and well executed. It was the first and last permanent success on the advanced position of Sickles' corps. There is glory enough for Crawford and his men without his claiming a share in the deeds of the officers and men of Vincent's and Fisher's brigades.

FISHER, THIRD BRIGADE

This brigade was composed of as good material—officers and men—as McCandless' brigade, which distinguished itself in its fight near the wheat-field. If given the opportunity, I have no doubt they would have done as well; but unfortunately, they did not arrive until the fight on that part of the field was done. The brigade was massed in the rear of Vincent's position. The last sentence in Fisher's report, is, "Taking it all in all, I have no hesitation in saying that my brigade fulfilled their mission to Gettysburg." The report appears to have been written with the purpose of preparing a way for this conclusion, but with too little regard for the facts. On his arrival, he did not engage the enemy, because that part of the enemy's force not killed, wounded, or prisoners was already out of sight. He says that soon after the close of the fight of the 2nd he discovered a hill in his front, from the summit of which the enemy was doing us great damage, and at 10 p. m. he took two regiments of his brigade and the Twentieth Maine and ascended the hill, which was occupied by a full brigade of the enemy. He went up in line of battle, taking about thirty prisoners during the ascent.

The fight against Vincent's brigade finished between 6 and 7 p. m. If he sustained the fire from this full brigade on the summit of Big Round Top for three or four hours without reply, his equanimity is surprising. He does not give the name of the full brigade of the enemy which he encountered. There was no Confederate brigade on the right of their line not fully accounted for elsewhere. The only soldiers of the enemy which could possibly have been in that location were one small company of Oates' Fifteenth Alabama, which followed a few of Stoughton's sharpshooters, drove them off the east end of the hill, and, as Oates says, did not return to the regiment until sometime during the night. The thirty prisoners which Fisher claims to have captured during the ascent may have belonged to this company, with possibly the addition of some men from the Fifteenth Alabama who left their places in line and climbed the hill while the Fifteenth Alabama was fighting the Twentieth Maine. The appearance of this full Confederate brigade, which somehow melted away, resembles Falstaff's "men in buckram."

Fisher certainly did not take the Twentieth Maine with his two regiments and ascend the hill. He had no jurisdiction over the regiments of Vincent's brigade. Rice would not have turned over to him the regiment of his brigade if asked for by Fisher. If a brigade commander had been needed for this expedition. Rice himself would have gone. He was satisfied, however, to send Colonel Chamberlain, with the Twentieth Maine, which he did an hour before the time when Fisher's men started. Chamberlain says that about midnight two regiments of Fisher's brigade came up the mountain beyond his left and took position near the summit; but as the enemy did not threaten in that direction he made no effort to connect with them.

The other two regiments of Fisher's brigade sometime during the night passed Vincent's brigade going down the valley on the north side of Big Round Top, and halted at the foot of the trail which runs up the mountain-side to the place where the observatory now stands and formed a line across the valley, which they slightly fortified during the night by piling up a wall of loose stones. A portion of these men went up this trail to a point near Chamberlain's right. Hearing the noise they made, Chamberlain supposed the enemy was coming from that direction, and made preparation to receive them. The Confederates had established a strong skirmish and picket line from north to south near the top of the western slope. The north end of this line was not far from the trail up which Fisher's men had come. The Confederates opened a brisk fire on them, and they soon returned to the valley.

The losses of Fisher's brigade at Gettysburg, as reported, were three killed and eleven wounded. It is probable that these losses occurred on the trail, although the fire of that full brigade of the enemy on the summit of Big Round Top may have been responsible for some of them.

In the publication entitled *Pennsylvania at Gettysburg,* near the close of the second volume is a list of the inscriptions on each of the Pennsylvania monuments on the Gettysburg battlefield. These inscriptions state the casualties of each of the regiments engaged in this battle. The following is the list of casualties in the four regiments of Fisher's brigade:

Fifth Pennsylvania Reserves, two men wounded. Ninth Pennsylvania Reserves, five men wounded. Tenth Pennsylvania Reserves, two men killed, three men wounded. Twelfth Pennsylvania Reserves, one man killed, one man wounded. Total casualties in the brigade, three men killed, eleven men wounded.

Above does not include the casualties in the Eleventh Pennsylvania Reserves, which fought with McCandless' brigade near the wheatfield.

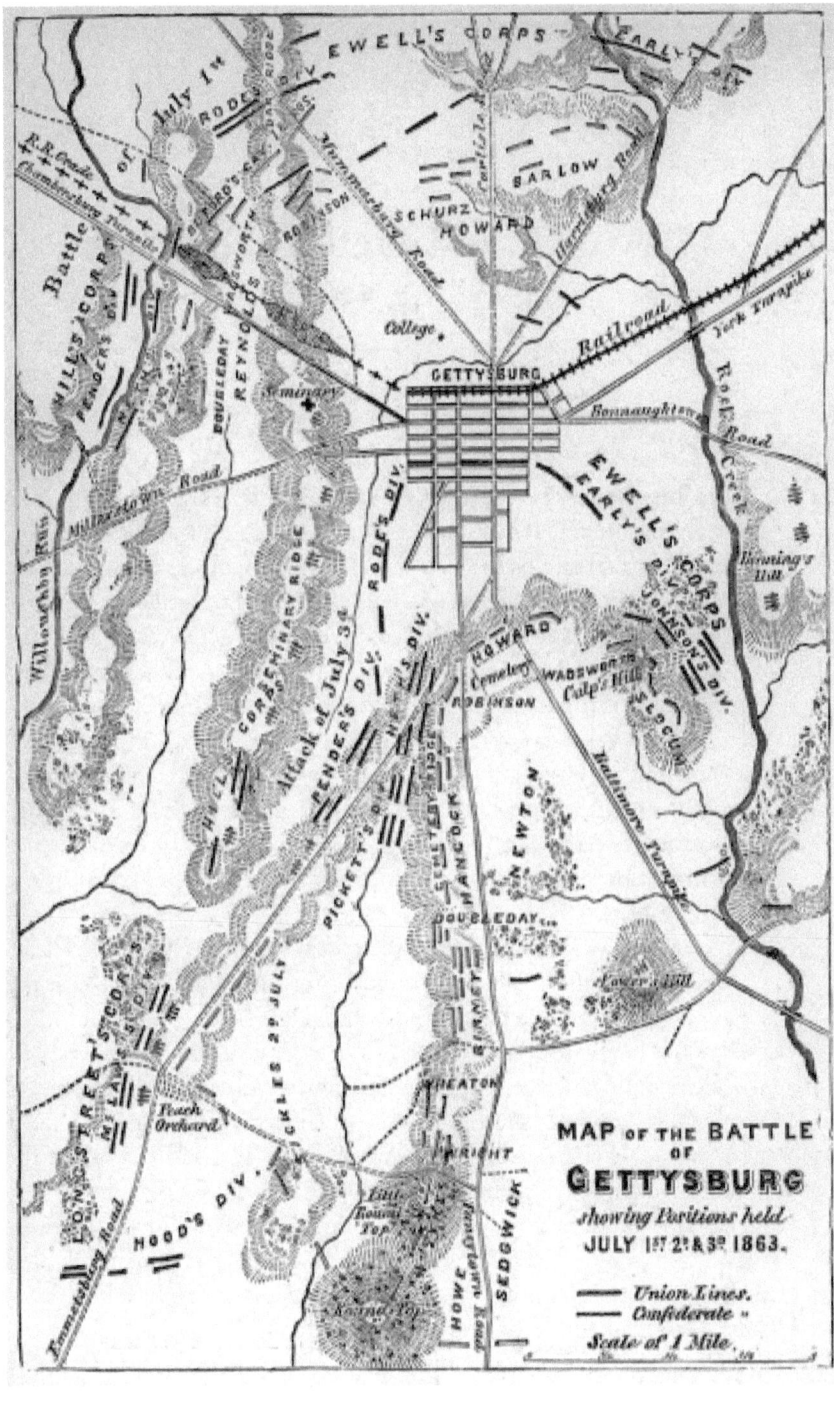

4. Attack and Defense of Little Round Top

THE ATTACK

On the morning of July 2 General Lee, after carefully examining the position on and about Cemetery and Culp's Hills, which the Union army had taken up at the close of the previous day's battle, decided to make his attack on the left of the Union line. Longstreet's corps had not been present during the battle of July 1, but McLaws' and Hood's divisions, with the exception of Law's brigade of the latter, arrived during the morning and were placed on Lee's right. Pickett's division had not yet arrived. Law's brigade came up later, and was placed on the right of Hood's division. After much marching and countermarching in the attempt to conceal their movements from the signal station on Little Round Top, they arrived about three o'clock at the Emmittsburg road at a point a considerable distance south of the Peach Orchard.

Meantime Sickles had posted the two divisions of his corps, Humphreys' on the right along the Emmittsburg road with his left near the Peach Orchard, his line facing Seminary ridge; Birney's division occupied a line facing south, with Graham's brigade at the Peach Orchard, De Trobriand in the centre, and Ward on the left among the rocks of the Devil's Den near the Plum Run valley, which separated his position from the western front of Little Round Top. Hood crossed the Emmittsburg road and formed his division in the woods on a ridge facing Birney's line. The division of four brigades was formed in these woods in two lines, Law's brigade on the right, Robertson's on the left in the first line, Benning's Georgia brigade on the right and Anderson's Georgia brigade on the left in the second line.

The four batteries of the division were massed on its left. McLaws'

UNION BREASTWORKS ON LITTLE ROUND TOP — BIG ROUND TOP IN THE DISTANCE. FROM WAR-TIME PHOTOGRAPHS.

THE "SLAUGHTER PEN" AT THE BASE AND ON THE LEFT SLOPE OF LITTLE ROUND TOP. FROM PHOTOGRAPHS.

division, consisting of the brigades of Kershaw, Semmes, Barksdale, and Wofford, was formed in the same order, with the division artillery of four batteries on its left. Law's brigade consisted of five Alabama regiments in the following order from right to left: Forty-Eighth, Forty-Fourth, Fifteenth, Forty-Seventh and Fourth. Robertson's brigade consisted of one Arkansas and three Texas regiments, arranged in the following order from right to left: Fifth, Fourth, and First Texas and Third Arkansas. Benning was in rear of Law and Anderson in rear of Robertson. As McLaws' division directed its attack on Graham and De Trobriand, and did not participate directly in the struggle for Little Round Top, we need not follow its movements.

Before crossing the Emmittsburg road Hood and Law had sent out trained scouts to the south and east to look for the Union cavalry. They found no sign of cavalry in that part of the field. Longstreet in the morning had urged Lee not to make a direct attack, but to move by his right around Meade's left to his rear, threatening his communications and forcing him to leave his strong position and attack the Confederates on ground of their own choosing; but Lee refused. Law's scouts had gone to the top of Big Round Top without encountering so much as a picket of the Union Army. They reported to Law that the Union trains of commissary and ordnance wagons were in plain view from Big Round Top, there were no troops on Little Round Top, and only a few wagon guards near the train.

Law reported this to Hood, and the latter urged Longstreet to permit his division to move around the east of Big Round Top and attack from that direction; but Longstreet replied to Hood's importunities, that Lee's order was to attack up the Emmittsburg road, and it must be obeyed. Hood had discovered the strong position of Birney's line, and made a formal protest against an attack in that direction, but finally yielded reluctantly and gave his orders for the attack. According to Longstreet's instructions the attack was to be made by the right *en echelon*, and taken up by the brigades in succession from right to left. The attack opened about half past three o'clock by a furious cannonade on Birney's line from Hood's and McLaws' batteries, which was answered by all the Union batteries which were in position to reply. After this bombardment had lasted about half an hour Hood's infantry advanced. During this artillery battle Hood was badly wounded by a shell while standing near his batteries, and was carried to the rear. It was not until the infantry had arrived near the Union lines that Law was informed that Hood was disabled. Upon receiving this informa-

GENERAL G. K. WARREN AT THE SIGNAL STATION ON LITTLE ROUND TOP.
FROM A SKETCH MADE AT THE TIME.

tion, as senior brigadier he assumed command of the division.

The ground over which the Confederates advanced was rocky and very rough, divided by numerous stone fences and other obstructions. As soon as their advance was seen, the Union artillery turned its fire on them, at first with shell, followed by canister as they came nearer. This made it impossible to maintain very good order in the advancing line. Robertson had been directed to keep his brigade closed on Law's left. For some reason not explained by Law, his brigade in advancing obliqued to the right. This movement was followed by the Fourth and Fifth Texas obliquing to the right, to keep closed on the Fourth Alabama.

Robertson's other two regiments, the First Texas and Third Arkansas, with Robertson himself, went straight on to the Devil's Den. Law's brigade had gone so far to the east that for more than half its length it faced the southern side of Big Round Top. To remedy this, instead of moving the whole brigade to the left, he directed the two regiments on his right to halt and then move to the left of the brigade. This was done; but they went so far that they came up on the left of the Fourth and Fifth Texas, thus leaving them in the middle of Law's brigade. This left the regiments in the following order from right to left: Fifteenth, Forty-Seventh, and Fourth Alabama, Fifth and Fourth Texas, Forty-Eighth and Forty-Fourth Alabama.

Ward, after getting his brigade into position at the Devil's Den on the left of Birney's line, had sent out the Second battalion of United States Sharpshooters under Major Stoughton as skirmishers to cover his front. This battalion consisted of eight small companies, not more than half an ordinary regiment; but the superiority of their arms and their skill in using them made them a formidable force. Stoughton crossed the little valley in front of Ward and deployed his men behind a stone wall covering Ward's front and flank. The right was in the air, but the left had a good position at the foot of the wooded western slope of the Big Round Top. The well-directed fire of this line from their position behind the stone wall checked the Confederates for a time, but their courage and superior numbers forced the sharpshooters to retire. The five companies on the right being outflanked and in danger of capture fell back to the main line of the brigade. The other three companies with Major Stoughton retired into the woods and up the western slope of Big Round Top, closely followed by the Fifteenth and Forty-Seventh Alabama.

Colonel Oates says that after he got in the woods he was ordered to wheel his line to the left, but he disregarded the order because the right of the Forty-Seventh was crowding in on the left of his regiment and he could not execute the movement without increasing the confusion. He did not dare to make a movement which would place his line in a position to be enfiladed by the sharpshooters on the mountain, so, straightening his line and that of the Forty-Seventh, which by direction of General Law was temporarily under his command, he advanced toward the top of the mountain.

When part way up the sharpshooters divided, the greater part of them going to the left around the Forty-Seventh, which, continuing, passed them. Another part of the sharpshooters moved to the right, menacing his right flank. He deployed Company A of his regiment as flankers, and with the Forty-Seventh pressed on to the top of the mountain. His Company A followed the sharpshooters until they drove them down the eastern end of the mountain, and he saw no more of this company until after the battle. Having reached the top of the mountain, he halted for a time to give his men opportunity to recover from the heat and from the fatigue caused by their exertions in climbing over the rocks.

Meantime the other regiments of Law's brigade, with the Fourth and Fifth Texas, had cleared the western slope of Big Round Top, and reached the narrow valley which runs along the northern side of Big Round Top and farther east separates it from Little Round Top. Colonel Perry, of the Forty-Fourth Alabama, which was then the left of the line, says that Law rode up and told him that he was expected to take that battery (Smith's battery on the Devil's Den) which had played such havoc with their line in its advance. He wheeled his regiment to the left until it faced the battery and then advanced directly against it. The other regiments of Law's brigade—the Fourth and Forty-Eighth Alabama and Robertson's Fourth and Fifth Texas—advanced up this narrow valley toward the east in columns of fours, without skirmishers, hoping to arrive before any Union troops reached that part of the field.

But Vincent's brigade had already got into position on the southern slope of Little Round Top and thrown out two or three companies in their front as skirmishers. The skirmishers of the Forty-Fourth New York and Eighty-Third Pennsylvania advanced down this valley toward the west. Captain Morrill's company of the Twentieth Maine went to the left to the east of Big Round Top. The skirmishers of the Forty-Fourth New York and Eighty-Third Pennsylvania had not gone

Round Tops

NORAMA, 1909

far before they met the heads of the Confederate columns. The latter were surprised, and both sides began firing. Captain Larrabee, in command of the skirmishers of the Forty-Fourth New York, was instantly killed and several of the men were killed or badly wounded. These skirmishers fell back to their regiments.

The Confederates quickly formed in line of battle, with the Fourth Alabama on the right, the Fifth and Fourth Texas in the centre, and the Forty-Eighth Alabama on the left. They advanced against Vincent, with the Fourth Alabama extending around toward Vincent's left, the other regiments in front of the western side of Vincent's position. Vincent's men were well protected by the rocks and boulders behind which they had sheltered themselves. Finding that they could not be driven from their position, the Confederate line wavered and fell back a short distance, sheltering themselves behind the rocks, which were numerous in that vicinity. After a time, they advanced again, this time moving a little further to their right and covering some of the companies on the right of the Twentieth Maine.

Meantime the Fifteenth and Forty-Seventh Alabama, under Colonel Oates, came down from the top of Big Round Top by the trail which leads to where the observatory now stands. They were discovered moving to the right in column along the foot of Big Round Top in the effort to extend the Confederate line and turn the left flank of the Twentieth Maine. They passed so far in this direction that Chamberlain was obliged to throw back the left wing of his regiment to a line nearly at right angles with his right wing. The Texas regiments and the Forty-Eighth Alabama finding they could not break Vincent's centre, determined to attack the right flank while Oates was fighting Chamberlain. They could not safely move to the left directly in Vincent's front; instead, they retired to the Plum Run valley.

By this time the other brigades of Hood's division had succeeded in driving back Ward's brigade from the Devil's Den and capturing three of the guns of Smith's battery. The other three guns which had been placed on a ledge further to the rear were drawn back. This opened the way for the two Texas regiments and the Forty-Eighth Alabama to advance northward under shelter of the large rocks between Plum Run and the western slope of Little Round Top, until they passed beyond Vincent's right flank, held by the Sixteenth Michigan. The Fourth Alabama did not fall back with the others. It continued fighting until its ammunition was exhausted, then retreated to the western foot of Big Round Top, and remained there during the night.

THE STRUGGLE FOR DEVIL'S DEN, (LOOKING TOWARD THE CONFEDERATE LINES). FROM A WAR-TIME SKETCH.

DEAD CONFEDERATE SHARP-SHOOTER IN THE DEVIL'S DEN.

The Forty-Eighth Alabama and Fourth and Fifth Texas having passed beyond the right of the Sixteenth Michigan, turned and, climbing the western slope of Little Round Top in a southeasterly direction, made a fierce assault on the right three companies of that regiment. The line of these companies was refused, so that they faced in a northerly direction with their right resting at the foot of the large rocks which formed the crest of the ridge. The steepness of the ascent and the loose stones which covered its surface made it impossible to maintain any orderly formation. They came up in a mass with great courage, without stopping to fire until they reached the Union line; here they engaged in a hand-to-hand conflict with the Michigan men, firing and using the bayonet. Their increasing numbers and the fury of the assault caused these three companies to fall back in disorder.

Vincent hastened to the spot, urging the men to stand fast, but he fell among them mortally wounded by a shot from one of the assailants, without succeeding in stopping the retreat. The greater part of these companies which survived the attack retired behind the large rocks, taking with them Lieutenant-Colonel Welch and the regimental colours. The remainder of the regiment stood fast and, although not well placed to resist such an attack on their right and rear, did good service in repelling the assault.

It was just at this moment that Colonel O'Rorke, with the One Hundred and Fortieth New York, came over the crest of the hill to the right of the Sixteenth Michigan. They charged down the hill against the Confederates, who were swarming up the slope, and drove them back to the valley. This unexpected reinforcement disheartened the Confederates, whose success in the first onset inspired the hope of being able at last to drive back Vincent's brigade. Many of them dropped their arms and surrendered, others were shot in their attempt to retreat. The fighting was severe for a few moments, but the hillside was soon cleared of the enemy, who retired to the valley and, sheltering themselves behind the rocks, there continued a desultory fire on the Union line. O'Rorke, who led his men so gallantly in this charge, was almost instantly killed within a few feet of where Vincent lay. The One Hundred and Fortieth New York formed an irregular line among the rocks, extending northward from the remaining companies of the Sixteenth Michigan, where they remained until the end of the battle.

In a map published by the authority of the Secretary of War, in 1876, revised in 1883, made from a survey conducted by Brevet Major General G. K. Warren, Major of Engineers, by order of Brevet Major

UNIFORM OF THE 144TH NEW YORK REGIMENT.

VIEW OF LITTLE ROUND TOP

General A. A. Humphreys, Chief of Engineers, showing the position of the Union and Confederate troops in the Battle of Gettysburg, the Forty-Fourth Alabama is shown on the left of the Forty-Eighth Alabama, in front of the position of the One Hundred and Fortieth New York. Whether the Forty-Fourth joined the Forty-Eighth in this flank movement is an open question. The official report of the Forty-Fourth Alabama, made by Colonel Perry, contains no mention of any fighting by this regiment, except the attack on the Devil's Den.

While this assault was in progress on Vincent's right, the Fifteenth and Forty-Seventh Alabama moved in column along the foot of Big Round Top until they had passed to the right of the Fourth Alabama, when they came into line and advanced against the Twentieth Maine. Adjutant Waddell, of the Fifteenth, with about fifty men of that regiment, continued further to the right, passing the Twentieth Maine, then advanced to a position from which he could enfilade Chamberlain's regiment and the left wing of the Eighty-Third Pennsylvania. To meet this attack Chamberlain refused his left wing to a position nearly at right angles with the remainder of his regiment. The Alabama men rushed upon Chamberlain in a furious assault. There was desperate fighting for some time. The Confederates made repeated charges, which were met with counter-charges by Chamberlain's men.

The Fourth Alabama by this time had retired, followed by what was left of the Forty-Seventh. Chamberlain's ammunition was nearly exhausted. Taking advantage of the apparent reluctance of the Confederates to advance again. Chamberlain fixed bayonets and ordered a charge. His left wing came forward into line with his right; then, reinforced by Morrill's company, which returned about this time with twelve or fifteen of the sharpshooters, he made a right wheel with his line, which cleared the valley of the Confederates. Some of the latter went back to the top of Big Round Top; others went down the valley in the direction of the Devil's Den. The force under Adjutant Waddell, which had been cut off by this movement, surrendered, although the adjutant made his escape. This was the last of the direct assaults on Little Round Top.

The Defense

The Fifth Army Corps, which came by the Hanover road, began to arrive on the field about 7 a.m. on July 2. The First and Second divisions were placed on the right of the Twelfth corps in the vicinity of Rock Creek. When the head of the Sixth corps arrived, about

GENERAL ROBERT E. LEE

2 p.m., it was ordered to the right to relieve the two divisions of the Fifth. These two divisions, with two brigades of the Third division under Crawford, which arrived about this time, were massed in rear of the centre near the point where the Baltimore Pike crosses Rock Creek. About 3 p.m. General Meade directed General Sykes to move his corps to the left and occupy that part of the line. General Sickles had been ordered in the morning to form his corps on the low ridge between Cemetery Hill and the northern foot of Little Round Top, relieving General Geary's division of the Twelfth corps, which had spent the night on the northern foot of Little Round Top, and which was ordered to rejoin its corps on Culp's hill.

In the middle of the day, being dissatisfied with his position. Sickles moved forward to the Emmittsburg road, where he placed Humphreys' division along that road facing Seminary Ridge, and Birney's division facing south, with his right at the Peach Orchard and his left at the Devil's Den near the Plum Run valley, which separates it from the western front of Little Round Top.

About three o'clock Meade rode to the left to examine his line. He rode out to Sickles' position, and from there sent General Warren to examine the left and report the situation. Warren continued on until he reached the signal station near the north end of Little Round Top. This must have been a little before half past three o'clock. No enemy was in sight from that position, but the signal officer told him he thought he had seen troops in the woods between Plum Run and the Emmittsburg road.

Warren had with him as *aides* three young lieutenants of engineers, Mackenzie, Reese, and Roebling, and some mounted orderlies. He sent an orderly to the commander of Smith's battery at the Devil's Den, directing him to fire a shot into the woods where the signal officer thought he had seen the Confederates. This shot, whistling over the heads of these men, caused them to make involuntary movements. The sunlight reflected from their glistening bayonets and gun barrels revealed a long line of infantry, far outflanking the left of Birney's line and in position ready to advance. At this time, no troops except Birney's division were in place to resist them. He sent a note by one of his *aides*, Reese or Roebling, to General Meade, with a request that a division, at least, be sent to occupy Little Round Top. He then sent Lieutenant Mackenzie with a request to General Sickles to send a brigade, but Sickles declined, saying that he could not spare a man.

While Mackenzie was interviewing Sickles, Sykes and Barnes ar-

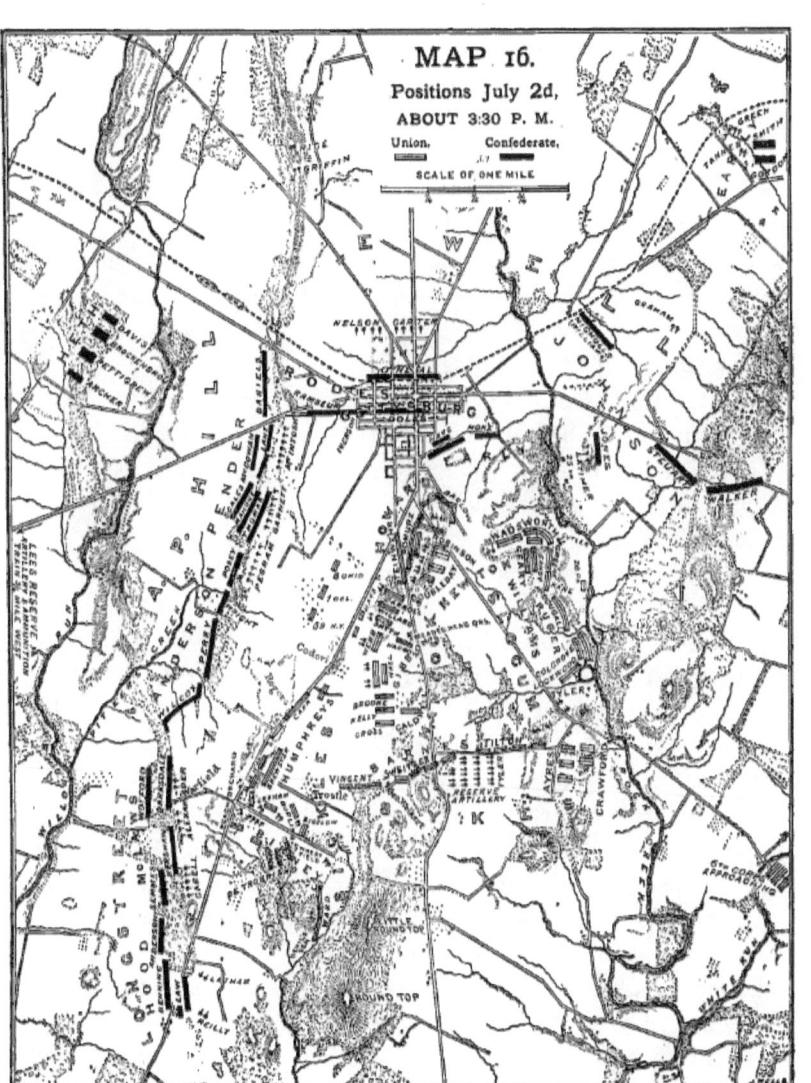

rived near the wheat-field with Barnes' division. The division was halted while Sykes rode forward with Barnes to select a position. Having found it, Sykes directed Barnes to bring on the division, and rode on to find General Birney and suggest to him to move some of his troops to the left, promising to fill the place vacated by them with Barnes' men. Mackenzie met Sykes while he was looking for Birney. Having explained to him the need for troops on Little Round Top, Sykes agreed to send one of Barnes' brigades. Mackenzie then returned to Warren and reported. Sykes immediately sent one of his staff to direct Barnes to send one of his brigades. Barnes had not returned to the division. Vincent was sitting on his horse at the head of the column, waiting orders. Seeing Sykes' *aide* approaching, he rode forward to meet him. I followed with the flag, and distinctly heard the following conversation:

"Captain, what are your orders?"

The captain replied, "Where is General Barnes?"

Vincent said, "What are your orders? Give me your orders."

The captain answered, "General Sykes told me to direct General Barnes to send one of his brigades to occupy that hill yonder," pointing to Little Round Top.

Vincent said, "I will take the responsibility of taking my brigade there."

Returning to the brigade, he directed Colonel Rice, the senior colonel, to bring the brigade to the hill as rapidly as possible, then rode away toward the northwest face of the hill. I followed him. Reaching the foot of the hill and finding it impossible to ride up to the top in that direction, owing to the steepness of the ascent and the loose stones which covered the surface, he turned to the left and, skirting the northern foot of the ridge, turned into the woods behind the ridge on the eastern side. He rode on until we reached the south end, where the line of great rocks which form the summit suddenly terminates by an abrupt descent of perhaps fifty feet. From the foot of this rock the ground slopes to the east, south, and west on a spur which is partly covered by scattered boulders and smaller rocks.

At the southern extremity of this spur is a ridge running east and west for a distance of about three hundred feet. From this ridge, southward toward Big Round Top extends a sparsely wooded valley which runs along the northern side of the mountain its whole length. There are many rocks and boulders scattered over the surface of this valley, far enough apart, however, to afford room between them for

Brigade Headquarters Flag
Third Brigade, First Division, Fifth Army Corps

the passage of troops.

Vincent rode around this big rock and halted a few paces to the west of it, at the place which was occupied a few minutes later by the Sixteenth Michigan. I sat on my horse behind him with the flag. Almost immediately a shell exploded to our right, followed by another just to our left. Vincent said to me, "They are firing at the flag, go behind the rocks with it." I rode behind the rock and stopped. Almost immediately he came and, dismounting, gave me the bridle of his horse. He then went down among the rocks, selecting a position for the brigade. In a few moments, the brigade arrived, with the regiments in the following order: Forty-Fourth New York, Sixteenth Michigan, Eighty-Third Pennsylvania, and Twentieth Maine. The field officers dismounted, leaving their horses with the mounted orderlies behind the rock.

Vincent said to Colonel Rice, "Form your regiment here, Colonel, with the right against the rock."

Rice replied, "In every battle in which we have been engaged the Eighty-Third and Forty-Fourth have fought side by side. I wish it might be so today."

Vincent understood and sympathized with this feeling. He replied, "All right, let the Sixteenth pass you."

The Sixteenth came forward and was placed in the position which Vincent had designated for the Forty-Fourth. The ground was too rough for much precision in movements, but the men came forward in as good order as possible. The Forty-Fourth formed along the western edge of this spur, with its right joining the left of the Sixteenth Michigan, the Eighty-Third next, with part of its line facing west, and the remainder facing south on the east and west ridge. The Twentieth Maine continued this line toward the east. Skirmishers were sent out by the Forty-Fourth and Eighty-Third down the valley toward the west, and a company from the Twentieth Maine toward the southeast to guard against an approach from that quarter. I think no skirmishers were sent out from the Sixteenth. The ground in their front was open to the foot of the hill, and an advance of the enemy from that direction could be plainly seen from the main line.

The position chosen by Vincent for his brigade was the best possible for preventing the Confederates from turning or capturing the hill. Had he placed his men on the crest of the ridge the enemy could have turned his flank and attacked from the rear. Or having opened the way, they could have held it for Hood's whole division to fol-

THE "SLAUGHTER PEN" AT THE BASE AND ON THE LEFT SLOPE OF LITTLE ROUND TOP. FROM PHOTOGRAPHS.

GENERAL BARNES

low, cutting Meade's communications, capturing his trains, and forcing him to leave his strong position and attack the Confederates in the open. Not all the troops that could have been placed on the crest of Little Round Top could have prevented this if the spur occupied by Vincent's brigade and the valley along the north side of Big Round Top had been left open.

In two respects justice, has never been done to Vincent. He would have gone with his brigade wherever he was ordered. He was thoroughly alive that day. A glance at Little Round Top was enough for him to realise its importance in relation to the field of battle and the necessity of occupying it without delay. Minutes were precious. In spite of all that Warren, Sykes, and Barnes did, it would have been too late had not Vincent moved without waiting for an order from his immediate superior. The instant he knew that Sykes had sent an order to Barnes to send one of his brigades, without designating any special brigade, he took the responsibility of taking his brigade there without waiting for the order to reach him through the ordinary channel. Had he waited for that, it would have been too late. He gave the order to Rice to bring on the brigade as rapidly as possible. He did not march at the head of the brigade, but preceded it, and when it arrived he had already selected its position.

The second respect is in not giving him the credit due for his knowledge and skill in the choice of a position. No general or staff officer directed or accompanied him. He knew only that Sykes had sent an order to Barnes to send one of his brigades to occupy that hill. Half the brigade commanders in the Army of the Potomac, if they received such an order, would have construed it as a direction to place their troops on the hill, where at that moment they would have been useless. Vincent used his discretion as to the manner of its occupation. The event proved that his instinct for the point of vantage was of the highest order.

The historians have vied with one another in telling how it was not done. Nearly all of them have credited Warren with taking the responsibility of detaching Vincent's brigade and placing it where it fought. In doing this they have relegated Vincent to the place of an officer who obeyed orders and stayed where he was put. Warren performed most important services that day. I yield to no man in my admiration and gratitude for what he did, but that is no reason for others to claim for him acts which he disclaims for himself, as I will show later by his own words.

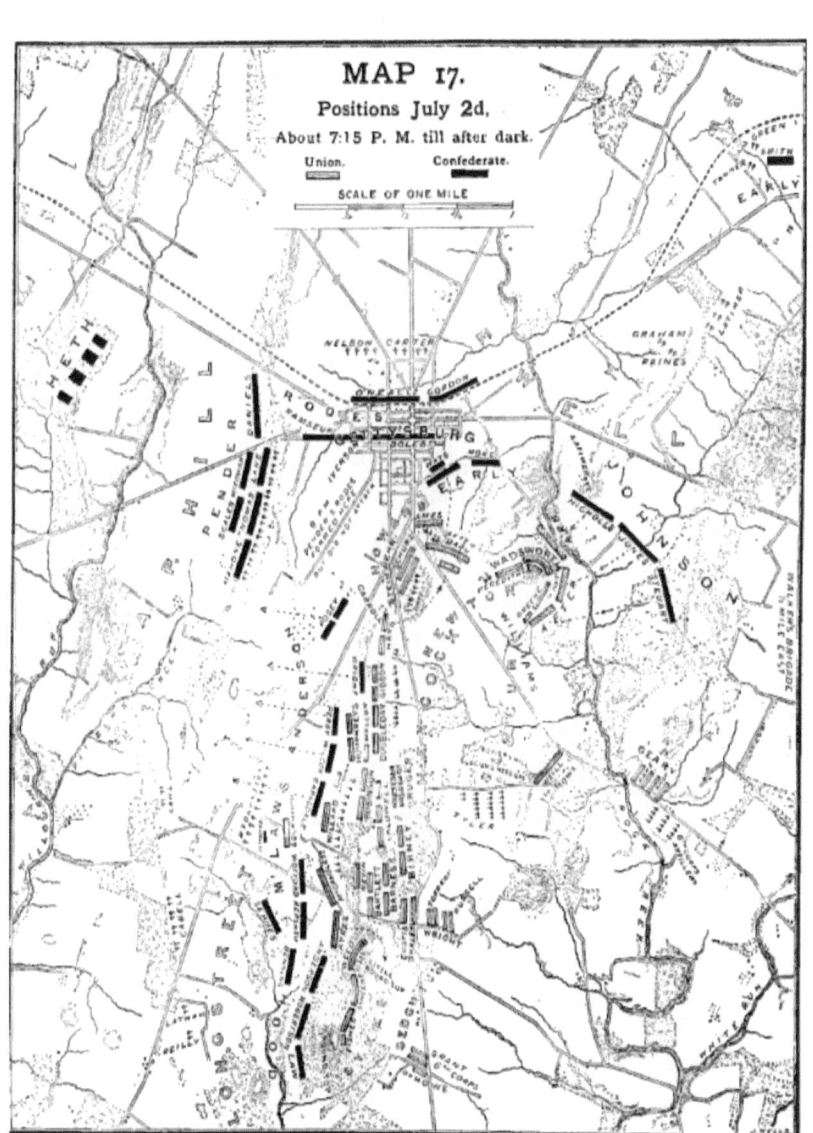

If I can show that the retention by the Union Army of this key to the battlefield on July 2, 1863, is due primarily to Strong Vincent and his gallant brigade, aided at the supreme moment by O'Rorke and his regiment, I shall feel that Vincent, O'Rorke, and the men of their commands who gave up their lives in that supreme effort did not die in vain.

In describing the Confederate attack, it has been impossible to separate from it the action of the Union troops in repelling it. After the Union skirmishers retired to their line, followed by the advance of the Confederates in line of battle, Vincent's brigade, with the exception of the charge by the Twentieth Maine at the close of the fight, confined itself until after dark to maintaining its strong position. It was there to hold Little Round Top, and it held it. It is doubtful whether any good could have been accomplished by following up the Confederate retreat. The failure of the repeated Confederate assaults, and their ultimate withdrawal, is sufficient justification, if any is needed. The time soon came for taking the offensive. The attack against the left of the brigade, under Chamberlain, had been vigorous and persistent.

Time and again the Confederates had succeeded in driving back Chamberlain's men a few paces, only to be forced to retire in their turn. The rocks where the Twentieth Maine was posted were smaller and less numerous than those behind which the Forty-Fourth New York and Eighty-Third Pennsylvania fought. At one time Chamberlain asked Captain Woodward if he could spare a company to enable him to close up toward the left his depleted ranks. Woodward could not do this; but, by taking advantage of the rocks and thinning his line in places where it was safe to do so, he extended it to the left enough to give material assistance to Chamberlain. Finally, with his ammunition exhausted and with no prospect of reinforcements, the psychological moment arrived, and Chamberlain seized the opportunity. He ordered a charge with the bayonet. I have described this in my statement of the attack. Its success put the finishing touch to the Union victory.

Colonel Rice, who assumed command when Vincent fell, had not been idle. After the temporary break on the right had been checked by the arrival of the One Hundred and Fortieth New York, order was restored on that part of the line. Realising the perilous situation of the Twentieth Maine, and the impossibility of sparing any men from other parts of the line. Rice sent an officer (not named in his report) to the corps commander to ask for reinforcements. Vincent had previously sent Captain Judson of his staff for the same purpose. While Vincent's brigade was fighting in this isolated position, the remainder of the Fifth corps had come up. The brigades of Sweitzer and Tilton, of Barnes' division, had been fighting along Birney's line. The two brigades of Regulars in Ayres' division had been sent to the vicinity of the Devil's Den. Weed's brigade of this division had been ordered by Sykes to Little Round Top, but by some misunderstanding of orders it went to the front to reinforce Sickles, except the One Hundred and Fortieth New York, which Warren detached as the brigade was passing.

When Sykes returned from the rear, where he had been to order up more troops, and found that Weed had gone to the front, he ordered him back to Little Round Top. The three regiments of this brigade, Ninety-First Pennsylvania, One Hundred and Forty-Sixth New York, and One Hundred and Fifty-Fifth Pennsylvania, finally got into position along the crest of the ridge on the right of the One Hundred and Fortieth New York, but they did not arrive until all the close fighting on that part of the line was done. Following Ayres, General Crawford, commanding the Third division, came up with two brigades of the Pennsylvania Reserves under McCandless and Fisher. McCandless' brigade, with one regiment of Fisher's, the Eleventh Pennsylvania Reserves, was sent to the front in the vicinity of the wheat-field. Fisher had five regiments in his brigade. He was sent with the remaining regiments to the support of Vincent, but did not arrive until the fighting was all done and the Confederates had disappeared from that vicinity.

About nine o'clock in the evening Rice sent Chamberlain with the Twentieth Maine to the summit of Big Round Top. They climbed the steep ascent directly south of the position of the brigade. On the way, up the mountain, they drove before them some Confederate stragglers, capturing on the way and at the top twenty-five prisoners, including an officer of General Law's staff. Chamberlain placed his men in a very strong position among the rocks, facing the western slope of the mountain, which was occupied by the enemy. He then sent back to Rice for ammunition and reinforcements. Meantime two regiments of Fisher's brigade advanced down the valley toward the west and formed line across the valley near the trail down which the Fifteenth and Forty-Seventh Alabama had come. Part of their force ascended this trail to a point near the right of Chamberlain's line. They were in close proximity to the enemy and some confusion occurred, as Chamberlain mistook them for the enemy and made disposition to receive them.

The Confederates opened fire on them and they retired to their line in the valley, where they piled up a breastwork of stone in their front. The entire loss of these four regiments of Fisher's brigade during the battle, as reported, was three killed and eleven wounded. This probably occurred in the ranks of the men who went up the trail in the direction of Chamberlain's right and encountered the strong picket line of the Confederates on the western slope of the mountain. After this encounter they retired to the valley.

Later in the night the Eighty-Third Pennsylvania, with a portion of the Forty-Fourth New York, went up the mountain and formed in line on Chamberlain's right, where they remained until the brigade was relieved in the forenoon of July 3, by the first brigade of Barnes' division. About midnight Colonel Fisher went up the mountain near the eastern end with the other two regiments of his brigade, the Fifth and Twelfth Pennsylvania Reserves.

It may be proper to say at this point a few words about the regiments which composed Vincent's brigade at Gettysburg. The Sixteenth Michigan was a good regiment, with a most honourable record. It entered the service at the beginning of the war and served to the end. With two other regiments of the brigade, the Eighty-Third Pennsylvania and the Twentieth Maine, it formed part of the line which, under command of General Chamberlain, received the formal surrender of the Confederate army at Appomattox. Its first commander was Colonel T. B. W. Stockton, a graduate of the Military Academy and commander of a regiment in the war with Mexico. He entered the Academy in 1823, was graduated in 1827, remaining in the regular army until 1836, when he resigned, with rank of first lieutenant. He was commissioned colonel of the First Regiment Michigan Volunteers, December 9, 1847, and was honourably mustered out July 9, 1848.

Commissioned as colonel Sixteenth Michigan September 8, 1861. Resigned May 18, 1863. As senior colonel, he commanded the brigade at the Battles of Fredericksburg and Chancellorsville. Lieutenant-Colonel Norval E. Welch succeeded him in command of the regiment. Welch's conduct at Gettysburg in leaving the brigade with a portion of his regiment was not creditable, but he was a good officer, and redeemed his reputation in all the battles of later campaigns. He was killed in action in one of the battles south of Petersburg while

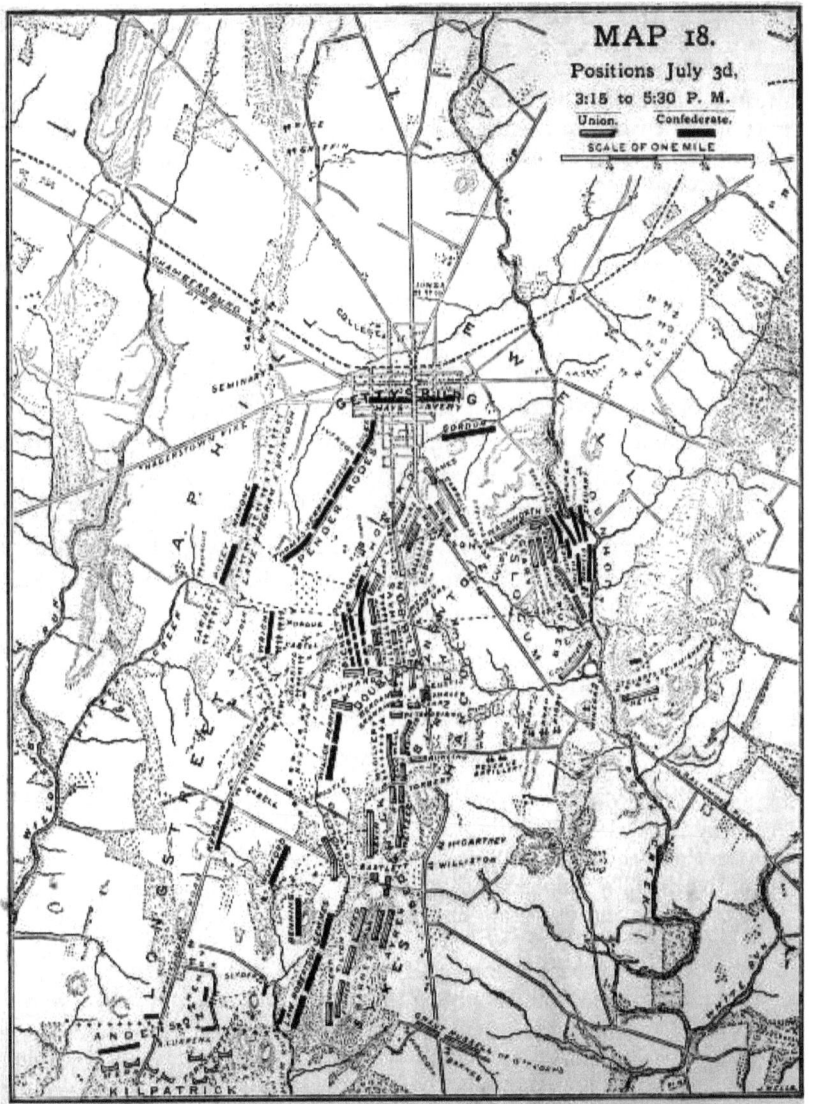

leading a charge of his regiment against the enemy's entrenchments.

The Sixteenth Michigan, Eighty-Third Pennsylvania, and Forty-Fourth New York entered the service at about the same time, in September, 1861. A brigade was being organised under command of General Daniel Butterfield. When the Eighty-Third crossed the Potomac, and went into camp at Hall's Hill, in front of Washington, it found the Sixteenth Michigan already there and pitched its camp in line with the Sixteenth. A few days later the Forty-Fourth New York arrived, about dusk, tired and hungry at the end of its first march into the enemy's country. The Eighty-Third had its camp in order and its cook fires burning brightly.

Colonel McLane had been informed during the afternoon of the approach of a new regiment to join the brigade. He called his officers together and suggested the propriety of inviting the officers and men of the new regiment to partake of our hospitality. The Forty-Fourth marched by our camp and, halting on the right, broke into column of companies and stacked arms. McLane with his field and staff officers called at the headquarters of the Forty-Fourth and invited all the officers of that regiment to take supper with the officers of the Eighty-Third. A deputation from the enlisted men of the Eighty-Third, headed by the first sergeant of each company, went over to the new regiment and invited the company with the same letter to come to the camp of the Eighty-Third and be their guests.

The invitation was gladly accepted, and there began a friendship between the officers and men of those two regiments which has not yet ceased and will not cease until the last survivors have passed over the river. These regiments were called "Butterfield's Twins." A generous rivalry sprang up, each regiment striving to outdo the other in drill, discipline, and all the manifold duties of a soldier's life. Although under different officers, the two organisations were like one great regiment. This explains Rice's request and Vincent's quick response that brought the two regiments side by side at Little Round Top.

The Twentieth Maine was organised in 1862. It joined the brigade during the Antietam campaign, after the army returned to Washington from the battlefield of the second Bull Run. Its first colonel was Adelbert Ames. He was graduated from the Military Academy July 1, 1860, and was second lieutenant and first lieutenant of artillery, serving part of the time with Griffin's, afterward Hazlett's, battery of the Fifth Artillery. He was commissioned colonel of the Twentieth Maine August 20, 1862. He was promoted to be brigadier-general of Volunteers May 20, 1863.

At the Battle of Gettysburg, he commanded a division in the Eleventh corps. Joshua L. Chamberlain, who had much to do with the organisation of the regiment, was commissioned lieutenant-colonel of the Twentieth Maine August 8, 1862. When Colonel Ames was promoted, Chamberlain succeeded him as colonel of the regiment. May 20, 1863. When Colonel Rice was made brigadier-general of Volunteers, August 17, 1863, and transferred to another corps, Chamberlain succeeded him in the command of the brigade. June 18, 1864, Chamberlain was commissioned brigadier-general of Volunteers.

******

The following is a copy of the special order of General Grant promoting Chamberlain to brigadier general, the verbal order having been given on the evening of June 18:

> Headquarters Army of the United States,
> June 20, 1864.
>
> Special Order No. 39.
>
> Colonel J. L. Chamberlain, Twentieth Maine Infantry Volunteers, for meritorious and efficient services on the field of battle, and especially for gallant conduct in leading his brigade against the enemy at Petersburg on the 18th instant, in which he was dangerously wounded, is hereby, in pursuance of authority of the Secretary of War, appointed Brigadier General United States Volunteers, to rank as such from the 18th of June, 1864, subject to the approval of the President.
>
> U. S. Grant,
> Lieutenant General.

******

On March 29, 1865, he was made brevet major-general of Volunteers for conspicuous gallantry and meritorious service in action on the Quaker Road, Virginia. He was honourably mustered out of the service January 15, 1866. August 11, 1893, he was given a medal of honour by Congress for daring heroism and great tenacity in holding his position on the Little Round Top, and carrying the advance position on the Great Round Top at the battle of Gettysburg, Pennsylvania, July 2, 1863.

Although the Twentieth Maine entered the service a year later than the other regiments of the brigade, the ability of its commanders, with the character and intelligence of its subordinate officers and men, soon placed it on an equality with the best.

Captain Woodward, who commanded the Eighty-Third Pennsylvania at Gettysburg, was made colonel of the regiment March 28, 1864. He lost a leg in the campaign of 1864, and was honourably mustered out September 20, 1864. He was given the brevet of brigadier-general of Volunteers March 13, 1865, for gallant and meritorious service during the war. General Rice was killed May 10, 1864, at the battle of Laurel Hill, Virginia.

Freeman Connor was a member of the famous "Ellsworth Zouaves." He was a captain in the.Chicago Zouave Regiment, April 22, 1861, and a first lieutenant in the Eleventh New York Volunteer Infantry, in which regiment he fought at the first Battle of Bull Run, July 21, 1861; resigned his commission and enlisted as a private in the Forty-Fourth New York Volunteer Infantry, August 8, 1861. He was commissioned captain of Company D, in this regiment, and in succession its major, lieutenant-colonel, and colonel. He served in this regiment until it was mustered out, October 11, 1864., He died in Chicago March 28, 1906.

Of the regimental monuments, which have been erected on the battlefield of Gettysburg, those of the Sixteenth Michigan and the Twentieth Maine are located on the lines where these regiments fought. That of the Eighty-Third Pennsylvania stands in rear of the centre of the brigade, and is surmounted by a bronze statue of Colonel Vincent. The monument of the Forty-Fourth New York stands on the summit of the large rock which forms the crest of the hill, a little to the right of the position occupied by the Sixteenth Michigan. It is a large circular granite tower forty-four feet high, with a spiral stairway in the interior leading to a platform at the top, which affords a fine view of nearly the whole of the battlefield. On the inside are bronze tablets giving the names of the members of the regiment.

POSITION OF VINCENT'S BRIGADE

5. Biographical

General Gouverneur Kemble Warren

General Warren was an excellent officer, a great engineer, an educated and polished gentleman of the old school. In the last years of the war he served as commander of an army corps, the highest rank obtainable except that of the commander of the army. He was greatly loved and admired by the officers and men of his command. After the war, he continued in the army until his death, using his knowledge as an engineer in the service of the country in many important works. His death was announced to the army in the following memorial notice recounting his career and services.

Headquarters Corps of Engineers,
United States Army,
Washington, D. C, August 9, 1882.

General Orders

No. 5.

It has become the painful duty of the Brigadier-General Commanding to announce to the Corps of Engineers the death of a brother officer. Lieutenant Colonel Gouverneur K. Warren, Brevet Major General, United States Army, who died at Newport, R. I., yesterday.

General Warren was graduated from the Military Academy and promoted to the rank of Brevet Second Lieutenant in the Corps of Topographical Engineers, July i, 1850. He served as Assistant Engineer on the topographical and hydrographical Survey of the Delta of the Mississippi, 1850-'52, and to the Board for the improvement of canal around the Falls of the Ohio, 1852-'53; in charge of Surveys for the improvement of Rock Island and Des Moines Rapids, Mississippi River, 1853-'54; in compiling the General Map and Reports (conjointly with Captain, now General, A. A. Humphreys) of Pacific Railroad Explorations, 1854; as Chief Topographical Engineer on Sioux Expedition, 1855, being engaged in the action of Blue Water, September 3, 1855; in charge of reconnaissances in Dakota Territory, and making Map and Report of same, 1855-'56, and in Nebraska Territory, 1856-'57, and preparing Maps and Reports thereof, 1857-'59.

He was Assistant Professor of Mathematics at the Military Academy, 1859, and Principal Assistant Professor, 18s9-'61

He entered upon his distinguished service in the late civil war (1861-'66) in the Department of Virginia, as Lieutenant Colonel of the Fifth New York Volunteers, being engaged in the action at Big Bethel Church, June 10, 1861. He was engaged on the defences of Baltimore, and constructing Fort on Federal Hill, 1861-'62, being temporarily detached on expedition to Northampton and Accomac counties, Va., 1861; in the Virginia Peninsular Campaign (Army of the Potomac), 1862, being engaged in the siege of Yorktown, April 11-May 4, 1862, and in command of Brigade, May 24, 1862; skirmish on Pamunkey River, May 26, 1862; capture of Hanover Court House, May 27, 1862; Battle of Gaines' Mill, June 27, 1862, where he was wounded; repulse of Wise's Division at Malvern Hill (in command), June 29, 1862; Battle of Malvern Hill, July 1, 1862, and skirmish at Harrison's Landing, July 2, 1862.

In the Northern Virginia Campaign, 1862, he was engaged in the Battle of Manassas, August 30, 1862, and skirmish near Centreville, September 1, 1862. He was in command of Brigade (Army of the Potomac) in the Maryland Campaign, 1862, being engaged in skirmishes and battle of Antietam, September 15-17, 1862; skirmish with the enemy's rear-guard on the Potomac, September 19, 1862; and march to Falmouth, Va., 1862. In the Rappahannock Campaign, 1862'-'63, he was in command of Brigade till February 4, 1863. He then became Chief Topographical Engineer of the Army of the Potomac, and was engaged in the battle of Fredericksburg, December 13-16, 1863; making reconnaissances, 1862-'63; action on Orange Pike, May 1, 1863; storming of Marye Heights, May 3, 1863, and battle of Salem, May 3-4, 1863, and as Chief Engineer of the Army of the Potomac, June 8-August 12, 1863.

In the Pennsylvania Campaign, he was engaged in charge of the re-embarkation of stores at Aquia Creek, 1863; reconnaissance and battle of Gettysburg, July 1-3, 1863, where he was wounded; and construction of bridges, and making reconnaissances while pursuing the enemy, July-August, 1863.

He was in command of Second Corps (Army of the Potomac), from August 12, 1863, to March 24, 1864.

In the operations in Central Virginia, he was engaged in movement to Culpeper and the Rapidan, September 13-16, 1863; combat at Auburn and Bristoe Station (in command), October 14, 1863; skirmish at Bull Run, October 15, 1863, and at Kelly's Ford, November 8, 1863; movement to Mine Run, with heavy skirmishing, November 26-30, 1863, and demonstration upon the enemy across Morton's Ford, February 6, 1864.

He was in command of Fifth Corps (Army of the Potomac), from March 24, 1864, to April 1, 1865.

In the Richmond Campaign, he was engaged in the battle of the Wilderness, May 5-6, 1864; battles about Spottsylvania, May 8-20, 1864; Battles of North Anna, May 23-25, 1864; skirmish on Tolopotomy Creek, May 29, 1864; battle of Bethesda Church, May 30,' 1864; battles of Cold Harbor, June 1-4, 1864; skirmish on White Oak Swamp, June 13, 1864; assaults on Petersburg, June 17-18, 1864; siege of Petersburg, June 18, 1864-April 2, 1865; Petersburg Mine assault, July 30, 1864; actions for the occupation of the Weldon Railroad, August 18-25, 1864; combat of Peebles' Farm, September 30, 1864; action at Chapel House, October 1, 1864; skirmishes near Hatcher's Run, October 27-28, 1864; destruction of Weldon Railroad to Meherrin River, December 7-10, 1864; combat near Dabney's Mill (in command), February 6-7, 1865; actions and movement to White Oak Ridge, March 29-31, 1865; battle of Five Forks, April 1, 1865.

He was in command of the defences of Petersburg and Southside Railroad, April 3-May 1, 1865; in command of the Department of Mississippi, May 14-30, 1865, and was at New York City preparing Maps and Reports of his campaigns, June 20, 1865, to July 31, 1866.

General Warren was promoted successively from the grade of Lieutenant to that of Lieutenant Colonel, Corps of Engineers, and Major General, U. S. Volunteers. He received the brevets of Lieutenant Colonel, U. S. Army, 'for gallant and meritorious services at the Battle of Gaines' Mill,' Va., 1862; Colonel U. S. Army, 'for gallant and meritorious services at the Battle of Gettysburg,' Pa., 1863; Brigadier General, U. S. Army, 'for gallant and meritorious services at the Battle of Bristoe Station,' 1863, and Major General, U. S. Army, 'for gallant and meritorious services in the field during the Rebellion,' 1865.

Since the close of the war he has been Superintending Engineer of surveys and improvements of the Upper Mississippi and its Tributaries, 1866-'70; of survey of the Battlefield of Gettysburg, Pa., 1868-'69, and survey of the Battlefield of Manassas, 1878; of Rock Island Bridge across the Mississippi, 1870, of the fortifications of New London and New Haven, Conn., 1870-'74; of the improvement of certain rivers and harbours on Long Island, 1870-'74; of construction of Block Island Breakwater, R. I., 1870-'82.

He was a member of Commission to examine Union Pacific Railroad and Telegraphic Lines, 1868-'69, and Member of many important Boards of Officers of the Corps of Engineers organised for the consideration of the plans and the execution of the works of the Corps, among which were the Board on Improvement of the Des Moines Rapids, 1867; Board on Bridge across Niagara River, at Buffalo, N. Y., 1870-'71; on Bridging the Ohio River, 1870-'71, and 1878-'82; on plan for docks constructed for Breakwater at Chicago Harbour, Ill., 1871; on the completion of Cincinnati and Newport Bridge over the Ohio, 1871; on the harbours of St. Louis, Mo., and Alton, Ill., and Banks of the Mississippi, 1872; on Bridging the channel between Lake Huron and Lake Erie, 1873; on Ship Canal from the Mississippi to the Gulf of Mexico, 1873-'74; to examine the St. Louis Bridge across the Mississippi, 1873; on the reclamation of the Alluvial Basin of the Mississippi, 1874-'75; on Mississippi Bridges between St. Paul, Minn., and St. Louis, Mo., 1876, and on the improvement of the Mississippi River, from the Falls of St. Anthony to Rock Island Rapids, 1878. He was engaged in the survey of the Battlefield of Groveton, Va., and in the preparation of campaign maps of certain operations in 1862-'63 of the Army of the Potomac in Virginia.

He was appointed a Member of the Advisory Council of the Harbour Commissioners of the State of Rhode Island, 1878.

In 1870 General Warren was assigned to the charge of the surveys and improvements of various rivers and harbours in southeastern Massachusetts; and in Rhode Island and Connecticut, on which duty and in the supervision of the construction and repair of the fortifications of New Bedford, Mass., of Narragansett. Bay and of Newport, R. I., he remained until the time of his death.

In scientific investigations, General Warren had few superiors; and his elaborate reports on some of the most important works which have been confided to the Corps of Engineers are among the most valuable contributions to its literature.

In the field, in the late civil war, he was a brave and energetic officer, and in the high command to which he attained by his patriotic valour and skill he merited the admiration of the army and the applause of his country.

He was kind and considerate in all the relations of life, and his family in its affliction will have the hearty sympathy of the Corps of Engineers.

As a testimonial of respect for the deceased, the officers of the Corps will wear the usual badge of mourning for thirty days.

George H. Eliot,
Major of Engineers.
By command of Brig.-Gen. Wright.

Strong Vincent, Brigadier-General Volunteers

Strong Vincent was born at Waterford, Erie County, Pennsylvania, June 17, 1837. He was the son of B. B. Vincent and Sarah Ann Strong Vincent. As the name indicates, Strong Vincent was of English Puritan and French Huguenot ancestry. During his childhood, his father removed from Waterford to Erie, Pennsylvania, engaging in business there as an iron-founder and banker. He was also largely interested in grain elevators in Chicago.

Strong Vincent entered the Erie Academy in 1843, remaining there until 1850; learned the trade of iron-moulder in his father's foundry 1850-1852; was a clerk in the foundry office 1852-1854; entered Trinity College, Hartford, Connecticut, 1854; entered Harvard College 1856, and was graduated at Harvard in 1859. He read law in Erie 1859-1860, with W. S. Lane, Esquire; was admitted to the Erie Bar in December, 1860, and practiced law until he entered the Army in 1861.

In April, 1861, he married Elizabeth H. Carter of Newark, New

Jersey, to whom he had been engaged since his college days.

Military Record.—Upon the call of the President in April, 1861, for volunteers for three months' service, he enlisted in Colonel John W. McLane's Erie Regiment of Volunteers; was elected second lieutenant of his company; was promoted to first lieutenant and adjutant of the regiment, serving as such until the muster out of the regiment at the close of its service in July, 1861.

Colonel McLane received an order from the Secretary of War, dated July 24, 1861, authorising him to raise a regiment of volunteers to serve for three years or during the war. About half the three months regiment re-enlisted and by the end of August the full complement of men and officers had been secured. The regiment was mustered into the service of the United States, September 14, 1861, as the Eighty-Third Regiment Pennsylvania Volunteers, with John W. McLane as colonel and Strong Vincent as lieutenant-colonel, to rank as such from July 24, 1861.

Colonel McLane was killed at the Battle of Gaines' Mill, Virginia, June 27, 1862. Vincent was promoted to be colonel of the regiment, ranking as such from June 27, 1862. When Colonel Stockton (who as senior colonel had commanded the brigade after General Butterfield's promotion) resigned, soon after the battle of Chancellorsville, Vincent, who was next in rank, was assigned to the command of the brigade and continued in command until he was wounded at the Battle of Gettysburg July 2, 1863. In consideration of his distinguished service at this battle General Meade telegraphed that night to President Lincoln, requesting that he be promoted to be brigadier-general. The President sent the commission at once by special messenger, but Vincent's wound was fatal, and he died a few days later.

Vincent without previous military training showed at the outset an appreciation of the need of discipline, precision, and accuracy in all military matters. My first recollection of him is his appearance as adjutant in forming the line of the regiment for its first dress parade. As I stood, a private in the ranks, and heard his command on the right, "To the rear open order, March!" and saw the line officers step to the front in an irregular line and heard him correct their faults, then saw him march to the centre, halt, turn on his heel, face the colonel, who stood like a statue at some distance with his arms folded, gauntlets reaching near to his elbows, salute with his sword and report, "Sir, the parade is formed," I confess my first impression of him was not favourable.

I thought him a dude and an upstart. I soon came to know that he

STRONG VINCENT

wished to impress on that mob of green country boys, by example as well as precept, the proper way for a soldier to stand and to move. It was the beginning for that regiment of its military education. By the end of its three months' service spent in continual drill and practice in all the duties of a soldier, that part of this regiment which re-enlisted for three years formed a trained nucleus for the Eighty-Third Regiment of Pennsylvania Volunteers, which placed it in the front rank of volunteers for the war, and kept it there.

Vincent had demonstrated his fitness for a higher position. McLane had seen service in the Mexican war and had kept up his training by the command of a militia company for several years in Erie. He was a tall, commanding figure, with a strong voice, and was glad to have Vincent as his second in command. McLane was a fine officer, and had he lived would have been worthy of, and no doubt received, higher rank; but he was instantly killed in the first great battle in which the regiment participated—Gaines' Mill.

The long and weary months of the fall and winter of 1861-1862 were not spent in idleness. The men and officers of this regiment, like those of the other regiments of the Army of the Potomac, were drilled and disciplined into a thorough familiarity with their duties. The company officers were as ignorant as their men. An officers' school was established, of which Vincent was the schoolmaster. He made a good one. What he did not know about tactics and army regulations he learned, and forced the junior officers to learn and practice. The result was that General McClellan, late in the fall, pronounced the Eighty-Third Pennsylvania the best drilled regiment in Fitz John Porter's division, if not the best in the army. Of course, this result cannot be attributed entirely to Vincent, although his quiet, persistent work had much to do with it. The regiment was fortunate in having McLane as its colonel and General Daniel Butterfield as its brigade commander, and from Hall's Hill to Appomattox the Eighty-Third Pennsylvania showed the effect of this early training.

Vincent was of medium stature, but well formed. He was a fine horseman, and when mounted looked much larger than when on foot. He was a gentleman by nature, quiet and considerate in his demeanour, deserving and receiving the respect of his men and officers, as well as that of his superiors in rank. Severe in discipline when severity was needed, no officer in the army was more thoughtful and considerate of the comfort and health of his men. Without the schooling of West Point, by the help of his trained mind, quickness of perception, and constant study, stimulated by his intense patriotism, his knowledge of the art of war made him equal to any emergency in which he was placed.

He was generally of a cheerful disposition, but during his last campaign he seemed to have a presentiment that it might be his last. On July 1, when after a long march the brigade went into bivouac just before reaching Hanover, expecting to spend the night there, news came of the battle at Gettysburg, with the order to continue the march in that direction. The brigade was quickly formed and in the road. Just before reaching Hanover Vincent sent back for the drum corps and the colour guard of the Eighty-Third to come to the front of the brigade with their flag. As the flag was unfurled and rippled in the breeze, he reverently bared his head, and said to Captain Clark, his adjutant-general, "What death more glorious can any man desire than to die on the soil of old Pennsylvania fighting for that flag?"

Just before leaving for the war, in April, 1861, he married Elizabeth Carter and left her with his father and mother in Erie. While the army was in permanent camps at Hall's Hill, Virginia, in 1861-1862, and in front of Fredericksburg, Virginia, 1862 1863, Mrs. Vincent joined her husband, and remained with him in the winter quarters until the army started on its campaigns, when she returned to Erie. She was a very handsome young woman, tall, graceful, and a superb horsewoman. When his duties permitted, Vincent loved to ride with her through the camps of the army and about the surrounding country. They were followed with looks of admiration wherever they appeared. Their love was ideal. She knew the risks of the service, but she always encouraged him to do his full duty. It was not military glory, but the purest patriotism which actuated both. At this writing Mrs. Vincent still survives him, one of the noblest of the noble women of our country.

Letters About Vincent and His Brigade at Gettysburg

In 1901 the compiler of this book, in response to his inquiry as to the character of General Vincent, his conduct at Gettysburg, and its effect in determining the result of the battle, received letters from the following gentlemen, with permission to publish them. Extracts from which are subjoined.

(From Major-General Daniel Butterfield, Chief of Staff, Army of the Potomac at Gettysburg.)

Hotel Royal Palm, Miami, Florida,
February 19, 1901.

No man who lived and fought in the Battle of Gettysburg did

more for his country than Vincent. I knew the whole matter from beginning to end. He was a magnificent soldier, a gentleman of high education and great ability.

General Tremain brought messages to General Meade and to me from the field, describing the exigency and great need for the immediate occupation of Round Top, and authority was given him to send the troops there. In my judgment, there was not another command on the field which could have been more effective in the matter of time and rapidity of movement in getting to the spot in time to have saved the day, owing to its wonderful efficiency, drill, and discipline under Vincent, who had been trained and educated with it.

(From Joshua L. Chamberlain, Brevet Major-General U. S. V., Colonel Commanding Twentieth Maine Volunteers at Gettysburg.)

Portland, Maine, November 18, 1901.

Colonel Vincent's conduct in taking his brigade to Little Round Top and placing it in position, and in throwing his great personal energy and determination into the fight there, are personally well known to me. I regard the timely occupation of that position, which was at that stage of the battle the key of the Union defence, as due to the energy and skill of Colonel Vincent.

(From Charles W. Eliot, President of Harvard University)

Cambridge, Mass., November 27, 1901.

I am, of course, incompetent to express an opinion about the precise value of Colonel Vincent's energetic action at Gettysburg; but I remember him as a student in Harvard College with perfect distinctness, and I should like to testify to anybody who wants to know what manner of man he was—that he was one of the manliest and most attractive persons that I ever saw. I remember thinking that his death was an unspeakable loss to the army on which the hopes of the country rested at the time, and to the country which he would have greatly served if his life had been spared.

(From General Ellis Spear, Major Twentieth Maine Volunteers at Gettysburg.)

Washington, D. C, November 23, 1901.

General George G. Meade

I have read carefully the foregoing statement in regard to General Vincent's services at Gettysburg. As to the greater part of the statement, I know of my own knowledge that it is strictly accurate. What happened on the right of the brigade when Vincent was mortally wounded I did not see, being then with the Twentieth Maine closely engaged on the left, but it was a matter of common report at the time, and beyond question the statement is strictly accurate. I had seen General Vincent in battle before and knew what he would do then. He was a very valuable officer and of great promise, and his death was a great loss to the army; but the success he achieved in averting the imminent and great danger on the left at Gettysburg on the second day of the battle, was worth what it cost, though the price was great.

(From General James Longstreet, C. S. A.)

Washington, D. C, December 6, 1901."It gives me pleasure to state in reference to the worth of Little Round Top to the Union Army at Gettysburg, it was everything to the success of the Union battle. General Vincent's prompt action in moving to save that point held it, and was the means of getting the battle to his side. Many minutes' delay would have given the Confederates the field.

Sketch of Colonel Patrick H. O'Rorke By Captain Porter Farley

Colonel O'Rorke was born in County Cavan, Ireland, on March 28, 1836. He was brought to America when he was only one year old. His parents settled for a year or so in Montreal, Canada, then moved to Ogdensburg, New York, where they remained about two years, when they moved to Rochester, New York, where they established their permanent home and where the survivors of the family still abide. Young O'Rorke attended No. 9 public school, and therein obtained such schooling as he had enjoyed previous to his entrance at the Military Academy at West Point.

About the year 1855 the University of Rochester established two free scholarships open on competition to the boys of the public schools of the city. O'Rorke competed with others, and stood first on the list at the close of the examination. His parents were devoted Roman Catholics, and objected to the denominational control of the

COLONEL PATRICK H. O'RORKE

Rochester College. On this account, he had to forego the educational advantages which were thus open to him. Soon after graduating from the public school he began to learn the trade of his father, which was that of marble cutter.

His general ability had by this time become well recognised and had attracted the attention of the congressman from the Rochester district, who obtained for him an appointment to a cadetship at West Point. He entered the Military Academy in June, 1857, with the class which was graduated in June, 1861. From the first O'Rorke took a high stand in his class and finally was graduated at its head, in a class of thirty-four. Among his classmates, the two best known for distinguished services during the Civil War were Lieutenant Alonzo H. Cushing, killed on July 3 at Gettysburg, and General George A. Custer, who fell in the massacre on the Little Big Horn in 1876.

Immediately upon his graduation O'Rorke was commissioned as second lieutenant of Engineers. He served on the staff of General Tyler at the Battle of Bull Run, July 21, 1861. Later he acted as assistant engineer on the defences of Washington and at Fortress Monroe. In October, 1861, he went to Port Royal as one of the staff of General W. T. Sherman. For his services on this occasion he received the brevet of captain. In September, 1862, he was commissioned colonel of the One Hundred and Fortieth New York Volunteers. During all the service of Colonel O'Rorke as commander of this regiment it formed a part of the Third Brigade, Second Division, Fifth Army Corps. It was due to O'Rorke's devotion and skill that this regiment attained an efficiency which was a source of pride to him and to the men who served under him.

During the Chancellorsville campaign O'Rorke was in command of the brigade, as our brigade commander, General Warren, had been assigned to duty as chief engineer of the army under Hooker. During the Gettysburg campaign, which closed his admirable and promising career, he was again in command of his regiment. He fell, instantly killed, on July 2, 1863, near the foot of the southern slope of Little Round Top. The last effort of his life was the gallant leadership displayed as he headed the successful charge down the slope up which Hood's impetuous men were already pushing their way. He died in the actual discharge of a service of the most vital importance to his country.

Colonel O'Rorke had been married to Miss Clara W. Bishop in July, 1862, only a few weeks before his appointment as colonel. He left no children. About a year and a half after his death his widow entered the religious order of the Sacred Heart. She died only a few years ago, being then Lady Superior in the convent of her order in Providence, Rhode Island.

Colonel O'Rorke's body was buried on the Bushman farm near Gettysburg. As soon as possible his wife came to the spot and caused its removal to Rochester, where it was buried in the cemetery on Pinnacle hill. It was later removed to a more eligible spot in the same cemetery, and still again some years later, when the old Pinnacle cemetery was abandoned, it was removed to the new cemetery of the Holy Sepulchre, north of Rochester. All this is mentioned to lead up to the interesting and remarkable fact that the body of Colonel George Ryan, who succeeded O'Rorke in command of the One Hundred and Fortieth New York, and who was killed at Spottsylvania, has also been four times buried, and now lies beside that of Colonel O'Rorke in his family burial lot.

Captain Porter Farley

Military Record—Extracts from the report of the Adjutant General of the State of New York.

> Porter Farley.—Age at enlistment, 22 years. Enrolled at Rochester to serve three years, and mustered in as Second Lieutenant Company G, One Hundred and Fortieth New York Volunteers, August 30, 1862. As First Lieutenant January 1, 1863. As First Lieutenant and Quartermaster, October 28, 1863. As Captain of Company B, January 16, 1864. Discharged for disability, August 4, 1864.

Lieutenant Farley served as acting adjutant of the regiment from the day the regiment left Falmouth for the Gettysburg campaign until October 28, 1863, when he was commissioned regimental quartermaster. He served in this capacity until he was commissioned captain of Company B.

Little Round Top, Gettysburg

6. Letters and Papers

Lieutenant Mackenzie to General Meade
(*Rebellion Records*, Vol. xxvii, part i.)

       Brandy Station, Va., March 22, 1864.
Major-General Meade:
Sir: I have the honour to submit the following statement of facts relative to the battle of July 2, at Gettysburg:
At the opening of the battle of July 2 there were no troops belonging to General Sickles' corps on Round Top ridge.
General Sickles, when called upon by General Warren through me, to furnish troops for the defence of that position, refused to do so, stating that his whole command was necessary to defend his front, or words to that effect.
General Sykes furnished troops for the object stated above as soon as called upon to do so.
I have the honour to be, very respectfully, your obedient servant,

       Ranald S. Mackenzie,
    First Lieutenant, Corps of Engineers.

  Lieutenant Mackenzie was one of three lieutenants of engineers serving on the staff of General Warren, chief engineer of the Army of the Potomac at the Battle of Gettysburg. This letter is evidently a reply to one from General Meade, which the writer has not been able to find in the *Official Records*. It is a link in the chain of evidence that Warren did not leave Little Round Top before the arrival of Weed's brigade, but remained there with the officers at the signal station, sending his requests for troops to occupy this position through the officers of his staff. He sent Lieutenant Mackenzie to General Sickles first. If it be objected that Lieutenant Mackenzie does not say that

Warren's request to Sykes was sent "through me," the inference is fair that it was, and that he would not repeat these words in a brief formal letter to General Meade.

A letter from the Adjutant General's office, War Department, informs me that, with one exception, all the officers of General Sykes' staff at Gettysburg mentioned in his official report are dead. Correspondence with the only survivor satisfies me that he is not the officer who carried the order from Sykes to Barnes, to send one of his brigades to Little Round Top, which was intercepted by Vincent and acted upon before it reached Barnes.

It is possible that when Mackenzie delivered to Sykes the request of Warren that a brigade should be sent to Little Round Top, Sykes agreed and sent the order to Barnes by Mackenzie and that, supposing that Barnes would be found with his division, Mackenzie rode there; and not finding Barnes, told Vincent of the order which Sykes had authorised him to deliver to Barnes.

General Sykes' Letter

(Copy of letter from General George Sykes, commanding Fifth Army Corps at Gettysburg, to Captain Porter Farley, Rochester, New York, dated Fort Snelling, Minnesota, August 5, 1872).

> Dear Sir: Your letter has just reached me through the War Department, and it gives me pleasure to answer such of the questions it asks as I can. I enclose a copy of my Report of the Battle of Gettysburg, which is confined exclusively to what I knew of events then taking place. The only error in it I have ever discovered, is that Birney did not close the gap I asked him to, near the battery on the left of his line. Through that gap the enemy in part forced his way. The Divisions of the Fifth Corps moved from the Baltimore pike where it crossed Rock Creek, as follows: First Division, Second Division, Third Division About 3 p.m. on the 2nd of July the Corps Commanders were at the headquarters of General Meade.
>
> After consultation, I was directed by him to establish the Fifth Corps on the left of the general line of the army, terminating at Little Round Top, and hold that part of the field. The crest of the valley sweeping from Cemetery Ridge around to the left and embracing Little Round Top was the general line of battle adopted by the commanding General. The position of the Third Corps was not known to me, and no staff officer was given me

to find it out. In looking for it, I found the gap spoken of in my Report, in consequence of which, I sought the commander of the troops nearest it, and asked that it be closed, promising to fill the interval he might make with my own troops.

To accomplish this, I hastened to the leading Brigades, Sweitzer and Tilton, First Division, and posted them on the edge of a wood in front of part of Birney's line, to cover the interval I expected him to make. How Vincent got to Round Top I do not know, unless hearing my *aide-de-camp* deliver the order for the Corps to take the left of the line, he made his way there of his own soldierly instinct. As I conducted the two leading brigades across the Taneytown pike to the position I gave them, I do not remember to have seen Vincent's troops. I was at the head, and he at the rear of the column, and a sputtering fire having commenced, I was anxious to get the foremost brigades in their place.

The interference with orders given by me to my troops occurred only in Warren's hurrying up Weed's Brigade to Round Top, which was very judicious, and an interference of General Sickles by which General Weed was withdrawn in part from Round Top, and placed *en route* towards the right, until I met him, and at once returned him to his place. Watson's Battery of regular artillery was likewise appropriated by Sickles without my knowledge, in consequence of which it was for a time lost. General Ayres took position to the right of Little Round Top until I ordered him to attack in the direction of the 'Den,' and Crawford was to be the right rear of Ayres until I moved him to the attack at a later hour.

You are right about two brigades of the First Division being out towards the peach orchard; I placed them there myself, and for the reason given. The rocky glen did not admit of troops being posted across it. If the left of the line of the Third Corps had not been thrust out into the valley, there would have been no interval near the glen, and I do not believe the enemy would have made the headway he did, but, being there, the glen enabled Longstreet to use it as a cover, and gave him power to turn the flank of the Third Corps. Had not the Fifth Corps held Round Top and the ground adjacent, nothing would have stopped him from reaching the Baltimore turnpike. Our Corps never got the credit it deserved that day. It simply saved defeat, and every fair-minded soldier knows it. The military politicians did not want one of their pets to suffer, and were strong enough to uphold 'their own.'

I have thus, Captain, replied to your letter as far as I am able. I cannot tell you much not known to you before. I am, Captain,

> Yours Very Respectfully,
>
> Geo. Sykes.

This letter was written nine years after the battle. In a measure, it confirms my statement. Warren sent Captain Mackenzie of his staff to Sykes, asking for troops for the hill. Sykes sent one of his staff to direct General Barnes to send one of his brigades. Vincent, learning of the order, in the absence of Barnes assumed the responsibility of taking his brigade. He would not have left the column except in anticipation of an order which he knew had been issued by Sykes to send one brigade. Mackenzie, in a letter to be found in Vol. xxvii, "Rebellion Records," says that Sykes responded promptly to Warren's request. As Sykes did not designate which of Barnes' brigades should be sent, he may well be pardoned for not knowing how Vincent got to Little Round Top. What he says in this respect shows a very high regard for Vincent.

Apparently, he thinks Vincent's brigade was the rear of the column, as he says he posted the two leading brigades himself. In fact, Vincent led the division with the third brigade, Sweitzer came next with the second, followed by Tilton with the first. Barnes' statement in his official report, that Warren in person came to Sykes is pure fiction. Warren remained on the hill at the signal station until Weed's brigade arrived and passed to the front to reinforce Sickles. Warren rode down the hill at this time and, detaching the rear regiment of the brigade, the One Hundred and Fortieth New York, sent it to the crest of Little Round Top, under the guidance of Lieutenant Roebling. Later the remaining regiments of Weed's brigade were ordered back by General Sykes and took position on Little Round Top, on the right of the One Hundred and Fortieth New York.

NOTES ON THE TAKING AND HOLDING OF LITTLE ROUND TOP, GETTYSBURG.

(Prepared for the New York State Commissioners of Gettysburg Monuments by Lieutenant A. P. Case, of the One Hundred and Forty-Sixth New York, acting as aid on the staff of General Weed, and after his death on the staff of Colonel Garrard).

This regiment, known as the Halleck Infantry, was commanded by Colonel Kenner Garrard of the regular army, who left the post of Commandant at West Point by request of General Halleck for that purpose. The regiment first joined General Warren's Third brigade, Second division, Fifth corps. This brigade was then composed of the Fifth New York, Colonel Winslow (Duryea's Zouaves), the One Hundred and Fortieth New York, Colonel O'Rorke, and the One Hundred and Forty-sixth New York. Warren, O'Rorke, and Garrard were together at West Point. The two other brigades of Sykes' Second division were all Regulars. But at the time of the Gettysburg campaign the brigade was commanded by General Stephen H. Weed of the regular army, and was composed of the One Hundred and Fortieth New York, the One Hundred and Forty-Sixth New York, and the Ninety-First and One Hundred and Fifty-Fifth Pennsylvania.

The Fifth corps, after marching nearly all night, reached the Gettysburg field about 6 a.m. July 2, and was stationed on the west side of Rock Creek, near the bridge of the Baltimore Pike, on the extreme right on the Union line. It was so posted, as we understood, because General Meade that morning contemplated an attack by the Fifth and Twelfth corps on Ewell's position at Benner's Hill. Soon after our arrival General Meade sent for General Weed, who had an excellent reputation as an artillery officer in the regular army, to visit the battery positions in this part of the line, including Culp's Hill. The writer, an extra *aide* on General Weed's staff, was ordered to accompany him. Several batteries were changed at General Weed's suggestion. But no attack was made on Ewell.

About 3 p. m. the Fifth corps was ordered in to support General Sickles, who held the extreme left of the Union line. At this time the Union line made nearly a horseshoe shape, so that the corps was marched from the right heel of the shoe across to the left heel. General Sykes himself took in Barnes' First division, going by the Peach Orchard cross-road. General Ayres' Second division followed, General Weed's Third brigade leading, the other two brigades following at quite a distance. The Peach Orchard crossroad connects the Taneytown and the Emmittsburg roads, and as it leaves the former it crosses over the north foot of Little Round Top. When the head of General Weed's column had reached the woods south of Trestles' house and near where the Third Massachusetts battery was placed, the smoke of the battle was so dense that General Weed rode ahead to see where he was wanted, and told his staff to bring the column along very slowly until he returned.

At this time the rear of the column, the One Hundred and Fortieth New York, had just passed the foot of Little Round Top, which was then bare of troops, and was occupied only by General Warren and the signal corps. They had just discovered a movement of rebel troops from the southwest, to occupy this hill, from which the whole left of the Union Army could be enfiladed. Realising the vital necessity of holding this point, and seeing the troops passing through the valley at its north foot. General Warren hastened down to them and found them to be his old brigade. The men greeted him with repeated cheers, for he was greatly beloved and respected by his old regiments. Detaching the One Hundred and Fortieth, he sent it up the hill, and then rode forward to the head of the column and, finding General Weed gone, ordered it halted for Weed's return. Weed soon came back with Sykes' order to take his brigade on to Little Round Top.'

He at once moved up the hill by a counter-march. The writer never learned whether he saw General Sykes or got the order from a messenger. A short time before this General Sykes had detached Vincent's brigade from Barnes' division and sent it to occupy the level gap south of Little Round Top and lying between it and Big Round Top, as that passage offered an easy route for the rebel troops to the rear of the Union left. I do not think that the occupancy or defence of Little Round Top was then thought of, for it appeared almost inaccessible. But the rebel troops that Warren had seen advancing towards the hill met Vincent's troops in the gap and at the south slope of Little Round Top, and had there a hard fight, in which Vincent was killed. His right was gradually driven back, and Hood's Texas brigade reached the southern summit of the hill, where they were met by the One Hundred and Fortieth New York, which had been rushed up from the opposite side. Never was there a more opportune arrival. A rebel occupancy of the hill would probably have been fatal to the success of the Union army.

The hill is sparsely covered with trees, and the ground thickly strewn with huge rocks, so that no deployment of troops could be made. A desperate hand-to-hand conflict ensued, the men loading and firing as they passed around the rocks. Colonel O'Rorke, two of his officers, and twenty-five privates were killed at the first onset. The Texans were driven down, Vincent's lines re-formed, with his right touching the left of Weed's brigade, now all on the hill.

The attack was renewed, and again repulsed. The regiments then took the positions they remained in until they left the Gettysburg field on the 5th of July. Their line, facing west, occupied the whole west crest of the hill in a north and south line, the One Hundred and Fortieth at the left, next the Ninety-first Pennsylvania, then the One Hundred and Forty-sixth, with the One Hundred and Fifty-fifth Pennsylvania on the right. The One Hundred and Fortieth lay partly down the south slope, and the One Hundred and Fifty-fifth Pennsylvania partly down the north slope.

There is some uncertainty as to which of the regiments first followed the One Hundred and Fortieth, but the writer thinks it was the One Hundred and Forty-Sixth. While the regiments were ascending the hill, Captain Hazlett's U. S. battery of four guns was also taken up, the horses being lashed to their utmost exertions, and the infantry assisting at the wheels. It was a terrible place for horses or guns, but the emergency had to be met. The ground on the west front of the hill was covered by the rocks of the Devil's Den, which were occupied by hundreds of rebel sharpshooters. This fight on Little Round Top took place between 4 p.m. and 5 p.m. The rebel sharpshooters were a great annoyance to both infantry and artillery. The guns of the battery could not be enough depressed to dislodge them.

Soon after 5 p.m. General Weed was instantly killed by a bullet, and as he sank to the ground Captain Hazlett, of the battery, who had been standing by his side, leaned over to speak to him, when he too was shot and fell by Weed's side, neither of them speaking a word, except that Colonel Jenkins of the One Hundred and Forty-Sixth thought he heard General Weed say 'My sister.'

During the whole of the next day, July 3, the rebel sharpshooters killed all who showed themselves on the hill. The men protected themselves as well as they could, the One Hundred and

Forty-Sixth piling up loose stones, which I am told still remain as they left them. As the hill made an excellent outlook over the field of the third day's fight, General Meade and his staff, with the signal corps, were there all day, occupying a rocky pen directly in the line held by the One Hundred and Forty-sixth. A company of Berdan's sharpshooters was brought up and afforded some protection. It was here that General Warren thought he could use one of the heavy rifles better than the man who had it. After firing it a few times, with what effect no one could tell, his own neck was grazed by a rebel bullet. He bound it up with his handkerchief and relinquished the rifle.

The writer, on going over that Devil's Den on the morning of July 4 to relieve the wounded Union soldiers who had lain there since the afternoon of July 2, found those rocky crevices full of dead rebel sharpshooters, most of them still grasping their rifles. Behind one short low ridge of rock lay a row of eighteen dead who had been tallied out one by one by our sharpshooters. One of the One Hundred and Forty-sixth brought in the sword of General Barksdale, of Mississippi, which was found by the side of his dead body. Colonel Garrard sent it to General Sykes.

During Lee's great charge on the afternoon of July 3, Hazlett's battery (commanded by Lieutenant Rittenhouse after Hazlett was killed) had a terrible raking fire on the rebel line, which was made with great effect. This caused a concentration of the fire of many rebel batteries upon Hazlett's position, their shell and shot crashing among the rocks as if the world was coming to an end. The Fifth corps hospital had been made at the house and barns of J. Weikart on the Taneytown road at the foot of the east front of Little Round Top, and during this cannonade many of the rebel shells came over the hill and struck our hospital, wounding some a second time. It was then moved to Lewis Bushman's, about a mile to the southeast. The losses of Weed's brigade were as follows: Staff, one; One Hundred and Fortieth New York, one hundred and thirty-three; One Hundred and Forty-sixth New York, twenty-eight; Ninety-first Pennsylvania, nineteen; One Hundred and Fifty-fifth Pennsylvania, nineteen; total, two hundred.

It was a curious coincidence that while the First and Second brigades of the First and Second divisions, respectively, of the

Fifth corps were supporting General Sickles, the Third brigades of those divisions should have been separately detached and sent by different routes to the defence of Little Round Top, these two brigades containing the only three New York regiments in the Fifth corps. Thus, the Forty-Fourth New York, Colonel Cross, of Vincent's brigade came shoulder to shoulder with Colonel O'Rorke's One Hundred and Fortieth New York and Colonel Garrard's One Hundred and Forty-sixth New York in one of the most critical moments of the Gettysburg fight. So, the New York men of the Fifth corps made a most gallant fight, and made it side by side.

And as General Weed's death left Colonel Garrard in command of one brigade, so did Colonel Vincent's death bring Colonel Cross in command of the other brigade. Colonel David T. Jenkins, afterwards killed in the Wilderness fight, succeeded Colonel Garrard in the command of the One Hundred and Forty-sixth. The Fifth corps left the Gettysburg field on the afternoon of July 5. Death has come to most of the leaders of the One Hundred and Forty-sixth—Meade and Sykes of the corps; Warren, Weed and Garrard of the brigade; Jenkins and Curran of the regiment. The One Hundred and Forty-Sixth had other ties which united it closely to General Warren, as one of his brothers was quartermaster of the brigade, and his youngest brother, Robert P. Warren, was a captain in the regiment, and he too is dead.

(Hazlett did not speak after he was shot in the brain, but Weed lived some time, long enough to give to Lieutenant W. H. Crennell, One Hundred and Fortieth New York, acting on his staff, minute directions as to disposition of his effects and messages to his family and to others. I believe the above account of movements of the brigade, and particularly of the One Hundred and Fortieth New York, is substantially correct.—Captain Porter Farley.)

Lieutenant Case in the preceding paper says:

A short time before this, General Sykes had detached Vincent's brigade from Barnes' division and sent it to occupy the level gap south of Little Round Top and lying between it and Big Round Top, as that passage offered an easy route for the rebel troops to the rear of the Union left.

Thus, the Forty-Fourth New York, Colonel Cross, of Vincent's brigade came shoulder to shoulder with Colonel O'Rorke's One Hundred and Fortieth New York and Colonel Garrard's One Hundred and Forty-Sixth New York in one of the most critical moments of the Gettysburg fight. So, the New York men of the Fifth corps made a most gallant fight, and made it side by side. And as General Weed's death left Colonel Garrard in command of one brigade, so did Colonel Vincent's death bring Colonel Cross in command of the other brigade.

Death has come to most of the leaders of the One Hundred and Forty-sixth—Meade and Sykes of the corps; Warren, Weed, and Garrard of the brigade; Jenkins and Curran of the regiment. The One Hundred and Forty-Sixth had other ties which united it closely to General Warren, as one of his brothers was quartermaster of the brigade and his youngest brother, Robert P. Warren, was a captain in the regiment, and he too is dead.

The greater part of the foregoing paper may be found in "New York at Gettysburg," having been read at the dedication of the monument of the One Hundred and Forty-Sixth New York on Little Round Top.

The paper contains much that is true, and some surprising errors. The statement that Sykes detached Vincent's brigade and sent it to occupy the level ground south of Little Round Top is an error, if it is to be interpreted that Sykes in person detached Vincent's brigade. If it means that the movement was made by Sykes' order, it confirms rather than disproves my statement. The ground on which Vincent's brigade fought is not level, but is the southern slope of Little Round Top. Vincent selected his own ground without direction or assistance. There is no record that Sykes saw this position at any time during the battle.

The statement that the three New York regiments fought side by side, and that Colonel Cross of the Forty-Fourth New York succeeded Colonel Vincent in command of the brigade, is contrary to all the records. The Sixteenth Michigan was between the Forty-Fourth and the One Hundred and Fortieth New York, and the Ninety-First Pennsylvania between the One Hundred and Fortieth and One Hundred and Forty-Sixth New York. Colonel Cross commanded a brigade of Caldwell's division, Second corps, and was killed on Birney's line near the wheat-field.

In his account of the movements of the divisions and brigades of the Fifth Corps, he sets the time of the arrival of General Weed, with three regiments of his brigade on Little Round Top, an hour earlier than I would.

Letters from the Comte de Paris to Captain Porter Farley

Chateau d'Eu, Seine Inférieure,
December 22, 1877.

Dear Sir: I thank you very much for your letter and the first instalment of your account of the campaigns of the One Hundred and Fortieth New York Volunteers, which I read with great pleasure. I am very grateful to General Warren for having suggested to you to send me that account, as especially the next part concerning the battle of Gettysburg will be most valuable for me in the task I have undertaken—to give an accurate narrative of that great fight. I have read already a great deal about the splendid achievements of the One Hundred and Fortieth New York on Little Round Top, but an account by a member of that regiment will be still more interesting for me. Believe me, Dear Sir,

Yours truly,

L. P. Orleans,
Comte de Paris.

Madrid, January 24, 1878.

Dear Sir: Your letters dated December 7th and 28th were duly received, and I beg you to accept my best thanks for the very interesting and valuable information which you have taken the trouble to supply me with in addition to your excellent account of the campaigns of the One Hundred and Fortieth New York Volunteers. The letter of Mr. Roebling is a striking and unexpected confirmation of your account, although, as you remark, he must have made a mistake about the position of the remainder of Weed's Brigade at the time he rode from Round Top to the Peach Orchard.

If I wrote a monograph of the Battle of Gettysburg it would afford me great pleasure to give a detailed account of all the incidents which are so graphically described by yourself and some other eye-witnesses. But my space is limited; the whole battle must be condensed into some fifty or sixty pages, and therefore every sentence must be reduced to its minimum. An act of heroism worthy of the admiration of the world must be quoted in a single word. The documents which are in my hands will enable me to give to each word a real value, but I feel it is a pity not to be able to do more out of these. Nevertheless, my task is already large enough and I cannot alter it. Believe me, Dear Sir,

    Yours truly,

            L. P. Orleans,
            Comte de Paris.

Address *Chateau d'Eu,*
Seine Inférieure, France.

        Chateau d'Eu, Seine Inférieure,
            April 20, 1878.

Dear Sir: I thank you very much for your letter of March 10th, and for the way in which you point out to me some serious blemishes in the translation of the first part of my history of the Civil War. The transposition of the word "only," occurring so frequently, must be especially annoying to the reader. The translator, Mr. Tasistro, is, I believe, a Pole, but the last correction ought to have been made by a native hand.

Having declined to revise the translation and to correct its mistakes, in order not to take the responsibility of every blunder which might remain, I did not take the trouble to read more than a few pages. But any blemish pointed out to me will be noted down for the next edition which Messrs. Porter & Coates may issue. Believe me, Dear Sir,

    Yours truly,

            L. P. Orleans,
            Comte de Paris.

7. The Warren Letters

The following letters from General G. K. Warren to Captain Porter Farley are copied from the original manuscript, and with the exception of part of the letter of July 13, 1872, have never before been published.

This 1872 letter, omitting some paragraphs at the beginning and at the end, appeared as a note to General Hunt's paper on the Battle of Gettysburg in the *Battles and Leaders of the Civil War*. It is also printed in full in the History of the One Hundred and Fifty-Fifth Pennsylvania Volunteers. The letter from Lieutenant Roebling to Captain Farley is inserted in this collection, because it is referred to by General Warren in subsequent letters.

These letters were not written for publication, but it is from just such letters that true history is made. It seems eminently proper that in the interest of the truth these letters should be taken from the files where they have slumbered for nearly half a century and be given to the public. They may contradict the statements of some historians who have attributed to General Warren deeds which he never claimed for himself.

It was not possible for any one man to have seen all of the Battle of Gettysburg. The most careful writers made use of such material as they had, to make their accounts correspond with the facts as nearly as possible. The differences between the various accounts show conclusively that some of them must be erroneous. The compiler of this book believes that the writers of accounts which he feels obliged to criticise would, in the light of later evidence, admit their errors. Some passages in General Warren's letters show the way in which these differences should be treated by fair-minded persons. This spirit does not oblige the treatment with tolerance of deliberate misrepresentation.

Newport, R. I, July 13, 1872.

To Captain Porter Farley,
One Hundred and Fortieth Regiment New York Volunteers, Rochester, N.Y.

Dear Captain: I have received your letter of the 8th inst. in relation to certain events at Little Round Top hill at Gettysburg on July 2, 1863. As nearly as I remember, "the light, almost yellow haired" officer that rode up the hill with your regiment, was Captain Chauncey B. Reese, of the Engineer Corps, U. S. Army. He and First Lieutenant Ranald S. Mackenzie of the Engineer Corps, U. S. Army, were serving with me at the time and it was like either of them to have done it. Both afterwards were promoted to the rank of Brigadier General for gallant and efficient services. General Reese (then Captain) went from Gettysburg to Charleston, S. C, and conducted the siege operations by which Ft. Wagner was reduced. He was one of the very best officers of the army. He died of yellow fever Sept. 22, 1870, at Mobile. General R. S. Mackenzie may be able to give you some interesting items about the matter, and you can address him care of the Adjutant General U. S. A., Washington, D. C.

Mr. John B. Bachelder has collected a vast deal of information about the order of occurrences at Gettysburg and you should write to him. I am getting engraved a Map of the Battlefield of Gettysburg, under direction of General Humphreys, and I will try to procure you transfer impressions to print with your book, if you desire it.

Your second question I will now answer as well as I can:

Just before the action began in earnest on July 2nd, I was with General Meade near General Sickles, whose troops seemed very badly disposed on that part of the field.

At my suggestion General Meade sent me to the left to examine the condition of affairs and I continued on till I reached Little Round Top. There were no troops on it and it was used as a Signal Station. I saw that this was the key of the whole position and that our troops in the woods in front of it could not see the ground in front of them, so that the enemy would come upon them before they would be aware of it. The long line of woods on the west (east) side of the Emmittsburg road, which road was along a ridge, furnished an excellent place for the enemy to form out of sight, so I requested the captain of a

GENERAL GOUVERNEUR K. WARREN

rifle battery just in front of Little Round Top to fire a shot into these woods. He did so, and as the shot went whistling through the air the sound of it reached the enemies' troops and caused everyone to look in the direction of it.

★★★★★★

(I think the word "west" is a slip of the pen, in a hastily written letter, for the word "east." The shot fired by Smith's battery, by Warren's order, was directed against Hood's division, then concealed in the woods east of the Emmittsburg road, between it and Plum Run, facing the Devil's Den.—O. W. N.)

★★★★★★

The motion revealed to me the glistening of gun barrels and bayonets of the enemy's line of battle already formed and far outflanking the position of any of our troops, so that the line of his advance from his right to Little Round Top was unopposed. I have been particular in telling this, as the discovery was intensely thrilling to my feelings and almost appalling. I immediately sent a hastily written dispatch to General Meade to send a division at least to me, and General Meade directed the Fifth Army Corps to take position there. The battle was already beginning to rage at the Peach Orchard and before a single man reached Round Top the whole line of the enemy moved on us in splendid array, shouting in the most confident tones.

While I was still all alone with the signal officer, the musket balls began to fly around us and he was about to fold up his flags and withdraw, but remained at my request and kept waving them in defiance. The first arrival I remember seeing was First Lieutenant Charles E. Hazlett, of the Fifth Artillery, with his battery of rifled cannon. He comprehended the situation instantly and planted a gun on the summit of the hill. He spoke to the effect that though he could do little execution on the enemy with his guns, he could aid in giving confidence to the infantry, and that his battery was of no consequence whatever compared with holding the position. He stayed there, you know, till he was killed.

I did not see Vincent's brigade come up, but I suppose it was about this time they did, and coming up behind me through the woods and taking post to the left (their proper place) I did not see them. The full force of the enemy was now sweeping the Third Army Corps from its untenable position, and no troops nor any reinforcements could maintain it. It was the dreadful misfortune of the day that any reinforcements went to that line, for all alike. Third Corps, Second Corps, and Fifth Corps, were driven from it with great loss. The earnest appeals for support drew, I suppose, the troops of the Fifth Corps away from where they were intended (that is, Little Round Top) out on the road to the Peach Orchard, and so it was that the Fifth Corps reached the vital point in such small detachments.

As soon as Hazlett was in position I rode down to the troops going out on the Peach Orchard road, and fortunately met my old brigade. General Weed, commanding it, had already passed the point with part of the command and I took the responsibility to detach Colonel O'Rorke, the head of whose regiment I struck, who, on hearing my few words of explanation about the position, moved at once to the hill top. I sent word to General Weed, or Colonel O'Rorke did, and he soon joined his command on the hill. I did not see General Weed, for soon after Colonel O'Rorke went into action General Sidney Burbank arrived with his brigade, and from that moment I felt confident the hill could be held by us. I was wounded with a musket ball while talking with Lieutenant Hazlett on the hill, but not seriously, and seeing the position saved while the whole line on the right and front of us was yielding and melting away under the enemy's fire and advance, I left the hill to rejoin General Meade near the centre of the field, where another crisis was at hand. This was finally settled in our favour by the determined bravery and gallantry of the troops posted there.

I am too much occupied now to make you a fair copy of this letter, but hope as it is it will do for your purpose.

I think General Vincent's brigade as well as your own, were, as you say, rushed up to Little Round Top after the enemy were seen making for that point.

Yours respectfully,

G. K. Warren.

Newport, R. I., July 24, 1872.

Captain Porter Farley,
Rochester, N.Y.

Captain: I have received your letter of July 21. I wrote my letter to you without consulting any notes, and I may not have given the strict order of occurrences in it. If you should wish to publish anything from me, I wish you would let me have time to revise it first. It was a time of most intense importance, while we were on Little Round Top, and it seems to me I can see everything now with the same distinctness, as if it were again before my eyes. Nevertheless, some important matters may have escaped my attention. I will not be sure that Hazlett's battery got up before I went down to Colonel O'Rorke. It may be that it was afterward, and that he, Hazlett, passed you, or it may be that only a section of the battery got there first. There was not room for more than two cannon on the hill top, and I and some stragglers from the Third Corps took hold of the gun carriage of one gun and lifted it bodily over the rocks where it was caught by a projecting piece on the summit.

If I detached Vincent's brigade I don't recollect it. General Barnes' report to General Sykes I think says something of the sort was done by me, which was Swinton's authority. Perhaps it was Reese or Mackenzie acting under my orders who did it. In fact, the whole Fifth Corps, I believe, was ordered to join me, and it was only by a miscomprehension of the situation or of orders, that any went to any other place. The authority I assumed was on the responsibility of my judgment, and I would not have hesitated to take any troops I could get hold of, to maintain ourselves on the hill. Yours respectfully,

G. K. Warren.

Newport, R. I., Oct. 12, 1877.

Captain Porter Farley,

Dear Sir: I have received yours of the 8th inst. I shall be very glad to receive the publications you proffer, and hope there will be no delay in the publication. I am specially interested about the fight at Gettysburg on July 2nd and the death of O'Rorke. If I had that part now I would at once send it to the Comte de Paris at *Chateau d'Eu, Seine Inférieure,* France. He is at present writing the account of the battle for his history, and I know he will give O'Rorke and your regiment the high credit they won there. You can send anything to him also, to the care of Theodore Lyman, Brookline, Mass.

Yours very truly,

G. K. Warren.

Newport, R. I, October 17, 1877.

Captain Porter Farley,
Rochester, N.Y.

Dear Friend: I have received your letter of the 15th and am glad you are going to send your account to the Comte de Paris. It will, I think, be in good season if you can send it before long.

I am very much interested in your two articles (which I have received) of the history of the One Hundred and Fortieth New York Volunteers. I shall grow very impatient for it from week to week. Such accounts faithfully written are the most important contributions to history. I remember Snicker's Gap that first night well enough, and my bones ached again with sympathetic cold, as they did at that time, in reading your account of it.

    Yours truly,

                              G. K. Warren.

Newport, R. I., October 23, 1877.

Captain Porter Farley,
No. 9 Rochester Savings Bank.

Dear Friend: I have received yours of the 21st inst. and the enclosure to the Comte de Paris. I venture to hold it till I can write to you about the order of march. You say, "When we reached the beginning of the rising ground at the northern extremity of Little Round Top, we being the rear regiment of our brigade, and our brigade the rear brigade of the division, General Warren," etc. This order of movement does not agree with my impression, nor with that of my brother, who was there and on General Weed's staff. I am making further inquiries about it. Are you sure of what you say, or do you derive it from someone else?

I do not know who was Swinton's informant, in particulars, if he had one. I did not furnish him any detailed information, first, because it would have been necessarily too personal, and I did not know what the greater part of the Fifth Corps did; nor have I seen any of the detailed official reports. You may be sure if I had given the account of my taking the responsibility of detaching troops and hurrying them at the last moment to the hill top, I should have said it was O'Rorke and his regiment that I detached. My recollections agree exactly with yours as to that matter after I met O'Rorke. General Sykes had ordered Vincent's brigade up, at my urgent request made some time before, but I did not see it come up, as it must have passed behind me in the woods. But then I think this brigade did essential service in holding the hill, because the troops they met and beat back would otherwise have turned the position.

I don't think Swinton's account does justice to the One Hundred and Fortieth New York and Weed's brigade; although I am willing to award all the praise to the brigade of Vincent that has been given it. O'Rorke and Hazlett, however, I saw, and I know they deserve all the praise that could be given them. I have so written to the Comte de Paris. He will not fail to divide the honours more evenly I am sure.

The battery that I directed to fire, which you inquire further about, was a battery of the Third Corps, Smith's Fourth New York, I believe, on Bachelder's map of positions. The word "requested" used by me seems to have misled you. I sent word by an orderly, I think, written on a slip of paper.

Your questions:

1st. I was Chief Engineer at Gettysburg. General Meade offered me the place of Chief of Staff, but I was not suited with it. It always kept a man away from the front in battle and the other took him there. My experience that was valuable, was in the fighting I had seen or taken part in.

2nd. The corps badge system originated with General Kearney, who had his men tuck a little piece of red flannel on their hats, cut diamond shape. When Hooker came in command he, through Butterfield, his Chief of Staff, took up the idea of making it general. I was asked, as I had many draughtsmen under me, to get up specimens of badges. I am not sure that some part of the Fifth Army Corps had not already adopted the Maltese Cross.

I made a lot of rude designs for badges, of simple forms, from which those adopted were selected. I have the originals yet. Such credit as attaches to the matter belongs to General Hooker and General Butterfield.

Swinton, I think, is in New York City. I have not seen him for many years nor written to him. Probably the editor of the *New York Times* would be a good address to send a letter to him to the care of.

I do not think the Comte de Paris will get through his history of Gettysburg very soon. I learn he is carefully investigating points in all directions, so there will be time to give him your account with all the distinctness that is attainable.

Yours truly,

G. K. Warren.

P. S.—When the point I have raised is settled I will send your letter to the *Army and Navy Journal*.—G. K. W.

Newport, R. I., October 26, 1877.

Captain Porter Farley,
Rochester, N.Y.

Dear Captain: I have a letter from Bachelder which states that Weed's brigade was leading, as shown by his notes made in the winter following, but that your regiment was in rear of the brigade. It is not an important matter in itself, but becomes interesting as illustrative of the different impressions preserved by different persons, of occurrences in exciting moments of battles, when there could be no motive for differing. Have you consulted official reports for your order of march?

Yours truly,

G. K. Warren.

Newport, R. I., October 31, 1877.

Doctor Porter Farley,
Rochester, N.Y.

Dear Friend: I have received this morning yours of the 26th, and at the same time one from Captain Marvin, who was, as you know. Adjutant of the Brigade. He wrote to me:

> I recollect the circumstances of our brigade's approach to Gettysburg. General Weed and one of his staff had gone ahead towards Sickles' Corps leaving orders with me to have the brigade follow him. The One Hundred and Fortieth New York Volunteers was in front with Colonel O'Rorke in charge of the brigade. Ninety-First Pennsylvania Volunteers next, and One Hundred and Forty-Sixth New York and One Hundred and Fifty-Fifth Pennsylvania. I well remember your riding rapidly down from Little Round Top as we approached it and inquiring of us what troops ours were and where General Weed was. You assumed the responsibility of taking away the One Hundred and Fortieth New York. I went

with the others and met General Weed, etc.

My brother was the staff officer that went with General Weed, and his recollection is the same as Marvin's. Marvin kept a journal. This recollection corresponds exactly with mine.

In view of all this, do you think still that you were the rear regiment of the brigade? I was in such anxiety to get troops that it seems to me impossible that I would have allowed a regiment even to pass me.

I would be very glad to get letters such as you refer to, when you have time to make copies.

I note what you say about your letter to the *comte*, only waiting to hear from you about this final route of order of march.

Yours truly,

G. K. Warren.

P. S.—I sent the Gettysburg map to you from this place, but it is well to acknowledge its receipt to the Chief of Engineers U. S. Army, Washington, D. C.

★★★★★★

(Marvin is all wrong in stating that the One Hundred and Fortieth Regiment led the brigade, and that O'Rorke was in temporary command of the same. On the face of it he is mistaken. If O'Rorke had been in command he would have been at the head of the brigade and would consequently have gone out to or near the Trostle House; whereas he and his regiment never crossed the northern end of Little Round Top by the roadway, but were deflected from it by Warren in person (to my certain knowledge), who then followed the balance of the brigade till he reached its head and halted it. Warren left Lieutenant Roebling with us, who accompanied our regiment to the crest at southern end of Little Round Top. See Lieutenant Roebling's letter. See statement by Lieutenant A, P. Case, of One Hundred and Forty-sixth New York. If O'Rorke had been at the head of the brigade, and in command of it, would Warren, when he met him as he did on the eastern slope, have ever allowed the balance of the brigade to pass out in the road to the Trostle House?—Porter Farley.)

★★★★★★

Newport, R. L, November 17, 1877.

Doctor Porter Farley,

Rochester, N.Y.

Dear Friend: Yours of the 8th inst. was received during my absence. I hope my "query" did not disturb your energies in the political battle you were engaged in, which must have been a very close contest, judging by the small margin of victory which you report. Your county must be a splendid field for fair play, with parties so evenly balanced.

I think your remarks about Marvin's statement are reasonable, but of course not conclusive. According to my ideas, Marvin's expression, "leaving O'Rorke in charge," expresses more than he meant. You know a general often leaves his command and goes ahead to learn about the use he is to make of his command, leaving some staff officer like Marvin to represent him, with the instruction that if any important emergency arises in his absence, to consider the next ranking officer in command. Such an idea of "in charge" might exist in Marvin's mind at the time without his communicating it to Colonel O'Rorke, and even if he did communicate it it was of such a temporary nature that O'Rorke would not disarrange his regimental organisation on account of it, preferring, as I always did, to hold the double charge until permanently assigned to the higher.

There is no reliance, however, to be placed on our memories, when their record is made to tally with our reason, based upon collateral experience; for instance, as when I wrote to you, as you quote, that my anxiety was too great for me to have allowed any troops to pass me. That is my impression now, and I was filled with restless activity at that time, so that I think no accidents of ground would have prevented my seeing, as your last letter suggests.

Let all those things go. My memory is supported by Marvin's statement and my brother's, both on Weed's staff. Your memory is sustained by General Garrard's and Mr. Bachelder's notes, so I see no reason why you should not hold to your own impressions, but give them the weight of the doubt which other memories cause. That is what I do, There is no special importance attached to the matter, that I know of, and it is a curious instance of the uncertainties of memory, for all were actors in the scene, and all truthful and disinterested.

General Garrard thinks I met General Weed, and that he consented to let O'Rorke's regiment go. But I did not meet Weed,

I am sure. And to back that up with an inference which I feel it is due to General Weed to use, I am sure that if I had met him he would have taken his whole brigade at once where I asked him. I have stood by him in trying places in battle, so that I know he would have done it at once, just as O'Rorke did, and just as I think General Garrard would have done, or any other man who knew me as well as they did.

I cannot tell you how grieved I was at O'Rorke's death. My earnest appeal appreciated and responded to was his knell. I would have died to save him if I could. If any honour attaches to what I did, it should all be given to him, for what I did would have been nothing but for him.

   Yours truly,

           G. K. Warren.

      Newport, R. I., November 20, 1877.

Captain Porter Farley,
Rochester, N.Y.

Dear Friend: I have today received galley proofs of Article IX, Gettysburg. I admire it very much and suggest several minor changes, which I make on the enclosed copy.

First: I correct the spelling of O'Rorke's name. It is thus on all the army registers.

Then, in "two" I have changed "pell-mell" to "rapidly." You can make it "excitedly," "furiously," or any other word you think proper; but not that.

Then, I have struck out six lines before the quotation from my letter, the words, "the discovery he had just made was the." I wish this done because many think I had just found the importance of the position, whereas I had been there and perceived it before it was attacked, as my letter shows.

Next, I have altered and a little shortened the quotation you made from my letter. I wrote that in a hurry, but I have lately looked over all the evidence I have and wish in it now, not to assert anything positively about points in which I differ from you. The point of difference is not great, and the change enables you to make your own statement without the necessity of reconciling an apparent inconsistency between us. I have thus struck out your explanation too. All this shortens and strengthens your articles.

Immediately after the quotation I strike out the word "just" again.

In the last paragraph, I strike out "entirely unknown to Warren," which may be a little too strong, and it does not weaken your narration to do so.

In the last paragraph of "four" I query the word "poor." (I had used the phrase "poor O'Rorke,"—P. F.) It is often used in the sense you use it, but as he was a hero "*mort dans le champ de bataille*," you better use a more exalted term of qualification. "*Dulce et decorum est pro patria*." Dickens makes little Paul Dombey wonder why they called him "poor little Dombey," and he felt hurt at the word even as a term of endearment.

Your article is very stirring and I don't think it will be injured by the changes I suggest.

     Yours truly,

                G. K. Warren.

P. S.—I think his classmates always called him Paddy O'Rorke., He was a man of noble character, and had nothing of the wild Irishman about him.—G. K. W.

Please send me another proof.—G. K. W.

         ******

(This letter was written commenting on, criticising, and correcting my first draft of the account of our going up on to Little Round Top. I sent him first galley proof, and after receiving this letter I sent him a corrected proof, and the article was not printed until after I got that back. So, my story had Warren's complete approval, and he ordered one hundred and fifty copies of it for distribution among officers of the Engineer corps.—P. F.)

         ******

(O'Rorke's Death)

         Newport, R. I., November 23, 1877.

Captain Porter Farley,
Rochester, N.Y.

Dear Friend: I have added a phrase accidentally left off in my change of my letter, and struck out an unnecessary "was," so that I think it now reads straight. The copy I kept was arranged this way.

I am such a poor writer myself that no one should feel hurt

at my effort to call attention to the propriety of using certain words in certain places. On this particular matter of O'Rorke's death I feel perhaps too much to be a good judge of the proper use of words. To me he was not poor, he was glorious. What was dear, became heroic. I love to think of him as Carthon in Ossian, when he exclaims, "Carthon dies unknown." "But thou shalt not die unknown," replied the king of woody Morven; "my bards are many, O Carthon! their songs descend to future times. The children of years to come shall hear the fame of Carthon."—"The beam of Heaven delights to shine on the grave of Carthon." "Happy are they who die in their youth when their renown is around them."

The subject you are treating of is, I consider, a very grand one; the simplest words of truth make it exalting. It requires some art in the narrator to bring us back to the consideration of the ordinary affairs of the campaign. Your last paragraph I think does this very handsomely, and is not bad just as it stands. The last three lines I think you may improve. I have indicated some changes for your consideration, although I am by no means certain that they would be improvements, and would not have done it if you had not requested it. I think the simple words "last look" will be understood by everyone to convey more than can be expressed. Poetry is full of illustrations of it.

Slowly and sadly we laid him down
On the field of his fame, fresh and gory," etc.
"He who hath bent him o'er the dead
E'er yet the day of death has fled
Before decay's effacing fingers
Have swept the lines where beauty lingers,
The first, last look by death revealed.

Yours truly,

G. K. Warren.

P. S.— I don't like the phrase "whiff of a bullet" as you use it. It was the bullet itself, and not the whiff, that was fatal. You see Shakespeare's use of it was to denote the feebleness of the "unnerved father." *Hamlet*, act ii, scene ii. You and I treat the subject differently. I would grieve as you do, but I would make the last act round up a perfect life. A great achievement by the greatest sacrifice. As the biographer of Nelson says, *"If the phaeton and horses of fire had been designed for his translation, he could not have departed in a brighter blaze of glory."*—G. K. W.

Newport, R. I., November 24, 1877.

Doctor Porter Farley,
Rochester, N.Y.

Dear Doctor: Your letter card of the 22nd is just received. I think there is no objection to putting the matter as you suggest. I have sent you answers to all your references heretofore, and if they do not accord with your ideas, use your judgment as to what to do, for I think it will be quite as good.

Be careful in statements of facts, for I see Longstreet, like everyone in the South, always gets whipped with overwhelming numbers, according to his own statement, which I know were quite as often just the reverse.

Yours truly,

G. K. Warren.

Newport, R. L, November 28, 1877.

Doctor Porter Farley,
Rochester, N.Y.

Dear Friend: I have read your revised proof, and think it very good indeed.

I would like to have you strike out the words "with part of the command" in my letter. It may have been so, but that is not according to the best of my recollection and belief. I would rather leave that an open question. My letter to you was written in great haste, without careful thinking over minute points, to give you a general idea of the situation as I comprehended it, and in which your regiment took such an important part. You must have overlooked my striking these words out before, or else I did not do what I meant to.

Yours truly,

G. K. Warren.

P. S.—Order for me one hundred and fifty copies of the papers containing No. IX. I want to send one to every officer of Engineers.—G. K. W.

Newport, R. I., December 2, 1877.

Dear Friend: I have received yours of the 30th, and note your kind offer to mail the papers for me, which would save some trouble and expense. But I want to send them in bulk to Washington, D. C, to be sent out from there. By doing this each officer will see that they are sent to all, and may take more special notice of them than if sent like newspapers ordinarily are. Moreover, I will write a short note and have it printed to accompany them.

If I can get time I shall soon write up my report of Gettysburg, and I shall do all I can to see that such a noble sacrifice as O'Rorke made is appreciated and his name honoured.

What has ever been done about his memory? Where is he buried? What kind of stone marks the spot? Where are his family? How many children did he leave? What circumstances are they in? I would like to know all about them.

Please send the one hundred and fifty papers by express, to William J. Warren, Esq., Office of Chief of Engineers U. S. A., Washington, D. C, and send me the bill for expenses, including expressage prepaid.

  Yours truly,

G. K. Warren.

Newport, R. I., December 5, 1877.

Dear Friend: Article IX came today, and I have sent a copy to the Comte de Paris. I thought perhaps you would like your own letter to go somewhat modified, so I return it to you. I believe I told you Swinton got his account very much from Bachelder, and he got it from Colonel Rice (afterwards General and killed at Spottsylvania in May, 1864), and from General Chamberlain.

I send you back also the reserved copy I had of the first proof, of which you sent me two.

  Yours truly,

G. K. Warren.

Newport, R. I., December 6, 1877.

Doctor Farley,

Dear Friend: I have just received your interesting letter giving me an account of the O'Rorkes. I remember Ryan well.

I enclose you a check for $5.50 for the papers.

In regard to the question you raise in the attached slip, I know nothing. I heard something of it at the time, but did not heed it. My brother recollects no special failure wait on the occasion. He was on his staff.

O'Rorke was about twenty-one years old when he entered the Military Academy, twenty-five years old when he graduated in 1861. Twenty-seven years old when he died at Gettysburg. I was thirty-three years, six months old at that time.

   Yours truly,

          G. K. Warren.

      Newport, R. I., December 16, 1877.

Dear Friend: I have received yours of the 14th, and enclosed letter from Colonel Roebling.(Reproduced further on). If I said the staff officer was Captain Reese, it was only a surmise, for I have no personal recollection. I had Reese, Mackenzie, and Roebling with me that day at different times, and they were all such bright, gallant men, proved on hundreds of trying occasions, that I might not recollect the special service of either of them. Roebling, however, was on my staff, and I think performed more able and brave service than anyone I knew.

It is singular that you should have received this information and sent it to me, for he is my brother-in-law, and I see him quite frequently, and this letter is written by my sister at his dictation. When we are together we never talk about the war, because it is an exciting subject. Colonel Roebling's health was very much injured by the air pressure in the caissons of the Brooklyn Bridge, and it requires all his strength to keep up with the management of the great bridge he now has charge of. So, all of us spare him from every exciting topic in conversation. He has a wonderful mind and memory, and as he says, "a slight hint sometimes brings up a whole chain of forgotten events."

I sent my sister a copy of your article, and they have very properly sent their acknowledgments of its merits to you.

I am very glad this matter has come out as it has, because it makes Roebling's recollections and mine free from any charges of collusion. Colonel Roebling married my sister in January, 1865.

I wish Colonel Roebling would write a narrative of the war, and perhaps when the bridge is finished he may do so. That bridge itself is as sad as a battlefield to us. Colonel Roebling's father lost his life in beginning it, and he is wearing himself out in finishing it, and all for the glory of the thing, for he has plenty of means and money, and brilliant education, so that "knowledge with her ample page rich with the spoils of time" is all unfolded to him.

I am very glad you received his letter, which I return to you.

Yours truly,

G. K. Warren.

P. S.—Are you not going to publish your articles in book form?—G. K. W. (Relating to *Battle of the Wilderness*)

                       Newport, R. I., December 22, 1877.

Doctor Farley,

Dear Friend: I have yours of the 20th. I cannot recall the number or designation of the section of the battery you refer to, nor the name of the officer in command of it. I well remember, however, that he was a gallant, brave fellow. I am very anxious to get time to write an account of this battle, which is so little understood and is so confused. I do not know whether you propose to comment on the matter or not, but I will tell you that it was my order that these two pieces should accompany the attacking force. Under orders I had moved every man that was up, in the assault, and I thought that when the enemy's line was taken these guns would give steadiness to the men by its firing, which would be heard all along it, and have a demoralising effect upon the enemy.

If General Grant would only have accepted my suggestion to let me deploy my whole corps, and wait till Sedgwick with one division could reach and assault the enemy's left flank, towards which I knew he was moving, then my advance would certainly, I think, have been a great success, and Ewell's corps alone and unsupported must have been driven from the field. Hill's corps could then have been beaten in its isolated position. I saw that, that day, and I was so astonished at General Lee's temerity in offering us such an opportunity. I think it is wrong to say the Wilderness did not allow of such grand tactics. We had become familiar with it by that time—at least I had. But all my suggestions were received with contumely and scorn that was positively insulting.

The guns were left on the road under the fire of both lines, so that neither could draw them off, and when we left the position we abandoned them. The officer in command, I think, was killed.

Write to General H. J. Hunt, U. S. Army, Charleston, S. C., for any information about the artillery. It is because I knew he kept so exact an account of everything relating to artillery that I have not more notes about it.

My sister, Mrs. Roebling, has sent me your letter to Colonel R., so that that cycle of correspondence seems complete. She says her first impression of Roebling was the same as yours, but singularly he never made that impression upon me. In fact, I got my impressions of men in the war very much from what they did and not from personal appearance. Every now and then I meet some small-sized, modest fellow in citizen's clothes, that I knew only on horseback in the field, where he appeared to me almost like a Centaur, and grand in physical strength.

    Yours truly,

            G. K. Warren.

      Newport, R. I., January 16, 1878.

Doctor Farley,

Dear Friend: I write to thank you for your considerate mention of me at Mine Run. I believe you spoke the general sentiment of the army about that matter. I never attend an army gathering that numbers of officers and men do not come forward and personally thank me for taking the stand I then did.

I have sent your Gettysburg number around, and one officer of Engineers writes me: "O'Rorke was two years my junior at West Point, but I remember him as a 'pleb' (name for new cadet), a noble, true, manly fellow, who wore a watch and chain presented to him by the Humane Society for heroism in saving a boy's life when he was drowning, at the peril of his own."

Such an act seems so to forecast his conduct at Gettysburg that I hope it is a true story, and would like to know all the details of it.

    Yours truly,

            G. K. Warren.

    No. 218 East Seventeenth Street, New York,

            April 10, 1878.

Doctor Porter Farley,

Dear Sir: I was pleased to receive your letter of the 24th *ult.*, and especially to learn your personal reasons for leaving the service when you did. There were a great many heart-breaking troubles which men in our war had to bear that few ever thought of, outside of it. But I knew them well in several instances, and I could often imagine them when I did not know the circumstances.

Separation from those dear to me, at that period in my life, was the greatest hardship I had to endure. I hope to hear from you occasionally at least.

Yours truly,

G. K. Warren.

Newport, R. L, May 15, 1878.

Doctor Porter Farley,
Rochester, N.Y.

Dear Friend: I have just returned here after two months' absence, and find your translation of Schweigger's *Ophthalmology*, which you have so kindly sent me with your compliments. I shall read it with much interest if it is not too technical for my understanding. I hope you will be rewarded for your labour pecuniarily, but think you cannot fail to add to your reputation. I hear your articles on Gettysburg and the whole series very flatteringly spoken of. It is a great pity that circumstances of ill health prevented your continuing them all the way through, and it makes us all regret with you that you could not have continued on to the end.

In talking with my sisters about O'Rorke's watch, they both say it was given to him for saving the life of another, though they do not know certainly whether it was his schoolmates or others who did it. What his classmate. Major Wilson, says, is therefore correct. Mrs. Roebling says she often had the watch in her hand and heard the whole matter talked over.

Hoping to hear from you now and then, I remain.

Very truly yours,

G. K. Warren.

LIEUTENANT ROEBLING'S LETTER

No. 110 Columbia Heights,
Brooklyn, December 13, 1877.

Porter Farley, Esq.,
Rochester, N.Y.

Dear Sir: I have read with much interest in the *Rochester Democrat* and *Chronicle* of December 3rd your graphic description of the critical episode on Round Top Mountain at the Battle of Gettysburg.

I was the mounted officer who accompanied General Warren on that occasion. I went with Colonel O'Rorke and your regiment to the top of the hill, where you at once became engaged with the enemy, who had almost reached the crest of the hill during the short interval which elapsed before we met your regiment, after we came down from the hill where the signal officer was. I had been on the summit of Little Round Top for half an hour with the signal officer, before we rushed down to call on you for help.

I left Colonel O'Rorke as soon as he went into battle, and started with a message to General Meade, to inform him of what had been done. I passed through the remainder of Weed's brigade and along the line of troops lying on the Peach Orchard road, who were already engaged with the enemy, and it seemed to me, before I had passed from one end of the line to the other, they had lost half their members, showing the severity of this onset and also the shortness of its duration, because it was all over in half an hour.

Vincent's brigade was to the back and left of the One Hundred and Fortieth regiment. They were marching through the woods, and arrived just in time to check the head of the rebel advance, which was coming up the ravine between the two Round Tops, but they did not become generally engaged until after your regiment had made its onslaught on the rebels.

So far as my memory serves me, your account is accurate in every respect, even down to very minute details which could only have been seen by two or three persons.

The tugging of the horses and men to get those guns up the hill, I remember as if it were yesterday.

If there are any points on which your memory may have failed you, I shall be happy to help you if I can. A slight hint sometimes brings up a whole chain of forgotten events. Yours very truly,

W. A. Roebling.

The statements by the historians about the battle for the possession of Little Round Top are so contradictory that their inaccuracy is evident. The discovery by me, a few months ago, of these letters from

General Warren, and Captain Farley's consent to their publication, led to the preparation of this book. If any further evidence is needed to show that the historians were misinformed, these letters furnish the proof. They were not written in any spirit of controversy. They were not written with any thought of their publication. Had Warren lived until some or all of these histories were published he might have had something to say about the matter; but he died in 1882. It is nearly half a century since the Battle of Gettysburg was fought. An earnest effort to relate the true story of Little Round Top justifies the publication of these letters, they prove by direct statement, or by fair inference:

First: That Warren was at the signal station on Little Round Top before the Confederate infantry or artillery made its appearance in front of Birney's line, and that he remained there until the arrival of Weed's brigade, which was then passing over the low ridge at the north end of Little Round Top into the Plum Run valley, on its way to reinforce Sickles, when he left the hill and detached from that brigade the One Hundred and Fortieth New York, which was the rear regiment of the brigade, sent it to the crest of the hill with one of his staff, Lieutenant Roebling, to conduct it to its position, while the remainder of the brigade continued its march to the front. Warren did not return to the hill, but rode away to join General Meade.

Second: That he did not go to Sykes and Barnes; that he did not detach Vincent's brigade and conduct it to its position on the southern slope of Little Round Top; that he did not see Vincent's brigade come up; that he used his *aides*. Lieutenants Mackenzie and Reese, in sending for troops to occupy the hill.

Third: That Warren, being unable to see the location of Vincent's brigade from his point of observation, knew very little, at the time, of the fight which Vincent's men made there, but later recognised its importance and gave full credit to Vincent.

The reader will find in these letters abundant evidence of Warren's generous spirit, with no attanpt to claim for himself all the glory.

The statement in Lieutenant Roebling's letter that Vincent's brigade did not become generally engaged until after O'Rorke's regiment had made its onslaught on the rebels, is a mistake. The attack on Vincent's right flank was not made until the troops which made it had been repulsed several times in assaults on Vincent's front and left. Roebling was with Warren near the signal station, and neither of them heard the noise of the fighting about Vincent's position, for reasons which I have stated elsewhere.

GENERAL JOSHUA L. CHAMBERLAIN

8. Appomattox

It seems fitting to close this account of a portion of the battle of Gettysburg, the high tide of the conflict for the preservation of the Union, with a description of the last scene between the Army of the Potomac and the Army of Northern Virginia, written by one of the regimental commanders at Little Round Top, who served to the end of the war and had the honour of commanding the parade which received the formal surrender of Lee's army.

This paper was read by General Chamberlain several years ago, at a reunion of the survivors of the old brigade, and is published by the kind permission of its author. It is entitled,

The Third Brigade at Appomattox

At two o'clock on the morning of April 9, 1865, the Third brigade, after a feverish march of twenty-nine miles, came to a halt, the rear brigade of the division column, which on such occasions has the hardest place of all. Worn out, body and spirit, by the vexations of a forced march over a course blocked every half hour by the nondescript and unaccountable obstacles of a lagging column in the road ahead, men made few preliminaries about "going into camp." That peculiar ingredient of humanity called the nervous system held an imperious precedence, not only over mind and matter, but over army regulations and discipline. There was no voice and ear for roll-calls, and even the command of empty stomachs did not avail with habit or instinct to grope among the jumbled remnants of the too familiar haversacks.

Officers and men alike flung themselves right and left along the roadside, whether it were bank or ditch, in whatever order or disorder the column had halted. Horses and riders exchanged positions, the patient animals, with slackened girths, dozing with drooping head just over the faces of their masters. In an instant, as it were, the struggling, straggling hosts were wrapped in misty darkness and silence.

But suddenly and soon the bugles rang out "The General!" Orders came to march within an hour's time. Word had come from Sheridan that he was at Appomattox Station, and that if we could hurry up he could cut the head of Lee's column, then near Appomattox Court House. Such a summons itself gave something of the strength it demanded. Spirit triumphed over body, and seemed to be on the alert before the latter could fully recover its senses. The time given was intended to provide for a meal, but that required also material, which indeed was now so simple as to quality and quantity as to make choice no task. Some of the younger regiments of the division were seen lighting dismal little fires to fry salt pork or steep some musty, sodden coffee.

The Third brigade, made up of veterans, spared their strength until the last for severer exercises. But this time patience did not attain to its perfect work. While sitting on their heels munching crumbs of hard tack and watching the coffee gradually "taking water," so as to produce a black liquid which could be sipped from the black tin dipper, word suddenly came that the Third brigade was to take the head of the column, and must pull out at once. The glimmering daybreak made still more weird the scenes and sounds which betokened that untimely departure, and the glimmering breakfasts must have evoked similar wild sensations for the benighted stomachs of the Third brigade. But a brisk march with a fight at the end was the best medicine for such a mood.

In three hours, we were at Appomattox Station, and then learned that Sheridan, with the cavalry, had pushed on to Appomattox Court House, leaving word for us to follow with all possible dispatch. Indeed, there was no need of orders to this effect, for we now began to hear the boom of cannon ahead, and we knew that Sheridan and our glorious cavalry had cut across Lee's last line of retreat. Every heart beat high. No "obstacles" hindered that march. The head of the Fifth corps ran past the rear of the Twenty-fourth, which had had the advance in the order of march. It was a triple column. The roads were taken mostly by whatever was to go on wheels, the men of both corps pressing along the fields on each side. We were evidently so near the "front" that General Bartlett thought it time to throw forward a "division" skirmish line, which he and General Griffin followed with characteristic eagerness. I was following with my own brigade and the Second

(Gregory's), when there dashed out of a farm road on our right an officer of General Sheridan's staff, who gave me a hurried order to break off from the column at once, without waiting for communication with any immediate superiors, and hasten to the support of Sheridan, who was that moment forced to fall back somewhat before the desperate onset of Gordon's old "Stonewall Corps."

Now it was the "double-quick," indeed. This movement, of course, brought me on the ground our cavalry occupied, and on the enemy's left flank, at nearly the same time at which our skirmish line had struck them in their proper front, the direction of the Lynchburg Pike. Reaching the ground, I wheeled into double line of battle and gradually replaced our cavalry, which galloped off to our right, while the Third brigade still poured in upon my left. In this way, we pressed the enemy steadily back upon Appomattox Court House. There was gallant and wild work done there by the Third brigade, as well as by the rest of the division.

Gordon had hoped to force his way through our cavalry before our infantry could get up, and reach Lynchburg with the resolute remnant of his famous old corps. But when there burst upon his front and flank these lines of ours they knew so well, that had so unexpectedly kept pace with the cavalry and marched around his retreating front, desperately as he had pressed his march, the veterans of Lee's army took in the situation as by instinct. Their resistance was mechanical and by force of habit or discipline. Their old dash and daring were gone. When our advance struck them at close quarters, they fell back in disorder or rendered themselves up as prisoners.

As an example of this feeling, all that was left of an entire brigade surrendered to a single staff officer of the Third brigade, who dashed up to them with the demand. It may well be believed that our men also were responsive to the logic of the situation. The end was now so near they could see through to it, and they were bound to "be there" themselves. Action there was of the most stirring kind, but of passion nothing. No man wantonly or in excitement struck at the life of his antagonist. It was an example of what is so strangely, and for want of an adequate word, called a "moral" effect.

When in the heat of the onset the flag of truce was seen coming in on our right, some deeper, inner sense seemed to stifle all the others. All was moving with such momentum, that when the order came at length to cease firing and to halt, it was next to impossible to stop the men. They saw well that we held the rebel army at bay, and what the consequence must soon be they did not need to be told; only whatever was to be done, they wanted to be there and have a hand in it. If there was anything to be seen, they had earned the right to front seats at the spectacle. But when at about four o'clock in the afternoon the brief, thrilling message was passed along the lines, "Lee surrenders!" there was a tumult as of an ocean let loose. Men went wild with the sweeping energies of that assurance, which answered so much of long-cherished hope and of long-endured suffering that had marked their loyal and brave career.

Now that they were no longer allowed to go forward and did not know how to go backward, there was no direction left but to go upward, and that way they took—to the top of fences, haystacks, roofs, and chimneys, that they might send their hallelujahs and toss their old caps higher toward heaven. The rebels over across the slender rivulets of the Appomattox were shouting their side of the jubilation, from whatever cause, whether cheering Lee as he rode over to speak a last word to them, or whether in deep truth they were heartily sick of the war and felt that their loyal spirit and manly energies were wasted in a hopeless and perhaps mistaken cause.

There is reason to believe the latter feeling was the motive of their exuberant demonstration, whose echoes rolled along the hillsides long after all was silent in our bivouac. For toward evening some of the rations that had been promised us for distribution at nine o'clock that morning, and from which we had double-quicked away, had now got up, and we could finish our breakfasts before lying down in peace at the close of that eventful day; and a certain deeper peace was ours, in that learning now of the starving condition of our surrendering foes, twenty thousand rations were sent over just as the day was done, into that camp of fellow-countrymen we had restored to brotherhood. Fitting token and emblem of the spirit in which that victory was won and that day ended! Here too was possibly one reason for the cheering that echoed in our ears as we fell asleep on that Palm Sunday evening.

All the next day, and the day after, measures were being determined as to the actual breaking up of Lee's army, and the return of ours. Grant and Lee had not lingered, after the main points were settled, nor indeed was Sheridan seen again on the field. Generals Griffin, Gibbon, and Merritt were appointed commissioners to arrange the final details.

All this while the visiting fever and the exchanging of tokens and souvenirs ran wild through both armies. Stringent measures had to be taken to prevent utter confusion in both camps, especially in ours, as it seemed to be understood that we were the hosts, and it was our "at home" reception. This spirit of exchange shortly passed into the spirit of trade; for our rations, after the best was done, were very short, and for three days afterwards it became necessary to forage the country far and wide to get even raw corn enough for man and beast. So, the market "went up" decidedly on all sorts of farm produce. Hard tack was a luxury, and coffee and sugar at a high premium.

How or why it came about, I do not know, but on the evening of the 10th of April I was summoned to headquarters, and informed that I was to command the parade which was to receive the formal surrender of the arms and colours of the rebel army the next morning. This was an order, and to be received and obeyed without question. One request only I ventured to make of my corps commander. It was that, considering this occasion, I might resume command of my old brigade, the Third, from which I had been transferred in June, 1864, with which I had served up to that time since my entrance into the service. My request was granted, and on that evening I yielded the command of my gallant First brigade, and went back to my veterans.

General Grant was a magnanimous man, great-minded and large-minded. He would have nothing done for show and no vain ceremony. He granted to officers the high privilege of retaining their swords, and all men who owned their horses were made welcome to keep them, as they would need them to plough their land. The rebels had begged to be spared the pain of actually laying down their arms and colours in the presence of our troops, and to be permitted to stack them in front of their own camps and march off, and let us go and pick them up after they had gone. But this would be to err too far on the side of mildness. So it was insisted that, while the surrendering army should be spared all that could humiliate their manhood, yet the insignia of the rebellion and the tokens of the power and will to hurt, lifted against the country's honour and life, must be laid down in due military form in presence of a designated portion of our army.

This latter office fell to our lot. It gave us, no doubt, a grateful satisfaction and permitted a modest pride, but it was not accepted as a token that we surpassed our comrades in merit of any kind.

We formed our line of battle on the southern margin of the principal street in Appomattox Court House. Massachusetts on the right—her Thirty-Second regiment, with all that was left to us of her Ninth, Eighteenth, and Twenty-Second; then Maine—her Twentieth regiment, with the delivered remnant of her Second and her First Sharpshooters; Michigan next—her Sixteenth, with interminglings of her First and Fourth. On the left Pennsylvania'—her One Hundred and Fifty-Fifth holding also filaments which bound us with the Sixty-Second, Eighty-Third, Ninety-First, and One Hundred and Eighteenth, an immortal band, which held in it the soul of the famous "Light Brigade," and of the stern old First division, Porter's, which was nucleus of the Fifth corps, men among them who had fired the first shot at Yorktown, and others that had fired the last at Appomattox, and who thus bore upon their banners all the battles of that army.

By the courtesy of General Bartlett the First brigade, which I had so long commanded, and the Second, which had been with me in this last campaign, were sent to me and held part in the parade, being formed on another line across the street and facing us. These were, with the exception of the One Hundred and Ninety-Eighth Pennsylvania, composed of New York regiments,—the One Hundred and Eighty-fifth, One Hundred and Eighty-Seventh, One Hundred and Eighty-Eighth, and One Hundred and Eighty-Ninth,—which in severe service had made themselves veterans worthy the fellowship of those sterling old New York regiments that had fulfilled their time and fame. Names and figures, all of these, dear to every heart that had shared their eventful and glorious history.

As we stood there in the morning mist, straining our eyes toward that camp about to break up for the last march, a feeling came over our hearts which led us to make some appropriate recognition of this great, last meeting.

We could not content ourselves with simply standing in line and witnessing this crowning scene. So, instructions were sent to the several commanders that at the given signals, as the head of each division of the surrendering column approached their right, they should in succession bring their men to "attention" and arms to the "carry," then resuming the "ordered arms" and the "parade rest." And now we see the little shelter tents on the opposite slope melting away and carefully folded, being things which were needed by men as men and not as tokens of rebellion. Soon the gray masses are in motion—once more toward us—as in the days that were gone. A thrilling sight. First, Gordon, with the "Stonewall Corps"; then their First corps,—Longstreet's,—no less familiar to us and to fame; then Anderson, with his new Fourth corps; and lastly, A. P. Hill's corps, commanded now by Heth, since Hill had fallen at one of the river fights a few days before.

On they come with careless, swinging route step, the column thick with battle flags, disproportionate to their depleted numbers. As they come opposite our right our bugle sounds the signal, repeated along our line. Each organisation comes to "attention," and thereupon takes up successively the "carry." The gallant General Gordon, at the head of the marching column, outdoes us in courtesy. He was riding with downcast eyes and more than pensive look; but at this clatter of arms he raises his eyes and, instantly catching the significance, wheels his horse with that superb grace of which he is master, drops the point of his sword to his stirrup, gives a command, at which the great Confederate ensign following him is dipped, and his decimated brigades, as they reach our right, respond to the "carry." All the while on our part not a sound of trumpet or drum, not a cheer, nor word nor motion of man, but awful stillness, as if it were the passing of the dead. Now and then a gust of wind would spring up from the south with strange greeting; our starry ensigns stiffen and fly out as if to welcome back the returning brothers. The ensigns of rebellion seem to shrink back and strain away from the fated farewell.

So, a division at a time covers our front. They halt, face inward, some ten paces from us; carefully "dress" their lines, each captain as careful of his alignment as if at a dress parade. Then they fix bayonets, stack arms, then wearily remove their cartridge-boxes and hang them on the pile; lastly, reluctantly, painfully, they furl their battle-stained flags and lay them down; some, unable to restrain themselves, rushing from the ranks, clinging to them, kneeling over them and kissing them with burning tears. And then the Flag of the Union floats alone upon the field.

Then, stripped of every sign of the rebellion and token of its hate and will to hurt, they march off to give their word of honour never to lift arms against the old flag again, and are free to go where they will in the broad Republic.

Thus, division after division passes, and it takes the whole day long to complete this deliverance. Twenty-seven thousand men paroled, one hundred and forty cannon and near that number of battle flags surrendered, but only about seventeen thousand stand of small arms. For sometimes a whole brigade, or what was left of it, had scarcely a score of arms to surrender, having thrown them away by roadside and riverside in weariness of flight or hopelessness of heart, or disdaining to carry them longer, only to be taken from them in token of a lost cause.

After this it remained only to gather up what was serviceable of this material of war and to destroy the rest. Nothing was left which could be turned to use against the Union armies. The cartridge-boxes were emptied on the ground for the most part, burned, and after the troops had withdrawn, at the first dusk of evening, it was a weird and almost sad sight to see the running flame with frequent bursts of lurid explosion along the lines where the surrendering army had stood; then only bits of leather writhing in the grey ashes.

All was over. With the dawn of morning the hillsides were alive with men, in groups or singly, on foot or horse, making their way as by the instinct of an ant, each with his own little burden, each for his own little harbour or home.

And we were left alone and lonesome! The familiar forms that had long so firmly held our eyes, until they almost demanded the sight of them for their daily satisfaction, had vanished like a dream. The very reason of our existence seemed to have been taken away. And when on the morrow, we took up our march again, though homeward, something was lacking in the spring and spice which had enlivened us through even the dreariest times. To be sure, the war was not over yet, but we felt that the distinctive work of the old Third brigade was over. We were soon to be mustered out; but never to be again as if the Third brigade had not become a part of our lives; a part of our souls. There were "thoughts that ran before and after," memories of things that cannot be told, and new purposes of manly living and hopes of useful service yet, in visions of a broader citizenship and the career of an enfranchised country.

Strong Vincent and His Brigade at Gettysburg
By Oliver W Norton

In the numerous histories of the civil war or accounts of the campaign and Battle of Gettysburg which have appeared from time to time, the writer of this paper has never seen one which did full justice to the important part enacted by Colonel Strong Vincent and his brigade on the extreme left of the Union Army on the afternoon of July 2, 1863, and which, if it did not decide the victory, contributed so much to it that but for this the battle would have been gained by the Confederates.

Some accounts state that General Warren, observing the importance of the position, entirely unoccupied, and the evident intention of the Confederates to seize it, took the responsibility of detaching Vincent's brigade from its division and personally conducted it to the place where it fought. Other accounts state that Weed's brigade was first placed on the hill by General Warren and that Vincent's brigade came up later and extended the line to the left. All accounts give great credit to Vincent's skill and the splendid fighting of the brigade, but they all miss the point which the writer wishes to make clear in this statement, which is that *if Vincent had not taken upon himself the responsibility of taking his brigade to that position without waiting to receive the order from his division commander as soon as he knew that his corps commander had ordered a brigade to be sent there, the arrival of his brigade would have found the enemy in possession of the ground, from which in all probability it could not have been dislodged.*

It may seem presumptuous for one who at the time of the Battle of Gettysburg was a private soldier of the Eighty-Third Pennsylvania Volunteers to question the accuracy of accounts written by officers of high rank or historians in civil life whose attainments have so well fitted them to write the story of the battle, but this presumption may be pardoned perhaps when it is known that the writer is the only living person, with the possible exception of a captain on the staff of General Sykes, who saw and heard what took place at the critical moment.

✶✶✶✶✶✶

(Note.—Where italics are used in these reports they do not appear in the original but are employed by the writer to call special attention to certain statements).

✶✶✶✶✶✶

The writer, although a private soldier, was on detached service at the time of the battle of Gettysburg, at the headquarters of the Third Brigade, First Division, Fifth Army Corps, acting as brigade bugler and bearer of the brigade headquarters flag. His duty was when the brigade was in the field to be always near the brigade commander, so that staff officers or others who had business with him could know by the flag where to find him, and to sound on the bugle orders for the brigade, when so directed by its commander.

The First Division, under command of General Barnes, with the other divisions of the corps, arrived on the field early in the morning of July 2 and was massed in rear of the right of the line. It made some changes of position during the day and about the middle of the afternoon, when Longstreet's attack on the Third Corps became very heavy, the Fifth Corps was moved to the left to reinforce the Third Corps. The First Division led the corps and the Third Brigade under Vincent led the division. The column was halted on the low ground in rear of the position of the Third Corps and General Sykes with General Barnes rode forward to select a position for the troops. Sykes and Barnes appear to have separated before any further orders were given to the division. While waiting for orders Vincent saw a captain of General Sykes' staff riding toward him from the front. Vincent, who evidently knew the captain, left the head of his brigade and rode forward to meet him; writer followed closely with the flag.

Arriving, Vincent said, "Captain, what are your orders?"

Without replying directly, the officer said, "Where is General Barnes?"

If Vincent knew he did not answer the question, but said with emphasis, "What are your orders? Give me your orders."

The officer replied, "General Sykes directed me to tell General Barnes to send one of his brigades to occupy that hill yonder," pointing to Little Round Top.

Without a moment's hesitation Vincent replied, "I will take the responsibility of taking my brigade there."

Vincent was a born soldier. Although not educated at West Point, he entered the service in April, 1861, as Adjutant of the three months' regiment that was raised at Erie, Pa., and upon the reorganization of this regiment, which was mustered into the service of the United States for three years, he became its lieutenant-colonel and when its Colonel, John W McLane, was killed at the battle of Gaines Mill, Vincent succeeded to the command of the regiment. A Harvard man recently admitted to the bar, he had the intellectual qualities which fitted him to command. With his quick eye, he appreciated as well as his superior officers the importance to our army of the immediate occupation of that commanding position. General Barnes was not with his division; writer had not seen him since early in the morning.

If Vincent knew where he was he also knew that if he waited for the officer of General Sykes' staff to find him and have the order sent through the usual channel, much valuable time would be lost, and it might be too late. At the risk of court martial for taking his brigade away from the division without orders from its commander, but understanding the order of the corps commander that some brigade of the division should be sent to that hill, he assumed the responsibility of taking his brigade there and he did the right thing at the right time. Returning to the brigade, he gave to Colonel Rice, the senior regimental commander, the order to bring on the brigade as rapidly as possible and started for the hill, closely followed by the writer.

Arriving at the foot of the northwest slope and finding it impracticable, he skirted the northern base of the ridge, then turned southward along the eastern slope where the ground was less difficult until he reached the point where the high ridge ends and the hill falls away toward the valley, between the two Round Tops. Riding around the large rocks which end the ridge at this point, we came out on the small plateau where the Sixteenth Michigan Regiment was placed in position a little later. We sat on our horses looking out toward the Devils Den and the country toward the Peach Orchard where the battle was then raging fiercely, but in our immediate neighbourhood not a Union or Confederate soldier was to be seen.

We had been there but a few moments when a shell exploded a few feet to our right, followed by another about the same distance to the left. Vincent said to me, "They are firing at the flag, go behind the rocks with it." I obeyed and in a few moments, he came and dismounting, left his horse with me. He then went over the lower ground on foot, selecting the position in which to place the brigade.

I think the regiments which had followed the same route we took, arrived in the following order: Forty-Fourth New York, Sixteenth Michigan, Eighty-Third Pennsylvania and Twentieth Maine. As the head of the column came up, Vincent said to Colonel Rice, "Form your regiment here, Colonel, with the right at the foot of this rock."

Colonel Rice replied, "Colonel, in every previous battle in which we have been engaged, the Forty-Fourth and Eighty-Third have fought side by side. I wish it could be so today."

Vincent appreciated the feeling and answered, "It shall be so, let the Sixteenth pass you." The order was sent back, the Forty-Fourth was halted until the Sixteenth had reached its place, then under Vincent's direction the Forty-Fourth, Eighty-Third and Twentieth took their respective positions and sent out skirmish lines to the front. Up to this time not a shot had been fired nor a Confederate soldier seen on that part of the field, but the skirmishers of the Eighty-Third and Forty-Fourth soon met the enemy advancing in heavy columns without skirmishers. They came on rapidly following the retirement of our skirmishers, and arriving within short range of our line, opened a heavy fire on the Eighty-Third and Forty-Fourth. This lasted for some time, when the enemy fell back but re-formed and with additional troops made another assault, this time reaching far enough to our left to involve the Twentieth Maine, but our men could not be moved.

While this was taking place, another force, supposed to be the greater part or all of Robertson's brigade of Texas regiments, passed to the north in the low ground between us and the Devils Den, and having gone beyond the line held by the Sixteenth Michigan, turned and advanced directly up the hill to attack this flank of our line. They came with such courage and such overwhelming numbers that the right of the Sixteenth Michigan wavered and broke. Colonel Welch and a large part of the right wing of his regiment left the field, taking his colours with him.

In trying to rally these men Colonel Vincent was mortally wounded and carried to the rear. Just at this time the One hundred and fortieth New York under Colonel O'Rorke arrived on the hill on our right and charged on the exultant enemy. O'Rorke and many of his men were killed and wounded, but the enemy was driven off, our line was re-established under the direction of Colonel Rice, who assumed the command, and no further assaults were made on the right of our line. Hazlett's Battery and the balance of Weed's Brigade, which came up after the One hundred and fortieth New York, extended the line along the crest of the ridge from Vincent's Brigade to its base at the north and held it until the end of the battle. The enemy continued its assaults upon the left of our line, making repeated efforts to turn the flank of Chamberlain's Twentieth Maine, but failed. The account of the battle at this point has been so fully described in the reports quoted elsewhere, that it need not be repeated here.

When the fighting opened, the writer left his horse and flag with the horses and servants of the mounted officers of the brigade and obtaining a musket took his place in the nearest point of the line on the right of the Forty-Fourth New York and remained there until the fighting ceased; reporting then to Colonel Rice he was directed by him to go to the hospitals in the rear to get ambulances and help to remove our wounded. Having no shoulder straps and being responsible for his brigade flag, he mounted and took that along as his badge of authority. He came to the road which passes east along the northern end of Little Round Top and found that road full of ambulances of the Second, Third and Fifth Corps and field hospitals of these corps located in every convenient spot for more than a mile to the east, but the ambulance officers and surgeons were so fully occupied that he received little immediate encouragement, although later help was sent and our wounded as well as those of the enemy which had fallen into our hands were cared for as well as they could be under the circumstances.

Returning he saw Colonel Welch with a large number of the men of the Sixteenth Michigan and the colours of that regiment at the road-side nearly a mile in rear of the battlefield. Being much surprised to see him there, he asked Colonel Welch where the brigade was. Welch replied that he did not know, that they were driven off the hill and that Colonel Vincent was in that farm house. After conversation with some of the men of the Sixteenth and being satisfied that Colonel Welch was mistaken, he entered the house and found Colonel Vincent on a bed in a room on the first floor. He was very pale and unable to speak, but held out his hand to me, and taking it I expressed in some way my sorrow at seeing him there. When I said "The boys are still there, Colonel," his face was lighted with a smile, but the sight was too painful to me and I hurried back to my place on the hill.

The writer has searched the official records and other accounts and presents herewith extracts from all the official reports relating to this matter, with certain letters and papers relating to the battle on Little Round Top. General Warren is entitled to all the credit which he would claim for himself, but he would be the first to disclaim credit for acts he did not perform. He went to the hill by the order of General Meade, accompanied by two lieutenants of Engineers and some mounted orderlies. Seeing from his position near the signal station a heavy force of the enemy very near the hill, he sent a written dispatch to General Meade, suggesting that a division be sent there at once. He then went to General Sykes, reported what he had seen and urged him to send there a portion of his corps which was then just arriving. He did not detach Vincent's brigade nor any other brigade, but acted in accordance with his military training by referring the matter to General Sykes commanding the Fifth Corps, the nearest available troops.

Sykes promised the troops needed and Warren returned to the signal station, where he found the officer folding his flags and preparing to leave. Warren directed him to remain and to continue waving his flags. He appears to have remained there until Vincent's brigade, which had repulsed the first assaults, seemed likely to be overwhelmed by the additional troops which the enemy was sending. He then descended the hill again and finding Colonel O'Rorke's regiment, the One Hundred and fortieth New York, bringing up the rear of Weed's brigade, the other three regiments with General Weed in advance, having already passed to the front, Warren took the responsibility of detaching O'Rorke's regiment and hurrying it to the crest of the hill, where it arrived just in time to repulse the assault of the Texas troops which had just driven back in disorder the right of the Sixteenth Michigan.

Sykes appears to have ordered first one brigade from the First Division to be sent there and then Weed's brigade of the Second Division, which was following at some distance in the rear, to take position on the hill also. Sykes then went further to the rear to order up Crawford's Third Division. On his return, he found that Weed's brigade, with the exception of O'Rorke's regiment, was moving to the front under orders from an officer of General Sickles' staff. He ordered it back to Round Top and Vincent's and Weed's brigades held this position until the fighting was over. Fisher's brigade of the Third Division came up later to reinforce Vincent's brigade, but did not arrive in time to take any active part in the battle.

Extract from General Hunt's paper on the Battle of Gettysburg, in *Battles and Leaders of the Civil War*, Vol. 3, in which he quotes a letter from General G. K. Warren:

..... As soon as General Longstreet's attack commenced, General Warren was sent by General Meade to see to the condition of the extreme left. The duty could not have been intrusted to better hands. Passing along the lines he found Little Round Top, the key of the position, unoccupied except by a signal station. The enemy at the time lay concealed, awaiting the signal for assault, when a shot fired in their direction caused a sudden movement on their part, which, by the gleam of reflected sunlight from their bayonets, revealed their long lines outflanking the position. Fully comprehending the imminent danger, Warren sent to General Meade for a division.

Before the Committee on the Conduct of the War, General Warren testified that he went to Little Round Top "by General Meade's direction." In a letter dated July 13th, 1872, General Warren says:

Just before the action began in earnest, on July 2nd, I was with General Meade, near General Sickles, whose troops seemed very badly disposed on that part of the field. At my suggestion, General Meade sent me to the left to examine the condition of affairs, and I continued on till I reached Little Round Top. There were no troops on it, and it was used as a signal station. I saw that this was the key of the whole position, and that our troops in the woods in front of it could not see the ground in front of them, so that the enemy would come upon them before they would be aware of it.

The long line of woods on the west side of the Emmitsburg road (which road was along a ridge) furnished an excellent place for the enemy to form out of sight, so I requested the captain of a rifle battery just in front of Little Round Top to fire a shot into these woods. He did so, and as the shot went whistling through the air the sound of it reached the enemy's troops and caused everyone to look in the direction of it. This motion revealed to me the glistening of gun-barrels and bayonets of the enemy's line of battle, already formed and far outflanking the position of any of our troops; so, that the line of his advance from his right to Little Round Top was unopposed.

I have been particular in telling this, as the discovery was intensely thrilling to my feelings, and almost appalling. I immediately sent a hastily written dispatch to General Meade to send a division at least to me, and General Meade directed the Fifth Army Corps to take position there. The battle was already beginning to rage at the Peach Orchard, and before a single man reached Round Top the whole line of the enemy moved on us in splendid array, shouting in the most confident tones. While I was still all alone with the signal officer, the musket balls began to fly around us, and he was about to fold up his flags and withdraw, but remained, at my request, and kept waving them in defiance.

Seeing troops going out on the Peach Orchard road, I rode down the hill, and fortunately met my old brigade. General Weed, commanding it, had already passed the point, and I took the responsibility to detach Colonel O'Rorke, the head of whose regiment I struck, who, on hearing my few words of explanation about the position, moved at once to the hill-top. About this time First Lieutenant Charles E. Hazlett, of the Fifth Artillery, with his battery of rifled cannon, arrived. lie comprehended the situation instantly and planted a gun on the summit of the hill. He spoke to the effect that though he could do little execution on the enemy with his guns, he could aid in giving confidence to the infantry and that his battery was of no consequence whatever compared with holding the position. He stayed there till he was killed. I was wounded with a musket-ball while talking with Lieutenant Hazlett on the hill, but not seriously; and seeing the position saved while the whole line to the right and front of us was yielding and melting away under the enemy s fire and advance, I left the hill to rejoin General Meade near the centre of the field where a new crisis was at hand.

Address of Captain Porter Farley

140th Regiment, New York Volunteers, at Dedication of Regimental Monument at Gettysburg.

September 17 1889
NewYork at Gettysburg,Vol. iii.)
EXTRACT.

. . . . It was while waiting there that a printed order was brought to Colonel O'Rorke. He read it and then handed it to the adjutant, as they both sat mounted in front of the regiment, and told him to read it aloud. It was from the general in command of the army and was as follows

Circular.
Headquarters Army of the Potomac.
June 30, 1863

The Commanding General requests that previous to the engagement soon expected with the enemy, corps and all other commanding officers will address their troops, explaining to them briefly the immense issues involved in this struggle. The enemy are on our soil. The whole country now looks anxiously to this army to deliver it from the presence of the foe. Our failure to do so will leave us no such welcome as the swelling of millions of hearts with pride and joy at our success would give to every soldier in the army. Homes, firesides and domestic altars are involved. The army has fought well heretofore. It is believed that it will fight more desperately and bravely than ever if it is addressed in fitting terms.

Corps and other commanders are authorised to order the instant death of any soldier who fails in his duty at this hour.

By command of Major General Meade,
S. Williams, Asst. Adjt. General.

The order was explicit that all commanding officers should address their troops; and, though doubtless much against his inclinations, as it was certainly contrary to his habit, O'Rorke, for the first and last time, there addressed a speech to his regiment. How well we all remember him sitting there on his horse in front of the regimental colours. His face, his form, his dress, all come up before us. His cheeks flushed as he spoke, but there was no hesitancy, and he closed with the ringing words: "I call on the file closers to do their duty, and if there is a man this day base enough to leave his company, let him die in his tracks. Shoot him down like a dog." The words were those of a man who intended to do his duty and who was equally determined that every man under him should do his. The speech was effective for its purpose, and a murmur of approval ran through the ranks. The scene, the action, and the words were of intense dramatic interest.

We soon changed our position, and during the greater part of the remainder of that day we lay with the whole of our corps upon Powers Hill, about a mile eastward from the spot where we now stand.

Throughout the day, the boom of an occasional cannon shot could be heard, but it seemed far away. Late in the afternoon, however, we could hear the artillery in lively play to our westward, but it still seemed much more distant than it really was. The battle of the day had actually opened, and we were soon set in motion towards the high ground which we could see to the westward, and which in fact was the very hill on which we now stand.

The First Division of our corps had preceded us, and so had the other brigades of our division and the other regiments of our brigade. It is my belief that we were marching that afternoon as the rear regiment of the Second Division. The whole of our division, therefore, was passing along the road which crosses this ridge at the foot of the northern extremity of Little Round Top; the two leading brigades had become engaged in the furious battle then raging on the further side; our own brigade was crossing the ridge, and we ourselves had about reached the point where the railroad now crosses the roadway, when an incident occurred which changed our line of march, and which proved to be an important factor in the result of that day's battle.

Just at that moment our former brigadier. Gen. G. K. Warren, Chief Engineer of the Army, with an orderly and one or two officers, rode down towards the head of our regiment. He came from the direction of the hill top, that is, from this point where we now stand. His speed and manner indicated unusual excitement. Before he reached us, he called out to O'Rorke to lead his regiment that way up the hill. O'Rorke answered him that General Weed had gone ahead and expected this regiment to follow him.

"Never mind that," answered Warren, "I'll take the responsibility." Warren's words and manner carried conviction of the importance of the thing he asked. Accepting his assurance of full justification, O'Rorke turned the head of the regiment to the left, and following one of the officers who had been with Warren, led it diagonally up the eastern slope of Little Round Top. Warren rode off, evidently bent on securing other troops. The staff officer who rode with us, by his impatient gestures urged us to our greatest speed. You will remember how some of the guns of Hazlett's Battery broke through our files before we reached the top, and the frantic efforts of the horses, lashed by the drivers, to pull their heavy pieces up that steep acclivity. A few seconds later the head of our regiment reached the summit of the ridge: war's wild panorama spread before us, and we found ourselves upon the verge of battle.

It was a moment which called for leadership, and we are here today the witnesses of the manner in which that leadership was fulfilled. There was no time for tactical formations. Delay was ruin. Hesitation was destruction. Well was it for the cause he served that the man who led our regiment that day was one prompt to decide and brave to execute.

The bullets flew in among the men the moment the leading company mounted the ridge, and as not a musket was loaded the natural impulse was to halt and load them. But O'Rorke permitted no such delay Springing from his horse, he threw his reins to the sergeant major; his sword flashed from its scabbard into the sunlight, and calling; "This way. boys," he led the charge over the rocks, down this hillside, till he came abreast the men of Vincent's Brigade, who were posted in the ravine to the left. Joining them an irregular line was formed, such as the confusion of the rocks lying thereabout permitted, and the line grew and was extended towards the right as the successive rearward companies came upon the scene of action. There while some were partly sheltered by the rocks and others stood in the open, a fierce fight went on with an enemy among the trees and underbrush. Flushed with the excitement and bravely led, they pushed up close to our line. The steadfastness and valour displayed on both sides made the result for some minutes doubtful, but a struggle so desperate and bloody could not be a long one. The enemy fell back; a short lull was succeeded by another onslaught, which was again repelled.

The story has been told in print that our colonel led with the regimental collars in his own hands; and that the men followed him and with clubbed muskets beat back the enemy. Such fictions provoke a smile, and are mentioned only to contradict them. O'Rorke carried only his sword, and you carried your muskets grasped by the butts and not by the barrels. History should record the truth without exaggeration. And this is the truth of the matter; that as the regiment came over the ridge its muskets were empty, and its leading companies rushed down the hill to meet the enemy without firing a shot. It was only when you came abreast the men of Vincent's brigade near the foot of the hill that you had time to load and return the fire which spit a deadly fusillade from the woods before you.

Those woods seemed to swarm with the gray-coated crowd. The enemy had almost enveloped Vincent, and had nearly seized this vantage ground on which we stand. Vincent's men, who for some minutes had maintained the fight, were outnumbered and outflanked.

Reinforcement was never more opportune. The arrival of the One hundred and fortieth Regiment at that crucial moment saved Little Round Top, and a glance at the surrounding topography carries conviction as to the supreme value of its possession.

While our regiment fought in the valley the guns of Hazlett's battery thundered from this hilltop, and its discharges swept the hostile lines which had forced back Sickles corps; so that by the time our regiments' fighting was over, not a battalion of the enemy remained in sight upon the opposite ridge, which had been the scene of that afternoon's chief battle Such, briefly told, was the struggle for the possession of this hilltop.

When that struggle was over the exultation of victory was soon chilled by the dejection which oppressed us as we counted and realized the cost of all that had been won. Of our regiment, 85 enlisted men and 6 officers had been wounded. Two of these officers, Lieuts. Hugh McGraw and Charles P. Klein, were fatally hurt. Besides these, 26 of the comrades who had marched with us that afternoon, had fallen dead before the fire of the enemy. Grouped by companies, a row of inanimate forms lay side by side beneath the trees upon this eastern slope. No funeral ceremony, and only shallow graves could be accorded them. In the darkness of the night, silently and with bitter dejection, each Company buried its dead.

Among the slain was one whose loss lay heavy on the heart of every one of us. Your thoughts anticipate his name. The artist's hand has reproduced his features, and his effigy upon this cenotaph now calmly gazes upon us, and for years to come shall remain the testimony to all who come this way, of the admiration and the love which this regiment accorded him. O'Rorke was among the dead. Shot through the neck, he had fallen without a groan, and we may hope without a pang. The supreme effort of his life was consummated by a death heroic in its surroundings and undisturbed by pain.

The spot on which he died is a most fitting place, and this circle of his comrades the most fitting presence in which to utter that tribute to his memory, which by grace of character, by natural talent, and by studious culture, he so truly deserves. To me he was as an elder brother beloved; and though since that time Death has struck near and hard upon my heart, he had never before struck so near as that July afternoon, when I looked down upon the placid features of O'Rorke's dead face and felt that he had gone from me forever Twenty-six years have passed, and time has tempered the grief which his death brought into our hearts; but we shall always cherish his memory with a loving regard and admiration, which only a noble nature could inspire. We have known many men since the day he died. Let each of us recall the list of those whose qualities have most attracted his regard.

Has there been one among them who possessed combined, the grace of form and carriage, the modesty, the purity and honesty of character, the amiable temper, the intellectual force, the commanding influence over others, the knightly accomplishments of his profession, and above all, the proved courage of Col. Pat O'Rorke, who here died at the head of his regiment? For myself I must say that I have never known one whose personality was so symmetrically developed, one so free from blemish, one who so well exemplified the ideal soldier and man.

"He was a very perfect, gentle knight." This cenotaph is a memorial of all our comrades who died in this great battle; but by the united wish of all of us who survived, it bears the face and name of the man whom we all most delighted to honour.....

Report of Gen. George Sykes, Commanding Fifth Army Corps,

dated July 31, 1863.
Rebellion Records, Series 1, Vol. 27

Extracts.

.....A rocky ridge, commanding almost an entire view of the plateau held by our army, was on our extreme left. Between it and the position occupied by Birney's division, Third Corps, was a narrow gorge filled with immense bowlders and flanked on either side by dense woods. It afforded excellent cover and an excellent approach for the enemy, both of which he promptly made use of. The rocky ridge commanded and controlled this gorge. In examining it and the ground adjacent, previous to posting my troops, I found a battery at its outer edge, and without adequate support. I galloped to General Birney, whose troops were nearest, explained to him the necessity of protecting the guns, and suggested that he should close his division on the battery, and hold the edge of woods on its right. I promised to fill the gap he opened, which I did with Sweitzer's and Tilton's brigades, of my First Division, *posting them myself*

In the meantime, Vincent's brigade, of this division, had seized the rocky height, closely followed by Weed's brigade, Second Division. These troops were posted under the direction of General Warren,

Chief Engineer of this army. After closing the interval made by Birney with the brigades of General Barnes, I rode rapidly to the Taneytown pike to bring up the remaining troops of the corps, and on my return with them found the greater part of Weed's brigade moving away from the height where it had been stationed, and where its presence was vital. I dispatched a staff officer to know of the general why he had vacated the ground assigned him. His reply was, "By order of General Sickles." I at once directed him to re-occupy it, which was done at the double-quick step. Hardly had he reached it before the enemy came on in tremendous force. Vincent's brigade and O'Rorke's regiment (Weed's brigade) were and had been sorely pressed. Both these heroic commanders had fallen; but Weed again in position, Hazlett working his guns superbly, and the timely arrival of Ayres' brigades of regulars, who were at once ordered to attack, stemmed the tide, and rolled away the foe in our front.

******

Night closed the fight. The key of the battlefield was in our possession intact. Vincent, Weed and Hazlett, chiefs lamented throughout the corps and army, sealed with their lives the spot intrusted to their keeping, and on which so much depended. . . . .

Report of Gen. James Barnes. Commanding First Division, Fifth Army Corps,

Beverly Ford, Va., August 24, 1863.
Rebellion Records, Series .1, Vol, 27.

EXTRACT.

I have the honour to submit the following report of the operations of the First Division of the Fifth Corps, from June 28 to July 9, including the battle of Gettysburg and the movements of the command during the few days previous and subsequent thereto *in conformity with instructions front headquarters:* . . . .

Between 4 and 5 o'clock in the afternoon, orders were received from General Sykes to move toward the left and to the front. The column was immediately formed, and moved rapidly up by the Taneytown road to the ground assigned to the division. *General Sykes and myself, preceding the advance of the column* upon the ground upon which it was to take position, reconnoitred the field, and the position to be held by the command was determined upon by him.

Soon after, the head of the column entered upon the field. At the same time, General Warren, of the staff of General Meade, came up, riding rapidly from the left, and, pointing out the position of the elevation known as the Round Top, not far off and toward the left, urged the importance of assistance in that direction. *General Sykes yielded* to his urgent request, and *I immediately directed Colonel Vincent, commanding the Third Brigade, to proceed to that point with his brigade.* Colonel Vincent moved with great promptness to the post assigned to him. The brigade consisted of the Sixteenth Michigan, the Forty-Fourth New York, the Eighty-Third Pennsylvania, and the Twentieth Maine Regiments.

The Second Brigade, commanded by Colonel Sweitzer, arrived next upon the ground. This brigade consisted of the Fourth Michigan, the Sixty-Second Pennsylvania, the Ninth Massachusetts and the Thirty-Second Massachusetts. The Ninth Massachusetts, however, was absent, being upon the special duty for which it had been detailed in the morning. Upon receiving his instructions, Colonel Sweitzer placed his command promptly in position.

The First Brigade, under command of Colonel Tilton, arrived next. This brigade was composed of the Eighteenth Massachusetts, the Twenty-Second Massachusetts, the One Hundred and Eighteenth Pennsylvania, and the First Michigan Regiments. The position assigned to it was on the right of the ground occupied by the Second Brigade, and was immediately placed by Colonel Tilton, in conformity with the instructions given to him. The division thus in position constituted the right of the Fifth Corps, and its place in line was on the left of the ground assigned to the Third Corps. The line was on the edge of a thick wood, the ground to the front being cleared of timber, but interspersed with rocks and some straggling trees. As the two brigades entered the wood, they passed over a line of troops, understood to be a portion of a brigade of the Third Corps; they were lying down upon the ground.

Upon the right of our position an open space, apparently unprotected, extended to some distance. Upon calling the attention of General Sykes to it, he remarked, referring to the part of the Third Corps over which we had passed, and then lying down in our rear, that those troops were to be removed. The remaining portion of the Third Corps was understood to be at some distance to the right, and much in advance of what seemed to be their natural and true position. This unguarded space was watched with great anxiety. There was little time, however, for deliberation. General Sykes, called by his duty to the left of the line, went toward that portion of his command. The attack of the enemy commenced almost immediately along my front. It was very severe, but was gallantly withstood.

After some time, during which the firing was very heavy, the enemy showed himself in great force on our right flank. He had penetrated through the unguarded space there, and commenced pouring in a destructive fire from the advantageous position he had gained, and without changing my front there were no means of checking his advance toward my rear. Colonel Tilton, commanding the First Brigade, which was on the right, was immediately directed to change his front to the right, and the order was at once executed, deliberately, yet promptly, and in good order. Colonel Sweitzer, commanding the Second Brigade, on the left of the First, was immediately notified of the change upon his right, and directed to fall back in good order, and to take up a new position a short distance in his rear, for the purpose of co-operating in opposing this heavy attack upon the flank. This brigade, consisting at that time of only three regiments, numbering in all, officers and men, 1,010, was placed promptly and in good order as directed. The First Brigade numbered in all, officers and men, 654.

Affairs being in this position, General Caldwell, commanding a brigade of the Second Corps, came up in great haste, and stated to me that his brigade, then in the woods a short distance to the left, was driving the enemy in his front, and urgently requested assistance. I immediately directed Colonel Sweitzer to go to his relief. He moved his brigade forward in line, to the front and left, his men giving cheers as they advanced across an open field to the edge of the wood; but the progress of the enemy upon our flank still continued, and this brigade was compelled again to change its front to repel his advance, and soon found itself in close conflict with him. The Fourth Michigan and Sixty-second Pennsylvania were in actual contact with him. Colonel Jeffords, commanding the Fourth Michigan, was thrust through with a bayonet while gallantly attempting to rescue his collars from the grasp of the enemy.

Finding himself unable to compete with numbers far superior to his own, and that the enemy was gaining ground in the rear. Colonel Sweitzer directed his command to retire slowly, but orderly, halting and firing as they retired, and took position on elevated ground a short distance to his rear and succeeded in preventing the enemy from making any further progress in that direction.

In the meantime, the movements of the First Brigade, under similar circumstances, corresponded with those of the Second. This brigade, small in numbers, fired and retired in good order, and succeeded in reaching the ground on the opposite side of the open field toward the left, and there halted. The darkness put an end to the conflict, and the enemy was foiled in his effort to get in the rear of the command. The Ninth Massachusetts shortly afterward rejoined the Second Brigade, having been relieved from the duty upon which it had been detailed early in the morning. In this position the two brigades remained during the night.

On the following day. the First Brigade was directed to relieve the Third Brigade at Little Round Top, where it also had succeeded in maintaining the position assigned to it, as will appear in the sequel.

I cannot speak in terms too commendatory of the bearing of the officers and men of these two brigades during the progress of this conflict. Skilfully directed by the two brigade commanders, they obeyed with cool intrepidity every order issued to them, under the most trying circumstances, and long resisted superior numbers with firmness. Partly surrounded by the enemy, they succeeded in preventing the left of the line from being taken in reverse, resisting an attack not exceeded, I am sure, in violence in any contest hitherto occurring. The exposure of their flank, arising from whatever cause, placed them in a most dangerous position and their heroic conduct alone saved the command at least, if not the entire left of the army, from disaster. The statement of the casualties of the contest is sufficient evidence of their gallant resistance, and it is alike due to those who have survived and to the memory of the gallant dead that this record should be made of their valour and devotion.

The Third Brigade, as above related, was detached from the division upon its arrival upon the ground, and was consequently removed from my immediate oversight. The record of its service, however, drawn principally from the report of its commander, belongs to this record of the service of the division.

Colonel Vincent, commanding the brigade, upon being detached, as above mentioned, proceeded promptly to the position assigned to him. It was upon an elevated and rocky hill known as Little Round Top. It was situated at some distance to our left, and near the extreme left of the line of battle. Its defence was of the utmost importance. When the brigade was placed in position, the Twentieth Maine occupied the left of the line, the Sixteenth Michigan the right, the Eighty-Third Pennsylvania and the Forty-Fourth New York the centre. *The*

Third Division of the Fifth Corps was posted on the right of the brigade. The enemy had concentrated a heavy force in front of the line, and began a fierce attack immediately after the troops were in position. Repeated charges were made upon the centre of the brigade, but the line was unbroken. A vigorous attack upon the right caused a temporary wavering there, but the One hundred and Fortieth New York coming promptly to its support, it was re-established at once.

It was at this time that Colonel Vincent, commanding the brigade, while rallying this part of his command, fell, mortally wounded. He was a gallant officer, beloved and respected by his command and by all who knew him. His death is a serious loss to the army and the country.

Upon the removal of Colonel Vincent from the field, the command of the brigade devolved upon Colonel Rice, of the Forty-Fourth New York Volunteers. The enemy, as stated, having in vain attempted to break the right of the brigade, renewed his attack upon the centre and left. The Twentieth Maine, Colonel Chamberlain commanding, was posted on the left. It consisted of 380 men and officers. While the enemy in front was making a fierce attack, a brigade was observed in the rear of their lines moving by its right flank and passing through a slight ravine on our left, with the evident purpose of gaining a position on the left flank of this regiment.

Colonel Chamberlain at once threw back his left wing, and extended his right wing by intervals toward the left, in order to avoid diminishing the extent of his front. The brigade of the enemy alluded to reaching a proper position, attacked him furiously on the left flank, advancing within 10 paces and rapidly firing. They were first checked and then repulsed by the left wing of the regiment, thrown back for that purpose.

A second, third, and fourth time the enemy renewed their attempt to break this line, and each time were they successfully repelled by that handful of men. Four times that little interval of 10 paces was the scene of a desperate conflict. The ground was strewed with dead and wounded men of both sides, promiscuously mingled. Their ammunition was exhausted; they replenished it from the cartridge boxes of the men lying around them, whether friends or foes, but even this resource soon failed them; the enemy in greatly superior numbers pressed hard; men and officers began to look to the rear for safety, but the gallant commander of the regiment ordered the bayonets to be fixed, and, at the command "Forward" that wearied and worn body of men rushed onward with a shout.

The enemy fell back. Pressing on, and wheeling to the right in open intervals, the left wing came again in line with the right wing, and then the whole regiment, deployed at intervals of 5 paces, followed up the advantage they had gained. The enemy threw down their arms and surrendered in large numbers; the others fled rapidly from the contest; 368 prisoners, including 1 colonel, 1 lieutenant colonel, and a dozen other officers of lesser rank were sent to the rear; 50 of their dead lay upon the field, and large numbers of their wounded; 30 of this gallant regiment were killed, over 100 were wounded, but not one was taken a prisoner, and none were missing.

It was now nearly dark. A portion of the enemy appeared to have occupied the summit of the rocky hill to the left. The men of this brave regiment, exhausted by their labours, had thrown themselves upon the ground, and many of them sunk at once in sleep. Colonel Rice, now in command of the brigade, directed Colonel Chamberlain to drive the enemy from this height. The order was at once given. Roused again to action, and advancing with fixed bayonets and without firing, lest the smallness of their numbers might be suspected, they rushed up the hill.

Twenty-five more prisoners, including some staff officers, were added to the number previously taken, with a loss to the regiment of 1 officer mortally wounded and 1 man taken prisoner by the enemy. It was ascertained that these troops occupying the hill had been sent from Hood's division, which was then massed a few hundred yards distant, and that their object was to reconnoitrer the position as a preliminary to taking possession of the height.

In addition to the prisoners above mentioned as taken by this regiment, 300 stand of arms were also captured by them. It is due to this regiment and to its commander that their service should be thus recorded in some detail.

Upon receiving a re-enforcement of five regiments of the Third Division, under command of Colonel Fisher, Colonel Rice detached two of them to the aid of Colonel Chamberlain, in order to maintain the position he had gained, and he was thus enabled to hold it, and the enemy, having been repelled upon every point of his attack, and night coming on, withdrew from the conflict.

Colonel Rice directed the Forty-Fourth New York and the Eighty-Third Pennsylvania to move to the front and gather up the wounded, who, including those of the enemy who had been left upon the field, were carefully brought in. The total results of the service of this brigade are stated by Colonel Rice to be 500 prisoners captured, including 2 colonels and 15 other commissioned officers, and 1,000 stand of arms. The brigade numbered about 1,000 men....

A tribute is due to the memory of Colonel Vincent, who fell, mortally wounded, early in the engagement. He lingered a few days after the engagement. His promotion as a brigadier-general was sent to him at once as an appreciation of his services by the government, but it reached him too late for his own recognition. He expired soon after its receipt. (July 7, 1863. O. W. N.) ....

Being disabled for further actual command of the division, the opportune arrival of General Griffin enabled me to relinquish it to him, and the division moved toward Middletown, where it arrived on July 8.

Report of Col. William S. Tilton, Commanding First Brigade, First Div., Fifth A. C.

Middletown, Md., July 9, 1863.
Rebellion Records, Series 1, Vol. 27

EXTRACT.

... At 4:30 p.m., on July 2, the brigade, under my command, advanced to the front, and was placed, by order of General Barnes, in order of battle in a piece of woods at the south of Mr. Rose's house. The Second Brigade was on our left, but there being no infantry upon our right, I made a crotchet by refusing the right wing of my right battalion (One Hundred and Eighteenth Pennsylvania Volunteers, Colonel Gwyn)....

No sooner was the line formed than the foe attacked our front. The onslaught was terrible and my losses heavy, so much so that I was somewhat doubtful if our line could withstand it. This fact I communicated to the general commanding division, who ordered me to fall back in good order if unable to hold the position; but my men behaved nobly, and twice repulsed the assailants. My colonels wished to advance. Being anxious about my right, however, I reconnoitred in person, and discovered the enemy in large force coming from the direction of Rose's house, with the evident design of outflanking me. I immediately retired and took up a new position (in two lines), at the left and rear of a battery which had been posted about 300 yards to my right and rear. The battery soon commenced to retreat, firing, followed by the rebels, who were now again upon my right flank. To avoid this flank movement, I retired, firing, a short distance in the timber, and then moved across an open field, took up a new position upon the right of the Second Division, and reported to General Sykes.

... On the 3rd we relieved the Third Brigade, on duty, holding the rocky hill upon the extreme left.

On the 4th, I advanced the brigade to the edge of the woods in our front and sent out a strong line of skirmishers to feel the enemy. The report of this reconnaissance has been made by order directly to Major-General Sykes.

Report of Col. Jacob B. Sweitzer, Commanding Second Brigade, First Div., Fifth A. C.

July 31, 1863.
Rebellion Records, Series 1, Vol. 1.

EXTRACT.

.... When we moved off from the orchard, the Third Brigade, being on the left of the division, moved first, the Second and First Brigades following in the inverted order.

The Second Brigade was placed in position in a wood fronting an open field, the woods bordering two sides of the field, the side in which we were and also that extending at right angles from our left toward the enemy, and in the last mentioned wood the First Brigade was posted, connecting with our left. Having formed the three regiments of this brigade in line of battle (the Ninth Massachusetts being still absent on picket duty) in their regular order from right to left, and finding this formation threw the Thirty-Second Massachusetts, which was on our left, into an exposed position beyond the woods in low, cleared ground, I directed Colonel Prescott to change his front to the rear, so as to give him the benefit of the elevated ground and the cover of the woods, which movement he executed.

We had not remained long in this position before an attack commenced by the enemy in front of the First Brigade and Thirty-Second Massachusetts. As there was no appearance of the enemy in front of the line formed by the Sixty-Second Pennsylvania and Fourth Michigan, I directed them to change front to the left, and form lines in rear of the Thirty-Second Massachusetts, to strengthen that position. During the execution of this order, the attack continued; the firing was very severe, and we lost many brave officers and men. Here fell

Major Lowry, second to none in all the attributes of a soldier and a gentleman.

When the attack commenced, word was sent by General Barnes that when we retired we should fall back under cover of the woods. This order was communicated to Colonel Prescott, whose regiment was then under the hottest fire. Understanding it to be a peremptory order to retire then, he replied, "I don't want to retire; I am not ready to retire; I can hold this place," and he made good his assertion. Being informed that he misunderstood the order, which was only intended to inform him how to retire when it became necessary, he was satisfied, and he and his command held their ground manfully.

Sometime after that, word was sent that the First Brigade was retiring, and General Barnes sent me word to fall back also, which I did in perfect good order, the regiments retaining their alignments and halting and firing as they came back. Having arrived at the road leading along the rear of the wheat-field, the brigade was formed in line in the woods in the rear of the road and parallel to it, the right resting on the corner of the woods toward the front. We had not remained here more than, say, fifteen minutes, when a general officer I had never seen before rode up to me, and said his command was driving the enemy in the woods in front of the wheat-field; that he needed the support of a brigade, and desired to know if I would give him mine. I referred him to General Barnes, and said I would obey his directions with pleasure. He spoke to the general, who was not far off.

General Barnes came and stated to me what had been said to him by General Caldwell (this I learned was the officer who had lately spoken to me), and asked me if I would take the brigade in. I told him I would if he wished me to do so. He said he did. The command was then called to attention. General Barnes got out in front of them, and made a few patriotic remarks, to which they responded with a cheer, and we started off across the wheat-field in a line parallel to the road, our right flank resting on the woods. We advanced to the stone fence beyond the wheat-field next to the woods, and took position behind it to support, as we supposed, our friends in the woods in front. The Fourth Michigan, being on the right of the brigade, extended beyond the stone fence, and was, consequently, most exposed.

We had scarcely got to this position before I noticed regiments retiring from the woods on our right, which I supposed were relieved by others who had taken their places, and would protect us in that direction. I observed also that there was considerable firing diagonally toward our rear from these woods, which I then thought were shots from our troops aimed over us at the enemy in the woods beyond and falling short. They were, however, much too frequent to be pleasant, and my colour bearer, Ed. Martin, remarked, "Colonel, I'll be —— if I don't think we are faced the wrong way; the rebs are up there in the woods behind us, on the right."

About this time, too, word was brought me from the Fourth Michigan and Sixty-Second Pennsylvania that the enemy were getting into our rear in the woods on the right. I directed those regiments to change front, to face in that direction and meet them, which they did, the firing in the meanwhile being rapid and severe. I at the same time dispatched Lieutenant Seitz, *aide-de-camp*, to communicate to General Barnes our situation. He reached the point where he had last seen General Barnes. He was not there. Lieutenant Seitz found the enemy had reached that point, and he came near falling into their hands himself; his horse was killed, and he made his way back to me on foot; reported that General Barnes was not to be found, that the enemy was in the woods on our right as far back as where we had started from, and along the road in rear of the wheat-field.

Finding that we were surrounded—that our enemy was under cover, while we were in the open field exposed to their fire—I directed the command to fall back. This was done in order, the command halting and firing as it retired. The Fourth Michigan and Sixty-Second Pennsylvania had become mixed up with the enemy, and many hand-to-hand conflicts occurred. . . . .

Finding, as we retired in the direction from which we advanced, that the fire of the enemy grew more severe on our right, I took a diagonal direction toward the corner of the wheat-field on our left and rear. We crossed the stone fence on this side of the field, and retired to the rear of the battery on the elevation beyond, where the command halted.

We had lost heavily in our passage across the field. The Fourth Michigan and Sixty-Second Pennsylvania had been surrounded, and a large proportion of those regiments were missing, either killed, wounded, or prisoners. What remained of the command formed in the rear of the battery, and we were shortly afterward joined by the Ninth Massachusetts, which had been absent all day on detached duty

It is difficult to conceive of a more trying situation than that in which three regiments of this command had lately found themselves, and from which they had just effected their escape; in fact, I have since understood that one of General Barnes' *aides* remarked to him shortly after we had advanced, when it was discovered the enemy was behind us on the flank, that he might bid goodbye to the Second Brigade. I was also informed by General Barnes that, learning soon after we had advanced, the situation on our right, he had dispatched an orderly to me with the information and a verbal order to withdraw, but the orderly, never reached me.

Every officer and man in the command, so far as I am informed, did his whole duty All stood their ground and fought unflinchingly until they were ordered by me to retire, and in falling back behaved with coolness and deliberation. We lost many of our best officers and men.

I subjoin a field report of the regiments engaged on the morning of July 2, and also a report of the same regiments on July 4. A nominal and tabular report of casualties in the command has already been forwarded.

About dark on the evening of the 2nd, the acting assistant adjutant-general of the First Brigade came to me and inquired for General Barnes; said he was directed by General Sykes to tell him to have the Second Brigade form on the right of the First in the position they then were. As General Barnes was not present, I received the order, and put the Second Brigade in the position indicated, where we remained until the evening of the 5th, when the division advanced toward Emmitsburg.

Report of Colonel James C. Rice, Commanding Third Brigade, First Div., Fifth A. C.

At Battle of Gettysburg., with Reports of Regimental Commanders.

Rebellion Records, Series 1, Vol. 27

July 31, 1863.

In compliance with orders from division headquarters, I have the honour to report the operations of this brigade during the battle near Gettysburg on the 2nd and 3rd inst.

The brigade, under the command of the late Colonel Vincent, was detached from the division and ordered into position at about 4 p. m. of the 2nd instant, on the extreme left of our line of battle. The Twentieth Maine occupied the extreme left of the brigade line, the Sixteenth Michigan the extreme right, connecting with the Third Division, under General Crawford, while the Eighty-Third Pennsylvania and Forty-

Fourth New York occupied the centre. The muskets taken into action by the brigade numbered about 1,000.

The ground occupied by the brigade in line of battle was nearly that of a quarter circle, composed mostly of high rocks and cliffs in the centre and becoming more wooded and less rugged as you approached to the left. The right was thrown forward somewhat to the front of the ledge of rocks, and was much more exposed than other parts of the line. A comparatively smooth ravine extended along the entire front, perhaps 50 yards from our line, while on the left and beyond a high and jagged mountain rises, called Round Top hill. That the disposition of the forces and the nature of the ground may be better understood by the general commanding, I send with this report a diagram of the same.

The brigade had scarcely formed in line of battle and pushed forward its skirmishers when a division of the enemy's forces, under General Hood, made a desperate attack along the entire line of the brigade. He approached in three columns, with no skirmishers in advance. The object of the enemy was evident. If he could gain the vantage ground occupied by this brigade, the left flank of our line must give way, opening to him a vast field for successful operations in the rear of our entire army.

To effect this object the enemy made every effort. Massing two or three brigades of his force, he tried for an hour in vain to break the lines of the Forty-Fourth New York and Eighty-Third Pennsylvania, charging again and again within a few yards of these unflinching troops. At every charge he was repulsed with terrible slaughter. Despairing of success at this point, he made a desperate attack upon the extreme right of the brigade, forcing back a part of the Sixteenth Michigan. This regiment was broken, and, through some misunderstanding of orders, explained in the official report of the commanding officer, it was thrown into confusion; but being immediately supported by the One Hundred and Fortieth New York Volunteers, the line became again firm and unbroken.

It was at this point of time that Colonel Vincent, commanding the brigade, fell mortally wounded. Of the character of this gallant and accomplished officer I will speak before I close this report.

The enemy again attacked the centre with great vigour, and the extreme left with desperation. Passing one brigade of his forces by the right flank in three columns, he pushed through the ravine toward the left of our brigade, came immediately to a "front," and charged upon the Twentieth Maine. Now occurred the most critical time of the action. For above half an hour the struggle was desperate. At length the enemy pressed so strongly upon the left flank of Colonel Chamberlain's regiment that he wisely determined to change the order of battle, and commanded his left wing to fall back at right angles to his right. He then ordered a charge and repulsed the enemy at every point.

On assuming the command of the brigade during this attack upon the centre and left, I at once passed along the line, and notified the officers and men of my own regiment that I was about to take command of the brigade and that they must hold their position to the last. I did this that no panic might arise. I then notified all the commanders of the regiments in person, and assured them of my determination to hold the line to the last. Colonel Chamberlain and other officers immediately informed me that their commands were out of ammunition. I had at this time neither an aide nor an orderly even to bear a message. (See P S.) The enemy was still pressing heavily upon the line. I immediately pressed into service every officer and man in the rear not engaged in the action, whether known or unknown, and made them pledge their honour that they would deliver in person every order that I should send by them. I sent four of them, one after another, with orders for ammunition. The ammunition came promptly, was distributed at once, and the fight went on.

The enemy was now attempting to take possession of Round Top hill, a commanding position overlooking our left. It was evident no time was to be lost, and I sent at once other officers, whom I pressed into my service, with messages to the general commanding the corps, asking for re-enforcements to support the brigade. The messages were promptly delivered, and five regiments were at once sent to my support from the Third Division, General Crawford, under command of Colonel Fisher.

Having, with the aid of this officer, properly disposed of three regiments of this force, I ordered Colonel Chamberlain, of the Twentieth Maine, to advance and take possession of the mountain. This order was promptly and gallantly executed by this brave and accomplished officer, who rapidly drove the enemy over the mountain, capturing many prisoners. Colonel Fisher at once ordered two regiments of his command to support Colonel Chamberlain, and the hill remained permanently in our possession.

The forces of the enemy being now repulsed on our left and front,

I ordered a detachment from the Forty-Fourth New York Volunteers and the Eighty-Third Pennsylvania to push forward and secure all the fruits of this hard-earned victory.

It was now 8 o'clock in the evening, and before 9 o'clock we had entire possession of the enemy's ground, had gathered up and brought in all of our own wounded and those of the enemy, and had taken and sent to the rear over 500 prisoners, including 2 colonels and 15 commissioned officers, together with over 1,000 stand of arms belonging to the enemy.

The following morning the prisoners of the brigade buried all of our own dead and a large number of those of the enemy

The fearful loss of the enemy during this struggle may be estimated from the fact that over 50 of his dead were counted in front of the Twentieth Maine Regiment, and his loss was nearly in that proportion along our entire line.

Although this brigade has been engaged in nearly all of the great battles of the Army of the Potomac, and has always greatly distinguished itself for gallant behaviour, yet in none has it fought so desperately or achieved for itself such imperishable honours as in this severe conflict of the 2nd instant.

A nominal and tabular list of the casualties of this brigade has already been forwarded to the major-general commanding, but it is fitting again to mention the names of the brave and faithful officers of the command who fell in this desperate struggle. Of the Forty-Fourth New York Volunteers, Capt. L. S. Larrabee and Lieutenants Dunham and Thomas; of the Twentieth Maine, Lieutenant Kendall, and of the Sixteenth Michigan, Lieutenants Browne, Jewett, and Borden were killed.

The brigade was relieved during the forenoon of the 3rd instant by the First Brigade, and ordered to the centre of the line, where it remained in reserve the balance of the day, exposed to a severe cannonading, but with no loss, from the security of its position.

The colonel commanding would commend to the favourable notice of the general commanding the following-named officers, for their gallant conduct in battle on the 2nd instant: Colonel Chamberlain and Adjutant Chamberlain, of the Twentieth Maine; Lieutenant-Colonel Conner and Major Knox, of the Forty-Fourth New York Volunteers; Captain Woodward and Adjutant Gifford, of the Eighty-Third Pennsylvania, and Captain Elliott and Adjutant Jacklin, of the Sixteenth Michigan.

Especially would I call the attention of the general commanding to the distinguished services rendered by Colonel Chamberlain throughout the entire struggle.

To the loss sustained by this command in the death of Colonel Vincent I can refer in no more appropriate language than that used in the general order announcing it to this brigade, a copy of which 1 herewith annex.

P S. In justice to the officers composing the staff, it gives me satisfaction to state, in explanation of my report, that at the time I took command, Captain (Eugene A.) Nash, inspector-general of the brigade, was, in obedience to orders received from Colonel Vincent, at the front watching the movements of the enemy, to report the same if he should attempt a flank movement that Captain (John M.) Clark, assistant adjutant-general, in obedience to orders, was absent for ammunition, and that Captain (Amos M.) Judson, by orders, was absent for re-enforcements. During the night, these officers rendered me the greatest service and I desire to commend each of them to the most favourable notice of the commanding general for their gallant conduct both under Colonel Vincent's command as well as my own.

(Enclosure.)
General Orders No. 5.

Hdqrs. 3d Brigade, 1st Div., 5th Corps,
July 12, 1863.

The colonel commanding hereby announces to the brigade the death of Brig.-Gen. Strong Vincent. He died near Gettysburg, Pa., July 7 1863, from the effects of a wound received on the 2nd instant, and within sight of that field which his bravery had so greatly assisted to win. A day hallowed with all the glory of success is thus sombered by the sorrow of our loss. Wreaths of victory give way to chaplets of mourning, hearts exultant to feelings of grief. A soldier, a scholar, a friend, has fallen. For his country struggling for its life, he willingly gave his own. Grateful for his services, the State which proudly claims him as her own will give him an honoured grave and a costly monument, but he ever will remain buried in our hearts, and our love for his memory will outlast the stone which shall bear the inscription of his bravery his virtues, and his patriotism.

While we deplore his death, and remember with sorrow our loss, let us emulate the example of his fidelity and patriotism, feeling that he lives but in vain who lives not for his God and his country.

Report of Col. Joshua L. Chamberlain. Twentieth Maine Infantry

Field Near Emmitsburg, July 6, 1863.

In compliance with the request of the colonel commanding the brigade, I have the honour to submit a somewhat detailed report of the operations of the Twentieth Regiment Maine Volunteers in the Battle of Gettysburg, on the 2nd and 3rd instant.

Having acted as the advance guard, made necessary by the proximity of the enemy's cavalry, on the march of the day before, my command on reaching Hanover, Pa., just before sunset on that day, were much worn, and lost no time in getting ready for an expected bivouac. Rations were scarcely issued, and the men about preparing supper, when rumours that the enemy had been encountered that day near Gettysburg absorbed every other interest, and very soon orders came to march forthwith to Gettysburg.

My men moved out with a promptitude and spirit extraordinary, the cheers and welcome they received on the road adding to their enthusiasm. After an hour or two of sleep by the roadside just before daybreak, we reached the heights southeasterly of Gettysburg at about 7 a.m. July 2.

Massed at first with the rest of the division on the right of the road, we were moved several times farther toward the left. Although expecting every moment to be put into action and held strictly in line of battle, yet the men were able to take some rest and make the most of their rations.

Somewhere near 4 p.m. a sharp cannonade, at some distance to our left and front, was the signal for a sudden and rapid movement of our whole division in the direction of this firing, which grew warmer as we approached. Passing an open field in the hollow ground in which some of our batteries were going into position, our brigade reached the skirt of a piece of woods, in the farther edge of which there was a heavy musketry fire, and when about to go forward into line we received from Colonel Vincent, commanding the brigade, orders to move to the left at the double-quick, when we took a farm road crossing Plum Run in order to gain a rugged mountain spur called Granite Spur, or Little Round Top.

The enemy's artillery got range of our column as we were climbing the spur, and the crashing of the shells among the rocks and the tree tops made us move lively along the crest. One or two shells burst in our ranks. Passing to the southern slope of Little Round Top, Colonel Vincent indicated to me the ground my regiment was to occupy, informing me that this was the extreme left of our general line, and that a desperate attack was expected in order to turn that position, concluding by telling me I was to "hold that ground at all hazards." This was the last word I heard from him.

In order to commence by making my right firm, I formed my regiment on the right into line, giving such direction to the line as should best secure the advantage of the rough, rocky, and stragglingly wooded ground.

The line faced generally toward a more conspicuous eminence southwest of ours, which is known as Sugar Loaf, or Round Top. Between this and my position intervened a smooth and thinly wooded hollow. My line formed, I immediately detached Company B, Captain Morrill commanding, to extend from my left flank across this hollow as a line of skirmishers, with directions to act as occasion might dictate, to prevent a surprise on my exposed flank and rear.

The artillery fire on our position had meanwhile been constant and heavy, but my formation was scarcely complete when the artillery was replaced by a vigorous infantry assault upon the centre of our brigade to my right, but it very soon involved the right of my regiment and gradually extended along my entire front. The action was quite sharp and at close quarters.

In the midst of this an officer from my centre informed me that some important movement of the enemy was going on in his front, beyond that of the line with which we were engaged. Mounting a large rock, I was able to see a considerable body of the enemy moving by the flank in rear of their line engaged, and passing from the direction of the foot of Great Round Top through the valley toward the front of my left. The close engagement not allowing any change of front, I immediately stretched my regiment to the left, by taking intervals by the left flank, and at the same time "refusing" my left wing, so that it was nearly at right angles with my right, thus occupying about twice the extent of our ordinary front, some of the companies being brought into single rank when the nature of the ground gave sufficient strength or shelter.

My officers and men understood my wishes so well that this movement was executed under fire, the right wing keeping up fire, without giving the enemy any occasion to seize or even to suspect their advantage. But we were not a moment too soon the enemy's flanking column having gained their desired direction, burst upon my left, where they evidently had expected an unguarded flank, with great demonstration.

We opened a brisk fire at close range, which was so sudden and effective that they soon fell back among the rocks and low trees in the valley, only to burst forth again with a shout, and rapidly advanced, firing as they came. They pushed up to within a dozen yards of us before the terrible effectiveness of our fire compelled them to break and take shelter.

They renewed the assault on our whole front, and for an hour the fighting was severe. Squads of the enemy broke through our line in several places, and the fight was literally hand to hand. The edge of the fight rolled backward and forward like a wave. The dead and wounded were now in our front and then in our rear. Forced from our position, we desperately recovered it, and pushed the enemy down to the foot of the slope. The intervals of the struggle were seized to remove our wounded (and those of the enemy also), to gather ammunition from the cartridge-boxes of disabled friend or foe on the field, and even to secure better muskets than the Enfields, which we found did not stand service well. Rude shelters were thrown up of the loose rocks that covered the ground.

Captain Woodward, commanding the Eighty-Third Pennsylvania Volunteers, on my right, gallantly maintaining his fight, judiciously and with hearty co-operation made his movements conform to my necessities, so that my right was at no time exposed to a flank attack.

The enemy seemed to have gathered all their energies for their final assault. We had gotten our thin line into as good a shape as possible, when a strong force emerged from the scrub wood in the valley, as well as I could judge, in two lines in echelon by the right, and, opening a heavy fire, the first line came on as if they meant to sweep everything before them. We opened on them as well as we could with our scanty ammunition snatched from the field.

It did not seem possible to withstand another shock like this now coming on. Our loss had been severe. One-half of my left wing had fallen and a third of my regiment lay just behind us, dead or badly wounded. At this moment my anxiety was increased by a great roar of musketry in my rear, on the farther or northerly slope of Little Round Top, apparently on the flank of the regular brigade, which was in support of Hazlett's battery on the crest behind us. The bullets from this attack struck into my left rear, and I feared that the enemy might have nearly surrounded the Little Round Top, and only a desperate chance was left for us. My ammunition was soon exhausted. My men were firing their last shot and getting ready to "club" their muskets.

It was imperative to strike before we were struck by this overwhelming force in a hand-to-hand fight, which we could not probably have withstood or survived. At that crisis, I ordered the bayonet. The word was enough. It ran like fire along the line, from man to man, and rose into a shout, with which they sprang forward upon the enemy, now not 30 yards away. The effect was surprising; many of the enemy's first line threw down their arms and surrendered. An officer fired his pistol at my head with one hand, while he handed me his sword with the other. Holding fast by our right, and swinging forward our left, we made an extended "right wheel," before which the enemy's second line broke, and fell back, fighting from tree to tree, many being captured, until we had swept the valley and cleared the front of nearly our entire brigade.

Meantime, Captain Morrill with his skirmishers (sent out from my left flank), with some dozen or fifteen of the U. S. Sharpshooters who had put themselves under his direction, fell upon the enemy as they were breaking, and by his demonstrations, as well as his well-directed fire, added much to the effect of the charge.

Having thus cleared the valley and driven the enemy up the western slope of the Great Round Top, not wishing to press so far out as to hazard the ground I was to hold by leaving it exposed to a sudden rush of the enemy, I succeeded (although with some effort to stop my men, who declared they were "on the road to Richmond") in getting the regiment into good order and resuming our original position.

Four hundred prisoners, including two field and several line officers, were sent to the rear. These were mainly from the Fifteenth and Forty-seventh Alabama Regiments, with some of the Fourth and Fifth Texas. One hundred and fifty of the enemy were found killed and wounded in our front.

At dusk. Colonel Rice informed me of the fall of Colonel Vincent, which had devolved the command of the brigade on him, and that Colonel Fisher had come up with a brigade to our support. These troops were massed in our rear. It was the understanding, as Colonel Rice informed me. that Colonel Fisher's brigade was to advance and seize the western slope of Great Round Top, where the enemy had shortly before been driven. But, after considerable delay, this intention for some reason was not carried into execution.

We were apprehensive that if the enemy were allowed to strengthen himself in that position, he would have a great advantage in renewing the attack on us at daylight or before. Colonel Rice then directed me to make the movement to seize that crest.

It was now 9 p.m. Without waiting to get ammunition, but trusting in part to the very circumstance of not exposing our movement or our small front by firing, and with bayonets fixed, the little handful of 200 men pressed up the mountain side in very extended order, as the steep and jagged surface of the ground compelled. We heard squads of the enemy falling back before us. and, when near the crest, we met a scattering and uncertain fire, which caused us the great loss of the gallant Lieutenant Linscott, who fell, mortally wounded.

In the silent advance in the darkness we laid hold of 25 prisoners, among them a staff officer of General (E. M.) Law commanding the brigade immediately opposed to us during the fight. Reaching the crest, and reconnoitring the ground, I placed the men in a strong position among the rocks, and informed Colonel Rice, requesting also ammunition and some support to our right, which was very near the enemy their movements and words even being now distinctly heard by us.

Some confusion soon after resulted from the attempt of some regiment of Colonel Fisher's brigade to come to our support. They had found a wood road up the mountain, which brought them on my right flank, and also in proximity to the enemy, massed a little below. Hearing their approach, and thinking a movement from that quarter could only be from the enemy, I made disposition to receive them as such. In the confusion which attended the attempt to form them in support of my right, the enemy opened a brisk fire, which disconcerted my efforts to form them and disheartened the supports themselves, so that I saw no more of them that night.

Feeling somewhat insecure in this isolated position, I sent in for the Eighty-Third Pennsylvania, which came speedily, followed by the Forty-Fourth New York, and, having seen these well posted, I sent a strong picket to the front, with instructions to report to me every half hour during the night, and allowed the rest of my men to sleep on their arms.

At some time about midnight, two regiments of Colonel Fisher's brigade came up the mountain beyond my left, and took position near the summit; but as the enemy did not threaten from that direction, I made no effort to connect with them.

We went into the fight with 386, all told 358 guns. Every pioneer and musician who could carry a musket went into the ranks. Even the sick and footsore, who could not keep up in the march, came up as soon as they could find their regiments, and took their places in line of battle, while it was battle, indeed. Some prisoners I had under guard, under sentence of court-martial, I was obliged to put into the fight, and they bore their part well, for which I shall recommend a commutation of their sentence.

The loss, so far as I can ascertain it, is 136—30 of whom were killed, and among the wounded are many mortally.

Captain Billings, Lieutenant Kendall, and Lieutenant Linscott are officers whose loss we deeply mourn, efficient soldiers and pure and high-minded men.

In such an engagement there were many incidents of heroism and noble character which should have place even in an official report; but, under present circumstances, I am unable to do justice to them. I will say of that regiment that the resolution, courage, and heroic fortitude which enabled us to withstand so formidable an attack have happily led to so conspicuous a result, that they may safely trust to history to record their merits.

About noon on the 3d of July, we were withdrawn, and formed on the right of the brigade, in the front edge of a piece of woods near the left centre of our main line of battle, where we were held in readiness to support our troops, then receiving the severe attack of the afternoon of that day

On the 4th, we made a reconnaissance to the front, to ascertain the movements of the enemy, but finding that they had retired, at least beyond Willoughby's Run, we returned to Little Round Top, where we buried our dead in the place where we had laid them during the fight, marking each grave by a head-board made of ammunition boxes, with each soldier's name cut upon it. We also buried 50 of the enemy's dead, in front of our position of July 2. We then looked after our wounded, whom I had taken the responsibility of putting into the houses of citizens in the vicinity of Little Round Top, and, on the morning of the 5th, took up our march on the Emmitsburg road.

Report of Lieut.-Col. Norval E. Welch, Sixteenth Michigan Infantry.

Near Emmittsburg, Md., July 6, 1863.

In reply to circular of this date from brigade headquarters, as to the part this regiment sustained in the action of July 2 and 3, I have the honour to report:

The regiment, under my command, lay with the Third Brigade, First Division, Fifth Corps, closed in mass, near and in rear of Gettysburg, to the left of the main road, during most of the day. The brigade was commanded by Col. Strong Vincent, Eighty-Third Regiment, Pennsylvania Volunteers.

About 4 p.m. we moved rapidly to the extreme left of our line of battle, and went into position on the left of the brigade, at that time circling the crest of a high, rocky hill. After deploying two of my largest companies as skirmishers—Brady's Sharpshooters from the left, and Company A from the right—I was ordered at double-quick to the right of the brigade, and to take my position on the right of the Forty-Fourth New York. Before this could be accomplished, however, we were under a heavy fire of the enemy's infantry We succeeded, however, in securing our places after some loss.

We remained in this position nearly half an hour, when someone (supposed to be General Weed or Major-General Sykes) called from the extreme crest of the hill to fall back nearer the top, where a much less exposed line could be taken up. This order was not obeyed, except by single individuals. From some misconstruction of orders, and entirely unwarrantable assumption of authority Lieutenant Kydd ordered the colours back. None left with them, however but three of the colour-guard. They followed the brigade colours to where Colonel Vincent, after being wounded, had been carried, where they remained all night, joining the regiment in the morning with 45 men, who had left the field during and after the fight. All the remainder of the regiment retained their position until relieved.

The two companies sent out as skirmishers numbered about 50. The number of muskets taken in line was about 150; the number killed and wounded 59—21 killed. Several wounded have since died.

On the 3rd, we took up a new line farther to the right, at the left of the brigade, and remained on our arms for twenty-four hours.

Captain Elliott and Adjutant Jacklin behaved with their usual gallantry. Captain Partridge, Lieutenants Borgman (wounded), Woodruff, Forsyth, Cameron (wounded, with arm amputated), Swart, Graham, Salter, and Captain Chandler, behaved nobly and handled their men with coolness and valour. Lieutenants Browne, Company E, Tewett, Company K, and Borden, Company F, died, bravely defending the flag they had sworn to support and that they loved in their hearts, and emulating the bravest. I had no truer or purer officers, and their loss cannot be replaced.

Report of Lieut.-Col. Freeman Conner, Forty-Fourth New York Infantry.

July 6, 1863.

I have the honour to submit the following report of the action taken by this regiment in the engagement of July 2:

About 4 p.m. our regiment. Col. J. C. Rice commanding, was placed in position on Round Top Hill, with the Eighty-Third Pennsylvania on our left and the Sixteenth Michigan on our right. Company B was immediately thrown out as skirmishers. When they had advanced about 200 yards they met the enemy advancing in three lines of battle.

Orders were immediately given by Capt. L. S. Larrabee, commanding the company, to fall back upon the battalion. It was while executing this order that that faithful and brave officer was shot through the body and instantly killed, being the first officer that this regiment had ever had killed in battle.

The enemy continued to advance until the first line came within about 40 yards of our line. Upon their first appearance we opened a heavy fire upon them, which was continued until they were compelled to retreat. After they had disappeared in our immediate front, we turned our fire upon those who had advanced in the hollow to our right, and continued it until we were out of ammunition.

After we had been engaged about one hour, Colonel Vincent, commanding brigade, was wounded, and the command fell upon Col. J. C. Rice, and the command of the regiment upon myself.

We remained in our position until the next morning about 8 a. m., when we were relieved by Colonel Hayes, Eighteenth Massachusetts. We were then moved to the right about three-eighths of a mile, and formed in line of battle, the Sixteenth Michigan on our left and the Twentieth Maine on our right.

I regret to add that in addition to Captain Larrabee, whose death I have already noted, the officers are called upon to mourn the loss of First Lieutenant Eugene L. Dunham, Company D, a brave and efficient officer, who was instantly killed during the heavy firing from the enemy in our front. Capt. William R. Mourne, Company K; Capt. Bennett Munger, Company C; Adjt. George B. Herendeen; First Lieut. Charles H. Zeilman, commanding Company F, and Second

Lieut. Benjamin N Thomas, Company K, were wounded, the latter, it is feared, mortally.

It affords me great pleasure to be able to state that both officers and men behaved with the greatest coolness and bravery, not a single case of cowardice having come to my ear

Report of Capt. Orpheus S. Woodward, Eighty-Third Pennsylvania Infantry

Near Emmitsburg, Md., July 6, 1863.

In compliance with orders from headquarters Third Brigade, First Division, Fifth Corps, I have the honour to report the following as the operations of my command during the battle of the 2nd, 3d, 4th and 5th instant.

On the morning of the 2nd instant, moved to the front. At about 2:30 p.m. was ordered into position on our extreme left, the Forty-Fourth New York on my right, the Twentieth Maine on my left. At 3:15 p.m. the enemy advanced and engaged my skirmishers, pressing on in force, with bayonets fixed. They soon drove in my skirmishers and engaged my regiment, posted behind rocks and stones hastily thrown up for defence. The contest continued lively until nearly 6 p.m., when the enemy fell back. I instantly threw forward a strong line of skirmishers, who captured between 50 and 60 prisoners and 200 stand of arms.

My men and officers acted splendidly. Where all did so well, I cannot discriminate.

My loss amounted to 10 killed and 45 wounded.

At 1:30 a.m. on the 3rd, moved to the support of the Twentieth Maine, which had succeeded in taking a high hill a little to the left of my former position. Remained here until 10 a.m., when, being relieved by a regiment of the Pennsylvania Reserves, rejoined my brigade, massed in the woods, just at the right of General Sykes' headquarters. Here I remained until 12 m., the 4th, when the brigade was thrown forward on a reconnaissance. We moved out, and occupied the position occupied by the enemy the previous day; threw forward skirmishers, but found no opposing force within 2 miles. I deem it but proper to state that but for the prompt and skilful disposition made by Colonel Vincent of the troops under his command (the Third Brigade), the enemy would have succeeded in turning our left.

I regret to state that Colonel Vincent was severely wounded. My command (his regiment) esteemed him highly as a gentleman, scholar, and soldier, and bitterly avenged his injury

Report of Gen Romeyn B. Ayres Commanding Second Division, Fifth Army Corps,

July 28, 1863.

Rebellion Records, Series 1, Vol. 27
EXTRACT.

.... In the afternoon, the enemy's attack on the left of our position being developed, the division, *preceded by the First Division*, was marched to the support of our troops engaged, the Third Brigade being placed in position on the general line of battle upon a rocky hill (usually called Round Top hill) of great importance, facing the Emmitsburg and Gettysburg pike. This brigade was ordered to hold this hill, which duty it performed well and effectually....

Report of Col. Kenner Garrard, Commanding Third Brigade, Second Div., Fifth A. C.

At Battle of Gettysburg after death of General Weed.
Rebellion Records, Series 1, Vol. 27, Part 1
EXTRACT.

....At this point the leading regiment, under the direction of General Warren, chief engineer Army of the Potomac, was led to the left, up on what is known as Round Top ridge. Hazlett's Battery ascended the ridge immediately in rear of this regiment (the One hundred and fortieth New York Volunteers, Col. P H. O'Rorke commanding), and went into battery on the summit. The One hundred and fortieth was formed in line, and was immediately closely engaged with the enemy at short musket range on the left slope of the ridge.

A portion of the First Division, Fifth Army Corps (Vincent's Brigade. O.W N.), was engaged to the left of the ridge, and this regiment and Hazlett's Battery were brought up to assist the First Division in repelling a heavy assault of the enemy, with the evident design of gaining this ridge. Colonel O'Rorke was mortally wounded at the head of his regiment while leading it into action.

The other regiments, One Hundred and Forty-Sixth New York Volunteers and the Ninety-First and One hundred and Fifty-Fifth Pennsylvania Volunteers, were led to the right and front some distance, and formed in line in a narrow valley to support a portion of the Third Corps and Watson's Battery, then severely pressed by the enemy. Before becoming engaged, however, orders were received for these regiments to return at double-quick to Round Top ridge, and secure and hold that position. The Ninety-First was posted on the left of the battery, connecting with the One Hundred and Fortieth. The One hundred and Forty-Sixth and One Hundred and Fifty-Fifth were posted on the right, extending from the battery on the summit, along the crest of the ridge, to the gorge on the right.

.... When the brigade and Hazlett's Battery seized the ridge, it was done under a heavy musketry fire, and was entirely unoccupied, excepting by a part of the First Division (Third Brigade under Vincent. O.W. N.). on the extreme left, and I am gratified to report to the general commanding the division that the order to secure and hold the ridge was faithfully executed.

Comments on Official Reports

In reports marked "extract," portions in relation to preliminary movements and in some cases recommendations of officers for good conduct and matters purely formal are omitted, but all which relates directly to the subject of this paper is given as reported by the several officers.

General Sykes

States that he posted Sweitzer's and Tilton's brigades of the First Division himself. He says that "In the meantime, Vincent's brigade, of this division, had seized the rocky height, closely followed by Weed's brigade. Second Division. These troops were posted under the direction of General Warren, Chief Engineer of this army." If by "these troops" General Sykes means to include Vincent's brigade, it appears to be an error. There seems to be no reference to Warren in any of the reports of Vincent's brigade and no evidence that Warren at any time went farther to the south than the ground occupied by the One Hundred and Fortieth New York of Weed's brigade.

The statement that Weed's brigade had been taken away from its position on the hill by order of General Sickles and ordered by General Sykes to return and reoccupy that position is not confirmed by the report of Colonel Garrard, who assumed command when General Weed fell, and made the report for the brigade after the battle. He must have been present and could hardly have failed to notice this change of position. It seems more probable that General Sykes had ordered the brigade to the hill before he went to the rear to bring up the Third Division and finding on his return that General Weed with all his regiments except the One Hundred and Fortieth New York were marching to the front by order of General Sickles, ordered them back to the position which he had previously assigned to them.

General Barnes

This officer's report was not made until August 24, nearly two months after the battle and then only after the receipt of positive instructions to make his report. It is a long document, composed largely of verbatim copies of the reports of his subordinate officers. It seems evident from the reports of his brigade commanders that they received very little assistance from him during the battle. General Sykes says that he personally posted the First and Second Brigades. The Third Brigade was removed from his immediate command and asked and received no advice or assistance from the Division commander. Barnes says that he was with General Sykes when General Warren applied to the latter for troops to occupy Round Top, that Sykes yielded to Warren's urgent request and that he (Barnes) immediately directed Colonel Vincent, commanding the Third Brigade, to proceed to that point with his brigade. In view of the writer's certain knowledge of the conversation between Colonel Vincent and the officer of General Sykes' staff and the enquiry of that officer for the whereabouts of General Barnes, the only plausible explanation of Barnes' statement is that General Sykes' *aide* found Barnes after leaving Vincent and Barnes sent the order after Vincent and his brigade had gone.

Some important discrepancies are found between General Barnes' report of the orders given and movements made by the First and Second brigades and reports of these movements made by the brigade commanders, some of which will be specified in comments on the Brigade Reports. Reading between the lines, it appears that Barnes' action as division commander was not efficient and did not inspire great confidence in him in the minds of any of his brigade commanders. Orders which he claims to have given in regard to some of the movements of the brigades, are reported by Colonel Tilton and Colonel Sweitzer to have been made under their own initiative and when they finally reached their last position they reported directly to the Corps commander. General Barnes says that "Being disabled for further actual command of the division, the opportune arrival of General Griffin enabled me to relinquish it to him, and the division moved toward Middletown, where it arrived July 8." He does not say what caused his disability. The only reference to him which writer has been able to find in the official reports, is that in 1864 he was relieved from duty on court martial and assigned to the command of a prisoners' camp at Point Lookout.

Colonel Tilton

After describing the position taken by his brigade and the attack on his front, states that "General Barnes ordered me to fall back in good order if unable to hold the position." He makes no mention of an order from General Barnes to change his front to repel the attack on his flank. Finding that the enemy was in great force on his right and rear, he made several changes of position apparently without orders from General Barnes, and at last, after crossing an open field, took up a new position upon the right of the Second Division, *and reported to General Sykes.*

Colonel Sweitzer

After detailing the various movements of his brigade, some by the direction of General Barnes and others by his own orders, in extricating his men from their perilous position, he adds these significant words:

> About dark on the evening of the 2nd, the Acting Assistant Adjutant General of the First Brigade came to me and enquired for General Barnes; said he was directed by General Sykes to tell him to have the Second Brigade form on the right of the First, in the position they then were. As General Barnes was not present, I received the order, and put the Second Brigade in the position indicated, where we remained until the evening of the 5th, when the division advanced toward Emmitsburg.

From this it would appear that at the close of the battle on the second day General Barnes was not present or in communication with any of the brigades of his division. From his conduct as reported by the commanders of the First and Second brigades, the reader may judge what would have been the result if Vincent had waited for an order from him before moving his brigade to Little Round Top.

Colonel Rice

As his report and those of his regimental commanders show so clearly the importance of the part taken by this brigade in securing the victory as Gettysburg, they are given in full. It will be noticed that neither Colonel Rice nor any of the regimental commanders make any reference to General Warren having conducted them to this position or taken any part in posting the brigade. The report of Colonel Chamberlain graphically describes the fighting of his splendid regiment. The promotion of Colonel Rice to be Brigadier-General and his transfer to another corps, left Colonel Chamberlain in command of this famous brigade and with his Twentieth Maine, the Eighty-Third Pennsylvania, and other regiments which had been added to the command later in the war. Chamberlain commanded the force which received the formal surrender of Lee's army at Appomattox. The brief reports of Lieutenant-Colonel Conner of the Forty-Fourth New York and Captain Woodward of the Eighty-Third Pennsylvania, are scarcely adequate to measure the splendid fighting of these regiments. The report of Lieutenant-Colonel Welch of the Sixteenth Michigan contains some statements which are not confirmed either by the brigade commander or the commanders of the other regiments. He says:

> About 4 p.m. we moved rapidly to the extreme left of our line of battle, and went into position on the left of the brigade, at that time circling the crest of a high, rocky hill. After deploying two of my largest companies as skirmishers—Brady's Sharpshooters from the left, and Company A from the right—I was ordered at double-quick to the right of the brigade, and to take my position on the right of the Forty-Fourth New York. Before this could be accomplished, we were under a heavy fire of the enemy's infantry. We succeeded, however, in securing our places after some loss.

This statement does not appear to be in accordance with the facts. When the brigade neared the position assigned to it, marching in column of fours, the Forty-Fourth New York headed the column, followed by the Sixteenth Michigan, the Eighty-Third Pennsylvania next, the Twentieth Maine bringing up the rear. At the request of Colonel Rice that the Forty-Fourth New York and Eighty-Third Pennsylvania might fight side by side, as they had in all previous engagements, Colonel Vincent assented, and directed the Sixteenth to pass the Forty-Fourth. This may have been done at the double-quick, but no skirmishers were thrown out at that time by the Sixteenth Michigan and probably at no time during the battle, as the ground in their front was open to the foot of the hill. As soon as the Sixteenth Michigan was in place the other regiments followed, taking position on the left in the following order: Forty-Fourth New York, Eighty-third Pennsylvania and Twentieth Maine on the left. The brigade was all in position before a soldier of the enemy had been seen. The skirmishers thrown out by the Eighty-Third and Forty-Fourth advanced some distance before a shot was fired by either side.

The Sixteenth Michigan was fully in place and at least two heavy assaults had been repulsed by the other regiments before the Sixteenth Michigan had received a shot from the direction of its front. After the attacks by the five Alabama regiments had been repulsed from our centre, the Texas regiments of Robertson's brigade passed north on the left of Law to a point some distance beyond the Sixteenth Michigan, then advanced in heavy force against that regiment. Its right wing fell back in disorder, while the left held fast. The Texans were within our lines for a few moments, when the timely arrival of the One Hundred and Fortieth New York and their charge down the slope, caused the enemy to retire, and our line was re-established. In his attempt to stop the retreat of Welch's men, Colonel Vincent was mortally wounded. Welch further states:

> We remained in this position nearly half an hour, when someone (supposed to be General Weed or Major-General Sykes) called from the extreme crest of the hill to fall back nearer the top, where a much less exposed line could be taken up. This order was not obeyed, except by single individuals. From some misconstruction of orders, and entirely unwarrantable assumption of authority. Lieutenant Kydd ordered the colours back. None left with them, however, but three of the colour-guard. They followed the brigade colours to where Colonel Vincent, after being wounded, had been carried, where they remained all night, joining the regiment in the morning, with 45 men, who had left the field during and after the fight. All the remainder of the regiment retained their position until relieved.

This is a remarkable statement evidently made to account for the unsoldierly conduct of the portion of the Sixteenth Michigan and its commanding officer. It is certain that neither General Sykes nor General Weed was near that position at that time. He makes no mention of the presence of the One hundred and fortieth New York with Colonel O'Rorke at its head, which charged down the hill and repulsed the enemy which had driven back the right of Welch's regiment. It is certain that Welch with his 45 men did not follow the brigade colours at that time to the house where Vincent was carried, because the brigade colours did not leave the hill until the fighting was all over, when the writer, who carried those colours, was sent to the rear by Colonel Rice to get assistance for our wounded.

It is certain that Colonel Welch told the writer near the farmhouse where Vincent lay, that the brigade had been driven off the hill and he did not know where it was. It is probable that Welch with a part of his regiment sought safety in the rear of the ridge, and went with his men nearly a mile from the scene of the fight of his brigade and remained until morning.

It is significant that in his report Colonel Rice commended for their gallant conduct Colonel Chamberlain and Adjutant Chamberlain of the Twentieth Maine, Lieutenant-Colonel Conner and Major Knox of the Forty-Fourth New York, Captain Woodward, commanding Eighty-Third Pennsylvania, and Adjutant Gifford of that regiment, but in the Sixteenth Michigan mentions only Captain Elliott and Adjutant Jacklin, omitting any reference to Lieutenant-Colonel Welch.

Colonel Rice in his kindness of heart seems to have accepted the statement made by Colonel Welch in his report, but could not commend his conduct. Possibly as he was engaged with his own regiment at the time this break occurred he had no personal knowledge of the facts. Welch continued in command of the regiment and in subsequent battles acted well.

Colonel Vincent gave up his life here, but his brigade, with the assistance of the One Hundred and Fortieth New York led by the gallant Colonel O'Rorke, maintained its position until the end.

In 1901 the writer sent substantially the same statement, in regard to Vincent's conduct at Gettysburg, to each of the officers named below, and received letters in reply with permission to publish them, from which the following extracts are made:

From Major-General Daniel Butterfield.
Chief of Staff, Army of the Potomac at Gettysburg.

Hotel Royal Palm, Miami, Florida,
February 19, 1901.

No man who lived and fought in the Battle of Gettysburg did more for his country than Vincent. I knew the whole matter from beginning to end. He was a magnificent soldier, a gentleman of high education and great ability.

General Tremain brought messages to General Meade and to me from the field, describing the exigency and great need for the immediate occupation of Round Top, and authority was given him to send the troops there. In my judgment, there was not another command on the field which could have been more effective in the matter of time and rapidity of movement in getting to the spot in time to have saved the day, owing to its wonderful efficiency, drill and discipline under Vincent, who had been trained and educated with it.

From Daniel E. Sickles, Maj.-Gen., U. S. V. Commanding Third Army Corps at Gettysburg.

New York, November 21, 1901.

Colonel Vincent's part in the operations of that day, on the left of the Union lines, was distinguished by excellent judgment, prompt movements and signal gallantry, for which he was promoted to the rank of Brigadier-General, before his death, on the 7th of the month. My own command, the Third Army Corps, was engaged in the immediate vicinity, and I had, therefore, an opportunity of observing Vincent's fight and can speak of it from personal knowledge. There is no doubt that the repulse of Lee's assault on our left flank, on the 2nd of July, '63, saved the Union Army from defeat at Gettysburg. This was accomplished by the Third and Fifth Corps and Caldwell's division of the Second Corps. I have always regarded General Vincent's cooperation as worthy of all praise.

From Joshua L. Chamberlain, Brevet Major-General, U. S. V. Colonel Commanding 20th Maine Volunteers at Gettysburg.

Portland, Maine, November 18, 1901.

Col. Vincent's conduct in taking his brigade to Little Round Top and placing it in position, and in throwing his great personal energy and determination into the fight there, are personally well known to me. I regard the timely occupation of that position, which was at that stage of the battle the key of the Union defence, as due to the energy and skill of Colonel Vincent.

From Henry E. Tremain, Brevet Brigadier General, U. S. V.

New York, November 23, 1901.

Upon reading the foregoing, I recall many reasons besides your own valuable testimony for believing that the account is correct, and that too much recognition cannot be given by this country to the skill and heroism of General Vincent's supreme effort and sacrifice.

From General Ellis Spear.
Major 20th Maine Volunteers at Gettysburg.

Washington, D. C., November 23rd, 1901.

I have read carefully the foregoing statement in regard to General Vincent's services at Gettysburg. As to the greater part of the statement, I know of my own knowledge that it is strictly accurate. What happened on the right of the brigade when Vincent was mortally wounded, I did not see, being then with the 20th Maine closely engaged on the left, but it was a matter of common report at the time, and beyond question the statement is strictly accurate. I had seen General Vincent in battle before and knew what he would do then. He was a very valuable officer and of great promise, and his death was a great loss to the army, but the success he achieved in averting the imminent and great danger on the left at Gettysburg on the second day of the battle, was worth what it cost, though the price was great.

From General James Longstreet, C. S. A.
Washington, D. C., Dec. 6, 1901.

It gives me pleasure to state in reference to the worth of Little Round Top to the Union Army at Gettysburg, it was everything to the success of the Union battle. General Vincent's prompt action in moving to save that point, held it, and was the means of getting the battle to his side. Many minutes' delay would have given the Confederates the field.

Position of Eighty-third Pennsylvania Volunteers on Little Round Top, Gettysburg.

ALSO FROM LEONAUR
AVAILABLE IN SOFTCOVER OR HARDCOVER WITH DUST JACKET

THE FALL OF THE MOGHUL EMPIRE OF HINDUSTAN *by H. G. Keene*—By the beginning of the nineteenth century, as British and Indian armies under Lake and Wellesley dominated the scene, a little over half a century of conflict brought the Moghul Empire to its knees.

LADY SALE'S AFGHANISTAN *by Florentia Sale*—An Indomitable Victorian Lady's Account of the Retreat from Kabul During the First Afghan War.

THE CAMPAIGN OF MAGENTA AND SOLFERINO 1859 *by Harold Carmichael Wylly*—The Decisive Conflict for the Unification of Italy.

FRENCH'S CAVALRY CAMPAIGN *by J. G. Maydon*—A Special Correspondent's View of British Army Mounted Troops During the Boer War.

CAVALRY AT WATERLOO *by Sir Evelyn Wood*—British Mounted Troops During the Campaign of 1815.

THE SUBALTERN *by George Robert Gleig*—The Experiences of an Officer of the 85th Light Infantry During the Peninsular War.

NAPOLEON AT BAY, 1814 *by F. Loraine Petre*—The Campaigns to the Fall of the First Empire.

NAPOLEON AND THE CAMPAIGN OF 1806 *by Colonel Vachée*—The Napoleonic Method of Organisation and Command to the Battles of Jena & Auerstädt.

THE COMPLETE ADVENTURES IN THE CONNAUGHT RANGERS *by William Grattan*—The 88th Regiment during the Napoleonic Wars by a Serving Officer.

BUGLER AND OFFICER OF THE RIFLES *by William Green & Harry Smith*—With the 95th (Rifles) during the Peninsular & Waterloo Campaigns of the Napoleonic Wars.

NAPOLEONIC WAR STORIES *by Sir Arthur Quiller-Couch*—Tales of soldiers, spies, battles & sieges from the Peninsular & Waterloo campaingns.

CAPTAIN OF THE 95TH (RIFLES) *by Jonathan Leach*—An officer of Wellington's sharpshooters during the Peninsular, South of France and Waterloo campaigns of the Napoleonic wars.

RIFLEMAN COSTELLO *by Edward Costello*—The adventures of a soldier of the 95th (Rifles) in the Peninsular & Waterloo Campaigns of the Napoleonic wars.

AVAILABLE ONLINE AT **www.leonaur.com**
AND FROM ALL GOOD BOOK STORES

www.ingramcontent.com/pod-product-compliance
Lightning Source LLC
Chambersburg PA
CBHW030218170426
43201CB00006B/128